CURTAINS GOING UP

by

ALBERT McCLEERY

AND

CARL GLICK

PITMAN PUBLISHING CORPORATION

NEW YORK   CHICAGO

To

PERCY MACKAYE

The Pioneer who pointed the way, and the
Prophet who did not speak in vain

This Is American Theatre!

It is the non-commercial and community producing groups, existing all across the country, that are responding to the desire of the American people for a non-merchandized, personal theatre. It is very largely through them that a national theatre is coming into being. They are closer to the people than any professional theatre can be and, therefore, at their best they present a truer and more fundamental reflection of American life and thought.

GILMOR BROWN

This is good C. I.

ACKNOWLEDGMENTS

The authors, believing in community participation in the drama, gratefully acknowledge their indebtedness to those friends who helped participate in the preparation of this book. Thanks to Percy MacKaye for his gracious permission to quote excerpts from his stimulating books. Thanks to Louise L. Mace and *The Springfield Republican* for permission to reprint certain portions of Carl Glick's weekly column on Community Theatre activities. Thanks to *Poet Lore Magazine* for permission to reprint excerpts from Carl Glick's article, "Art for God's Sake," published in the 1923 summer number. Thanks to Marian Robertson for her sane advice to young movie aspirants. Thanks to Glenn Hughes for his inspiring comments on his Penthouse Theatre. Thanks to Barrett H. Clark for permission to quote from his article, "West of Broadway." Thanks to those friends who gave us advice and assistance; to Sue Ann Wilson, to Lydia Ayers, to Garrett H. Leverton, to John Hanrahan and *Stage* magazine, to Mrs. Mabel Foote Hobbs. Particularly thanks to the Lux Radio Theatre, Cadwell Swanson, Thomas Luckenbill and Sandy Barnett for making possible two extensive trips throughout the country during which more than a hundred and fifty theatres in America were visited. An indebtedness must be acknowledged to John Paxton, Curtis Rudolf, Patricia Bradley, Allen Churchill, and Harry J. Cummings, who have all aided and helped in this Community Theatre research these past two years. And certainly to the many friends throughout the country who, during the hot summer months, prepared and mailed to us the stories of their Community Theatres—one and all, we thank you. And to the newspapers, whose comments on their local groups we have quoted, also thanks. And last, but not least, thanks to the postman who, ringing the doorbell and delivering bulky packages of photographs too big to be put into the mail box, said, "Are you writing a book on Community Theatres?" And when we replied that we were, said, "I wish you'd mention my group." We do. It's a band of Players at the Church of All Nations on Second Avenue in New York.

CONTENTS

CURTAINS GOING UP

I. THE THEATRE OF DEMOCRACY IS BORN

Street Scene of Today

One fine spring morning we stood on the corner of Main Street in a fair-sized city one thousand miles from the Broadway of Times Square. It was a typical American town of some thirty thousand inhabitants; a business district with a court house set in a green lawn with trees, a new post office looking architecturally like an imitation of a Greek temple, parks named after the early pioneers, schools, a public library, homes with gardens, and at the edge of the city—the country club.

A chubby, rosy-faced young man getting out of a car turned and waved.

"There goes Bill Smith," said our guide. "He's one of our best actors."

He didn't look like an actor. He wasn't romantically handsome and he didn't strut. He appeared to be on first glance what we later discovered he was—an average young American.

"What does he do for a living?" we asked.

"Insurance business. He's married. Got a couple of kids, too. Lives out in Elmwood. His wife's on the play reading committee. She went to college. Bill's a good worker. Swell with the paint brush. When he's not acting, he helps the backstage crew, and I guess he's painted as much scenery as anybody in town. He's on the Board of Directors, too. And, oh boy, when he starts selling tickets—people buy. Come on now, I want to show you our theatre. It used to be an old garage."

"Who owns this theatre?" we asked.

"We do," was the answer.

"Who's 'we'?"

"Everybody—the townspeople."

"Who does the acting?"

"We do!"

"The work backstage?"

"We do!"

"You mean you own the theatre, act in it, shift scenery, and all that?"

"Sure. It's our Community Theatre. In the past ten years we've given over fifty plays. Six hundred different people have taken part. More than that have painted flats, hustled props, made costumes, sold tickets, and done all the other jobs necessary for the presentation of a play."

"But just who are these people?" was our next question.

"Oh, a cross section of the whole town. We've got bankers and auto-

3

mobile mechanics, doctors and factory workers, dentists and business men, school teachers and plumbers, society matrons and stenographers, housewives and grocery clerks. They're all busy during the day—got their jobs to attend to. We rehearse our plays evenings. Bill Smith's a typical example. Our actors and backstage workers are townspeople—no different from anybody else."

And here they are—over five hundred thousand Bill Smiths in towns and cities throughout the United States—from Maine to California, Washington to Florida. Their hobby is producing plays. And they are proud of their theatres. They should be. They built them themselves, stone by stone and word by word.

And a new kind of theatre was born in America. It was, to borrow the words of Abraham Lincoln, "A theatre of the people, by the people, and for the people." It was something new in the history of world drama.

Community Theatre—even the Greeks didn't have a name for it.

The golden age of Greek drama, that for all time ennobled tragedy, even though it wailed aloud that mortal man was but the plaything of the gods, contributed the first great corner-stone in the development of the theatre.

In England the Elizabethan Period, which gave to the world its greatest literary genius, laid another corner-stone of enduring worth.

In between and up to the present day there have been such solitary figures as Terence and Plautus, Racine and Molière, Sheridan and Ibsen, Belasco and the Shuberts, who have done their part. But the history of the theatre has been one of individual, often lonely, figures each making his contribution. It has been one man against his own age, against his own time, blazing a trail for others to follow.

But it is in our own age and time—right now—that the greatest corner-stone of enduring drama has been laid. It hasn't been one man's work alone. It's been the efforts of countless thousands. All of America—the Bill Smiths and Mary Roes of practically every town and city in the United States. They've turned play producers, actors, stage hands, and playwrights —because they loved it. It's been some fifteen million people—one eighth of the nation—the Community Theatre Movement.

In the archives of the Vatican there is a priceless fragment from the Greeks that antedates the birth of Christ by some four hundred years. The writer of it sincerely lamented the fact that the grand old days of the theatre were dead, and every carping critic from then to now has echoed him.

But it's not true today. The theatre is not dead. It is more alive today than it has ever been in the history of the drama. There are more plays being produced in the United States—more people taking part—more people going to the theatre—than at any time since the first playhouse was opened on these shores in South Carolina some time in the early 1700's.

The theatre of commerce, of the Max Gordons, of the Theatre Guild, of the Gilbert Millers, of all Broadway producers may have its woes and doubts, its moments of hesitation—but not the Community Theatres of America.

The theatre of the "tank towns" and "one-night stands" of forty years ago may be dead. But a new theatre has sprung into being in these neglected byways—a theatre in all respects quite different from that of the days of the old "Opery House."

It's all happened since the turn of the century.

Troupers in the Tank Towns—1900

Those were the good old days in 1900. The Gay 'Nineties were drawing to a close. "The theatre was theatre then," wail the old timers who now haunt the sidewalks of Broadway like ghosts from that by-gone era.

Along the Great White Way in New York theatrical producers sat in quite magnificent offices, furnished with genuine antiques and suits of armor. Just inside the outer door was the waiting room, where lounged the eager actors seeking engagements. On the walls hung signed photographs of the stars more or less under contract. Beyond, in the sanctum sanctorum, was his huge mahogany desk with a quill pen, and a couch where he sometimes did his casting.

Dignified gentlemen, those producers, astute and elderly, with derby hats, silky black moustaches, fur coats and large diamonds in rings on their fat fingers and in pins in their cravats. Some of them had been prize fight promoters, real estate agents, cloak and suit merchants. They came into the theatre to make money—and they did.

They hired actors. They fired actors. They hired scene painters, stage hands, musicians, and put on a show. They ran the whole thing single-handed from their luxurious offices overlooking the bright lights of Broadway.

If one of their productions ran a month in New York, it played the rest of the season on the road. But if they had a success on their hands, several companies took the play to the hinterlands the next year.

In the theatrical season of 1900-1901 over one hundred and fifty-five plays were produced in New York. (In 1937-38 the total was about ninety, according to John Hutchens.)

The big hit that year in New York was the musical comedy, "Floradora." Blanche Bates was appearing under the management of David Belasco and the Frohmans in the play seen on the screen over thirty-five years later with Claudette Colbert and Ronald Colman: "Under Two Flags." Maude Adams was starring in "Quality Street"; Grace George in "Under Southern Skies"; E. H. Sothern with Cecilia Loftus as his leading lady in "If I Were King"; David Warfield in "The Auctioneer." Alice Fischer starred a few years later in "Mrs. Jack," a play written especially for her.

Clyde Fitch was the popular playwright of the day. Three of his plays were running simultaneously on Broadway: "The Climbers" with Amelia Bingham in the leading part, "Lover's Lane," and "Captain Jinks of the Horse Marines" with a young actress by the name of Ethel Barrymore, who was making her first big hit.

Other popular actors and actresses of the day were May Robson (that young ingenue), Maxine Elliott, Blanche Walsh, Kyrle Bellew (the Clark Gable of his day), Tim Murphy, and Mrs. Fiske, an actress who was never so happy as when she could pack a bag and go on tour throughout the length and breadth of the country.

On the road Richard Mansfield was playing "Monsieur Beaucaire," by Booth Tarkington. Julia Marlowe was also on tour in "When Knighthood Was in Flower," with William Harcourt as her leading man. James O'Neill was somewhere abroad in the land, and with him was his young son, Eugene. This boy later turned playwright and several of his dramas have been produced, so we have heard, on Broadway.

In Buffalo, New York, the manager of the Opera House was Dr. Cornell. Perhaps then—certainly later—who wants to say?—his daughter, Katharine, was whisking her pigtails about the lobby.

From New York and Chicago the touring companies went forth. Troupers all—living in trunks and handbags. Some—the top-notchers—in their private cars. Others in the day coaches. Town after town, one night in each. In the big cities, perhaps a week. But mostly "one-night stands."

It was a great day when the troup arrived in town. The villagers all flocked to the railway station to see the company come in, strange people from a strange land. There was the old character woman lugging her own suitcase in fair weather or foul; probably doubling at the hotel with the ingenue, a cute and somewhat frightened little thing with dimples, being protected and saved from danger by the wise old character woman who had played this town before. There was the character man who had once been with Booth, and the "heavy," often the kindest gentleman of them all off stage with a friendly word for everybody. Then there was the haughty leading lady, looking neither to right nor left, for she knew in her heart that next season she'd be playing on Broadway. And the leading man, so handsome you doubted his morals, also a trifle superior, but causing a flutter in the bosoms of the village maidens as he cast an admiring but distant glance in their direction. He had an overcoat with a fur collar, a low, soft-brimmed, graceful hat, spats, and sometimes even a walking stick. (He's grown old now, that leading man of 1900. For a long time he was without an engagement. Then came the WPA and the Federal Theatre. He's acting again on Broadway, and has got his coat with the fur collar back from the pawnshop, and all's well with the world.)

Sometimes, as in the case of "Uncle Tom's Cabin," there was a parade through the streets with Little Eva in a chariot drawn by white ponies, and a band leading the way resplendent in red uniforms with much gold braid. Minstrel shows did the same thing, and even gave a free concert on the sidewalk before the evening performance. One night only, then they moved on, taking all their glitter and tinsel with them.

There were countless repertoire companies, too—"The Ten-Twenty-and-Thirt." They stayed a whole week. "The May Dorsey High Class Repertoire Company" with May as leading lady, still playing ingenue roles and looking sixteen on the stage even though she had a grown daughter back home in high school who wasn't—"so help me, going to lead this kind of a life if I can help it!"

Ten-Twenty-and-Thirty—with ladies admitted free on Monday night with every thirty cent ticket. For the Saturday matinee all seats were ten cents and unreserved—how the youngsters scrambled for the front row downstairs!

Yes, those were the halcyon days of the old theatre, when the drama was brought to Kalamazoo, Burlington, Louisville, Macon, and other cities. And save for the stock companies which dotted the land in the larger cities such as Denver and St. Louis, the theatre came from the outside. The players carved their statues in snow and then departed, and the opera house was dark until another traveling company appeared.

Murder in the Opera House

All the townspeople had to do in those days was simply attend the theatre, cough and sneeze, rustle their programs, and applaud when the curtain fell. The drama was laid on their doorsteps and they took what was given them from Sarah Bernhardt making one of her periodic farewell tours to "Tom Shows" and minstrels.

They were ornate in design, those old opera houses. Outside were massive Doric columns, sometimes statues in niches in the lobby, and on the inside lots of red plush. Hung on the walls of the foyer were signed photographs of the visiting stars.

"To my dear friend, and many thanks for a happy time in your delightful city," they read. When the old opera houses were torn down or abandoned, those priceless photographs were lost, given to near-by bar-rooms, or, as in the case of Louisville, Kentucky, salvaged.

There were two entrances: one through the main foyer, past the box office, and the other outside, up long flights of stairs to the topmost gallery.

This was "Nigger Heaven" or peanut gallery, 'way up next to the roof. Here, in knee-pants and gingham dresses, the present generation of theatregoers hung onto the rafters, ate peanuts between the acts and more often than not with careful aim hit with a spit-ball the bald head of the banker seated in the front row downstairs. The gallery was noisy, rude, and boisterous. But silent, too, and breathing deep in the great moments of the play, free with its applause, and freer still with its tears when Camille lay dying, or Lady Isobel in "East Lynne" bent over the bedside of her small son and uttered that classic line, "Dead, my little Willie, dead—and never called me 'mother.' " Virtue triumphed in the theatre in those days, and the gallery was always ready to acclaim it with thunderous approval.

In the balcony below sat the more conservative citizens; the young drug-clerk anticipating matrimony, holding his sweetheart's hand during the tender love scenes; and the better behaved boys and girls who could afford something more than a seat in the peanut gallery, but not a seat downstairs.

In the orchestra squatted the uppercrust of the town; the bankers, the lawyers, and the merchants. And in the boxes—usually four, two on each side—in complete evening dress sat the social leaders, bowing and smiling to their friends on the main floor. They came to be seen more than to see. Their seats were the most expensive in the house—and the worst. It was a snobbish theatre, this old opera house. Where you sat determined your social position.

The boxes had heavy velvet drapes which, year after year, gathered their quota of dust. In the orchestra pit the town band played between the acts. Nobody moved from their seats. There wasn't a general mingling in the foyer. If anyone left his seat it was not the desire for conversation which moved him. If the manager of this opera house had served coffee between the acts, they'd have locked him up in the insane asylum.

On the ceiling of the theatre and above the proscenium arch were either Cupids in dignified poses or little angels dropping rosebuds. The front curtain had on it an elaborate scene, the favorite one being a gondola gliding through the canals of Venice, with the maker's name, LEE LASH STUDIOS prominently displayed in the lower right-hand corner. No matter where the locale of the play you were seeing, England, Russia, or our own wild west, when the curtain dropped, you were always back again in Venice.

The curtain had a wiggle to it, too. Often this was the stage manager shaking the corner gently as a signal to the audience the lights were about to go out and the play was to begin. Then the gallery whistled, stamped its feet in glee, and the dowagers downstairs looked up and muttered something about rowdies.

Forever, possibly, these opera houses might have continued to offer the spoken drama to the theatre-lovers throughout the country. But something happened.

Somebody invented the camera. Somebody else made the taken pictures flicker and move. Wise men saw the possibilities of entertainment in these moving pictures. It was something new, and the public paid their money.

As the movies grew in popularity—and were called the "bastard" child of the theatre—the legitimate received a knock-out blow. During the following years traveling company after company was stranded in "the sticks." Actors no longer alighted from the day coaches and played one-night stands. They stayed home, and about the only theatre left was that of Times Square. Oh, yes, players still went to towns and cities outside of New York. But they didn't go in person. They arrived in express cars in tin cans. The movies had come to stay.

The old opera houses were either sold to the moving picture people, or closed. More dust gathered on the velvet drapes, the plush seats fell into ruin, the beautiful front curtain with its Venetian scene remained forever down. The day of the opera house was over.

And Marlowe's mighty line was no longer heard from behind the footlights. What spoken drama there was in cities miles from New York was confined to elocution teachers who presented pageants and gave recitals— very dreary for the most part. There was no more theatre in the one-night stands.

The Revolt of the Dowagers

Of course this made the dowagers mad. They liked the spoken word. Hadn't they for years been having Drama Study Clubs, reading the plays they were to see behind the footlights, entertaining the visiting stars at luncheon when the stars would consent to come, and expressing their opinions of plays and playwrights as freely as if they were the wisest critics on the best metropolitan newspapers? They had always been a little stage-struck, too. But now there was no theatre. No handsome Kyrle Bellew in the flesh to see and admire. No Sarah Bernhardt to weep over and discuss her private life in hushed tones.

Out in Pasadena, California, there was Gilmor Brown, a stranded actor. He wasn't any too happy, either, over the state of affairs. In North Dakota there was a young college professor. It had been a long time since he had seen a play. His name was Alfred G. Arvold.*

Over in Europe a few lusty pioneers had started a new kind of theatre. A Russian by the name of Stanislavsky had a group of amateur actors who became professional and were doing fine things in Moscow. A young man in Germany, Max Reinhardt, had rented a tiny hall and was putting on plays. In France, Andre Antoine, previously a clerk in a gas company, gathered together some other clerks and artisans and a few playwrights and began producing plays on his own. Later France was to award him the Legion of Honor for his services to the theatre. In Dublin, Ireland, some patriots had their own theatre where they produced their own plays. And there were others.

In 1911 or thereabouts pioneers began to experiment in this country. In Chicago Maurice Browne opened a Little Theatre seating ninety-one persons on the fourth floor of an office building. Mrs. Lyman W. Gale in Boston turned a stable into a Toy Theatre. Out in Wisconsin, Thomas H. Dickinson created the Wisconsin Players in Madison, and Laura Sherry had a Little Theatre in Milwaukee. In Lake Forest, Illinois, Mrs. Arthur Aldis built on her estate a tiny playhouse where she started producing her own plays. She even published them.

The idea spread. Other groups in other cities started up. By 1917 there were, according to Constance D'Arcy Mackay, over fifty established groups in existence in the United States. They called themselves "Little Theatres."

The reason was obvious. They *were* little—small auditoriums and small stages. Like mushrooms they sprang up over night. Some sank into oblivion the next year. Some grew and flourished. But the spoken drama was restored to the byways of America—and plays were being produced.

The dowager took command. She surrounded herself with faithful henchmen, and the amateur theatre in this country was born. There was the literary lady, who thought anything short of Pirandello, Chekov (this was before the Russian Revolution and the threat of communism), Shaw, and other playwrights whose plays she didn't understand was a compromise with art. There was the elocution teacher who, born with a middle-western accent, discovered the Italian "A" and the Delsarte school of gestures. There was the arty young man who was a misfit among the hometown boys and girls,

* See Fargo, North Dakota.

and dyed batiks whether he had a use for them or not. There was the mother with the plain debutante daughter, who, having failed matrimony, attempted to console herself with the stage, since the convent was no longer feasible. There were a dozen or so ladies of indefinite age who always hovered around the edge of any movement whether they knew what it was all about or not.

These the dowager assembled in her drawing-room and over tea cups founded the Little Theatre. The American matrons of that period, said Edith Wharton, "Met culture in bands, since they were afraid to face it alone."

That they ultimately put on a play is a miracle. But the play went on, tickets were sold, and the husbands slept soundly through it all. Nobody got the chance to act on the tiny stage unless they first produced their birth certificates and proved they were socially house-broken.

Those were hilarious, raucous, mirth-producing days. "Charlie Blair," for example, was one of the first directors in the field. Since then he has gone on to higher and better things. Maybe he's out in Hollywood now with a megaphone in his hands, instead of a tea cup on his lap.

Art for God's Sake

The story of Charlie's Little Theatre is typical of the day.

"Holding aloft the banner of the ideal," he hastened to a middle-western city, in 1923, in response to a call from the local Drama League, to become director of their Little Theatre. He remained one year, and then vanished—a nervous wreck.

"I have failed," he murmured, before he left. He had a clear, crisp accent. You could always hear him prompt—even to the tenth row. "But there are others who will feel the urge. Tell them, for me, the story of my Little Theatre; its pitfalls, its tragedies, its mistakes. Someone else may want to try it. Let them know, while they are still young, the real problems of a Little Theatre.

"Books on the subject are useless. If you must organize a Little Theatre in your town, avoid such treatises as *How to Produce Amateur Plays*. In the end they tell you nothing. And the real problems of a Little Theatre are not—to quote a few of the chapter headings from such books—'Where to send for plays,' 'Vocal technique,' 'Gesture,' 'What can be done with cheesecloth and old sheets,' 'Tempo and finesse,' 'The Art of make-up.'

"There is sure to be an elocution teacher, who has never been behind the scenes, to give you all the advice needed on such matters. Since her appearance as the Spirit of Something-or-Other in the annual pageant given by the School of Expression—a framed diploma testifying to her ability as a competent actress can be found in her studio—she knows everything worth knowing about stage technique, and sometimes a little bit more."

That is what Charlie Blair advised in 1923. He was a great man in his day. He was the first to use a completely dark stage, and he never had a good word to say for footlights. When he failed to get a job on Broadway —he was willing to do anything, shift scenery or sell candy in the lobby— he threw himself heart and soul into the Little Theatre Movement. He was only too glad, at any time, to tell the "real truth" about the commercial theatre and Broadway.

For, to Charlie, scenery and lights meant nothing. Nor did acting ever bother the members of his group of players. The real difficulties were keeping a fat, fifty year old matron, the mother of six children, from playing Paula Tanqueray; persuading the leader of the local Four Hundred, who took the part of the maid, not to wear all the family jewels; convincing the bashful leading lady that the leading man didn't really mean it when he kissed her in the love scenes.

These were the problems that broke Charlie's spirit.

His Little Theatre was supported, and financed, by a group of really worth while citizens. Their purpose was to bring the drama close to the hearts of the people: not those in their own particular set, but the masses, the great body of people who did their shopping on Saturday night, had Sunday picnics on the river bank, believed what they read in the newspapers, and flocked to the movies. They were to be shown that musical comedy was not art, and that the average Broadway play was trash.

Heaven only knows the worth while citizens did what they could. They gave the best of the Continental Drama, the gloomy plays of the Russians, and the sinister tragedies of France, England, Germany, and Italy. But the masses didn't respond, and it was discouraging to Charlie and his supporters to find only half of the hundred and sixty seats in their Little Theatre taken, and those by members. That year there was a deficit of three thousand dollars.

"We were most democratic," said Charlie. "No one was ever turned away. When we began our movement we had to have a slogan. After a committee meeting—in which one person was decidedly nasty and domineering—we finally decided on 'A theatre of the people, by the people, and for the people.' Someone objected because it was trite and had been used before, she didn't remember exactly where or how, but she was certain it was one of those expressions that have been used so often nobody believes it any more. The only other dissenting voice maintained that if we said 'by the people' there would be a lot of social climbers who would try to get in and run things. We found out later she was right. But at the meeting we silenced her. We told her most emphatically that this was to be a democratic, civic affair, and anyone who paid fifty dollars could join our Little Theatre, we didn't care who, what, or why they were."

The slogan selected, they elected officers. Charlie advised that every supporter of the Little Theatre be given an office. They lost one of the wealthiest women in town because no one nominated her for president. But she never missed a performance. She came and brought her family and all her friends, who talked loudly, and left at the end of the second act.

For a theatre they remodeled an old livery stable; put in just less than two hundred seats, to avoid the fire laws; hung the windows with cretonne, made scenery out of burlap, and decorated the walls with photographs of the Board of Directors.

One of Charlie's greatest stumbling blocks was the Play Reading Committee. It consisted of the librarian (she should have known how to select a good play), a minister's wife (so there would be no complaints about vulgarity, but they selected the wrong minister's wife), and one other woman who had seen all the good shows in Chicago and knew a thing or two about the private lives of the prominent movie stars. They never agreed. The librarian wanted to do Ibsen. The minister's wife had her heart set on Oscar Wilde or "The Maid's Tragedy" by Beaumont and Fletcher. And the other member wasn't certain what she wanted to see. So Charlie had to call a meeting and move that the Play Reading Committee be disbanded, and he alone select the plays, for praise or blame. He was always blamed.

The next stumbling block was the casting committee. They all wanted their particular friends to have the leading part, whether they were suited or not. In vain did Charlie explain to them what "type" meant. And when at last he did convince them, half the people he asked didn't want to take part.

They gave "The School for Scandal." First of all, the president didn't like the title. (She had been talked about the year before—but how was Charlie to know that?) She admitted it was a classic, but why not call it "Husband and Wife" or something sweet? So "Husband and Wife" it became, for she had subscribed five hundred dollars to the Little Theatre.

Charlie selected the play because it had many parts, and gave them all a chance to dig around in the attic for old-fashioned clothes. But the women didn't want to wear their old clothes. So the scene of the play was changed to New York in the year 1923.

For Lady Teazle—they decided to keep the titles—they wanted someone whose name would give the play the proper prestige; some woman who would draw a crowd because of her social position. More than one performance before this had been spoiled by a leading woman who was unpopular socially.

The woman Charlie finally selected didn't exactly look the part, and was quite unable to act it; still she had a magnificent home, gave splendid dinners, kept four servants, and had her own car. It meant a great deal from a publicity standpoint to advertise her as taking part. Trouble started, however, when the Lady Teazle insisted that they get a man plumper than herself to be Sir Peter.

There were only three men in town larger than Lady Teazle. One was a barber. He was out of the question, of course. Another was the lady's own husband. And that would never do. It would be no inspiration to her. The other really fat man in town was the Methodist pastor. Could he be persuaded to take part? He could not! He explained his position thoroughly on the matter. In vain did Charlie argue. The Methodist pastor was firm. Charlie was in despair.

Finally he showed Lady Teazle that young Jim Dawson, the handsomest man in town, would be an excellent Sir Peter, and might play the part if approached by the right persons. Jim did agree to act, after seven dinners, three luncheons, and four bridge parties.

For the rest, they managed to get a fairly representative cast. But Lady Teazle didn't like the girl who was to play Maria. They weren't speaking. Charlie urged that personal motives be laid aside.

"Our purpose," he said, "should be enough to make us forget all personal grievances."

But Lady Teazle was firm, and he had to get someone else. He soothed Maria by promising her the leading part in the next play, for which she wasn't suited.

He wasn't able to get as many men as he wanted, so he filled up the rest of the cast with high school boys who proved willing to work and were much more earnest than the young business and professional men of the town.

He had difficulties, too, with the husbands. There wasn't one who trusted him. Perhaps it was because he was an artist. But he never walked home in the evening with the married women of the cast. Or if he did, he left them a block from their homes to avoid suspicion. And he never called private rehearsals for fear someone left out would cause a scandal. Yet, in spite of precautions, one husband called him a "parlor ornament," because he tried to be polite.

Finally, his spirit broken, he vanished from the scene. Nobody knows exactly what has become of Charlie Blair. Someone said they heard he was at Yale taking a course in the drama. Someone else said they thought they

saw him playing one of the Senators in a current production of "Julius
Cæsar." If untrue, that, of course, is libelous. Nobody really knows for
certain. It probably doesn't matter.

A Prophet in the Wilderness

Of course, this was only one Little Theatre. The others were different.
Maybe they were worse. But certainly the state of affairs does not exist
in the Community Theatres of today. In 1923, the Little Theatres had just
begun to sprout wings.

And during that frightening period two things were happening. One
was that the boys and girls who used to sit in the peanut galleries of the
old opera houses were growing up. The other was that a prophet began
to point the way.

He was Percy MacKaye, the son of Steele MacKaye, one of our first genuine American playwrights. Percy MacKaye, himself a playwright and a poet
of the first order, was busy delivering lectures and writing books on the
state of the theatre in this democracy of ours. More pointedly he was looking into the future, and blazing the way for others to follow.

His first book, *The Playhouse and the Play*, appeared in 1909. In this
book he made the revolutionary statement, "The highest potentiality of the
drama can never be realized until the theatre—the drama's communal instrument—shall be dedicated to public, not private, ends."

He also included in this book chapters on "The Drama of Democracy,"
"The Dramatist as Citizen," "Self-expression and the American Drama," and
"Art and Democracy."

In the introduction he said, "The present book seeks to help clear the
ground for the upbuilding—not in one city only but in all our greater American communities—of a permanently endowed theatrical institution, dedicated
solely to dramatic art as a civic agency in the democracy; *a civic theatre for
the people.*"

And he also asked the question, "What local societies have been formed
in our towns and cities for the purposes of investigation, study, statistics,
public suggestion, regarding the conditions of acting, playwriting, theatrical
management, as these are related to the public welfare?"

This was in 1909. And now some thirty years later, the writers of this
present book are endeavoring, in part, to answer that question of Mr.
MacKaye's.

In his next book, *The Civic Theatre, in Relation to the Redemption of
Leisure,* published in 1912, Mr. MacKaye wrote further:

were   /"The Civic Theatre idea, as a distinctive issue, implies the conscious awakening of a people to self-government in the activities of its leisure. To this end, organization of the arts of the theatre, participation by the people in these arts (not mere spectatorship), a new resulting technique, leadership by means of a permanent staff of artists (not of merchants in art), elimination of private profit by endowment and public support, dedication in service to the whole community; these are chief among its essentials, and these imply a new and nobler scope for the art of the theatre itself. Involving, then, a new expression of democracy, the civic theatre—in the meaning here used—has never existed in the past, and has not been established in the present. An institution, potential yet actual, its conception is peculiarly the outcome of present and near-future needs in America."/

On December 13, 1916, Percy MacKaye delivered an address in Washington, D. C., before the American Civic Association. In 1917 it was published in a slim volume entitled, *Community Drama,* with a subtitle, *Its Motive and Method of Neighborliness,* wherein may be found a definition for Community Theatres: something which in a few words expresses its ideals, its aims, and its goal:

"With Community Drama—there is participation; there is creative expression; there is neighborly ritual."

Meaning, of course, in Community Theatres there should be participation of all the people in creative endeavor, resulting in neighborliness.

Mr. MacKaye's words should be placed over the doorway of every Community Theatre in the country, and printed in gold on every program.

And the three books he has written should become part of the library of every group in the country. They should be read and re-read, quoted and discussed. For he has stated the ideals and aims of Community Drama— the Theatre of Democracy.

Slowly, but surely, his prophecies are coming true. In the meantime, so far as we know, there is already one Civic Theatre in the United States, supported solely by taxation—the Community Theatre of Palo Alto, California.

Whether or not others will follow remains to be seen.

The Menfolk Declare Their Independence

Some twenty or thirty years ago the average American male, when Art with a capital "A" was mentioned, said firmly, "Leave it to the ladies—God bless them!"

The menfolk of the nation back in the days of Charlie Blair's Little Theatre were too busy making money, learning to play golf, and keeping the factory free from labor troubles to bother about music, painting, or acting. Then, too, it wasn't considered becoming in those days for the hairy-chested male to indulge openly in such "sissy" occupations. And so it was the dowagers and the wives in most communities who organized the Little Theatres, and then literally forced their tired husbands to spend an evening in a badly ventilated tiny playhouse dozing over Ibsen and Shaw, or perhaps even Aeschylus.

Then came "the depression." And there wasn't much anybody could do about anything. By that time, however, in many communities the men had already discovered that there was fun in producing plays; that painting scenery was a grand hobby and acting a perfect leisure-time activity.

So about 1930 the men of the nation came boldly forward and claimed the Little Theatres as their personal discovery. They did even more than that. They were tired of having the playhouses referred to as "little." It sounded "arty"—and in some places it had been. So they began changing the name to Community Theatres or Civic Theatres, or some such title denoting community participation.

The ladies sat back and smiled and said, "Go ahead! We showed you the way—and sometimes you laughed at us. But now—take the theatre! It's yours! But please let us tag along, and continue to help all we can!"

Percy MacKaye prophesied in *Civic Theatre:* "The use of a nation's leisure is the test of its civilization . . . Till now our people, through their public opinion or government, have never recognized the vocations of their leisure as related to labor; nor the vocations of their labor as related to recreation . . . Utterly divorced from art in their industrial labor, it is indeed no wonder that the people are slow to conceive art as their only salvation in leisure . . . For the redemption of leisure by an art participated in by the people on a national scale would create such a counter-demand for craftsmanship in the humblest things as would revolutionize the present aspects of the machine-made world. Every property, costume, symbol, insignium, banner and humblest buckle would ultimately become the product of the people themselves, under leadership of their fellows—the artists of the civic theatre. This appears a visionary goal, but it is inherent in the idea at stake. In its beginnings the idea has already been vindicated. Organized with clear vision, the rest may follow."

And it has followed, for it may truthfully be said that the Community Theatres of America belong to the men—and the women—of the nation.

Recently, the president of a group of mid-western community players made a declaration of independence. He shall be nameless, for after all he has to live in the town, but he said, "Out our way, the presence of fluttering society women does much to discourage progress, although these kindly ladies make much ado about their efforts for Community Drama. If we more red-blooded adherents of the Community Theatre game could organize and divorce our interests from the patronage of nervous society women, we'd find a lot more zest in the work and, I think, once rid of the patronage of these dowagers we'd manage our problems much better. Our theatre is dominated by men whose position in town commands respect. Perhaps that is why I speak out against the sissy influence of the women and resent having the Community Theatre stamped as one of their cultural stepchildren."

When the ladies read this, they'll have another private chuckle, but the wise ones will not say, "I told you so!"

It's the men of the nation who today are flocking to the stages of the Community Theatres: doctors, lawyers, bankers, preachers, business men, and politicians.

In San Antonio, Texas, several years ago, Maury Maverick was skeptical about acting, but after a few of his cronies survived the stage of the San Pedro Playhouse, he called up the director and said, "Could you use a tame armadillo? If you can, you'll have to take me, too, because he won't follow anyone else."

So Representative Maury Maverick and his armadillo played in "The Bad Man" and they both loved it. Senator John F. Healy acts in the Denver Civic Theatre. State Representative Harry E. Glass appears with the Civic Theatre of Grand Rapids, Michigan. John M. Vorys, who ran for Congress in Columbus, Ohio, is always on deck when the Players Club there gives its yearly Gilbert and Sullivan opera. And in Harrisburg, Pennsylvania, they think nothing at all of having a politician or two in the casts of their plays. State Senator George Kunkel is one of their best actors.

Lawyers are grand stage material. The three past presidents of the theatre at Charlotte, North Carolina, have been attorneys. Director Thomas Humble of this group says, "I believe that the local attorneys have found the theatre an asset to them, not only as a source of recreation, but more as a schooling for diction and ability to read."

Physicians have the problem of uncertain hours, but when Burtt F. McKee, director of the theatre at Birmingham, Alabama, gave "Men in White," he cast three prominent doctors in main parts. No less than five medics and three dentists starred in "Yellow Jack" in Shreveport, Louisiana.

Clergymen? In Denver, Canon C. W. Douglas of St. John's Cathedral gave a memorable interpretation of Thomas à Becket in "Murder in the Cathedral." Two well-known clergymen of Memphis are actors, and the Rev. Steward Meacham of Birmingham played the lead in "Biography" there. In many communities the clergy have taken an active part in the founding and organizing of Community Theatres.

Nor do the business men say, "That's all very well for professional men, but we're too busy—got too many things to do—and besides, we'd get razzed good and plenty if we went gallivantin' around a stage."

Business men founded the theatre in Chattanooga, Tennessee. One of their presidents has been John E. Gilbreath, former newspaper man now handling insurance. A vice president of a wholesale notion house in Lynchburg, Virginia, R. M. Woodson, is the town's chief character actor, and when Stokes McCune gave Drinkwater's "Bird in Hand" in Columbus, Ohio, the entire cast was made up of business men. A manufacturer in Quincy, Illinois, C. Arthur Fifer, writes plays and acts in them as well.

In New Orleans, Harold Levy, president of a box factory, can be found in Le Petit Théâtre du Vieux Carré most any afternoon, and Henry Garic, prominent insurance man, plays an average of three to four roles a year there. John Oulliber, ex-New Orleans and Cleveland Indian baseball player, now with a New Orleans bank, is prominent in the affairs of the theatre. Leo C. Zinzer and Felician Y. Lozes, former newspaper reporters and now attorneys, handle the publicity.

Look at the Playhouse in Summit, New Jersey, to see what business men can do. They once put on a play written by an engineer, Walter F. Faust, and acted by business men: Theodore Kenyon, patent lawyer; John H. Clark, insurance broker; Victor A. Traub, steamship line official; Leonard R. Barrett, of the Better Business Bureau of New York, and Ralph Williams, cigar manufacturer.

There are others, whose names you will find scattered through the following pages.

Again was Percy MacKaye right when in *The Playhouse and the Play* he said, "True democracy is vitally concerned with beauty, and true art is vitally concerned with citizenship."

Pioneers of Today

These are the boys and girls—or the sons and daughters of them—who hung over the railing in the peanut galleries of the opera houses in the 1900's. The old opera houses have gone. But a new theatre has been created. And they are the ones who have done it.

The descendants of those men and women who crossed the plains in covered wagons, fought off the Indians, dammed the rivers, cleared the forests, made homes in the wilderness, and founded a nation: they, too, are pioneers.

But they are pioneers of a new order with a new frontier to conquer—the frontier of creative endeavor in the arts. How they have created Community Theatres is a story of struggle and triumph, of discouragement and fulfillment. And the end is not yet, for Community Drama in America is still in the making.

But the pioneers of today, undaunted, are going forward. Community Theatres are dotting the land. "Community participation in creative endeavor for neighborliness," is their creed.

One more word from *Civic Theatre* by Percy MacKaye:

"The audience of the civic theatre, participating to varying extent in its productions, would come to be a very different audience from that of the present day commercial theatre. It will feel a proprietorship and pride in its own institutions, new and stimulating both to its critical and creative capacities. Sharing in its art activities, the people would naturally share in acclaiming the achievements of its art."

And so they do. For now they tell the story of their Community Theatres.

II. COMMUNITY THEATRES OF THE NORTHEAST

Allentown, Pennsylvania
Bangor-Brewer, Maine
Bethlehem, Pennsylvania
Boston, Massachusetts
> Buffalo, New York *33*
Candlelight, Pennsylvania *36*
Dobbs Ferry, New York
Dover, New Jersey
> Erie, Pennsylvania *43*
Fitchburg, Massachusetts
Great Neck, New York
Harrisburg, Pennsylvania
Hartford, Connecticut
Longmeadow, Massachusetts
Mount Vernon, New York
Philadelphia, Pennsylvania
Pittsburgh, Pennsylvania
Rochester, New York
✳ Short Hills, New Jersey *66*
Springfield, Massachusetts
Summit, New Jersey
Torrington, Connecticut
Utica, New York
Washington, Pennsylvania
Waterbury, Connecticut
York, Pennsylvania
And Other Theatres of the Northeast

*Allentown, Pennsylvania. Formed to Satisfy the Average
Theatre-goer.*

Few productions of the road days failed to get as far as Allentown. No
producer's shoestring was ever quite so short that it didn't reach the ninety
miles out of New York. And so Allentown got the good with very much
of the bad, the latter including no end of strange assortments of actors and
actresses offering the two or three year old hit "exactly as presented in New
York" as well as innumerable tryouts; an affliction shared with Stamford,
Connecticut, and Atlantic City, New Jersey.

Permanent stock companies also came, sometimes to flourish gloriously
for a season or two or to die ignobly within the first weeks. So, when the
road dried up, there were mourners left who found the offerings of the Civic
Little Theatre "not bad at all."

The twelve year history of the Allentown Little Theatre may be divided
into equal periods. Since 1932 it has been in its present home; before that
existence was precarious.

Mr. Kohl, aided by a fellow newspaperman, called a meeting in 1927.
In grand democratic fashion they invited everyone in town who had been
even remotely associated with things theatrical.

Practically everyone came to the meeting and immediately started paying
dues!

But meeting followed meeting and the only activity was talking. Highly
explosive factions and rugged individualists kept the movement from "jell-
ing." The first season ended with a social affair at which "Suppressed Desires" became the initial offering.

One by one the various factions dropped out. One marched out when
the late Theodore Roberts, veteran of the stage and screen, in addressing the
group, urged that amateurs realize their limitations and not rush in where
angels of the profession feared to tread.

The local Fine Arts Club, struggling to maintain its rooms, had a drama
section it didn't know what to do with. So finally a deal was negotiated to
use their quarters and add the membership of the club's drama section to
the now meagre ranks of the group in return for the theatre's treasury.

Two sets of one-act plays were presented but, by the end of the season,
the Fine Arts Club was dispossessed and the Little Theatre was on the
street—sans treasury.

The group carried its problem to the municipal recreation commission which had been conducting drama classes. Again a merger, a score of new members and the use of a building on the fair grounds, which were then under municipal control. The commission provided funds for renovating part of the main exhibition building and it was there amid building paper partitions that the fifth season was launched, offering two sets of one-acts, a full-length play, a travesty on the old-time melodrama, and a municipal tournament.

The urge for a real theatre took form with this partial success. The Allentown mind, however, either in the group or its audience, can envision only a theatre that is like a theatre: no rough walls, no rude benches, no inadequate sets, no drafty barn, no jerky lights; but a velvet curtain, leather-cushioned chairs, concealed illumination, reserved seats and a box office regularly manned for three days prior to and all through the run of a play.

Next season, the fall of '32, the group jumped off the deep end. They moved into a neighborhood movie theatre. They contracted to pay $500 a year rent, to purchase enough coal to feed the big heater, to move their stage, luckily portably designed, again to use building paper to close off proscenium and dressing rooms and to offer a subscription season.

This theatre has remained the home of the Civic Little Theatre of Allentown.

These things came slowly with the years, but until each arrived their absence was a handicap for which apologies were in order.

Perhaps this is the reason for the turnover in membership and officials. The weight of constant debt has tired many, but ever there have been new enthusiasts to take their places—and to create new debts, for each new regime had its own idea of "what this theatre needs."

John K. Kohl, the founder of Allentown's Little Theatre, proclaims that they hope very soon to have all the things they need and may then settle down to an easier life. Perhaps then will come some of the experimental plays that need not always spell profit, but must be good theatre.

Only one or two of the original little band were left: a few who came with the Fine Arts Club and a handful of municipal dramatic classes. Most of the rest have come since the rental of the movie theatre. Many of the factionists of the early days rejoined when it became apparent that Allentown's Little Theatre Movement was going on without them.

They were welcomed back because the group has always welcomed contributors to its activity. Allentown's Little Theatre has remained a community enterprise in its broadest sense.

Two of the members of the group have written plays: Warren E. Smith and Mr. Kohl, who at last found time to finish his original opus. A third member-playwright is to have his play presented soon.

The Allentown Civic Theatre likes to cite the following successful productions: "The Dover Road," "Broadway," "The Butter and Egg Man," "A Doll's House," "Murray Hill," "The Return of Peter Grimm," and "Jane Eyre."

Bangor-Brewer, Maine.   Two Cities Combine Their Efforts.

Directly across the river from Bangor is Brewer, and it is the combined efforts of the theatre-lovers in these two towns that make the Bangor-Brewer Little Theatre.

The moving spirit in the organization of this group was Rebecca Chester, girls' work secretary of the Y.W.C.A.   She proposed, at a meeting of the Business Girls' Club, that a Little Theatre group be formed.   Announcement was carried in the newspapers, with a date of the proposed meeting, and an invitation to attend was issued to those interested.   Twenty-five persons responded, and discussed the possibilities of forming a group strong enough to be self-supporting and to meet the competition offered by the local moving picture theatres, and the church and school plays.

The first three meetings were uninteresting.   Members of the group, with true Yankee caution, were slow to ally themselves with any new movement.   Accordingly the attendance varied, both as to number and personnel.

But in December of 1935 they had settled down to an average of fifteen members with some ten present at every meeting; the assistant manager of one of the hotels, a high school teacher, a reporter, a shoe clerk, the manager of the local branch of a chain store, a bank clerk, a secretary, two primary school teachers, a mill worker, the motorman of a trolley car, and a couple of stenographers.

The dues for that first season were twenty-five cents, an amount which did not even cover the purchase of play books for their first production.

The Y.W.C.A. offered the free use of one of their rooms for meetings and rehearsals and advanced the money to cover preliminary costs of the first play.   Since then they have been self-supporting, apart from the use of the Y.W.C.A. rooms, and at the beginning of their second season they started to pay for the use of their meeting rooms, although they were not yet able to pay rental for rehearsal rooms.

On their first production, Miss Chester, assisted by the cast, handled publicity, tickets, properties, business and all the production details.   But by the second offering they had established committees to take care of this work.

From the beginning the casts have worked under terrific handicaps in the presentation of their plays.   The stage in the hall they were using was eighteen by eleven, its light facilities were inadequate and there was no provision for installing their own lights. The floor was not ramped, the chairs were borrowed, and the ventilation was very bad.

Then, in the fall of 1937, they gave Molnar's "The Guardsman." On the first night there was a good house, the second night was packed. The third night had out the sign, "Standing Room Only." And the Bangor-Brewer Little Theatre was a success, for Oscar Shepard, of *The Bangor Daily News*, one of the foremost dramatic critics in the state of Maine, took up the cudgel in their behalf.

Up to this time he had maintained an indulgent attitude toward the players and had not hesitated to score any and all faults in their productions. But the smoothness of the production of "The Guardsman," directed by Russell C. Hobbs, so inspired Mr. Shepard that he interceded with the manager of one of the moving picture theatres to obtain this theatre for future productions. Permission was granted.

And so for the first time this group was to have the advantage of a true theatre atmosphere, adequate stage and lighting facilities, a ramped auditorium, and all the advantages which a real theatre offers. Also they were removed from the class of most amateur groups presenting shows for granges and churches, and placed in a position where they could and would be compared with various professional companies.

There was considerable anxiety in the heart of every member of the organization. Failure in this step would mean the collapse of the structure they had labored so hard to build through three long years. Success would mean that they had made a tremendous stride toward their ambition: the establishment of their own theatre for the production of plays in a worthwhile manner.

They selected "The Amazing Dr. Clitterhouse." From the beginning the show seemed to be "jinxed." First, the books were slow in arriving, losing a week of valuable rehearsal time. Several of the best players were unavailable and it was necessary to place in important roles two actors who were completely untried insofar as their own productions were concerned; and the play itself proved to be more difficult mechanically and involved more intricacies of timing than they had realized. The script called for four separate sets with six changes. In order to eliminate unnecessary waits between scenes and to cut down production costs, they decided to produce the show with six changes apparent to the audience, but with actually only two sets. This was done by lighting effects, and the switching of door or window flats occasionally.

The business department had outdone itself and so pushed the sale of tickets that four days before the date of production the ticket manager had to recall all reserved seats in the hands of the members.

In these circumstances, it can well be understood that the cast and director awaited the day with trepidation.

A climax to the efforts to establish a true theatre atmosphere was the hiring of an orchestra to play in the pit which had been unused for years.

At 8:15 on the evening of April 29, 1938, the curtain of the Bijou Theatre went up on the first scene of "The Amazing Dr. Clitterhouse." Whether it was the effect of the packed house, the stage and lighting facilities, or the work of the cast and director themselves—everyone knew in the first few moments that their show was a success. On the strength of that production alone they had that spring at least three hundred unsolicited requests for season tickets for the 1938-39 season from new patrons.

Twenty-five and more years ago, Bangor was well known as a good "road" town. And the "Opery House" is now having spoken drama again—but this time it's by a Community Theatre group, and the actors and actresses of Bangor and Brewer speak their lines from the stage where once trod the stars of Broadway.

"From the very beginning," says Helen M. Hobbs of this group, "we have steadfastly refused to ally ourselves with any other organization and have consistently refused remunerative offers to present some play under the auspices of any other organization. I do feel, however, that we are serving the community by offering an outlet for the energy and desires of those interested in theatrical work, and by offering to the community at large the opportunity of seeing plays that would not otherwise be presented in Bangor and Brewer."

Bethlehem, Pennsylvania. They Proclaim Their Purpose in a Magazine.

Three times a year the Plays and Players of Bethlehem issue an attractive little magazine called *Asides.* It's an emotional outlet, this magazine, a sort of safety valve, for in its pages the players say what they think about matters theatrical; not only about what is going on in foreign territories such as Broadway, but also the events in their own circle.

Kenneth Llewelyn, writing in *Asides,* and taking as his subject the well known theme of which came first, the chicken or the egg, turns the spotlight upon the origin of the actor, saying, "Did the theatre have its origin because people without mirrors wanted to see themselves as other people saw them, or did it have its genesis in some long-defunct Thespian's seeking to show other people how he felt they should see him? To answer the question 'How do I look?' the artificial mirror is sufficient, but to answer the question, 'How do I behave?' we seek the opinion of our fellow-men, either directly or indirectly, on the street, in books, in the universities, in the art galleries or in the theatre!"

And that might be one way of explaining what's behind all this participation in community drama.

This group was organized in October, 1930, by the Rev. Mr. Moore of Trinity Parish. There was at that time in Bethlehem, on vacation, an actor who had been playing various roles in Broadway productions.

"I have a group of talented young people who want to start a community theatre," the Rev. Mr. Moore said to this actor. "We need a director—and you're it!"

So W. Everett Moll became the group's first director, and has stayed at this post during the past eight years. So far he has produced for Bethlehem twenty-three plays—and in each production fifteen to twenty persons have participated.

The organization is simple. There is a Board of Directors composed of two school teachers, a banker, a radio engineer, and Mr. Moll. The members are actors or backstage technicians. They play a part—or shift scenery. Then they become members.

They have no subscription audience. Admission to each play is fifty cents. Tickets are placed on sale before each play, and can also be bought at the door. There is no other source of revenue. But they have jogged along for eight years in this manner at Bethlehem.

The plays are given in the Trinity Parish House, and include every type of drama from the current popular successes to Ibsen, Wilde, and other stand-bys of the modern drama.

Meetings are held monthly at the Trinity Parish House. Comments and criticism are welcome at all times and will be acted upon to the best of the club's ability.

One of the reviewers on a Bethlehem paper, Judson Shaeffer, wrote for *Asides* his opinion of critics. He says, in part:

"The art of play reviewing goes back to the guy who first got kicked out of a Greek chorus. He next tried his hand at playwriting, but the public was prejudiced in favor of a citizen by the name of Aeschylus. Kicked out of the chorus, disliked as a playwright, what was there left for him but to become a critic?

"The toughest assignment in 'critic-sizing' is to review the performance of an ingenue whom you have subtle ideas of dating—afterwards . . .

"Juveniles are troublesome, too. They're so sensitive. In fact, one Little Theatre lad got so mad because of a little error in the composing-room (the review of his performance appeared 'accidentally' under the obituaries) that he stopped bumming extra copies of the paper at the office.

"Leading ladies—and men—are swell. All you have to do is mention them first, give them the most space and use only complimentary adjectives. Sometimes they'll even thank you, if you run large enough pictures of them.

"When I get right down to thinking about it I wonder if I'm wasting my time writing reviews—when and if. Sometimes I wonder if I shouldn't be acting. Last year I wrote a show and the morning-after review wasn't half bad. I wrote it myself."

So Community Theatre actors and actresses take heart. The same morning-after heart throb that troubles you also exists in the bosoms of Thespians in Bethlehem.

Incidentally, Mr. Shaeffer's play was a one-acter, one of the three best submitted in an original play-writing contest held by the Plays and Players last season; and the contest for original plays is to become one of the features of this group.

Speaking in defense of community theatre groups, Kenneth Llewelyn says, "Why should audiences feel that because a drama is given in Bethlehem, or any like city, it will surely follow as Monday does Sunday that the play will no longer have the significance it had in New York or London or Copenhagen? It is probably more logical to conclude that a play performed in a LITTLE theatre will have gained more in intensity than it had lost in immensity.

"And who will say that you may not be watching tonight, in this Little Theatre, as earnest an actor or actress as ever dreamt of Broadway? One who, no matter how small the stage, is as sincere in his work and thrills as much to the lines he speaks as if the setting were Broadway itself . . . but with one difference . . . here he plays for the sheer love of his work; on Broadway he would no doubt wish to be remunerated for his pains.

"Great oaks from . . . !"

Boston, Massachusetts. Sixty-one Years of Play Production.

On January 4, 1877, a group of young people met in Jamaica Plain, a suburb of Boston, to consider forming a small local dramatic club for the amusement of themselves and their friends. The founder of the Club and the person at whose suggestion this group met was Miss Caroline H. Morse. It was she who was the inspiration of the whole undertaking. A curious commentary on the times is that she did not become the club's first president, perhaps because in those days it was regarded as more fitting that a man should hold this office. But probably it was modesty which kept her in the background.

So it was Mr. Thomas B. Ticknor who became the first president, a position which he held for twenty years. This group, however, elected Miss Morse to the office of vice president and for a brief period of a year and four months, until April 30, 1878, she served in this capacity. With her untimely death, the office was appropriately discontinued. Her portrait hangs in the club room to serve as an inspiration to the newer members and to be a connecting link between the past and the future history of this theatre.

By good fortune, the founders of the Footlight Club elected to be creators and not mimics. In the cramped and inadequate quarters of the old German Theater on Boylston Street, they presented plays in a fashion that won for them the devotion of their audiences and the respect of their contemporaries.

Critics of those days are reported to have said that the Footlight Club's first performance of "A Scrap of Paper," even then a time-honored relic of the theatre, was acted with such sincerity and conviction "that it became a finer piece of artistry than Hamlet, played in halting imitation of professionals."

Mr. Ticknor retired in 1897 and Parkman Dexter succeeded him and the change occurred so naturally and the traditions of the Club were so carefully maintained that the break was almost unnoticed. There is a saying that "prosperity has no history." During all Mr. Dexter's term of office, the Club moved smoothly along its accustomed way.

It was not until 1913 that there was even a ripple on the smooth surface of the Club affairs. Then Mr. Dexter felt it necessary to give up his duties as president. There was no one in sight to take his place, and there appeared the first indication of waning interest on the part of some of the members—life was much more complex than in the early days, and other amusements and preoccupations took the time that used to be reserved exclusively to the Club. Many thought that this was an appropriate time for the Club to disband and rest on its well-earned laurels. Many of the actors who had borne the brunt of the work were growing older and were willing to retire. The suggestion to disband was most unwelcome, but it seemed the best and only solution. At this point as clever and adroit a move was made as ever sprang from the active brain of a seasoned politician. An informal meeting was called—as the founder was a woman, so this epoch-making meeting was also suggested by a woman. There were only two or three men and the rest of this gathering were women, none of whom had ever held office in the Club. Most of the men were either too busy to attend or thought the whole effort futile. Later it developed that the more discouraged and pessimistic of them (women's intuition working) had not even been invited to attend.

The whole situation was discussed, and while the few men in attendance vacillated and feared to go ahead, the women announced that the Club was to go on and they intended to see that it did. They knew exactly what they wanted to do. They outlined the method of procedure, suggested a new slate of officers, fired the doubting men, and then adjourned. A subsequent meeting of the Club ratified everything they proposed, elected their slate of officers, and the Club was saved. The Club continued despite the fact that the first play, under the new administration, has gone down in history as probably the worst performance the Club ever perpetrated.

With varying fortunes, but on the whole with some measure of success, the Club went on and it was not until the war dislocated life for everybody that troubled times again loomed. But at that time Mr. Jenkins was president, and by the exercise of the greatest patience and utmost ingenuity the lean years were survived.

Audiences at the early performances at the old German Theatre were composed of friends and neighbors of the Jamaica Plain community. The quality of the plays presented brought more and more auditors, and after two years the Footlight Club left the German Theatre and moved to Eliot Hall, its present home. Here there was more room, a slightly larger stage, and more conveniences. But the Club labored under disadvantages of very limited theatrical machinery. In fact, the building was in such bad repair that in 1924 the owners decided to tear it down and use the plot of land on which it stood for more productive purposes. As soon as this was announced, the people of Jamaica Plain, in practically a spontaneous movement, demanded that some action be taken in the interest of the Footlight Club.

An association was formed to finance the purchase of Eliot Hall and one thousand shares of stock were issued. A Board of Trustees was chosen to operate it, and in a few weeks the Footlight Club was assured of a permanent home.

The organization of the Footlight Club has been about the same since 1877. There was, and is, a hard-working secretary, treasurer and a small board of directors invested with extensive and somewhat arbitrary powers under the chairmanship of the president of the Club proper. But the real strength of the Club lay then, as it does now, in a devoted active membership. At first this was made up almost entirely of Jamaica Plain people, but little by little recruits were drawn from an ever-widening circle. It is interesting to note that in the list of active members of 1938, the date of their election appears as follows: Miss Grace Chandler, June 4, 1894; Arthur Wallace Rice, June 4, 1894; William O. Safford, June 4, 1894; Archibald R. Tisdale, June 4, 1894; William Stanley Parker, February 10, 1903; Henry M. Goodrich, December 10, 1906; Mrs. James S. Lee, February 10, 1913; Joseph A. Locke, December 5, 1917; Mrs. Franklin H. Nichols, February 26, 1919.

The associate membership was enlarged from time to time to permit the election of applicants. Originally seventy-five, it was increased during the first year of the Club's life to one hundred. But it was not until 1878 that the associate list was full and a modest waiting list appeared. From then on, the membership was enlarged from time to time, until it numbered 275 and a high water mark was reached in 1906 when the list was full and there were a hundred and sixty-two impatient souls on a special waiting list.

Little by little over the years there was developed an esprit de corps that has made this organization unique. "It comprised an unfaltering allegiance to the best interests of the Club, a cheerful acquiescence to the will of those directing the performance, an entire readiness to sacrifice, as far as possible, all matters of personal preference or pleasure to the duty in hand."

In the life of the Footlight Club there is one outstanding and surprising fact. Never in its long history has it postponed or omitted a performance, save once, and then in respect to a beloved member who died during dress rehearsals.

Mr. MacGregor Jenkins, in a very interesting and beautifully written brochure, recalls the old days of the Footlight Club with such nostalgia and affection that a few passages of it are included here:

"The little meeting for organization, the first hazardous venture in the German Theatre, the transfer to Eliot Hall, the simple stage with its gas footlights. The theatre, at least for some of us, lost one of its most endearing charms when the introduction of electricity robbed it of its characteristic odor of escaping gas. Miss Alice Morse playing a solo overture on a hired piano before a talkative and inattentive audience; the last frantic efforts of the stage crew to have everything in its place and in the right place; the long table in the men's dressing room with its cool bottles of beer and boxes of crackers and pounds of cheese; the acting manager assailed with doubt as to whether the ladies of the cast would complete their toilettes in time for the curtain; and over it all and through it all a delicious tingle of excitement which set us all on edge . . .

"Then little by little, the improvements came; gas gave way to electricity, Miss Morse resigned in favor of the Footlight Orchestra, and for the first time we, back stage, heard the intoxicating tuning of violins and the soft moans of wind instruments as they prepared for their part in the evening's entertainment. When all was ready, Roger Scaife, in faultless evening dress, stepped to the conductor's rostrum, tapped his music stand with professional dignity, waved an authoritative baton and the orchestra crashed into an inspiring overture.

"Then back stage, the director's last inspection of the set, hurried visits to the dressing rooms, tactful suggestions to this or another actor that he pick up his cues a bit quicker and contrive to appear when the action of the play required his presence, and when the orchestra was being applauded, the familiar orders: 'House Lights'—'Borders'—'Ring Up.' The stage manager steps into the shadow of off-stage with a prayer in his heart, a bell rings, the curtain slowly rises, polite applause greets one of Russell's incomparable sets, and the play is on.

"From then on the fate of the evening, and in a larger sense the fate of the Club, is in the hands of the active members. Directors may read countless plays, they may cast and recast a piece, the secretary may wade through a maelstrom of requests for the exchange of tickets, the treasurer may gasp at the demands of the producer for this or that piece of scenery or some special lighting, the director may labor at rehearsal, encourage, correct and exhort, but this is now all in the past. It is as if it never was, for now the active member, for better or worse, is in command, and upon him and him alone the success of the piece depends."

The list of plays given by the Footlight Club in the past sixty years is practically a history of playwriting.* In fact, it is more than a history of playwriting. It is a commentary on the taste and dramatic appreciation expressed by a serious group of cultured and artistic people.

Buffalo, New York. The Combination of Dramatic School and Community Theatre.

Looking through the society pages of the Buffalo newspapers, one can trace the interest in amateur dramatics through the past fifty years by watching the rise and fall of the many groups organized for this purpose. Among the latest of these groups, The Little Theatre of Buffalo was organized in 1922 and came to an unhappy financial end in 1927. Soon after this, Miss Jane Keeler resigned from the State Teachers College and organized the Studio School of the Theatre, now known as The Studio Theatre School, which combines a Little Theatre and a dramatic school.

This organization is unique in America in being at the same time a dramatic school and an honest Community Theatre. The premise on which the usual Community Theatre is based is that any person in the city may have the right to join by becoming a member and participating in its activities as an actor or technician. A Community Theatre must also present its plays to a representative audience of such size as to warrant its claim of community interest. However, there is no rule in this definition of a theatre that people participating in the production activities should not pay for that privilege and thereby aid in the subsidization of their theatre. That is what is done in Buffalo. More than three hundred people now attend the Studio Theatre School throughout the year and lend their aid to the six or seven productions that are given each season. It is only natural to note that they pay for such privileges of the school as courses in acting, make-up,

* See Appendix.

costume, fencing, and so forth. This large number of students allows the Studio to have a staff of nine which means that the productions of the Studio will be more efficiently directed and produced than if they had to struggle along with one person doing all the work.

The Studio Theatre School took over the equipment of their immediate predecessors and had its theatre workshop and school on the second floor of a building on Elmwood Avenue, where even in this limited space they achieved a city-wide reputation by outstanding productions of such plays as "Liliom," "The Critic," and "Trelawney of the Wells." During these early years when the Studio Theatre was doing some six to seven plays each year, Miss Keeler had associated with her as an art director, Sheldon K. Niele, whose experience and training in the theatres of Berlin, London and Rome, added much to the success of the studio's first productions.

From 1927 to 1933, life was fairly tranquil for the Studio Theatre in their Elmwood Avenue home. But fire laws enacted in 1933 made a new location essential. Just when the group was almost completely discouraged at seeking a home, Michael Shea offered the use of the Gaiety Theatre, a former burlesque house. Although much too large, with tremendous overhead, it was the only solution that the Studio Theatre could find at that time. However, their troubles were not over, for just as they had got their audiences used to coming to this new address, a burlesque company offered to pay so much more rent that the Studio Theatre again found itself homeless. This time they were forced to take the offer of some storage space over the old Teck Theatre which was probably one of the most unattractive locations possible for a community theatre and theatrical school.

Miss Keeler's office could then be reached only by a long flight of steps which surely must have kept many of the older patrons away, and the floor squeaked even after many applications of oil and driven nails, and a cover of heavy rugs. Heavy suburban cars passed frequently, shaking the building and making it impossible to hear the actors. But even so the Studio Theatre kept a great portion of its local following and was able to carry on with determination to get a new home at the first opportunity, even though the depression years made such a dream practically impossible.

In 1936, the Trustees of the School met and made plans for a drive to create a building fund. A small church was discovered at the corner of Hoyt and Lafayette Avenues, which the owners were eager to sell at a reasonable price. With earnest determination a drive was launched with Mrs. Howard W. Cowan as chairman. Within a few weeks there were sufficient contributions to make the theatre seem a certainty and, with accumulative eagerness and optimism, the drive was carried through to a successful finish. In order to give every member of the community an opportunity to share in the building of this theatre, a plan of selling bricks at $1.00 each was in-augurated. How the bricks went out and the dollars came in! The little church was purchased and the ground was broken for rebuilding in the middle of August, 1937. Final alterations were completed the first of December. At last the Studio Theatre had a permanent home.

The auditorium in the new theatre seats two hundred and sixty-four in comfortable and modern theatre chairs. The building itself, mellowed with age, with beautiful beamed ceilings enhanced by the use of attractive indirect lighting, is a joy to all those who have been loyal in much less pleasant surroundings these many years. Since the start of the Studio Theatre in 1927, more than seventy-five major productions have been given; over four hundred actors and one hundred and twenty-five people working back stage have participated in the theatre's activities.

Miss Keeler believes that a community theatre should be "able to reach out and touch people in all walks of life . . . giving potential actors an opportunity for expression . . . also stimulating in the public an interest and understanding of the arts of the theatre."

The Costume Department contributes a touching story of a large old fashioned trunk which was left on their door-step one day by some unknown friend. This "Treasure Trunk," as it is now called, is the center of the theatre's greatest mystery, for upon opening it they found a complete trousseau of the 1880's. There was a bridal dress with a slightly soiled train, a white evening gown, a red going-away dress with a green cape, a pink evening dress, and many other small articles of wearing apparel. All were wrapped in beautiful home-spun linen. Apparently nothing but the bridal dress had ever been worn. Many are the imaginative stories which have been woven about the contents of this trunk, perhaps none of them half so romantic as the real one. For all Buffalo would like to know what happened to the bride. Was she . . . ?

The Studio Theatre claims with some pride that more than sixteen of its former students are now engaged professionally in the movies, on the stage or in radio, and point with particular pride to Robert Wilcox and Reed Herring who have been doing well in Hollywood, Charme Allen and Katherine Clark active in radio work in New York City, and James Corbett, Helen Gardner and Bel Benstock, active in the professional theatre in New York.

At Green Lake, Orchard Park—a small resort near Buffalo—the Studio Theatre also has a summer theatre, and for five years has been playing to capacity audiences almost every night during the warm months. The stage is roofed over, but the audience sits out under the stars. In spite of discomfort when it rains, the audience insists on the play going on—even in the midst of thunder and lightning! They seem to resent even the suggestion of rain checks, for they consider the whole experience very much of a lark. One revival is always given at the close of the summer season, which runs as long as two or three weeks. By that time the weather is so cool that people bring blankets and generally fortify themselves against frost.

The Studio Theatre has found a real audience in the city of Buffalo. And this, probably more than anything else, makes it unique throughout the country, for few dramatic schools or even university theatres can boast of a real civic following.

Candlelight, Pennsylvania. A Farmyard Becomes a Community Theatre.

You won't be able to find this town on any map. In fact, it's not a town at all—it's a farmhouse. But there's a Community Theatre here that deserves attention.

To reach this spot go first to York, Pennsylvania. From there inquire your way. Three miles from York turn off the main highway onto a rough-stoned, treacherously sloped road. This road is so bad that patrons, driving their own cars, probably whoop with joy to find it only about two city blocks in length.

The only indication that one has arrived at the theatre is the end of the road, which turns uphill to a private residence, and a white-painted, tall tin can, with the letter "C" cut in front, suspended from a three-foot pole.

At the turn of the road stands one of the actors in greeting. He parks automobiles and directs patrons to the box office, a cleverly constructed replica of the shoe lived in by the old woman of story-book fame; with its characteristic roof, stove-pipe and lantern, it is large enough to shelter a table, a chair and two persons. The hollow toe of the shoe can accommodate three sleeping actors. It was first used in the Christmas parade in York, and donated to the Candlelight Players by the man who built it.

A short distance from the shoe, at the rear of the house, which, incidentally, is the home of the director, is the theatre.

The stage is merely a grass plot against the house. On the sloping terrace beyond, facing the "stage," are placed seven sixteen-foot benches (with back supports) used as seats for the audience. The benches aren't firm because they are placed on uneven ground, the kind one finds in so many back yards. The benches aren't even painted, because the group hasn't the money to paint them.

The footlights, borders, floods, and other stage lights are candles. Tin cans are used for all purposes. Small cans, cut vertically and separated, are the footlights; larger cans cut open in the front and separated are the overhead lights; bucket and wastepaper cans serve as floods. The usual illumination is the glow of tallow-dips. As a precaution, however, electric light fixtures are arranged; sometimes it gets very windy and the candles won't stay lit. The "house lights" of the theatre are tall tin cans with the letter "C" cut in front, suspended from three-foot poles and placed at the four corners of the audience section.

To the rear of the audience is a miniature brick house, from which tea and cookies are served the patrons between the acts. This house, like the shoe, was salvaged from the floats of the York Christmas parade, and is large enough to allow four persons to prepare the refreshments comfortably on a big kitchen table.

Outside the "tea house" are posted the names of the plays and the characters; this, however, is not the only program. The programs are cut from ordinary paper in the shape of a candle and candle holder with the names of the play, the scenes and other notes written on them.

The tickets are cut from file cards in the shape of a shoe. On one side is a linoleum block print showing what roads lead from York to the theatre, on the other side the usual ticket phraseology.

The theatre is not without farmyard atmosphere. On the same plot is a chicken coop, a geese pen, and a shelter for ducks. Before the performance begins, the fowls unite in something similar to a hog-calling contest, but, strangely, not one of them makes any sounds during the performance.

On the night of the theatre's premiere performance during the summer of 1938, it was necessary to wait until nine o'clock when it became dark enough to get the effect of the candlelight. Sharply at nine o'clock it began to rain. The audience ran for shelter under the garage roof and into the house. But, after ten minutes, the rain ceased and the audience resumed its seats. The play was begun. The rain began again. The play was halted and the audience was asked to return the following night—when all went well!

The plays are presented with a minimum of stage properties and no scenery whatsoever. The group started with no capital and realized $12.00 on its first performance. And they are struggling courageously on. They cannot be discouraged.

The players are composed of young people from York and the surrounding countryside. They earn their livelihoods by day and act by night. The membership is limited to those persons who hold the theatre second to their daily bread.

Their aim is to satisfy the desires of the community for spoken drama. The audiences are city folk from York and farmers from nearby, in overalls and muddy boots. But under the stars and the candlelight they have their own theatre. True pioneer spirit—the young people of today creating the theatre of tomorrow.

The director and organizer of this group is an enterprising young man, Robert Olewiler, a product of the York Little Theatre. This Candlelight Players group is the third Community Theatre he has organized. The first was at Dallastown, Pennsylvania, seven miles from York. He named the theatre group there the Dallastown Community Playhouse, and under his direction presented ten full-length plays among which "Little Women" and "Smilin' Through" were the most successful. The next was at Red Lion which is only one mile from Dallastown. There's a friendly rivalry between the two communities, so when Dallastown started a Community Theatre and borrowed actors from Red Lion, the citizens of Red Lion organized a Community Theatre and borrowed players from Dallastown. This is more interesting when one realizes that the combined population of these communities is only five thousand.

Mr. Olewiler made an interesting experiment in Red Lion when he produced "Ladies of the Jury." In casting the play he selected his actors according to profession. Among the roles which were given to persons from their respective walks of life were the prosecutor, which was played by one of Red Lion's lawyers; the judge, played by the town's justice of the peace, and the maid, enacted by one of Red Lion's most competent.

It was anticipated that the performance would be stilted, shop-worn. But the acting had fire, and the performance being "true-to-life" had an individuality which is remembered in Red Lion.

With such enterprising young men working in the Community Drama field, experimenting and pioneering, how can anyone say that the theatre is dead? It is more alive and flourishing in the byways of America than it is in the highways.

Dobbs Ferry, New York. The Methods of the Moscow Art Theatre in Practice.

A Community Theatre that has made an enviable reputation for itself is the Civic Theatre of Dobbs Ferry in Westchester County, New York.

In the fall of 1935 at the suggestion of Sherwin Cody, well-known educator and a resident of Dobbs Ferry, John W. Timen opened the Washington Theatre as an art theatre and training school for those interested in stage arts. This theatre, one of the most unusual of its size anywhere in the country, seats approximately two hundred in its comfortable auditorium, and has a stage sixteen by twenty-six feet with excellent lighting equipment and ample dressing room and stage space.

The Civic Theatre has a board of directors composed of outstanding people of Dobbs Ferry and vicinity. But the director, Mr. Timen, for the most part guides the policy and, knowing best the possibilities of his acting group and his stage, he chooses the plays to be produced.

Mr. Timen is a pioneer in the Little Theatre Movement, with which he has been associated for twenty-five years, and has been responsible for the establishment of a long list of art theatres in various parts of the country. In direction he follows the realistic school and uses the methods of the Moscow Art Theatre of his native Russia, adapted and modified to meet the needs of his American actors. No character is too small to receive careful analysis and interpretation, and he inculcates in his actors the maxim that "There are no small parts, only small actors." Thus, an individual in the group may play the lead in one production and have only a line or two in the next, yet feel as important a part of the whole as in the former play.

The Civic Theatre gives five productions a season. It is Mr. Timen's policy to produce plays of various countries, and to avoid, except in rare instances, a recent Broadway success. He feels that it is the duty of Community Theatres to produce only plays of literary and dramatic worth, whether they be comedies or dramas, and that those plays should, if possible, be works that are seldom or never produced on the commercial stage. With such plays, he believes, the director can do his best creative work; the actors find material for study and the employment of their full capacities for interpretation and characterization; and audiences and actors alike gain a wider knowledge of dramatic literature.

He is also interested in producing plays by unknown authors, but, though he has read dozens of manuscripts during the past three seasons, he has not yet found a play that meets his requirement of significant content, dramatic and literary worth, yet suitable for production on a small stage. However, he has not given up hope of finding such a script!

The acting group of the Civic Theatre is drawn not only from Dobbs Ferry, but from other Westchester towns such as Hastings, Tarrytown, Irvington, Yonkers, and from New York City. It is composed of business men and women, housewives, doctors, lawyers, teachers, and men and women from almost every walk of life. Season subscriptions are open to all who are interested as actors, stage mechanics, or audience. More and more people from nearby towns, as well as from more distant ones, are inquiring how they may become part of the acting and stagecraft groups, and audiences have steadily increased both in numbers and enthusiasm. The directors as well as the members of the group are always glad to add to their number anyone whose interest and theatre ideals correspond to theirs, and scarcely a month goes by that a new man or woman does not enter the Civic Theatre family.

There has been a growth in the dramatic taste of both audience and actors. All now demand only the best in dramatic literature, and subscribe whole-heartedly to the director's ideals as to what an amateur art and Community Theatre should represent.

The Civic Theatre in its three years of existence has accepted no dona-tions. Mr. Timen and his wife, Irene A. Timen, who acts as associate director, have assumed all responsibility for the financial as well as the artistic success of the theatre.

Thanks is due, however, to Colonel and Mrs. Franklin Q. Brown of Dobbs Ferry, owners of the Washington Theatre and always prime movers in anything of civic interest to their Hudson River town, for having donated the use of the theatre until such time as it shall be self-supporting.

Dover, New Jersey. First Nighters Attend a Play in a Morgue.

Eleanor Brigham Shattuck reports: "The Dover Little Theatre is a Com-munity Theatre in a small town forty miles from New York, not a commut-ing town and not a town of wealth." It got its start one sultry evening in June, 1933, sponsored by the president of the Woman's Club and an in-terested group of theatre-minded people. Lawyers, doctors, engineers, car-penters, electricians, photographers, store keepers, grocers, jewelers, clerks, teachers, stenographers, dressmakers, business men and women, college stu-dents, and homemakers, all pitched in together with the one idea of building for their town a dramatic enterprise which would not only satisfy each one's desire to work out his particular hobby but would add a successful unit of entertainment to the life of the community.

This new child was put into the hands of Ruth Beth Watts, whom the group was so fortunate as to find available as director. Miss Watts, while teaching dramatics and public speaking at Texas State College for Women and also at Winona State Teachers College in Minnesota, had organized little theatre groups. It was indeed fortunate for this newly organized band of Thespians and backstage workers that she was at hand to become the motivating power in the new enterprise for her home town.

Though homeless, the theatre grew and flourished. While some mem-bers scoured the countryside for a possible old barn, inn, mill or vacant shop to house the theatre, others were busy in the immediate production of plays. On September 25, 1933, "Ladies of the Jury" was admirably presented to a capacity audience in the auditorium of the high school. One milestone had been passed.

By the beginning of 1934 the housing problem had been solved. A long, low red brick building on a side street, near the center of town, piled high with storage machinery, was vacant. Formerly it had been a morgue!

"That's our theatre!" declared Ruth Beth Watts.

The zoning law requirements were satisfied and the lease executed. The theatre had its home.

The rent was paid and there was nothing left in the treasury. All hands set to work to dig out cobwebs, seal up doors, open new doorways, tear out walls, build up partitions, paint the plaster and brick work, lay flooring at a slight angle, make a greenroom, a lobby, dressing rooms, and best of all, a modern stage. The dressing rooms were built in the basement out of the old horse stalls. Time and patience, blisters and dusters, tools and good will, all had parts. Before the flooring was laid or the stage built, a masquerade barn dance was held. Monthly meetings and one-act plays were given in the theatre despite its half-finished condition.

On May 2, 1934, "Lady Windemere's Fan" by Oscar Wilde was presented in the permanent home of the Dover Little Theatre. Members proudly hailed this first full-length play in its own building, and the last major production of its first fiscal year. The season closed in June with a fine record: three full-length plays under the direction of Miss Watts, several one-act plays under the direction of different members, regular monthly meetings and a membership of one hundred and fifteen.

The second year, through a membership campaign, the number of members was increased to one hundred and sixty-eight, classified as active members, active subscribers, subscribers and patrons. This drive for members with their dues paid in advance supplied a bit of capital, which was used for improvements in the heating system, additional scenery, and stage necessities. The second year was most successful, witnessing four three-act plays; a Christmas pantomime, which has since become an annual affair; three one-act plays contests of three plays each directed by members; forty one-act plays, three of which were original, given not only as programs at the monthly meetings but also as entertainment for various outside social clubs and community projects; the organization of a string ensemble from among the theatre numbers; and a mimeographed monthly bulletin of theatre news, the *Curtain Call*, mailed to each member.

Also in this year began the custom, since fostered by the Dover Little Theatre, of inviting visiting groups from other Community Theatres, the first being that of the Point Pleasant Play Shop, whose leader, S. Iden Thompson, was a pioneer in the Little Theatre Movement in this country. Visiting groups from other theatres and professional theatres, too, have continued to flock to Dover from all parts of New Jersey.

They participated in the "Little Theatre of the Air Contest" on Station

WOR in Newark, sponsored by L. Bamberger and Company, with "Back of the Yards." The Dover group was one of twelve chosen from fifty-four competing groups.

Toward the end of the season an opportunity for securing permanent seats came to the attention of the theatre. Discards from the high school auditorium were bought and installed. Previously the local undertakers had lent chairs for the theatre which, although in keeping with its original morgue status, were rather a nuisance to borrow and set up for each meeting and play.

In the fall of 1935 the membership drive raised the number to two hundred and ten. The theatre was growing. New faces kept appearing in important roles. Difficult plays were attempted and proved successful. Theatre members worked hard, and the results were appreciated by large audiences. Plays had to run three nights to accommodate the playgoers. The theatre seats a hundred and seventy, and more often than not the house was sold out.

In July of 1936 a new idea was brought in. The young people of high school age wanted to share in the dramatic interest, and so a Junior Little Theatre began for those between thirteen and eighteen. Under Miss Watts, forty joined this organization, elected officers, and held meetings through the summer. Several one-act plays were put into rehearsal and by September a one-act play contest, open to the public, was carried out with great credit to the juniors who not only were the actors but the scene and property designers and stage managers.

The opening of the fifth subscription year was appropriately celebrated by a campaign which brought the number of memberships up to five hundred. Never was the treasury so full at the start of a year. The lobby was improved by the addition of two high-backed benches and doors to separate the box office from the lobby itself. The ladies' dressing room was overhauled and redecorated. (Remember it was once a couple of horse stalls!) The stage wiring was improved and a set of footlights were donated and installed.

In the season of 1937-1938 they produced seven one-act plays and five three-act plays using sixty-one different members as actors and thirty-five different members as stage crew. In the three act plays forty-eight different members took part. Many of these acted or worked backstage in more than one play in the year but the fact that so many different people were available makes them feel the success of their theatre in Dover. In addition to monologues and short plays at their regular monthly meetings they have had visiting lecturers, visiting monologists, dancers, musical programs, and monologue contests.

The record for their five years of existence in play producing is sixty one-act plays, including four originals by members, and twenty-one full length plays with a total of fifty-six performances. The average attendance per performance has been one hundred fifty-one. Quoting Miss Shattuck again: "We, like everybody else, have to watch our budget but have always been self-supporting. This is accomplished by our dues system and subscription memberships. Our money for the most part is in at the beginning of the season so we pretty well know how much expenditure we may run."

Two members, still active, are doing professional work now; one in summer theatres and one on Broadway. Kenneth Alpers, a student in the New York School of Interior Decoration, who has been very active in the Dover Little Theatre since its beginning, is designing sets for summer theatres. And Franklin Heller, a graduate of the Carnegie Institute of Technology, who worked with the original group in Dover, has been assistant stage manager and played a small part in "You Can't Take It With You."

Miss Shattuck states further: "The playgoers are not all local people but come from far and near, including several counties. Our theatre is well organized and one which we think bound to thrive. There are a Board of Directors, a slate of officers changed every two years, a business manager, a program committee, a stage manager and technical crew, a committee chairman for every particular line from scenery design down to the vacuum cleaning jobs.

"New talent keeps appearing, sometimes fifty or more trying out for parts at a play reading. New faces are often found behind the footlights. New hands try their luck at directing plays and still there are many of the original interested group from back in 1933 working in their spare moments in the theatre, their hobby.

"Who knows but that Broadway or Hollywood may see more of us some day! The Dover Little Theatre is growing!"

Erie, Pennsylvania. The Erie Playhouse.

The forerunner of the present Playhouse was "The Little Playhouse" founded in 1916 by Henry B. Vincent and a group of associates.

Seating only one hundred people, and with a very tiny stage, The Little Playhouse at first operated only when someone had time to sweep out, dust, make scenery and rehearse a play. Nevertheless, in a very short time it became a lively dramatic and musical center for the city. Its actors, rapidly gaining experience, turned in increasingly excellent performances; its artists painted novel and effective scenery; its orchestra and choral society made good music; and it imported many famous people for lectures and intimate recitals. During the first year of the war it sponsored city-wide community sings, entertained soldiers and sailors, adopted a French war orphan, and was invited to send a company of its players abroad.

One of the greatest charms of The Little Playhouse was its air of informality, good cheer and friendliness. Its audiences learned by experience always to expect the unexpected. In its lighter plays the actors occasionally overflowed into the audience and continued their performances from there; scenes sometimes were set with the curtain up. Nothing was done in a hackneyed way. It may have been (and probably was) very poor theatre, but the neighborly spirit of the place was contagious; everybody felt at home and everybody had a good time.

Finally, however, the war-time demand for space compelled the abandonment of the premises, and on May 14, 1918, the curtain was rung down for the last time in The Little Playhouse.

Almost immediately search was begun for a new location and within a few weeks a building was offered for the continuance of the Playhouse idea. This building had successively been Erie's first electric light plant, a brass foundry, and a war-time automobile barracks. Extensive alterations, financed by the War Chest of Erie, made it possible to open the new and much larger "Community Playhouse" in March, 1919, with an ambitious program of community drama and opera: community sings, dances, and open forums; a settlement art and music school for those who could not otherwise afford to study; a children's theatre and story-telling hours; and other activities designed to encourage talent and to promote general friendliness. In particular, the Community Playhouse organized dramatic and musical groups in many of the larger stores of the city.

Back of this Community Playhouse was a tangible idea and a definite purpose. It sought to discover and to encourage every phase of artistic endeavor in the city; to promote neighborliness by bringing people together and interesting them in each other; to add something to the joy of life by the production of good plays and good music. In its emphasis on community drama, music, and art as socializing influences, the Community Playhouse discovered and developed unsuspected abilities and unused resources. It sought to make active participants instead of passive observers—to capitalize people's leisure time. In one season alone, nearly three hundred and fifty people appeared on its stage in some capacity, and its general admissions numbered over a hundred thousand.

The Community Playhouse, like many other institutions of its kind, was rich in ideas but poor in purse. It derived its entire support from the people it served. In the beginning it attempted to secure this support by cooperation rather than coercion. A barrel was placed at the entrance and people were trusted to contribute voluntarily. A year's experience showed that this touching faith in human nature was not wholly justified. The barrel was too convenient a receptacle for buttons, hairpins and other small matters, and constituted a hazard which many otherwise good people found it impossible to surmount.

Finally the Community Playhouse found itself compelled to abandon its more altruistic activities and to put increasing emphasis on that which produced the most satisfactory and concrete return—the production of good plays. These productions already had begun to have a more than local reputation when the building was sold and on May 27, 1927, the curtain was rung down for the last time in the Community Playhouse.

A widespread public interest in providing a comfortable and well-equipped home for a permanent theatre company made possible Erie's third Playhouse. During the fall of 1927, Erie people very generously contributed to a fund for a new building. Ground was broken on July 6, 1928, and on January 3, 1929, the curtain was raised for the first time in the present Erie Playhouse—the attraction being "The Queen's Husband."

With the inauguration of the new building that much overworked word "community" was eliminated from the title. To many people the word "community" seems to indicate the pleasing possibility of getting something for nothing. Intelligent people know that one seldom gets anything for nothing in this imperfect world, and the Playhouse is no exception to the general rule. It is an amusement enterprise and charges for its wares as does any other enterprise. It does propose that its wares shall be exceptional; and it must stand or fall by its ability to deliver the goods.

The present Playhouse is almost the last word in theatre comfort, convenience and equipment. While it is small it is complete in every detail. Its semi-professional company operates continuously every night, except Sundays, from September until June of each season. It has, in addition, a Saturday afternoon Children's Theatre staffed by, and playing to, children. Also there is a school giving instruction in all phases of theatre activity, including dancing.

In September, 1938, the Playhouse began its twenty-third season. The opening was the two hundred eightieth and the opening performance was number two thousand three hundred five. What began twenty-two years ago as little more than a plaything has developed into a well-established public theatre, housing a permanent acting company and playing to an annual audience of between forty and fifty thousand people.

While the Playhouse is commercial insofar as it is self-sustaining, it is operated primarily for the pleasure it can give. It is dedicated, as the inscription over its foyer fireplace indicates, "to the making of happiness."

Fitchburg, Massachusetts. Ten Nationalities Join Hands in a Community Theatre.

Here is a Community Theatre truly cosmopolitan in scope. Its membership of some hundred and fifty persons includes Finnish, German, Jewish, Swedish, Irish, French, Italian, Greek, Russian nationalities, and of course, New Englanders of old Puritan and Pilgrim Father's stock.

Organized in 1924, it has managed every since to be self-supporting but not profit-making. Any small balance is spent for educational purposes, such as lectures on the drama by prominent speakers, classes for students, and preparation for succeeding productions. And it continues to operate within the bounds of its pre-determined budget.

To Mr. and Mrs. Charles T. Crocker of Fitchburg much of the success of this group of players is due. Through their kindness, interest, financial support and encouragement The Workshop has forged steadily ahead. In 1934 Mrs. Crocker purchased for the players what is known as "The Barn." Part of an estate in Fitchburg, it was redecorated and remodeled; the former horse stall became a tiny kitchen where refreshments are served, the walls are gay with pictures of successful productions, and there's a fireplace around which the players sit while resting from rehearsals. The building is home.

Besides this charming clubhouse, the players rent a large storage room where they make their own scenery. The sets are designed and usually executed by Aarne J. Parker, a talented artist and young business man of Fitchburg. The major productions are given in one of the downtown theatres. But numerous one-act plays and informal evenings are held at the Workshop.

This group has never conducted a membership drive; enrolment is open to persons sincerely interested in the work. Each member is expected to take part in at least one play during the season, either one of the major productions or a Workshop evening.

Three secret judges, two appointed by the executive committee and the third by the first two members, judge the work of each player and, at the season's end, prizes are awarded for the best performance.

In January of 1938 this group made a momentous decision: to retire from a public theatre and drop "box-office" appeal. On the ninth of March the Board presented to the membership the plans drawn up by their vice-president, Aarne Parker, for remodeling their barn into a small theatre.

This plan involved the purchase of adjoining land, and a ways and means committee of eight members was appointed to study plans in cooperation with their sponsor, Mrs. Charles T. Crocker.

Both active and associate members were interviewed for contributions, as were a few former members and friends of the players. The campaign was successful, and the interior of the barn is being remodeled.

A stage is being built, and an auditorium seating about one hundred. Here in the future the plays of The Workshop will be given, running two or three nights. And since the seating capacity is limited, the general public when they wish to attend the plays in this new playhouse will have to obtain guest tickets from the members. And if there aren't any left, their names will be put upon a waiting list for the next production.

One of the features of this group is the yearly presentation of an out-of-doors play on the grounds of the beautiful estate of Mr. and Mrs. Crocker. Usually given in the spring when the gardens are in full bloom, the event is attended by hundreds of persons, many of them coming from other states.

Most of the directing of this group is done by the members, although occasionally they bring in a guest director. Mrs. Cristobel Kidder, well known throughout New England as a dramatic reader, has directed many of their plays. They have given almost forty productions, with several hundred different people participating at one time or another.

From this group of players several have gone to Broadway or Hollywood. Albert Cairns appeared in the motion picture, "Calvacade." Ernest Sonis has played with summer theatres. Frederick Thompson made his professional stage debut with Katharine Cornell in "Romeo and Juliet," and was with Orson Welles in "Julius Caesar." Santy Syrjala was a scenic aid on "Pins and Needles."

And now, with their own new playhouse, opened during the fall of 1938, they are making plans for a permanent Community Theatre in Fitchburg.

Great Neck, New York. Community Players Thrive Where Broadway Actors Live.

Again a generous patron of the theatre. Again a discriminating patron of the arts who has the discretion to create a living monument to herself rather than an empty shell of grandeur. For a few thousand dollars, Mrs. Roswell Eldridge has been able to give to her community a structure which will bring more pleasure, enjoyment, and beauty into the lives of her friends than anything else she might have given them. Very recently Mrs. Eldridge came to the aid of the Great Neck Players by enlarging their theatre and amplifying its physical plant until today it is a model community theatre.

Edith Hay tells the story best in her own words when she says:

"Ever since Great Neck became something more than a spot on the map, it has been known as a 'dramatic' town. Way back, about the turn of the century, when the drama meant something, some of Broadway's gayest luminaries chose this rapidly growing town as a haven of rest and Great Neck became what some choose to call an artists' colony. As time progressed, followers of the other arts joined and people, weary with life in typical suburban villages or large cities, created their homes in Great Neck. The town reached its greatest peak of unadulterated joy and excitement in the late '20's but something happened in 1929. Since that time, the physical aspect of the town has changed but the spirit, which was permeated with the love of the theatre, and good theatre at that, has lingered.

"Undaunted by the decline of the stock market and general panic, the Great Neck Players went ahead with plans and introduced their first production to the public on December 12, 1929. The opener was an A. A. Milne comedy, 'The Romantic Age,' and it was directed by Mildred Whitney, who still is a member of the board and one of the leading spirits of the group.

"Since the first production, the Players have plunged bravely along, giving three plays and five green room nights a year. Originally, the Players planned to be an experimental theatre. They wanted to produce new scripts. However, they soon were discouraged in this idea because there was a dearth of scripts that were worth the effort. Rather than lower their standards, the Players turned to established successes. During their nine years of playing they have found only five new scripts worth production—'Places,' 'The Cradle,' 'Dear Youth,' 'Postscript,' and 'Maybe Tomorrow,' a play written and directed by a local newspaperman, Donald Oatley. All of these plays were successful.

"The greatest pride of the Players is their theatre. They do all of their work in what was formerly called the Union Chapel, a picturesque seventy-year old building, once a church, once a meeting place of the Woman's Club. Until last year, the building was one unit with 'community' dressing rooms and a small kitchen. Before each performance there was typical backstage pandemonium and when it was warm enough and the cast large enough, it was not an unfamiliar sight to see them oozing from the doors as they sought room to turn.

"The house was small; the floor was level. The seats, about 150 of them, were of the kitchen variety; the kind that grew uncomfortable by the end of Act One and by the final curtain were in an entirely different row than originally. The stage was tiny and often when it was necessary for any person to move backstage, between the wall and a flat, there was a bulge visible to the audience. Upstage center, there was a chimney that constantly hindered almost all attempts at unusual scenes from the windows of a set.

"However, in 1938, the honorary chairman of the board, Mrs. Roswell Eldridge, induced the board of the Union Chapel to allow her to make several alterations on the Chapel. They assented and soon the Union Chapel was transformed from one of the most clumsy, but best loved little theatres, to one of the most modern ones of its size in the surrounding territory.

"In the first place, a wing, fifty by thirty feet, was added at the back of the small building as a stage. This left the house large enough to seat 215 comfortably in regular theatre seats that were installed after the floor was made on an incline. The proscenium opening is thirty feet leaving a space of ten feet all around back stage. Since scenery may not be flown, this gives the stage crew ample space in which to work. The second play of the 1938 season was 'The Beaux' Stratagem,' a piece that requires numerous scenery changes.

"The scene designer, David Bryant, a teacher of art in the high school, devised a system of scene shifting, using rollers, that enabled a complete shift in a few seconds. Before the new theatre was built, the Players presented 'Fashion' and still are wondering how they managed the twenty-nine scene changes.

"In the stage wing was built a large dressing room with mirrors and dressing tables at each end. When a play is being given a large wooden screen divides this room, making it into men's and women's dressing rooms. There also is a small room which is used by the star. In this wing, too, is a kitchen, used for the refreshments served during the green room nights. However, this invariably turns either into a dressing or a costume room, depending upon the play and the number of people in the cast.

"The theatre, now called the Chapel Theatre, is situated on the main road of Great Neck, in what is called the Upper Village. It is surrounded by spacious grounds, artistically planted with ample space for parking. No taxes are paid on the building which is controlled by a board of executors— a non-profit group. For the past five years until 1936, the Woman's Club of Great Neck and the Players both contributed toward the upkeep of the Chapel. However, the Woman's Club was given a building of its own which left the Players as the sole lessee.

"Attendance at the Players' productions was dropping off, people complained of the theatre, the seats and sometimes the plays. With the building of the new theatre, these faults were removed. The Players increased their attendance at plays more than one hundred per cent. Also a new plan of membership was inaugurated. There are active members who must work and subscribers who are entitled to six tickets a season. The active membership is less than the subscription, but the holder of a membership is permitted one ticket to each production, free admission to the green room night and the privilege of working with the group. Gradually, the Players hope to weed out all of the non-productive members and put them on the subscriber list.

"The set-up of the Players is entirely democratic. Each year there is an election for four of the twelve board members who have a term of three years. The board itself elects officers and assigns the members to various committees. Each one is given a definite job such as costumes, publicity, tickets, workshop and others covering every phase of production. It is not necessary for the director of a play to be a member of the board and in the past, the rule has been that an interested member usually takes over his job. An earnest effort has been made every year to have the entire membership actively at work in one phase of the production or another, but as is the case in most groups of this kind, the enthusiasm runs high for the first weeks, then the work is done by a few people and soon the organization is criticized for showing favoritism. However, during the last year, the Players were successful in having more than fifty per cent of the total members of a cast newcomers or comparative newcomers.

"When the Players realized that they were to be the sole tenants of the Chapel Theatre and were expected to be largely responsible for the heavy carrying charges if the building were to remain at their disposal, they looked around for a source of revenue. The source and the Players found each other almost at the same time. With the theatre in its present condition, it made a perfect setting for a Summer playhouse.

"The result was that after several months of consideration a company was chosen for the 1938 season. A ten week program was announced and has been carried out as successfully as any 'barn circuit' theatre playing its first season. However, the Summer theatre has met with the same problem that the Players must constantly face. Great Neck is not more than a half an hour by train from New York City. Plays must be carefully chosen in order not to conflict with recent New York successes that may have been seen by a large majority of Great Neck residents. The Summer theatre has filled its houses best with the appearance of such stars as Blanche Yurka, Effie Shannon, Donald Brian, Elissa Landi, Fay Wray and Helen Vinson. When the plays are poor, the Great Neck audiences, who know a great deal about the theatre, do not come; when the plays are good they do come. Word gets around.

"Of course for a local amateur group there is always the problem of money matters, filling the house even when the play is good, producing a play that meets the requirements of the audience. But these are the problems of every small theatre, no matter where it is located. If the Players can maintain their money average of 1938, they will be able to continue in their new home with the aid of the Summer theatre which will probably return. This is a case of one theatrical group helping the other.

"When it was decided to have a Summer theatre in Great Neck there was but one thing lacking to make the Chapel Playhouse complete. That was a nearby workshop where sets could be built easily and without too much cost. Mrs. Eldridge, realizing this, constructed a large and complete workshop with an office, adjoining the theatre itself. Thus, the Great Neck Players are housed in a modern plant fully equipped. It is entirely up to them to make it successful and there seems no reason, if everyone cooperates, why the Great Neck Players cannot be one of the most outstanding groups of its kind in its territory. It has met and conquered every obstacle so far. The Players were organized primarily for those residents who had a keen interest in the theatre, but worked in other professions. Those who work consistently with the group, do so because they love the theatre whether it is amateur or professional. They have no terrors about stagecraft, except that anything attempted should be done as well as it is possible for the group to do it. Most of the productions are done in the conventional manner because it takes money, not available through an audience, to maintain a purely experimental theatre."

Two of the group have made their marks on the professional stage. One is Philip Truex, son of Ernest Truex, a Great Neck resident, who has played in several Broadway productions, including acting with the Maurice Evans Shakespearean group. The other is Patricia Palmer, a Bayside resident, who has appeared for two years with George Abbott both on the road and in New York. Both of these youngsters received their first training and encouragement with the Players.

Harrisburg, Pennsylvania. One Thousand Members in One Week.

In one week the Community Theatre of Harrisburg tripled its membership!

It was that dreary spring of 1934, and the players were suffering from a hang-over of the depression. The group was slowly accumulating a list of debts. Interest in the theatre was lagging, attendance was dwindling, subscriptions were not renewed, and the death of the little group was foreseen. But as a last try, Henning Nelms, the director, and a telephone squad hung onto their phones and sold the idea to enough members to pull through another season.

Not that this meant very much. The director hadn't been paid for months. So over the summer the players dodged bill collectors.

And then in September of 1935 there was one last concentrated effort to obtain members. The theatre planned an elaborate campaign, patterned after the welfare campaigns, under the leadership of John M. Crandall. Division heads and team captains were named, and more than one hundred volunteer workers dedicated themselves to the cause of the theatre. The Civic Club was used for daily report luncheons, and after one exciting week, the membership of the Harrisburg Community Theatre was tripled.

For the first time in its history, the books showed a membership of nearly eleven hundred members, and each succeeding year since then more theatre lovers have joined the group.

All this has been told in detail by Henning Nelms in his booklet, *Building an Amateur Audience*, published by Samuel French of New York. Copies can be had for the asking.

Ironically, this large membership brought on a new problem in Harrisburg. It was not practical for them to present their plays for more than three nights in a rented auditorium. That meant that the audience must be equally distributed over the three performances if the members were to be accommodated. In the past, with few exceptions, members who attended a performance without reservation were fairly sure of finding seats. With increased membership this was no longer true. Therefore as many as possible were urged to come to the first showing, as it usually had been the least attended, with the last nights playing to crowded houses. So now Harrisburg is first-night conscious.

This group started in 1923. A drama group of the University Club, some twenty-five women, met for the sole purpose of self-expression. Each of the twenty-five members contributed twenty-five dollars, and their plays were presented in the homes that boasted the largest living rooms, before a few select guests.

Came the revolution. The group divided into two factions; those who wanted to expand into a civic organization, and those who wanted to continue as a closed organization limiting the membership to Harrisburg's Blue Book. The first group won!

In the spring of 1926 they presented their first play for the general public. Fifteen hundred persons attended and pronounced the offering a success. Some of those who appeared at that time are still trouping with the Community Players.

They soon had their own theatre, an old church which they remodeled

The New Bedford (Massachusetts) Players: Set designed by Robert J. Wade for "The Bishop Misbehaves."

Design by Robert J. Wade for "The Tempest" as produced at Emerson College in 1937.

The Spouters, New Bedford, Massachusetts: Set designed by Robert J. Wade for "When Ladies Meet."

Rochester Community Players, Inc.   Rochester, New York.

"Jane Eyre" at the Civic Little Theatre of Allentown, Pa.

"Penny Wise."

The Footlight Club
Boston, Massachusetts.

(Photos by Henry S. Adams.)

"Viceroy Sarah."

"Bees on the Boat Deck."

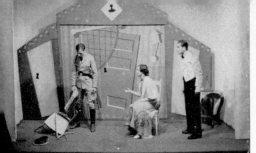

"A Leghorn Hat."   Theatre League, Philadelphia.   "The Feud."

Longmeadow, Mass., Community House—home of the Longmeadow Players.

A women's matinee at the Bangor-Brewer Little Theatre in Maine.

Set designed by John Lee Clark for "Accent on Youth" at the Players' Guild, Springfield, Massachusetts. (Photo by Art Photo Co.)

The Studio Players of Essex County, Montclair, New Jersey. "Behold We Live." (Photo by Guy G. Clark, Jr.)

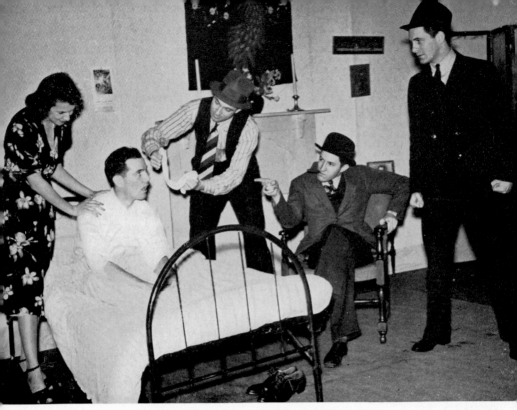

Plays and Players Little Theatre Group, Bethlehem, Pennsylvania.
"Three Men on a Horse."

Jersey City Little Theatre: "Street Scene."

Dobbs Ferry, New York.

Sketches by Richard Hurd.

Civic Theatre.

Lobby.

Rehearsal.

Performance.

Stage Crew.

The Dover Little Theatre
(New Jersey) was formerly
a morgue!

"Ah, Wilderness!"

"The Importance of Being Earnest."

Pittsburgh Playhouse. Musical review: "Hold Your Hats."

"Accent on Youth."

Civic Theatre of Waterbury,
Connecticut.

"Excursion."

"Hotel Universe."

"Excursion."

The Mark Twain Masquers,
Hartford, Connecticut.

"The Swan."

A standing custom:
serving coffee and cakes
to all patrons!

Fitchburg, Massachusetts.   (Photos by Donald Barton Studio.)

"Crime at Blossoms."

Fitchburg: "The Queen's Husband."

(Frederick New, Photographer.)

Studio Theatre School,
Buffalo, New York.

"Libel."

with great good will. Then, after five pleasant years, the building was again put to use as a church and the theatre was forced to vacate.

A workshop of their own was set up, and the public performances given in the Jewish Community Center. And when the curtain fell on the last play of the 1937-38 season, the Harrisburg Community Theatre counted seventy-two productions to their credit.

Each season more than one hundred actors appear in the plays, and those who work back stage are too numerous to be counted. They try each year to have at least thirty or forty new people take an active part in the productions.

Chester Good, the president, says, "This theatre does not exist by fits and starts. Instead it is a civic enterprise established for a purpose, well organized, having a trained director, a board of governors representative of the best in the community, and a program of plays planned one year ahead. Every cent of its finances is accounted for, and its books are audited by able accountants. These, and many, many more factors, all carefully planned, make up this Community Theatre."

The organization is composed of committees. The board of governors engages the director, makes final decisions about play selections, finances, and all matters pertaining to general theatre policy. The president appoints all committees.

Their first director was Adele Eichler, who found romance in the theatre and married the leading man of one of her productions. She now lives in New York and sends them news of the Broadway stage in a column published in their twenty-page program. The next year Gordon Ruffin was at the helm. And then in 1931 came Henning Nelms from Yale.

The director for the 1938-39 season, Alfred Rowe, had been with Jasper Deeter's Hedgerow Theatre the preceding nine years. They say in Harrisburg that Mr. Rowe brought something to the Community Theatre beyond a knowledge of what the public wants and an intuitiveness for good productions. He brought excitement—that buoyant, fourth-dimensional thing that means life to an organization.

Preliminary plans for a suggested Community Auditorium have already been drawn in Harrisburg. Many organizations are being approached, for it is the purpose of the Community Theatre to make this a building in which everyone can have a share. When it is finally completed they hope it will be a civic center to house every group that seeks a home.

Hartford, Connecticut. They'd Rather Stay Home Than Try Broadway.

Back in 1933, Merrill E. Joels, of Hartford, decided he wanted to become an actor. So he came to New York, and managed to obtain an interview with Lee Strasberg of the Group Theatre.

"What is your background?" asked Mr. Strasberg. "What books have you read on the theatre? What methods have you studied?"

In reply Mr. Joels could only shrug his shoulders. He hadn't read many books on the theatre. So he went on back home to Hartford and spent the rest of the summer in the public library.

In his reading he came across books on the Community Theatres of the country; his imagination was fired. Here was something he hadn't anticipated. Something different from becoming a Broadway actor. And soon his enthusiasm was fanned to a roaring desire to establish in Hartford a Community Theatre that would equal organizations already flourishing in other cities.

Feeling certain that Hartford could and would support such an organization, he approached the theatre lovers of that city. He was greeted with various reactions. Some were enthusiastic. Others contended that Hartford would not support such an organization, citing as proof that there never had been a successful Community Theatre group in the city.

But eventually he succeeded in interesting a number of people, and through the courtesy of Mr. and Mrs. Joseph Dolgin, a meeting was called at their home on September 9, 1933.

At this meeting, after discussion of the many difficulties facing such a project, it was decided that: based upon an honest effort to present fine plays and bearing in mind the need for an efficient, business-like and progressive theatre, it definitely was a worth-while undertaking to establish in Hartford a non-commercial civic theatre organization. The group selected as its name "The Mark Twain Masquers," in honor of the man who had contributed so much to the enjoyment of the world and had brought honor to Hartford through his residence there. At the close of this meeting, the group realized that they had begun a work that would require many years before realizing its main purpose: the construction of a Community Theatre building as a monument to all connected with the venture.

First the founders discovered a two-room studio on the third floor of a dilapidated old building. The members pitched in and painted the walls. A truck went to each member's home, picking up a chair here, a table there, an old phonograph, and little by little the place began to take on a livable appearance.

The Avery Memorial had just been completed and the Masquers desired to be the first to present a play on its new stage. Jay Ray was secured as director. Their production was a success, financially and artistically, and the Masquers had a feeling of security, knowing that they were on the right track.

But soon they found that they could not continue presenting plays in settings of velvet drapes. It was necessary to build and paint scenery. Through the courtesy of C. H. Dresser and Son, a workshop was established at their woodworking plant, and the group learned what it meant to take wood, muslin and a bit of paint and build sets of an author's dream scenes.

All this time the Masquers were growing. Their studio was too small. So at the end of the second season they moved to their present quarters. This consists of four rooms at 262 Trumbull Street: a main rehearsal room, a reception room, a Board of Directors' room, and a Green Room.

No longer in the experimental stage, the Masquers in their third season began to accomplish a few of their main objectives. One was a memorial play of Mark Twain's for the benefit of the Mark Twain home on Farmington Avenue. The second was production of a new play.

Raleigh Dresser was appointed business manager for the production of Mark Twain's "Puddin' Head Wilson." Mr. Dresser put in five months of constant work to perfect the final presentation at the Bushnell Memorial in November, 1935. With the cooperation of Joseph C. Gorton as head of the Mark Twain Memorial Commission, Mr. Dresser began his work, which included a nation-wide search for the original play, and a trip to Maine to interview and obtain permission to produce it from Edward A. Huse, who had the only original copy. Mr. Huse supplied some of the properties used with the original show when it was first produced by the play's co-author, Frank Mayo, in the late 'Nineties. Through the cooperation of the Board of Education, Fred Wish, and other civic-minded individuals such as Professor Odell Shepard and Lester B. Scheide, a poster and essay contest was introduced into the schools of Hartford.

At the Tercentenary Parade the Masquers were represented by a float consisting of an old horse pulling an ancient buggy in which was seated Raleigh Dresser with the make-up and costume of Mark Twain, and Cedric Thompson, who played the title role in "Puddin' Head Wilson." Tagging along behind was an old hound dog.

A cast of thirty-five under the competent direction of Jay Ray presented a superior performance that justified all the work and effort the Masquers put into it.

For the closing play of that season they realized another ambition: the

presentation of a new play. This was "Love My Island," by Alfred Etcheverry. It proved highly diverting and a grand conclusion to a busy, hectic
season.

During the 1937-38 season, financially successful, the Masquers decided
on two steps. First a substantial deposit was made in one of Hartford's
banks for the building fund. Second, a checking account was opened. The
appreciation of the Hartford people has given the Masquers the courage to
go on to the ultimate fulfilment of their ideal.

Early in the life of the Masquers an anonymous civic-minded citizen
announced that each season he would give a $5.00 prize to the Masquer
doing the most for the organization. This is called "Old Bill" prize. The
first season it was awarded to Merrill E. Joels, the second season to Cedric
G. Thompson, and the third and fourth seasons to Samuel Gold, who served
the group as president.

"Acting is just one small phase of Community Theatre work," says Merrill Joels. "Those people who just want 'to act and act' and persist in this
attitude and do not gradually become immersed in the whole ideal of the
work of the Community Theatre, which means also constructing scenery,
making costumes, selling tickets, and doing dozens of other jobs, soon find
themselves left behind, disillusioned and, perhaps, a little wiser. One of
the most important contributions of the Community Theatre movement is not
the discovery of new talent for Broadway, but the awakening of realization
in the individual with nothing but an illusion of ability that the professional theatre is not their life's work—but community drama is!"

Concerning their production of popular plays of the Broadway success
type, such as "Boy Meets Girl," "Brother Rat," and "Night of January 16th,"
Raleigh Dresser says:

"I can't stress too strongly the selection of plays. It wasn't until the
Masquers began to do modern comedy and plays with snappy lines that they
began to earn money. At the conclusion of one season of 'arty' plays, there
was only one hundred dollars in the treasury. After a season of currently
popular hits and only one 'Drama' of the doubtful era the nest egg of the
Masquers leaped up to a very few dollars under one thousand, without debts.
Avoid the lurid plays that deal with the sordid side of life. Labor troubles
are fought during the day and the tired business man doesn't want to hear
the communists bark across the footlights in the evening. Mr. and Mrs.
America want to laugh and enjoy life, and the Community Theatre should
help them do those very things."

Mr. Dresser also believes in having personal suggestions put into a suggestion box and discussed at a general meeting rather than be lobbied through.

"You may not get your way if your thought is talked over, but you will get some side-lights on the subject that you never dreamed of and the chances are 100 to 1 that the discussion will definitely improve the original.

"A Community Group should be as the Three Musketeers—'One for all, and all for one.' When all hands join in the fun, each one forgetting his or her personal likes or dislikes, it will amaze you how grand a group you can have and what polished work you can present."

Longmeadow, Massachusetts. The Town Fathers Cooperate with a Community Building.

A group of about twenty-five people met on October 7, 1925, in Longmeadow, and decided to start a Community Theatre. Just as simple as that. Among the citizens assembled at this meeting were ministers, bankers, editors, teachers, society matrons, and insurance men.

And from the very beginning they engaged as their director William Thornton Simpson, who lived not far away in Springfield. They started their work by having classes in voice, stage technique, and stage deportment. The scenic end of the Longmeadow Players, as they called themselves, was managed by the people who did the acting, as the group was very small. Meetings were held monthly, one-act plays were read, and speakers on the problems of play production were imported.

In February of that season they felt they were ready for a public performance of "Enter Madame," which was announced for two evenings. The second performance had to be postponed because of a blizzard. Nevertheless the production was a great success, and the Longmeadow Community House, where the Players have since given all their plays, was filled to capacity.

In subsequent years, even through the depression, the group has grown steadily. They now have about ninety members. In the summer of 1938 they decided to canvass the town in a house-to-house campaign. This proved most successful, and they discovered in Longmeadow that people like to be asked personally to join the Community Theatre.

About three years ago Mrs. Philip A. Perkins, a graduate of Mount Holyoke College, active in the Play Shop there and one of the group which established the New London summer theatre in New Hampshire, came to Longmeadow. She developed a backstage crew of which the Players are very proud. There are about twenty of these scene shifters. And since acting personnel has grown proportionately, they are going to attempt four productions each year, instead of two as formerly. They have also, in their monthly meetings, given one-act plays.

For the city of Longmeadow each Christmas they give a special program, and the entire community cooperates. At the request of the town fathers they have given several children's plays. In addition to this service to the town, they also present one-act plays for church groups and the various woman's clubs.

"For a group of its size we have certainly kept extremely busy," says Ruth Miller. "I think because we have shown our willingness to cooperate we are about to reap our reward in that our last membership drive for at least three hundred and fifty members we hope will bring in around five hundred."

Because Longmeadow is small, with a population of some five thousand, they feel it is their duty to present plays that will amuse and entertain. Once in a while, however, they do a serious play just to prove it can be done.

The Longmeadow Community Building is, of course, owned by the town, but the town fathers always cooperate fully with the Players.

It was in this Community Building in May of 1935 that a Community Theatre Conference of groups operating within motoring distance was held.* Neighborliness at home that leads to neighborliness among surrounding towns and cities is the ideal of this group.

Mount Vernon, New York. The Theatre Stands Ready to Serve the City.

In their fifteen years of existence the Community Players of Mount Vernon have produced over two hundred plays. And with an average of fifteen people appearing in each production, it becomes apparent not only that there is a theatre-going public in Mount Vernon, but also that you can't walk down the shady streets without running into an actor.

The active membership of the Players is composed of teachers, lawyers, housewives, stenographers, engineers, artists, authors, clerks, editors, and executives. Anyone who has the urge to help promote the cultural development of the community is welcomed into the Community Players. The Mayor, the Superintendent of Schools, the Chairman of the Recreation Commission, the President of the Woman's Club and many other leaders in the city endorse the aims and purposes of the Players. And a subscribing membership costs only four dollars a season.

In fifteen years receipts from dues and ticket sales have totaled $30,892.82.

* See Chapter IX.

And outside of royalties on plays, all this money has been spent in Mount Vernon. Well, not quite all, for they have about one thousand dollars in the savings bank.

They have won three first prizes in the Little Theatre contests in Westchester County. They have conducted two play-writing contests, and have produced about twelve plays written by their own members. They have given eighteen guest and benefit performances.

Public performances are those in which the Community Players do their serious work and are given at the Westchester Woman's Club. Studio performances are those in which the Players do their experimenting and training. Here new members are given an opportunity to show whether they can act or direct plays, or whether they have potential abilities that may be developed. Members with writing ambitions are encouraged to present their plays for production in the studio.

According to Genevieve Cheney, one of the founders of this group, who has also served in capacities of both actress and president, "I believe in the importance of the organization as an artistic and recreational project. There is a place in every town and village in our country for a like organization, one offering an artistic outlet to those individuals who seek to create in the line of drama and offering also aesthetic satisfaction to those lovers of the theatre who are not themselves creators. The Community Players stand ready, as always, to serve our city."

Philadelphia, Pennsylvania. A Cooperative Venture of the Theatre-minded.

No endowment.
No outside subsidy.
No sponsors.
No permanent list of subscribers.
We are completely and entirely independent.

When a small group of Philadelphians, whose mutual interest in the theatre had brought them together from time to time for discussion meetings, found themselves continuously tempted by the question—"Why not start a cooperative Little Theatre in Philadelphia?"—they began to inquire about the city to get the lay of the land. From every side they heard that it would be impossible to create a permanent producing group in Philadelphia unless it were largely subsidized by some "angel."

The fall of 1933 found this group taking definite steps to create what they chose to call The Theatre League of Philadelphia. They say with pride that all physical work of production, the executive management, the cleaning of the building, the direction of and participation in productions, and the planning and execution of the entire program of the organization is done by the active membership, which averages fifty each year. The fact that they have no obligation to any outside group, and that their only responsibilities are the payment of rent and expenses incident to the life of the organization, means that they have freedom of choice in the selection of material and membership, and that the entire responsibility for their program rests upon their own shoulders.

That there has been no shirking of this responsibility is proved by the fact that the Theatre League has had five successful years and looks forward to an excellent future.

The Theatre League is housed in an old stable adjoining the Wanamaker mansion in the heart of Philadelphia. Since 1933 more than two thousand people have been interviewed for membership in the organization, out of which nearly five hundred have been accepted probationally as members. Of this group more than two hundred have been associated with the organization for a period of a year or longer.

The nature of the organization has been such that it has attracted to it for permanent association a number of individuals with specialized theatrical and organization training whose abilities have been donated impersonally to the work of the association. The "no-star" system is an integral part of the plan of work and cliques, personal animosities and friction are at a minimum.

The production schedule from September to June calls for one new production and one revival each month. The League plays every Saturday night, and one Sunday of each month. In addition they give benefit performances in their own auditorium and elsewhere, selling the productions to organizations interested in raising money or in providing entertainment for their members.

The spring of 1938 saw the establishment of a Junior Workshop for Children, which policy will be continued.

At present the organization is run by an executive committee of seven to which the remaining members are responsible for the performance of assignments.

Thomas Erskine and Ada Funcke are the directors of the League and members of the executive committee. The production record to date is three hundred and seventy-one performances:

188 performances of 44 full-length plays,
183 performances of 62 one-act plays.

Of these eight were first performances of plays by unknown playwrights. In addition to these, thirty-four were Philadelphia premieres.

The League, centered in one of the few cities in the United States that still has an active theatrical season, takes great pride in being able to contrast its own productions with the plays that visit Philadelphia. For example, professional productions of "Ghosts" and "The House of Connelly" have been done in Philadelphia by excellent companies. Therefore, the League thought it worth while to produce "Rosmersholm" and "The Field God" by the same playwrights. This contrast naturally afforded exciting interest to League audiences.

There are features about the Theatre League that should be brought to the attention of all Community Theatre people. One is the active membership which forms the basis of the group. They charge a fee of $4.00 a month during the season and offer an associate membership with limited privileges for $12.50 for the entire year. Technical membership for those interested in the theatre or set design and construction is offered at $7.50. Another is their definite effort to maintain a repertoire of plays that are kept in rehearsal at all times. To date their repertoire includes "The Father," by Strindberg; "Leghorn Hat," by Labiche and Michel; "Ladies and Hussara," by Fredro; "Rosmersholm," by Ibsen; "Love and Geography," by Bjornson; "Wide Awake Nell," by Dumont; and "The Concert," by Herman Bahr.

The Theatre League is thoroughly a cooperative community theatre depending upon its active membership for its main body of sustenance, and considers the box office an auxiliary source of income which may be devoted to expand its activities and ambitions.

A benefit of a cooperative form of subsidization and government is that a group is allowed higher standards in the choice of plays and the manner of their presentation; dependence on the box office is substantially reduced.

Mr. Erskine says that a community theatre should ultimately become the meeting place of artists in every field so it can use to best advantage their contributions. At the same time it must encourage talented beginners to continue their work and develop their special abilities. By careful planning of programs it can educate the community to new cultural values—it should present the best in the theatre both modern and classical; striving to foster an understanding of the universality of human nature and an appreciation of various peoples and cultures.

Pittsburgh, Pennsylvania.   From Speak-easy to Thespian Temple.

1928.
A sinister looking
building fronting two
heavily trafficked thoroughfares;
heavy, many-paned doorways and drawn
shades over small-paned windows lend a
furtive air to the entire structure. Venturing inside, one would find several large rooms
gaudily decorated in the most Parisian cubistic
style; particularly would your attention be called to a
large gaming room, which was so soon to have such a
different meaning; for this entire structure was a speak-easy
and its demise was probably accompanied by the shrill whine
of police sirens and the crashing axes of a prohibition squad.

The year is now 1938.
Slick, streamlined limousines
pull up to the self-same structure
whose appearance from the outside
has still a certain speak-easy quality, but
whose wide double doors show forth gleams
of hospitality not associated with illicit undertakings. For today this once brawdish speak-easy
is now the Pittsburgh Playhouse and on the inside,
instead of the gaudy aura of the 1928's, we find walls
tastefully decorated in becoming shades of gray.   That
self-same gaming room is now converted into a handsome
oval auditorium seating two hundred and forty of the best-
dressed people of Pittsburgh.   From the ceiling of this room
hangs a beautiful and delicate crystal chandelier which has shed
light over the assembled audiences of Pittsburgh since the year 1935.

But this story begins in 1933, when a group of twenty prominent people
founded the present well-established Pittsburgh Playhouse. Many of these influential, civic-spirited persons were also responsible for the forming of the
present Pittsburgh Symphony Orchestra.   They engaged, as their first director
of the Playhouse, Mrs. Frank Stout, who served for two seasons and whose

wide acquaintance with Pittsburgh talent enabled her to organize casts and crews for the six productions that marked her regime.

During these two years, the productions were presented in the Theatre of the Frick Training School for Teachers through cooperation of the Board of Public Education. The Playhouse at the beginning was financed solely by the sale of subscriptions for the productions, which were presented for one full week each.

At the beginning of the 1935-36 season, the Board in its infinite wisdom deemed it wise to enlarge the interests of the Playhouse and to try an experiment professionalizing what had started out to be a healthy community theatre. They leased the aforementioned speak-easy and, with borrowed funds, undertook the remodeling and equipping of an auditorium.

Mr. Herbert V. Gellendre was engaged as director, and while Gellendre's shoulders bore most of the responsibility of the next two years' undertakings, nevertheless he must have started with the full knowledge and probably at the prompting of the Board of Directors.

Gellendre instituted many changes. The plays were experimental, often beautifully mounted and superbly produced, but unfortunately almost always of continental variety.

During Gellendre's second year, he formed an apprentice group and hired a "prominent" company of Equity actors. The productions during this season were presented for two full weeks with Saturday matinees. Gellendre deserves credit for very ambitious and idealistic experiments, but his experiments must be held up to the American Community Theatre as an example of what no Board of Directors should ever be tempted to do. Community Theatres can be over-professionalized, and in being so, they commit suicide. With but two exceptions—the Cleveland Repertory Playhouse and Jasper Deeter's Hedgerow Theatre—there is no existing commercial community playhouse in the United States, and it is not likely that there ever will be because: First, the type of actor which a group west of Broadway may hire for a reasonable salary is certainly no better than the local talent available in almost every American city. This point can be proved by enough examples to overcome completely the vanity and pride of any theatre traditionalist who devoutly believes in the superiority of a forty-dollar-a-week ham actor on Equity rolls as compared with the superior university trained amateur. Second, the audiences of a Community Theatre soon lose interest in a professional company because it lacks variety and the personal contact with the community life.

If this experiment were to work in any American city, it certainly had a fair chance in Pittsburgh. Thousands of dollars went down the drain, and the result was total apathy on the part of one of the most theatre-conscious centers in America. It cannot succeed because it would destroy the essence of the American spirit of democracy inherent in every Community Theatre.

In the summer of 1937, Mr. Frederick Burleigh, formerly of the Indianapolis Civic Theatre, became the director at Pittsburgh. There he found himself faced with the tremendous problem of re-interesting the general public, re-persuading the newspapers of the theatre's civic value, and of presenting plays which would have a popular appeal. Mr. Burleigh has had a remarkable success in doing, for the past season has been by far the most successful year experienced by the Pittsburgh Playhouse, and the astute showmanship in closing his season with a musical review culled from the talents of popular Pittsburgh actors and actresses marked a high point in the return of the Pittsburgh Playhouse to the paths of democracy.

Rochester, New York. A Church Remodeled in Elizabethan Style.

The starting point of a Community Theatre often lies in the mind of a single capable person. In Rochester, Mary Finycane felt in 1923 that the time was ripe for her city to have an organization and perhaps a theatre of its own in which those with talents and interest might have an opportunity to express themselves. From the beginning, she declared that it must be very democratic and, for that reason, self-supporting. Her idea found sympathetic response in the minds of many people who were willing and able to give her wholehearted cooperation. Through sheer hard work and persistence, enough memberships were sold that fall to warrant renting a small office and engaging a secretary. The office was used at night to present one-act plays and a hall was engaged for the two-night runs of the several full-length plays presented that year.

The next season saw such an increase in membership that Robert Stevens was engaged as director and six plays were given. Mr. Stevens has been with the Community Players ever since.

Encouraged by their successes the second year, it was felt that the group should have a home of its own. An option was taken on a building, originally a church; bonds were sold and a mortgage put on the property, which was soon completely remodeled into a very cozy and workable little theatre from plans made by James B. Arnold, one of Rochester's leading architects and president of the Rochester Community Players. The public gave the Players full support almost from the first day and, besides making ends meet, they have been able to lay aside each season a substantial sum toward retirement of the bonds sold during the building campaign.

The cost of a membership is $10.00, which amounts to two memberships in that each subscription holder is entitled to two tickets for every production. It also entitles the two seat-holders to take part in all activities of the theatre without further charge. These activities include courses in diction, make-up, scene designing, costuming. There is also a children's class, the members of which each year give a play for other children and adults that are properly chaperoned by a child.

In 1935 a Workshop Theatre was created by the more enterprising Players. It has since devoted its time to plays written and directed by members, and played by members who wish to get extra training to be eligible for the regular productions.

The Rochester Community Players are definitely interested in encouraging local playwrights, and in reading full-length dramas by anyone who cares to submit manuscripts.

A few years ago, after a visit to the Folger Shakespeare Library in Washington, Stevens was fired with the idea that a reproduction of the Globe Theatre could be made easily in the theatre in Rochester. On his return he inspired the production crew to outdo themselves in building a false proscenium and platform for the outer stage; and in covering the sides of the theatre with huge canvases on which balconies and heads and shoulders of the various grandees of the Elizabethan period were painted. The work was volunteer and created piece-meal, and many were startled to note, at the last minute, that one of the painters had expressed his individuality by drawing one row of people looking away from the stage. A royal box was built for the local Queen Elizabeth who attended each performance with her ladies-in-waiting. It is worth noting that, after the first night, every audience respectfully rose at her entrance and contributed its bit in creating an atmosphere of congeniality for the revival of "Twelfth Night."

The actors of the Rochester Community Players are, as in most theatres, drawn from all walks of life. The only qualification is ambition to be a sincere and useful member of the organization.

Nature has decreed that we must creep before we walk, and the same ruling is true in other activities in life. Radio has promoted a real interest in music, through a long process of musical education these past ten years. This principle applied to the drama is bearing results in many localities throughout the United States. In Rochester it was found at first that farce comedy was the most popular, but as years went by the taste of the general audience changed so that today comedy drama has the best box-office appeal. In the past fifteen years, Rochester's audiences have had an opportunity to enjoy plays by Anatole France, Molière, Shaw, Martinez Sierras, Lewis Carroll, Dickens, O'Neill, St. John Ervine, and Maxwell Anderson.

Rochester is one of the few cities still favored with road show productions of Broadway plays and, after many years of theatre-going both in Rochester and New York, Stevens says that he would like to send a word of warning to the Broadway managers who are tempted to water their casts with second-rate players and shoddy scenery: "If the community theatres have done nothing else, they have created great audiences of people who are interested in the technicalities of the theatre . . . The 'sticks' today knows the difference between a first-rate production and a shabby presentation . . . The day of getting by in the 'sticks' has passed."

He says that the greatest problem facing the directors of Community Theatres is "how to make idealism a practical reality," which in prosaic words is "merely the search for a way to promote an intelligent and real interest for more thoughtful plays in a large and ever-increasing sustaining group."

The Players have contributed several charming people to the professional theatre, including Eve Symington, Oliver Barbour, Rhea Cooke and Charles Ainsley. Judy Abbott, daughter of George Abbott, made her first stage appearance with the Rochester Community Players.

Short Hills, New Jersey.   Historic Paper Mill Becomes a Theatre.

The Paper Mill Playhouse is the beginning of the realization of an ideal— a permanent repertory theatre and art center in New Jersey. Seven years ago a group, headed by Frank Carrington, started to work toward such a theatre. Under the name of the Newark Art Theatre they presented plays at the Newark Art School and at the Montclair Theatre. Through the busy seasons of play production they kept up a constant search for a permanent building of their own. Since their subscription audience was drawn from every town from Newark to Morristown and from Plainfield to Montclair, they felt that the theatre's location must be central to this great residential district.

In September, 1934, they discovered the century-old paper mill in Short Hills, an ideal location. The property was purchased and the corporate name of the group was changed to Paper Mill Playhouse. Located in a charming rural section of Short Hills on Brookside Drive, a short distance from Millburn Center and near the southern entrance to the South Mountain Reservation, the Playhouse is accessible to all neighboring communities. Residents of northern New Jersey can see from a map how easy it is to reach the Playhouse from their homes, and can find ample parking facilities. Those coming by train find the Playhouse a short walk or taxi drive from the Millburn station of the Lackawanna.

In the plans for remodeling, Henry D. Scudder, the architect, has skilfully combined the charm of the old mill with the comforts of a thoroughly modern fireproof theatre. The exterior, of brick, field stone and white timbers, will be restored as nearly as possible to its appearance over a hundred years ago, when the mill was operated by water power. Eventually the long-unused race-way will be cleared and the old water wheel rebuilt. The two and one half acres surrounding the Playhouse will ultimately be laid out in a series of old-fashioned gardens. Various garden groups have become interested in designing the different sections of the property as a means of furthering the development of the whole project. A Shakespearean garden is being planned, also a wild garden; a garden making a feature of the spring and wishing-well, and a water-garden along the brook. The original owner of the paper mill took great pride in his garden near the old well, and it was here that he courted and won his wife. He overlooked the beauty of the brook when planning the grounds for the reason that the water was always discolored with mash from nearby distilleries. The name Rum Creek had a real meaning in Revolutionary days.

The lobby and auditorium are included in the main building of the old mill. The southern entrance has been remodeled into a beautiful colonial doorway. Through white-paneled doors one enters the lobby—a room of austere simplicity, but suggestive of the gracious hospitality of the early American home. The walls are finished partly with plaster and partly with pine paneling. The ceiling is of pine planks supported by heavy hand-hewn beams. Similar wide boards are used in the floor. Five-foot logs can be used in the big fireplace, and if we did not know that there were concealed radiators in the room we could well believe that the blazing open fire supplied sufficient heat. The room is furnished entirely in American antiques, which were collected and given to the Playhouse by the Short Hills Committee. The grandfather's clock on the landing of the stairway keeps time as it did over a century ago. A family of twelve could be seated easily at the long pine table in front of the fireplace. There are several fine ladder-back chairs, a dower chest, a spinning wheel, and a Shaker rocker among the collection. This room has been designed so that it can be used for other activities when plays are not being given. Lectures, chamber music, dance recitals and meetings have been held in the lobby.

The lobby opens into the main auditorium. Here the same early American design has been followed; the walls are finished with pine paneling, and the ceiling with sand-finished plaster. The original windows have been preserved, and inside shutters added to match the walls. The only color in the auditorium is from the velour of the chairs and the proscenium curtain. The simplicity of the room is very satisfying and the feeling of intimacy has not been lost even though the six hundred and fifty seats are on one floor. A pipe organ has been presented to the Playhouse and will be installed above the auditorium, with the sound grill in the ceiling over the orchestra pit.

The Exhibition Gallery is in the main building, just above the lobby. It was opened to the public in November, 1936. There will be several exhibitions during the winter season. It is gratifying to the founders that so much interest has been shown in these exhibitions. The Gallery is contributing to the purpose of the Playhouse: cultivating and encouraging appreciation in painting, music, and sculpture as well as drama.

The Administration Wing is a new fireproof building adjoining the stage. It replaces part of the rambling old mill which was too far gone to restore. Brick has been used in this construction to match the main building, and again the colonial has been followed in the architectural design. The graceful white columns of the portico and the lovely doorway add greatly to the charm of the whole place. The entrance to this wing opens into the general business office. Other offices adjoin this room for the director and theatre staff. A dining room has been provided for the staff. At stage level, in this wing, the whole floor is given over to dressing rooms, stage models, properties and costumes. On the second floor a studio has been included for Miss Antoinette Scudder, President of the Playhouse.

Construction has begun on the stagehouse of the Paper Mill Playhouse in Short Hills. The stage will have a proscenium opening thirty-five feet wide by seventeen feet high and fifty feet from proscenium to back wall. This is deeper than the stage of any New York legitimate theatre, according to Mr. Scudder.

The stagehouse which is now being built is a permanent structure, adequate in size for play production, but forming only a part of the stage-house to be constructed ultimately. The visible part of the stage will be of full size, but the present working space in the wings and overhead is only one third of the final structure. The roof is permanent and will be raised, when the building is completed, to its full height of seventy feet. Wings at the left are twenty-eight feet, which is full size, but on the right they are only fourteen feet, later to be expanded to forty-eight feet.

The Playhouse structure embodies the latest developments in the theatre. "A new building, designed solely for theatre use, can take advantage of the newest discoveries in theatre technique," says Frank Carrington. "Although the stage itself will not be in its final form, much of the lighting equipment can be installed. This will be flexible in arrangement, and will be responsive to any artistic demands we may put upon it."

The building is of steel and concrete block construction, and when completed will be faced with brick to harmonize with the other Playhouse buildings. With the removal of the platform in the auditorium, which served the Playhouse as a temporary stage last year, the interior of that building will be completed. Two more rows of seats will be installed, and the orchestra pit put in readiness for use.

The west wing is still to be built. In this wing a puppet playhouse has been planned for children—or rather a children's theatre. There will be a small stage and an auditorium seating one hundred. Here children may develop creative ability by writing and staging plays themselves, as well as witnessing performances designed especially for them.

An Apprentice Group will receive training in all branches of the theatre, under professional guidance. The Paper Mill Playhouse is interested in the serious young person who wishes to make the theatre his life work. Those with the necessary qualifications may be admitted to this group, which will have the opportunity to learn by actual work in the various departments of the Playhouse.

Under Frank Carrington's direction, the group has already presented: Maeterlinck's "Blue Bird," Shaw's "Heartbreak House," Barrie's "Quality Street," Ibsen's "Lady from the Sea," Noel Coward's "Hay Fever," Sierra's "Take Two From One," and Drinkwater's "Mary Stuart." Work is now under way on fifteen plays to be added to the repertory. Included in this list are: "Midsummer Night's Dream," Shakespeare; "Paolo and Francesca," Phillips; "March Hares," Gribble; "Snow Queen," Scudder; "The Brontes," Sangster; "Cavalcade," Noel Coward; and "Madame Pepita," Sierra. The productions will be completely professional, being created, designed, costumed, built, and staged by Frank Carrington and the Playhouse staff of designers, costume makers, carpenters, scene painters, and technicians.

The Paper Mill Playhouse is interested in building a dignified and distinguished organization for the practice of theatre as an art. It believes that the theatre rightfully belongs to the artist and not to the world of commerce, that theatres should not be required to make profits for private interests, that theatres should be established on the basis of their vital importance in community life for cultural and civic advancement. Beyond the point of making the organization self-sustaining, the Playhouse is not interested in profits, and is legally a "non-profit-making corporation." The whole purpose of the Playhouse is service to the community through its plays, concerts and art exhibitions.

Springfield, Massachusetts. From a Burlesque House to an Art Center.

In the Community Theatre Movement, Springfield is distinguished for two things. One is *The Springfield Republican*; its dramatic section, edited by Louise L. Mace, is outstanding not only for her refreshing comment on the state of the theatre and her vigorous reviews of current plays, but also because in this paper Miss Mace has had the foresight and the courage to run for the past seven years a weekly column devoted to the activities of the Community Theatres of America.

The other reason that Springfield is kept on its toes in matters theatrical is the Players Guild, now beginning its fifteenth season. During the years since November, 1924, the Guild has presented practically everything from "Heartbreak House" to "George and Margaret." It has no permanent home, producing its plays in church and Masonic Temple; but for the past three years it has had the use of the splendid auditorium and stage of the Springfield Museum of Fine Arts.

Mrs. Chester Neal (Julia Delmonico), the founder of the Guild, came to Springfield from New York in 1922. She had had experience with some of the strong amateur dramatic groups in New York, and quickly became associated with the South Church dramatic group. While appearing in one of their plays she met William Thornton Simpson, the director. He had also come to Springfield from New York, where he had appeared as an actor and had directed some of the well-known stars of the day.

Mrs. Neal saw an opportunity to form the Little Theatre she had been dreaming of for years. She gathered a group of men and women who had been active in dramatic circles in college and church. A board of directors was elected. Mr. Simpson was made director—and Shaw's "Heartbreak House" was put into rehearsal.

The performances were given at the old State Theatre. This house had for years been playing burlesque. When it was found that the theatre was available for three nights a week, the Guild rented it and two plays were given on its stage. The experiences at the burlesque house were chastening.

The filth of the dressing rooms and other evidences of a second-rate company of professional players dampened the ardor of some of the Guild actors. The plays were successful despite the unsanitary surroundings and the few hilarious gentlemen who wandered in by mistake and could not understand why the actresses didn't go into a strip tease.

So started, the Guild has gone on producing four plays a season, giving two performances of each play. A workshop, play readings, lectures, luncheons in honor of visiting professional players, have been included in their yearly program.

For years the Guild has had a membership of approximately three hundred. There had never been any concerted effort made to increase this number until 1937, when a drive for members was undertaken and patterned after that outlined in Henning Nelms' booklet, *Building an Amateur Audience*. A committee of forty-five workers was organized and, without difficulty, the membership was more than doubled.

In making choice of plays for their major productions, the Guild has mixed the fare, so that comedy and serious drama would find place on its bill.

As the years have gone by, there has been evident a tendency to lighten the character of the productions, conceding to the demand for entertaining comedies.

"Is it right to make such concessions under the conditions the Community Theatres have had to meet during the past ten years?" asks William Simpson. "This question looms large for all community theatres with the problem of establishing a policy which will satisfy both the audience and the artist. Shall a group be experimental, doing new plays, experimenting with odd vehicles which offer difficult but interesting problems to the producing staff? Or shall the group do the successful Broadway plays, avoiding everything that may not satisfy the amusement seeking audience, picking only plays which can easily be cast and which present no great difficulties to the producing staff? Different concepts cause rifts and defections. The Guild has therefore tried to steer a middle course, feeling that it is wise to be conservative in the selection of plays and sane in the choice of acting and directing technique."

Mr. Simpson also has this to say: "For the sincere worker in the theatre there comes the strong conviction; Community Theatres have a function more nearly akin to that of the dramatic organizations of the past. Drama has flowered and become significant only when it has had a purpose beyond that of the business manager's quest for gold. In such a Community Theatre anthology of history and opinion each group can contribute something of value to the movement as a whole.

"The Springfield Players Guild has learned that a play more nearly achieves its purpose when it becomes under careful, considered, and tempered direction a well-integrated organic whole. When the players realize fully the importance of team-play there develops a spirit of congenial cooperation. This in turn fosters a companionable harmony accompanied by an intense artistic concentration on the work in hand.

"Rehearsals become play as well as work. It is here that the Community Theatres make departure from the commercial theatre, and herein lies the hope of the THEATRE, for the verity of spirit in drama is cooperative effort.

"When the theatre is divorced from the shriveling influence of the box office and from the corruption which accompanies exhibitionism and nepotism still rampant in many groups, there is then hope for a true renaissance in the theatre."

During the life of the Guild many players have been developed, others have come from college and other dramatic groups. Few have gone into the professional theatre. Several, however, have found openings in radio work. John S. Young, in charge of all radio programs for the New York 1939 World's Fair, is a Guild product.

Summit, New Jersey. Professional Standards the Aim.

In 1917, during the World War, a few persons in Summit assembled to raise money for the Red Cross. They decided to give a play. And, finding their production a success, they decided to continue producing plays.

There was at that time an old library building in Summit which had been standing idle for twenty years. Built sixty years earlier, it was a well-loved landmark in the community. The owners, in their will, had left it to be used only for educational purposes. And with the library grown and moved to larger quarters, what was more natural than to turn this vacant building into a community playhouse?

The drama lovers rolled up their sleeves and plunged in. The girls scrubbed and cleaned. The men built, tore down, and electrified. Someone gave an old railroad switchboard. A stage was built where the book shelves used to be. The roller shades, sewn together and painted, were used for the first scenery.

The Playhouse faces a small park with trees outside the doors and a spacious surrounding lawn. Inside, the walls of the auditorium have been touched with the magic brush of Jack Rose. He has painted murals, the illustrations of scenes from one of the early plays, "Behind a Watteau Picture." So Pierrots, Harlequins, and Columbines give their gay inspiration to the Summit players and audiences. In the basement are dressing rooms, property room, and Green Room.

During the first years of the Playhouse, Norman Lee Swartout guided its destinies, and several original plays were given at one time or another. It was under his direction that Milne's "The Romantic Age" had its first performance, later being presented on Broadway.

From the first Mr. Swartout established professional standards. The theatre was run according to the rules and regulations of Broadway. And by his quiet and skilled direction, his fine character, and his rigid discipline, a precedent of professionalism was established which has run through the years.

At first there were a few subscribing and sustaining members. Now the Playhouse is supported only by subscription. Tickets are not placed on sale to the general public, but members may buy extra tickets if they so desire. This plan was put into effect because of the small seating capacity of the theatre. There are seats for only about a hundred, but at times a hundred and twelve have witnessed a play. Each production is given for five nights, with a matinee on Saturday.

Personalities are kept rigidly out of the theatre. "Jane Smith's" husband is not allowed to be the butler because she wants him in the play and it is such "a small part." Cliques have never been allowed to form, or personal dislikes to grow and flourish. When animosity is found anywhere, the people are put to work together on the same committee. Almost invariably, they discover in Summit, the animus disappears.

The actors are trained to think always of the play. That is why, they feel, they have no quarrels and no factions. Each one in a department thinks "What is best for the play?"

For the past eleven years the director of this group has been Mrs. Marjorie Cranstoun. She believes that casting should ignore social standing as an influencing factor.

"Even though Mary Jones has five hundred influential friends," she says, "and Anne Smith none, in the long run the five hundred friends of Mary Jones prefer to see Ann Smith, who can act, than Mary Jones, who can't. In our theatre our most popular actors are those who were completely unknown in the beginning."

From this group several have gone on to the professional stage. Beatrice Miles played on Broadway with Henry Hull and H. B. Warner. William B. Miles has directed in summer theatres. And Viola Wydner and Dorothy Harrower have also acted professionally. Many more have been offered opportunities, but as business men or housewives they have not been free to accept. They'd rather play leads, anyway, in Summit, than a bit on Broadway.

Concerning Community Theatres Mrs. Cranstoun has this to say: "Ours is not a Community Theatre—it is a theatre in a community. A group theatre presenting plays to the community. Theatre is one thing that cannot thrive under a communistic plan. Communistic control means mediocrity. Theatre must be 'best.' Even in Communistic Russia the theatres are despotisms of the first order. And when they succumb to communistic ideas they are inferior."

And this when we are writing a whole book to prove that the Community Theatres of America are based on democratic participation. Tut, tut, Mrs. Cranstoun.

Torrington, Connecticut. Civic Players Wax Dramatic in a Haymow.

A bunch of the girls were whooping it up over tea cups one afternoon in 1935. It was a club. The name, to be exact—the Torrington Sisterhood. When they weren't knitting sweaters and chatting about matters of local interest, they gave their time and attention to the discussion of art, literature, and other cultural subjects.

One of the members, Laura Halberstam, had written a play, a rip-roaring melodrama. She read it aloud. The club members all liked it and were unanimous in the opinion that it should be produced.

"We'll do it ourselves," said one member.

"How can we?" suggested another member timidly. "There are men in the cast!"

"If men are needed," was the grim reply, "we'll get them!"

They did. The play was produced. And that was how the Torrington Civic Players were born.

The production proved such a success that, with the cast as a nucleus, a community theatre group was formed. All during the next winter this group met at odd times at different places, and then Margaret Graham announced that the second story of her barn was available for a studio workshop; the old barn where hay used to be kept in the days when there were horses in Connecticut.

Thereupon one Sunday afternoon, the boys and girls of Torrington, armed with mops and brushes and dressed in overalls, descended upon the Graham barn. They sloshed away the cobwebs and the dust and proceeded to decorate the walls with masks, hangings, and sketches, all the work of the members. This was in May, 1936.

But they needed chairs, curtains at the windows, ash trays and tea cups. So to raise money for these necessities, a bridge party was held in the new studio, with pantomimes by the members for entertainment. It was a huge success.

"Can your actors talk?" the guests asked.

"Certainly," was the reply. "We're going to give some plays next winter to prove it!"

"If your plays are as much fun as your parties—save me two seats on the aisle in the fifth row."

Civic minded, it was part of their original purpose to be sponsored by local organizations which might be seeking means of raising funds by producing plays with equal division of the profits. In this way they would be free to expend all their energy on behind-the-footlights activities, leaving the business matters in the hands of the sponsoring organization. The local Lions Club backed them for the benefit of their health camp for Torrington children. Another sponsor was the Torrington Creamery Sick Benefit Association.

Their activities are varied. At their formal monthly meetings, programs are planned dealing with discussions of some phase of the theatre. Sometimes speakers are brought from out of town. Sometimes, too, they all jog to nearby cities to see the plays being done by other community theatres, and come back to discuss them. The Mark Twain Masquers of Hartford invited them to attend the dress rehearsal of "Brother Rat." And the Civic Theatre of Waterbury reserved a whole block of seats for them for the production of "Pride and Prejudice."

"We learned a lot from both these experiences," says Miss Burns. "There seems to be a growing connection among the Little Theatres of Connecticut with helpful exchange of ideas and plans."

Sometimes at their meetings, without benefit of scenery, a few of the members present a one-act play. Usually these are original dramas written by the members. Laura Halberstam has written several, and Judith Burns found a hit on her hands with her sketch, "Thundering Without Blood Through Deadman's Gulch." This was in the style of the old silent movie with much horseplay and heaving of chests.

With their feet firmly on the ground, and a schedule of three to four productions a year (they are using the high school auditorium as a theatre), the Civic Players are making plans for the future.

In the past the theatre-goers of Torrington have preferred definitely light comedies. But with money in the treasury the Civic Players are now planning to give Torrington stronger dramatic fare.

They say, "Let our souls revel in dramatic freedom, which is the life and strength of an independent theatre group—the new thought and enthusiasm which emanate from a breaking of the bonds. Attempt what we feel we must do—not because of audience appeal or sanction—but because our hearts compel us to. How can we grow and learn unless we plow into a serious play or tragedy and experiment with ourselves?"

Margaret Graham is a guiding light of the Torrington Civic Players. Laura Halberstam is another. Both these ladies help direct the plays. Another enthusiastic member is Judith Burns.

They lay particular stress upon community participation in Torrington, and also believe that a community theatre should be a lot of fun.

"After every play, the Civic Players blow themselves to a party," says Judith Burns. "All work and no play, you know—besides, one of the principal factors in the success of our organization is the social activity. These shindigs are always terribly gay after the strain of putting on a play.

"Although all of us belong to many other clubs and societies, we find the Players the most agreeable and sociable. Half of the parties are impromptu—very much on the spur of the moment—and everyone joins in with right good will. After the dress rehearsal of 'Three-Cornered Moon' on Sunday morning, we rustled around and had a skating party on a pond belonging to one of the members. Then we all ate together at a long table in the Grill and went to the movies. This is just an example of what may happen any time."

Utica, New York. The Players.

The Players of Utica issued a silver-coated program in the spring of 1938 to celebrate their Silver Jubilee. For the program they asked five members who had been closely associated with as many different periods in the Players' life to submit a résumé of the years with which they were most intimately concerned.

Julia H. Cummings mentions that the Players were originally known as the Amusement Club, and operated under that title for several years up to 1913. Apparently the Amusement Club was exactly what its name implies: a little organization formed for amusement only. However, love of the theatre so impressed many of the members that a more serious attitude began to appear; by 1913 this had accumulated into the definite organization of the Players.

Their first production, "The Workhouse Ward," by Lady Gregory, made such a sensational hit in Utica that a New York theatrical manager begged for an opportunity to bring the Club to New York for a week.

After this initial success they gave full-length plays each year in the auditorium of the New Century Club. In 1916 a deepening interest in stagecraft reached a climax when the policy of the group was broadened to include two lecturers of international reputation: Granville Barker, English playwright and authority on stagecraft, and Lady Gregory, of the Abbey Theatre.

In 1916 Frank Sterling directed his first production for the Players and the future of the group became linked with this gentleman: its guide, philosopher, friend and, most important of all, professional director.

Mrs. Walter Gibson recalls the hectic days of 1917 when the Players gave a fiesta and bazaar. Again proving the everlasting elasticity of a Community Theatre, we find that this group (long before the rise of the "proletarian theatre," which prides itself on being so much the mouthpiece of its generation) is able to treasure among its memos this following letter written in France during the bitter winter of '17: "The Allied Fiesta Ambulance (which the Players had bought and supplied for a year) followed the Germans all along the Chemin de Dames, driven by Miss Curtis. It has saved many lives and was attached to a French evacuation hospital that kept moving toward the retreating German lines. Our driver and two French nurses, with the surgeons and orderlies, saw and cared for many French wounded. The fighting was very bitter. [Signed] Bien être du Blessé, Mrs. S. Thompson, Secretary."

Mary C. Gordon reports that in 1921-22 the Players were chiefly concerned with the problem of achieving a membership drive of one thousand subscribers. During these interesting years the Players determined to combine with their own production schedule others, both amateur and professional, from outside the city. The first of these was Walter Hampden in an afternoon performance of "Romeo and Juliet" and an evening performance of "Hamlet." The second was an invitation to the Comedy Club of New York to visit them and give a production of "Passers By." The Players of Utica and the Comedy Club are closely linked by ideas of membership and expressed purpose, so this experience as host to the Comedy Club was entirely successful and the gesture was repeated for several years.

The foundations of the theatre were strengthened during the years of 1919-23, when there was definite growth and change. The Players Club found itself emerging from a small social group into a city-wide organization. In 1923, through the foresight and courage of Bernie Gordon, the Players Club took what is probably the major step of its twenty-five years of existence. They assumed the responsibility of a home of their own. As Charles W. Childs points out, it was only a barn on Mandeville Street, but a stage was built, a new heating plant installed, and the Players found themselves with a complete little theatre seating about two hundred people, which had both charm and atmosphere. Due to its downtown location, the workshop soon became a rendezvous.

However, Francis M. Wheeler says the Players had outgrown this humble home by 1929, when George Sicard, with a few deft passes, relieved the active members of the Players of their bank balances, hypnotizing them into a state of pleased acquiescence. The money thus "nefariously" obtained was for the purchase and remodeling of an ex-movie theatre. This new enterprise was carried out in the nick of time, because with the Players' first production in their new building, a counterpoint was enacted on Wall Street in which, although not by choice, many of the Players were cast. This little opus was entitled "Crash of 1929" and after it Mr. Sicard would have had poor picking from the pockets of the Players. His anticipation enabled the Players to weather the years of the depression in their own comfortable home.

During the past nine years they have produced more than fifty plays and drawn the curtain upon dozens of one-act plays. The last few seasons they have maintained a free dramatic school under the direction of Mr. Le Sueur and have rejoiced in an ever-faithful and beloved orchestra, the history of which is practically a book in itself, so much is it a part of the atmosphere of any opening night at the Players.

The Munson-Williams-Proctor Institute, after planning how to aid in the development of the arts in the city of Utica, recognized the Players and extended them cooperation, greatly encouraging and enlarging their possibilities of production and instruction.

The Players of Utica represent the most substantial type of community theatre endeavor and their twenty-five years of theatre life may be pointed out as an example of a substantial slice of the life of the real American theatre.

Washington, Pennsylvania. Union Stage Hands Sit with the Audience.

In every community there have been always a large number of individuals interested in the theatre and willing to take part in or support the production of plays. Washington, Pennsylvania, was especially play conscious because within the community there were many institutions of learning presenting plays as part of their school programs. Many taking part in the school plays remained in Washington after graduation and retained their interest in dramatics, so there grew up a nucleus around which a community movement might be built.

It was in the late fall of 1926 that they met together in the public meeting room of the court house in Washington to discuss the formation of a permanent organization. Out of this meeting grew a temporary organization which accomplished very little due to the inactivity of the hastily selected officers. About December of the same year a reorganization was effected at a meeting in the Chamber of Commerce rooms, a constitution and by-laws were adopted, committees and officers selected and the play, "So This Is London," chosen as the first production of the new group.

But the troubles of this new organization multiplied rapidly, partly because of the inexperience of all connected therewith and partly because of unforeseen occurrences over which they had no control.

The original name was "The Washington Centre of the Drama League of America." They affiliated immediately with "The Drama League of America," and continued to be so connected until that organization changed its name to "The Church and Drama League," whereupon the local group correspondingly changed its name. As the activity and influence of the national organization diminished the local group dropped the name "Washington Centre of the Church and Drama League of America" and was for several seasons active under the title of "Washington Drama League." About three years ago this was again changed to the present one of "The Community Theatre of Washington, Pennsylvania."

The activities of this group have been financed and advanced by voluntary memberships which are sold annually in a membership campaign. The number of memberships has varied from two hundred and fifty to nearly one thousand in 1934. The members have always been made to feel that they have as much responsibility for the success of the organization as do those who produce the plays. At the end of each year a questionnaire is distributed on which members are asked to express their opinions on the choice of plays and other problems.

There is usually a turnover of between 20 and 25 per cent in the membership each year. This is due to change of residence, the intervention of other interests, or, to a small extent, dissatisfaction with the program of plays produced.

In the beginning plays were given only one evening, but later two in succession, and during the time when the membership reached its maximum three performances were given with two evenings of dress rehearsals. The season's program has usually consisted of plays produced once a month for six months during the winter.

When this group undertook to produce its first play in December, 1927, it came in contact with the Stage Hands Union, of which there were two members in Washington. These men demanded that they be employed to handle the scenery and be paid regular union wages, including time and one half time for Sunday rehearsal. Since the production was being given in a local theatre—where the stage hands officially worked about once a year—it was necessary to yield to their demands.

However, since the members wished to do the work themselves, the stage hands were paid their wages and given reserved seats in the audience and invited to sit there and not interfere with the "amateur" stage hands.

This did not end the troubles of the first play. In its last week of rehearsal, an effort to discipline one of the cast resulted in the dismissal of the directress and the indefinite postponement of the production. Several months later the cast was reassembled and a second date set for production. A week before that opening night the death of a relative of a member of the cast caused a second postponement. But the play was finally given in December without a professional director.

The two stage hands caused considerable difficulty at a later date when they demanded that a local organization cancel its contract with the Community Theatre group unless it agreed to use union stage hands. This demand was refused and resulted in the local owners of the building being placed on the black list as unfair to union labor and no union orchestra was permitted to play in the dance hall during that winter.

The first play was produced in the town's "Opera House." The first regular program was attempted on the platform of the Masonic Temple, which proved to be inadequate. The following two years found the group in the auditorium of the Elks Temple. Since 1930 the Community Theatre has occupied the auditorium of a newly constructed building owned by the Y. W. C. A., the stage having been to some extent constructed to meet the needs of the group.

The promotion of a building to house the Community Theatre has been discussed almost from the first meeting. But there are many factors locally which make it inadvisable at this time, not the least of which is the presence of a growing municipal consciousness of the need for an auditorium which, if constructed, could be used by the Community Theatre without building a home of their own.

For nearly five years the scenery purchased for the first play was used without objection on the part of the audience. However, the more recent policy has been to construct the scenery to fit the needs of the particular play.

The Washington Community Theatre is operated by a directorate of nine persons, three of whom are elected each year, thus preserving a continuity of experience on the board. Each season is self-sustaining and there is no subsidy or endowment upon which to rely if a deficit is incurred. As long as finances permit, competent professional directors are employed, and when finances are low experienced members of the group carry on the direction; there are eight or ten members who can fill in when needed.

"We give five productions each year," says Mrs. C. E. Carothers, president of this group, "and when it is considered that about one hundred people besides the members of a cast take part in producing each play, it can be appreciated how many people derive pleasure and recreation from membership in the Washington Community Theatre."

It has been thought better to furnish entertainment and offer an opportunity to a large number for self expression than to develop a favored few for professional careers. This policy has developed a limited number of experienced and active participants over the years and has enabled several hundred others to take part in the productions, thereby increasing audience-interest. But there has existed for years a sharp difference of opinion as to whether or not the playing group should be confined to a small number of experienced persons in the nature of a stock company, producing finished work. This difference has made for a healthy condition and lively interest.

In the spring of 1929 the group became interested in the annual one-act play contest sponsored by the Pittsburgh Drama League. They entered the contest and in spite of the fact that they had never contested before were successful in winning the Samuel French Trophy for the first place together with a cash prize of $100.00. The next year they took third place, and the third and final year in which they competed they received honorable mention.

In the beginning the group was fortunate in being able to secure the very able direction of such men as Chester M. Wallace, head of the Department of Drama at Carnegie Institute of Technology, Theodore Viehman, also of Carnegie Tech, Edward S. Day of Trinity High School, Robert Allen Greene of Broadway and Kilbuck Theatre, Robert Hayes of the Wheeling Little Theatre, and in addition to the directors the group had in the beginning the expert advice of Harold Burris-Meyer, at that time connected with the English Department of Washington and Jefferson College, and now at Stevens Institute, an authority on sound equipment.

Waterbury, Connecticut. Visiting Firemen Always Welcome.

Probably he'd always been a little bit stage-struck. Anyway, in the late 1920's he decided that he would like to attend the Yale Drama School. He did so—a rather unusual venture for a man of his years. After graduation he came back to Waterbury and continued the publishing of his newspapers, *The Waterbury Republican* and *The Waterbury American*. A query in one of these papers as to what Waterbury stood most in need of brought the suggestion of a Community Theatre.

This struck a responsive note in the publisher's mind, and so the enterprise was on. His name—William J. Pape. He gathered about him some hopeful souls; they hired Helen Schoeni, Yale School graduate, as director and away they went!

This was in the fateful year of 1929, a significant date throughout the country and probably not the most propitious time to try to thrust culture down the throat of a factory town. But the determination of Mr. Pape, Mrs. Murray Beebe, and Edward H. Davis, his co-enthusiasts, struck right at the top figure that U. S. Steel and General Motors and the rest had so abjectly slumped from, though it was touch-and-go financially year after year. Yet, as William W. Vosburgh, Jr., president of the Civic Theatre of Waterbury, so aptly puts it, "This noxious artistic weed persisted in this pharisaical garden and here, by the grace of God, to everyone's resounding wonder the damn thing stays and flourishes."

Miss Schoeni was the director for three struggling years, then followed Alan Wallace, another Yale School graduate, and former director at Duluth and Indianapolis. He was with them for two years. Still drawing on Yale they had Gordon Giffen the next year, lost him to Duluth, and there came another Big Blue product, James N. Furness, who is now in his third year at Waterbury.

They haven't their own theatre. The best they can do is maintain a workshop, rehearsal room, offices, and so forth in—you've guessed it—a commodious barn. But the depression baby has won a place in Waterbury, and during the 1937–38 season when business was looking up for a change, they put on a campaign that boosted their membership close to the thousand mark, and their records show that this same season about two hundred and fifty of these members were active workers of one sort or another. They are very happy over that in Waterbury, and they feel if they can hold onto something like those figures they'll soon begin thinking in terms of a theatre of their own.

The only special problems they face are the everlasting financial ones and the one of catering to a community of mixed population. But Waterbury has a theatrical background and tradition. It was a dog town back in the hey-day of the road and old timers there are fond of recalling the memorable night when due to a failure of costumes to arrive Edwin Booth played "Hamlet" in modern dress—a forerunner of the later vogue. And it is partly that old affection for the spoken drama, and partly the type of plays they offer that have enabled them to prosper.

"We strike for the most part a popular note with such incidental contributions to sweetness and light as we think the market will stand," says Mr. Vosburgh. "Our program for 1937-38 included 'Excursion,' 'Boy Meets Girl,' 'Pride and Prejudice,' 'Biography,' and an original revue, 'Speak of the Devil.' We really made 'Pride and Prejudice' an eye-filling thing, and 'Biography' gave the local intellectuals a chance to cheer. The rest was more down the local alley, though 'Boy Meets Girl' puts us a bit in the moral element's doghouse."

"Pride and Prejudice" had the largest attendance and box office in the theatre's nine years of existence. On stage was twenty thousand dollars worth of authentic antiques; a sixteen-piece orchestra dispensed appropriate music. For the dress rehearsal of this play they invited neighboring groups, and the scenery was shifted from one set to another in full view of the audience to show the backstage end of a difficult play as well as display a number of technical innovations in the construction and rigging of scenery. Most interest was aroused over the making of decorative, floral, rococo moulding out of plain paper toweling and glue, over the wagon stages, and walls, canvased on both side with all props, draperies and appurtenances, attached thereto, allowing for minute shifts on a stage with inadequate overhead rigging and only sixteen feet deep.

They often do original plays, one-acters by the members of the group, and a few seasons ago did a full-length play by William W. Vosburg, Jr., that was under option for a Broadway production.

They are particularly interested, in Waterbury, in exchanging news with other Community Theatres. They maintain a billboard in their workshop where programs, announcements, and notes from other groups are posted. This keeping up of friendly relations, particularly with nearby theatres, is a healthy sign of progress. It points the way to the next important step to be taken by Community Theatres—state and ultimately national organization.

York, Pennsylvania. The Drama Gets in Dutch.

The enthusiasm of youth and the spirit of adventure characterize this group of players.

York is in the heart of the Pennsylvania Dutch country. Three major conflicts of historical interest have swept through this city. During the Revolutionary War Benjamin Franklin came to York to assemble wagon trains for General Braddock's expedition, General Anthony Wayne made his headquarters here in a house that still stands, Continental Congress was in session here for nine months, and Thomas Paine wrote much of his Revolutionary propaganda in York.

During the Civil War the city was invaded by General Early's division of Confederate troops. Turmoil reigned in the city during its occupation, and then General Early moved on to Gettysburg after camping in what is now one of York's city parks.

The third major conflict was when the young people of York started a Community Theatre. This occurred in 1928 when the Department of Recreation, under the leadership of Sylvia Weckesser, began to sponsor dramatics as a community project. Charles Wells, Drama Organizer for the National Recreation Association, was brought to York for a three weeks' institute on drama. An underlying interest in drama existed at that time in the sixty-some churches of York and in numerous other organizations. This was demonstrated by the fact that over one hundred and fifty persons enrolled in the institute.

Following the drama institute, community dramatic work was further sponsored by the Recreation Department through the organization of a Civic Drama Committee, which annually conducted a city-wide one-act play tournament. This tournament interested church groups mostly. A junior tournament stimulated interest among high school groups and the boy and girl scout organizations.

While the tournament was a splendid means of creating a community interest, it was, of course, of transient value. It provided no permanent organization for the many people in the city who were especially interested in dramatics and wished to spend their leisure time in study and participation. So in January, 1933, a group of young people began organizing a permanent community dramatic group.

These were for the most part teachers in the public schools; others included a sprouting young lawyer or two to advise cautious procedure and sometimes delay matters by the lengthy legal terms of "whereas, inasmuch as, heretofore, and aforesaid."

At this time the Recreation Board discontinued the annual tournaments and lent its interest and support to the York Little Theatre. Space for a workshop and club rooms was provided in a downtown recreation center. The services of the Recreation office and $25.00 were provided for typing, mimeographing, and sending out notices.

During the first year the York Little Theatre made no public appearance but confined its activities to workshop classes and plays. This was a period of growth and discovery of talent. At the end of this year over two hundred persons were listed as active members and the organization had grown beyond the powers of local volunteer leadership. The problem of centralizing the activities of so large a group; the training of actors, and the staging problems demanded more time and resources than the Recreation Department or any members were able to supply. Consequently, in the spring of 1934, a professional director was employed, and the Little Theatre began its career of public performances.

And community participation has been the ideal of this group ever since.

Even the Mayor of the city recognizing this made a proclamation. He said, "Appreciation and participation in the drama is a healthful and essential activity in any well-rounded community and realizing what the York Little Theatre has accomplished in its existence in promoting democratic and discriminating appreciation of the best in the theatre, I, the Mayor of York, officially recognize Friday, September 21, to Friday, September 28, as York

Little Theatre Week. During this week, I hope that the ideals of the Little Theatre may be called to the attention of the people of York in such manner that they may be inspired to become a part of and support this organization, which is open to everyone. The sole purpose of the Little Theatre is to utilize and develop in a fruitful and profitable fashion talents among our citizens that otherwise would have no opportunity for expression."

Whereupon the members and the workers of this group held a parade in automobiles, carrying banners, through the town. But they tooted their horns, and had forgotten to obtain a permit. The Chief of Police requested them to stop in a moment at the City Hall, and they were told that they could drive about town singly if they wished, but they couldn't toot their horns, and they couldn't drive through the center of town in parade formation.

The Board of Education cooperates fully with this band of players. From the beginning it has granted the use of the stages in the schools; first in one of the junior high schools at the edge of town, and later in the senior high school in the heart of the city.

The headquarters and workshop are located in the old York County Academy Building, built in 1787, one of many historic spots. Here rehearsals are held and scenery is painted. Then the scenery, properties, and furniture are loaded onto a truck and taken to the high school for the dress rehearsal and public performances.

During drayage of one of their plays an "antique" table broke. Borrowed property! The committee had nervous prostration. They were not cured, either, upon inquiring at the various antique stores in town and discovering that the price of this type of table ranged from five hundred to a thousand dollars.

At a consultation it was decided that the prettiest girl, dolled up in her Sunday best, was to call upon the owner and make a complete and full confession. This she did, with lagging feet and thumping heart.

When the owner saw the table, he said, "Swell! The breaks look natural. I'll have them mended and can now sell this for a thumping good sum as a genuine antique!"

During the dress rehearsal of "The Bad Man" a genuine tragedy was narrowly averted. Those who have given the play recall that the lead twice in one evening shoots at the villain.

The director on this occasion said to the actor, "Got blanks?"

"Sure," was the reply.

"Let's see," and breaking the revolver—real bullets fell out.

"I guess I made a mistake," said the actor weakly.

The moral is that a director cannot be too cautious.

The Little Theatre now wants a home of its own in this city where the players will be able to rehearse their plays on the stage where the performances are given. A committee was selected in the winter of 1938 to look over the situation and find a suitable place.

From this group of players three young men have gone forth to seek fame and fortune elsewhere. William Lucus toured with Clare Tree Major's Children's Theatre. And Bob Flinch, after experimenting with marionettes in the workshop turned professional, and his "Personettes" appeared on the stages and in night clubs in Baltimore, Washington, and Montreal. Kay Wilt joined forces with the Barter Theatre in Abington, Virginia.

And Robert Olewiler, inspired by the community theatre ideal, has gone forth and organized three community theatres. The story of his achievements is told elsewhere.

And Other Theatres of the Northeast

Arlington, Massachusetts.

The Arlington Friends of the Drama, Incorporated, are housed in their own club, formerly an Episcopal Church. The chancel has been rebuilt into a stage, the choir room into a Green Room, the rector's study is now a kitchen, and the cellar has been converted into a between-the-acts lounge off which are dressing rooms, workshop, paint room, etc. The regular season program includes eight productions with an active interest in workshop programs adding an incentive for their four hundred subscribers. The productions on the main stage play for three nights each and have an average attendance of seven hundred.

Belmont, Massachusetts.

The Belmont Dramatic Club was organized in 1903 and is typical of many New England Theatres, producing plays in the Town Hall. They give two or three productions a year and have no hesitancy in tackling such plays as "Stage Door," "Kind Lady" and "The Royal Family." The three hundred fifty members put in a year's hard work participating in the Dramatic Club's activities.

Bloomfield, New Jersey.

This community theatre was the outgrowth of a dramatic club in Bloomfield called "The Comedy Players." Originally it was the banding together of a group of actors. Their first official meeting was held in October, 1936, in the Bloomfield Public Library. Melvin H. Searfoss was the first director.

Bristol, Connecticut.

Twenty-one years of age and more than one hundred productions to their credit is the proud boast of the Bristol Community Players. They have at various times had professional direction and have given some attention to original plays by local playwrights.

Burlington, Vermont.

The Theatre Club, Inc., was founded in 1920 and has averaged three major productions each year since that time. It has an active workshop which in the past seventeen years has given a total of three hundred fifty presentations. Four hundred subscriptions at $3.00 each allow a budget sufficient to pay a professional director, Wilnetta S. Taggart, and maintain a modest production schedule.

Cambridge, Massachusetts.

The Cambridge Social Dramatic Club was organized in 1889. The four hundred members of this organization give three productions each year in Brattle Hall.

Chinatown, New York.

In 1932 a number of young Chinese in New York started making plans for a Little Theatre group. For six years they thought it over carefully, and finally in the summer of 1938 decided to make a definite start. Calling themselves the New York Ching Wah Players, they gave their first production on December 29, 1938. Among the enthusiastic organizers and workers in this group are William S. Chin, Wood Moy, Charles Young, Tom Poon, Eddie Lee, Roland Lee, and Thomas B. Goon. Their plans for the future include the production of several plays each season.

Cohasset, Massachusetts.

The Cohasset Dramatic Club has twenty-six active years of community endeavor behind it. Activities center in the Cohasset Town Hall which has a seating capacity of about four hundred fifty. The two hundred fifty subscribers underwrite a season of three productions each year.

Concord, Massachusetts.

The Concord Players, organized in 1919, occupy a club house jointly with other civic activities. Their plays are produced in the Veterans' Building which has a seating capacity of five hundred fifty. Two public productions are given each season, and three or four private workshop productions are done during the year. About three hundred fifty members subscribe.

Before the Civil War, Louisa May Alcott was giving plays in Concord. At first she did them at home and with her neighbors and a few friends. But gradually more neighbors joined in. Later several plays were given in the Town Hall and from this small beginning grew the Concord Dramatic Club which flourished for a great many years. When the World War came, interest in the Club waned and for a few years no plays were given. Then the late Samuel Merwin came to Concord. Under his direction and with his knowledge of the New York stage, a group of men and women reorganized the Dramatic Club into the present day Concord players. Since then a conscientious attempt at progressive improvement has been made in acting and stagecraft. The Concord Players' regular productions are open to the public. Besides the public performances given, there are the private workshop productions featuring sketches and one-act plays written by members and the season is always closed with a frolic which includes, besides a gala dinner, a series of sketches which lampoon and satirize the season's activities.

A feature of the Concord Players is their periodic revival of "Little Women," which, because of the local appeal, is always a high point in the Concord social calendar.

Lenox, Massachusetts.

The energetic and talented director of this group of players, known as the Lenox Brotherhood Club, is Robert Dixon. They have their own workshop, where scenery is painted; also a print shop of their own where bulletins concerning the coming plays and notes on production are issued. Besides being a gifted director, Mr. Dixon is also a talented actor, having played with Jane Cowl and other well known people from Broadway.

Milton, Massachusetts.

The Milton players were organized in 1932. They give four major productions a year and produce their plays at the Women's Club which has a seating capacity of some four hundred. They have approximately fifty active members and depend upon the box office for support of their activities.

New Britain, Connecticut.

The Little Theatre Guild in four short years has produced three one-act plays and three full length works by local playwrights. They have found these very successful financially because of local interest in the pen-work of neighbors and they report that it has been a stimulating experience to both the writers and the actors who work together. Paul Neil Desole is very active in directing the productions of this group.

Pawtucket, Rhode Island.

The fall of 1938 will be the seventeenth season of active producing by the Pawtucket Community Players. This group, like so many others, has expressed interest in doing original plays and despite a modest budget of four hundred subscription tickets at $2.00 each, estimates that $1960 has been spent in royalties the past seventeen years. The Pawtucket Community Players also sponsors studio readings of current Broadway attractions and a series of children's plays which are done in cooperation with the local Junior League.

Plattsburg, New York.

The Little Theatre of Plattsburg was founded in 1927. Mr. John Meyers is conspicuous as the director of a number of its outstanding productions. From time to time the Little Theatre has cooperated with Bennington College in producing such ambitious productions as "Electra."

Quincy, Massachusetts.

The Community Players of Quincy have been in existence about ten years and have been presenting four plays a year since their inception. They present each play two nights and build and decorate all of their own scenery. Such plays as "Biography," "Berkeley Square," and "Accent on Youth" are found to be the most popular with the four hundred ninety subscribers that this organization boasts.

Reading, Pennsylvania.

The Reading Community Players celebrated their nineteenth birthday in the fall of 1938. During these years they have managed to squeeze out eighty-three productions with casts averaging about ten each. They report that they have given several plays by local playwrights during the past few years and have produced from a number of manuscripts sent to them by the National Theatre Conference. Matthan Gery supervises the productions for the Players which are given in a renovated barn about one-third of a mile outside the city limits. This barn has been remodeled on the strength of the Players taking a rental lease with an option to buy in five years. Housed here they can inaugurate semi-repertory theatre in Reading.

Schenectady, New York.

Here the Civic Players (1938 saw the opening of their eleventh year) have their own playhouse. Four nights are given over to each production. They issue a most attractive magazine, containing not only news of their productions and activities, but also pertinent articles on the theatre. They do not have a professional director.

South Hills, Pennsylvania.

This group, the South Hills Community Players, was organized in 1933. Being in a suburb of Pittsburgh, they were entirely independent of and unidentified with any other civic or community organization. Their aim is to afford an adequate opportunity for self-expression to everyone who is interested in acting. Edward Blaine, experienced both on Broadway and in Hollywood, was the first director of this group.

Spring Lake, New Jersey.

Here the Monmouth Community Players hold forth in a theatre in a building which is the gift of former Mayor O. H. Brown, one of the founders of Spring Lake. This building was donated as a memorial to "those who served in the World War." An endowment fund was raised among both summer and winter residents of the town. The directors are Hudson Faussett and Mary Thomas.

Wellesley, Massachusetts.

The Wellesley Players Club was organized twenty-seven years ago and at the present time is giving productions in the Bardwell Auditorium. Three full length productions are presented each season, supplemented by numerous one-act plays. Approximately two hundred seventy-five members are listed as the average season's subscribing list.

West Newton, Massachusetts.

The Players, Incorporated, have been presenting plays for fifty-one years. They have three hundred memberships and give three productions each year.

Westport, Connecticut.

Here is one of the new groups of community players. Up to four years ago the Westport Players gave an occasional production. Now some of the founders and organizers of this group have banded together again, and in the fall of 1938 definitely planned a season's schedule of three plays a year. They also have play readings. Frances Mason designs the sets, and is also writing original plays which these players are planning to present.

White Plains, New York.

The Spotlight Players' activities of several years were climaxed when they won the Westchester Drama Association Tournament with an excellent production of "Bury the Dead." White Plains will long remember "Liliom," which is considered by all Spotlight Players the finest show that they have ever given.

Wilton, Connecticut.

The Wilton Players, a group organized in 1937 by the business and professional men of Wilton, present three major plays each year. They also have a laboratory and give programs of one-acters. Wilton being an artist's colony, the artists here design all the sets. The actors are all from within the town limits. Their plays are given in the Town Hall, and their season continues during the summer months as well as during the winter.

Yonkers, New York.

The Studio Players of Yonkers are not averse to trying out new scripts. They did "East River Romance" by Edwin Gilbert, with the stage settings designed by Gretel Urban, daughter of the late Joseph Urban. They give their plays in the Waverly Terrace Auditorium. This auditorium was originally the studio of Joseph Urban; but the Studio Players, after his death, remodeled it into a Little Theatre well equipped even to a bar from which refreshments are served during intermissions.

III. COMMUNITY THEATRES OF THE SOUTH

Ashland, Kentucky
Baltimore, Maryland
Birmingham, Alabama
Bowling Green, Kentucky
Charleston, South Carolina
Charleston, West Virginia
Charlotte, North Carolina
Chattanooga, Tennessee
Columbia, South Carolina
Dallas, Texas   116
Del Rio, Texas
El Paso, Texas
Gainesville, Florida
Jacksonville, Florida
Johnson City, Tennessee
Lake Charles, Louisiana
Louisville, Kentucky
Lynchburg, Virginia
Macon, Georgia
Memphis, Tennessee
Mobile, Alabama
Nashville, Tennessee
New Orleans, Louisiana
Orlando, Florida
San Antonio, Texas
Sarasota, Florida
Savannah, Georgia
Shreveport, Louisiana
Tyler, Texas
Washington, D. C.
Waycross, Georgia
And Other Theatres of the South

Ashland, Kentucky.   Seventy-five Dollars for a Corner-stone.

You save money by being married in Ashland, Kentucky. The annual dues for a bachelor or a single person to the Little Theatre are $3.00 a year. A married couple can belong for $5.00, thereby saving a dollar and encouraging matrimony.

Perhaps this is because the group was started by the Reverend G. W. H. Troop, Rector of the Calvary Episcopal Church. It was in April, 1935, and Rev. Troop in an effort to find an interest for the young people of his church called together a small group and suggested the formation of a dramatic club. Nine young people attended. They elected officers. And two of those, sprouting lawyers, were appointed to draw up a constitution and by-laws. The name, "The Parish Dramatic Club," was chosen. All that summer meetings were held. Line by line, comma by comma, and period by period, the constitution was discussed, and finally by fall it was approved and adopted.

But they suddenly realized that nine members weren't enough to carry on a dramatic club, so it was decided to invite people outside the church to join. Membership jumped to over one hundred. The name was therefore changed in October to the "Ashland Dramatic Club" and the Community Theatre of Ashland was launched.

They proceeded cautiously. During the winter standing committees were appointed for finance, casting, scenery, reading, publicity, costume, properties, program, and makeup, and three one-act plays were produced and directed by the members. These were given most informally in the Parish House.

It wasn't until Christmas of that year that they gave their first public performance. Henry Van Dyke's "The Other Wise Man" was dramatized and presented in the Episcopal and Presbyterian churches. There were eleven characters in this play, and costuming them presented the first real hurdle this group had met. They were entirely without experience, but they had great enthusiasm and a firm belief in the purpose of their club.

In a copy of *The National Geographic* they found pictures of "The Passion Play," which they copied using unbleached muslin dyed in bright colors. Sandals were made from imitation leather, cut to fit the sole of the foot and laced with strips of felt. Soldiers' uniforms were cut from cardboard and painted with aluminum paint. Properties, too, were improvised.

As this was their initial bow to the public they were all apprehensive of the outcome. But their fears were groundless; the effect entirely surpassed their expectations, and the costumes, which had caused so much work, came in for special mention. An offering was taken each night and enough money received to defray all expenses and leave a little over for each church.

After this venture the group was much encouraged and began laying plans for a three-act play to be presented the following spring. But the quarters in the Parish House were limited, so early in March they moved to the auditorium of the American Legion building for meetings and rehearsals of their first major production. This was "The Whole Town's Talking." But the whole town didn't, and after expenses were paid there was only ten dollars left in the treasury. Undaunted, they felt themselves lucky to have cleared expenses.

The summer was spent in revising the constitution. And in the fall they brought out their first year book, a very modest one, but containing the constitution and by-laws, the lists of standing committees, the names of the charter members and the membership. That helped, for it made Ashland fully aware of this Community Theatre springing up in their midst and struggling to be heard.

Then they obtained, through the kindness of the manager, the ballroom of the Henry Clay Hotel, where there was a small stage. They resumed production of one-act plays; throughout the winter they put on one each week. This gave them publicity and valuable experience. Also they began broadcasting some of the plays over the local radio station WCMI. That helped spread the news of a growing Community Theatre.

Two of the one-act plays presented were written by members of the club, and in December they gave their second Christmas play, "Emmanuel," also written by a club member.

When the Ashland Public Library was completed, a new building with club rooms and an auditorium, the players moved their headquarters to it and presentation of one-act plays was continued.

But being a stepchild didn't appeal to some of the members. They wanted their own home, something entirely their own where they not only could meet socially, hold their business meetings at times of their own choosing, but also could have room to store their rapidly growing assets of properties and scenery. So finally, over a store, they found a large room. The rent was $25 a month with an additional $4 for heat and light. They moved in, and have been there ever since. Having their own home, they are now making their greatest progress.

They changed their name again, too; this time to the "Ashland Little Theatre" to distinguish themselves from the various school dramatic clubs in town and to identify themselves with the Community Theatre Movement.

Next they went over their membership list, talking to each member personally, and dropped a number who had lost interest or who had failed to pay their dues. This reduced the rolls to sixty-two, of whom twenty-five are the real workers of the club. Now they are moving slowly and building up a membership composed of people seriously interested, having the future of the club as their guiding purpose.

A person applying for membership is asked what he wishes to do in the club. The application is endorsed by three members in good standing and then submitted to the Board of Governors where it is voted upon. If accepted, the name is read at the next regular meeting. Two weeks later, if any member knows why the proposed candidate is not a good worker, he speaks or forever holds his peace. Provided there is no dissension, the candidate pays the dues and immediately is placed upon a committee and given a job, which naturally increases his interest in the club.

"Only workers allowed!" is what they believe in Ashland will give a solid foundation for their Community Theatre.

Of course they have patrons, too, at $5.00, whose names appear upon all programs and in the year book. Patrons are entitled to vote in all club matters and are admitted to all activities. Season tickets are sold to the general public also. So with three sources of income, the Ashland Little Theatre manages to keep out of debt.

Mrs. H. S. Scott, one of the founders of this club, asked what she considered a Community Theatre should be, replied, "I have several ideas, because this is a venture in which I'm deeply interested. As set forth in our year book, the purpose of our organization is 'the promotion of community interest in amateur theatricals,' which, of course, is very broad and takes in a great deal of territory. While the Community Theatre should be rightfully considered a source of entertainment both to its members and to the public, it also has a responsibility in connection with the cultural side of the life of its community. There is also the social aspect. People drawn together by a common interest are sure to have contacts and form friendships they might otherwise miss. Too, they are given an opportunity to express themselves . . . and often they discover talents they never knew they possessed. It is good for people to have a hobby which takes them away from their daily jobs and I can think of no more fascinating one than the Community Theatre, or one which pays larger dividends in pleasure and excitement, and real satisfaction."

So here in a city of thirty thousand is a small and serious band of workers, with their present program: one-act plays for members and full-length plays for the public—three a year. But they are looking ahead and some day hope to have their own theatre. Already they have put aside $75 in a special fund for that purpose.

Baltimore, Maryland.   The Vagabond Players.

The Community Theatre that probably has afforded the most pleasure and amusement to its active membership during a long and useful life is the Vagabond Players of Baltimore. Now approaching their twenty-second season, they have a record of almost two hundred and fifty plays and about fifteen hundred performances.

The theatre that the Vagabond Players now have is in a barn in the heart of the downtown district—where an aristocratic mayor of Baltimore formerly housed his prancing bays. The theatre has been reconstructed to seat two hundred persons and its total equipment is insured for more than $35,000.

Art exhibits are held in the Green Room which was once the hay loft; visiting theatre celebrities are entertained there with receptions; Sunday afternoon teas are held; musical and dance recitals and one-act plays are frequently given on the stage of the Vagabond Theatre which has seen a catholic assortment of talent pass across its boards.

The Vagabond Players are a shining example of a Community Theatre that has attained success without the aid of a professional director. Rita Swann, their historian, summarizes their financial set-up by simply saying that there "are about eight hundred subscribers, generally secured after a strenuous spring festival subscription drive." She continues— "Once we made $2,000; once we went into debt . . . but we generally manage by the skin of our teeth to cover our $4,000 annual budget."

From the very birth of this enterprising theatre, its destiny has been bolstered up by the enthusiasm and devotion of its president, Mrs. Nicholas Penniman. This theatre to her has been child, avocation and main interest. She has made cushions for the theatre seats, translated plays from foreign lauguages, fought Broadway managers for releases on restricted plays; she has moved scenery, painted sets, taken parts at a moment's notice, held the book, directed, supervised elections (and, we suspect, railroaded them), swept the theatre, washed the windows, guided the financing and, last but not least, has footed the bills when necessary.

Inspired by her leadership is also a nucleus which has been with the theatre most of its life. However, they have always held an open door to new talent and, from time to time, have welcomed such people as Evelyn Varden, the noted Broadway player, who came to Baltimore to live after her marriage and was a tower of strength directing and acting, participating in the activities of the Board of Governors.

Since the beginning, the ambition of the Vagabond Players has been to give Baltimoreans an opportunity to see good plays which they otherwise would not see or have brought to them by the professional theatre. In their more than twenty years of existence, they have brought to the Baltimore audiences the works of Strindberg, Masefield, Mencken, Conrad, Bennett, Chesterton, Benelli, Gogul, Sierra, Keats, Coward, and innumerable others including many novices.

Recently we heard a prominent actor lamenting the lapse of the stock company system, and he pointed out Baltimore as an example of a "little theatre" which had contributed to the demise of the sacred stock company. It was pointed out to him that while in 1924 the stock company in Baltimore was probably giving "Getting Gertie's Garter," "Up in Mabel's Room," "Little Miss Bluebeard," and "Baby Cyclone," the Vagabond Players were giving productions of Ibsen, Coward, Hauptmann—which are seldom found in the offerings of the average stock company. The actor was unimpressed by this argument.

The Vagabond Players of Baltimore may, with all the pride in the world, claim to be the typical American Little Theatre and, while the authors of this book have hailed the gradual disappearance of "little theatres" per se, nevertheless, they are glad that the cultural life of Baltimore is such that a little theatre, in the old sense of the word, may continue to function and to serve the cultural life of that city in the finest possible manner.

Birmingham, Alabama. Little Theatre Week Proclaimed.

Last winter a young man came to Birmingham to see his first stage play. He could talk glibly about theatre, he had read a lot of plays, he had seen hundreds of cinemas, but he had never seen a play acted by real people on a real stage. He lives in a small town in Alabama, where road companies never go and where the Little Theatre idea has not yet been born. He read a story in his local paper about the Birmingham Little Theatre's coming production of "The Masque of Kings." He boarded a bus and came to the big city for his first theatre thrill—the curtain going up on his first real play! His enthusiasm and excitement interested one of the members of the Little Theatre so much that he made inquiries and learned that many young people had seen their only plays on the Little Theatre stage.

During the good years, Birmingham folk were great travelers and lovers of drama. Many families made annual trips to New York to see the season's crop of plays. But the young people of this generation were the children of our late adversity, so during the hard years they stayed at home, as did their parents. Depression may drive people into churches, but it also drives them into the theatre if there is one at hand and if the price is low enough. Escape from the stern realities of life is nowhere so simple as in the make-believe of the theatre. It has been the Little Theatre's purpose to serve as a "playhouse" in the real sense of the word, for their community. They adopted "Let Us Be Gay" as their slogan and for the most part have adhered to it. Consequently their doors have been kept open (when many other theatres were dark) during the lean years as well as in the early days of their prosperity. They have profited greatly, if not in money, certainly in friendships.

The Little Theatre has just finished its fifteenth season—a very successful one. Their audiences demand recent Broadway plays—the ones they have read about in theatre magazines. This year they saw "Call It a Day," "Excursion," "High Tor," "Stage Door," "Storm Over Patsy," and as grand finale, "The Masque of Kings," a typical list appealing to diverse interests.

Fifteen years ago, the "Drama League" was a live organization in Birmingham. Famous dramatic readers were imported—learned lecturers came to outline drama courses. The membership was six hundred. After eight years a small group felt that the time had come for expansion into the actual production of the living drama. So in 1923 an invitation was sent out to all the prominent people in the city, urging them to attend a mass meeting at the Chamber of Commerce to discuss the organization of a Little Theatre. The success of the idea was immediate. A constitution was drawn up, a small auditorium was rented and Mrs. Vassar Allen was elected president.

The next business was to secure a director, and Bernard Szold was employed. Fresh from Carnegie, a pupil and friend of Thomas Wood Stevens, enthusiastic and gifted, he gave great impetus to the theatre during his five years directorship. In three years the audience outgrew the small auditorium, seating two hundred, and the productions outgrew the little stage. The demands for a new building were insistent. Mr. Eugene Fies made it possible to pay twelve thousand dollars for the lot and to build the present theatre at a cost of forty thousand dollars. Twelve friends of the theatre bought life-memberships at five hundred dollars and, in the fifth year of its history, the Little Theatre moved into its own beautiful building.

The location is ideal. Away from the noise and confusion of the congested city district, it is adjacent to a spacious, landscaped City Park, providing ample parking space and assuring an attractive setting. The large lobby gives entrance to the auditorium with a seating capacity of four hundred and twenty. An overall dimension of fifty feet by twenty-eight feet, makes the stage suitable for most any kind of production. The huge dome, modeled after the one in the Goodman Theatre, has recently been removed, enlarging the stage considerably.   In addition to the run-of-mine equipment backstage, the auditorium is equipped with a unique arrangement for the electrician in charge of the production.   They have employed the old French Opera House idea and installed an elaborate bank of dimmers below the stage floor, thus permitting the electrician to stand in what used to be the prompt box, invisible to the audience, and at the same time able to secure an unobstructed view of the set and receive light and curtain cues from the action.   A complete fly gallery and gridiron enables them to "fly" almost all the scenery and greatly facilitate scene changes, utilizing valuable floor space for properties and furniture.

Such is the story of the beginnings of the Little Theatre.   Its further history can best be told through a résumé of the work of its four directors. Bernard Szold left after five extraordinarily successful years.   Szold had a unique gift for friendship.   He believed that a Community Theatre should really represent that community and he went out into the highways and byways to make friends for the theatre.   He cast for ability and not for social prestige.   The quality of deep sincerity which marked all his work gave it something much to be desired, but not often found, in the theatre.

During these first five years, the Little Theatre sponsored an original play contest.   A prize of fifty dollars was given for the best play and smaller amounts for the two next best.   All three plays were produced on the stage. The Children's Theatre was also organized and carried on under the sponsorship of the Junior League.

When Szold left, Hubbard Kirkpatrick, also a student and friend of Mr. Stevens and a product of Carnegie, took his place.   He came directly from the Goodman Theatre, where he had been leading man.   Prior to that he had been acting with Ethel Barrymore, Emily Stevens, and other famous stars. Mr. Kirkpatrick combined a keen intellectual view of the drama with an almost uncanny "sense of the theatre."   During his career he produced several Shakespearean plays with a rare touch of authority and beauty.   Under his direction the Little Theatre did its first O'Neill—"Beyond the Horizon." His comedies were always paced like professional plays.   Perhaps the high mark of all his work was the beautifully directed "The Sea Gull" which was given as an extra performance.   Mr. Kirkpatrick was also an actor of high merit, and played in many plays to their great success.

After his five years of excellent work, Mr. Kirkpatrick left for Youngstown, where he still is.

For the next two years John McGee directed the plays.   Mr. McGee revived a waning interest in original plays and produced several, among them one of his own.   Perhaps his most outstanding contribution was his production of Hallie Flannigan's "The American Plan," done on a series of interesting levels. His "Yellow Jack" and "Men in White," also done on a series of levels, marked him as especially gifted in the directing of the episodic type of play. His "The Royal Family" was another big success.

The present director, Mr. Burt F. McKee, Jr.—also a Carnegie man—in 1938 began his fourth season with the Little Theatre. He has been in the theatre all his life and knows it from many angles. He has worked with the Globe Theatre at the Chicago Fair, on the West coast and again in Cleveland and Dallas. He came to Birmingham from the Little Rock Theatre. A writer in reporting her first impression of him for the *Birmingham News,* said, "He seems the answer to prayer—the artist, the intellectual, the man of the theatre, the actor, the show-man, and—praise be—a business man!" And so he has proved to be. During the worst years of the depression and the "worser" years of the recession, he has kept the doors open with fine productions of fresh, stimulating plays. Besides the plays of past season mentioned earlier in this story, Mr. McKee staged and acted in his own play, "Two Fields," which was enthusiastically received by audiences and newspapers alike.

Besides the directors whom this story has praised, there are many others who should be given high commendation. All the work in the Little Theatre, except that of the director and the janitor, is voluntary. Through the years rich talent has been uncovered and developed. The whole intricate machinery of the theatre has been operated by devoted workers. They have sent out into the professional world several actors: Helen Walpole, who toured with Katharine Cornell as Henrietta in "The Barretts" and appeared with Eva Le Gallienne in New York repertory productions: Gail Patrick of movie fame; Henry Richard, many times a juvenile on Broadway; Natalie Levinge, now under contract in Hollywood; Adeyn Owens.

Human interest stories? There are many crowded into the years. There are anecdotes galore; one that was particularly amusing. During a heavy stage-rainfall, a member of the audience stole quietly from the auditorium to the telephone in the lobby—"Nurse, nurse, be sure to close the nursery windows—it's raining cats and dogs outside!"

The Birmingham Little Theatre states that its greatest problem is: "Finding out what the public wants! In an industrial city like ours tastes are as queer and varied as the animals that went into the ark. We have two large colleges, we have a state university sixty miles away, we have more would-be authors than any city of its size in America, we have capitalists, we have communists, we have steel workers and day-laborers, and we want them all in the Theatre. But some want all comedies, some want all tragedies, some want 'nice' plays, some want a bit risqué plays, some want DRAMA, some want

—bless my soul—burlesques. Some like it hot and some like it cold. But they all want a show! The public is a hydra-headed monster, as Mr. Stevens once said. To try to feed each head to its special taste is the thankless, exciting, heartbreaking, thrilling, greatest problem of our Little Theatre."

We think it fitting to close this résumé of the activities in that southern city by showing you what appeared as an editorial in the *Birmingham News* on May 18, 1938:

ONE WEEK THAT DESERVES OBSERVANCE

"The multiplicity of special 'weeks' has tended to detract from what is basically a good idea. The 'weeks' have become the butt of jokesters.

"But one such week now confronts Birmingham, and the justice of its cause and the worthiness of its object demand that it be taken seriously and earnestly. By proclamation of Commission President Jones, the period from Thursday through Sunday has been designated as Birmingham Little Theatre Week, in honor of the year's closing presentation.

"For fifteen years (with the possible exception of this year) the Little Theatre has been Birmingham's chief source of theatrical entertainment. During this time it has presented outstanding plays that otherwise Birmingham would not have been permitted to see. Because of its reputation for high artistic performances, it receives consideration from playwrights and producers not ordinarily granted. Illustrations of this fact are seen in the permission given this year to produce the two Maxwell Anderson plays, 'High Tor,' which was an event of midwinter, and 'The Masque of Kings,' with which the Little Theatre closes its second season this week.

"Entertainment has not been the only function of the Birmingham Little Theatre, however, and perhaps, from the long view, it has been the lesser function. The Little Theatre, because it works on a nonprofit basis, does not have to restrict itself to assured box-office successes. It can experiment; it can do pioneer work; it can be a builder of a larger artistic appreciation and a finer understanding of the stage.

"Moreover, the Little Theatre offers opportunities for acting to hundreds of persons in the city who find pleasure and a deep satisfaction for the creative urge in being members of Little Theatre casts.

"And consequently, in remembering the Birmingham Little Theatre this week (and remembrance means, among other things, attendance), Birmingham citizens will be giving themselves a present treat as well as aiding an organization whose influence for good radiates in many directions."

Bowling Green, Kentucky. Hurricane Tears Off Roof, but the Play Goes on.

They worked hard to present their first play to the public in Bowling Green. They painted their own scenery, hustled tickets, did all the many jobs necessary, and finally presented "Dulcy" in the basement of the Metho-

dist Church. Sixty dollars was cleared, including profits on program adver-
tising sold to local merchants. But, unfortunately, the treasurer absconded.
However, they wrote it up to profit and loss, and got a business manager.
Now no check can be signed by one person alone.

Their next production was also given in the Methodist Church, with the
women serving coffee between the acts.

"This beautiful friendship was dissolved eventually," says Muriel Hawks
of this group of Players, "because the cast and various workers could not be
dissuaded from smoking during rehearsals, and you can readily see that the
Sunday School classes were not improved in any way when the floor was lit-
tered with cigarette stubs. In addition, as long as we were playing in a
church, each script had to be rewritten considerably, and swear words had to
be avoided as the plague, and anything resembling a kiss had to be changed
into a firm and friendly handclasp, thereby losing some of the punch originally put there by the play's author."

They gave "Double Door," which proved to be their most successful venture, without having had a rehearsal on the stage they were to use. Rehearsals were held in homes, the basement of the hotel, and woodsheds.
While they rehearsed in the hotel one warm night with the windows open, a
traveling salesman, tired and sleepy, phoned the desk to say, "Please, mister,
go down there and put some gal named Caroline to bed. I gotta get my
rest."

On the night of production a hurricane blew part of the roof off, but
the audience thought the noise was sound effects warning of Victoria's doom
and the applause drowned out the noise of the storm. When the lights
finally went out, candles were used on the stage, which helped the melo-
dramatic effect.

The Bowling Green Players Guild was organized in January, 1933, by
a small group of kindred spirits. Now each year they present three full-
length plays and seven workshop programs. Associate memberships are $1.00
a year, with reserved seats to all major productions. Active memberships are
priced at $1.50, with patron memberships at $3.00.

The list of plays they have given in Bowling Green is proof that this community sees the best in drama: Ibsen's "A Doll's House" and Martinez-
Sierra's "The Cradle Song," together with recent Broadway successes, make
up their bill of fare.

Mrs. Philip Binzel, who had directed the dramatic work at Eastern State
Teachers' College of Kentucky, has been the Guild's director from the beginning. With her practical idealism and a sense of humor on the part of
the workers, this Players Guild forges ahead. It feels that any organization
which can bring together so many people of varied talents and unite them,

democratically and harmoniously, in a non-profit endeavor to produce worthwhile plays, has a definite place in the modern social order.

According to Russell H. Miller, president, their greatest problem is the lack of a theatre. At various times they have used churches, school auditoriums, downtown theatres, the armory—at all times they have been an orphan seeking some sort of home.

"But," he says, "although we are a long way from the center of the nation's dramatic activities away out here in the edge of the bluegrass section, we still believe that we've got somethin'."

The purpose of this group is: "To give to those throughout the city and surrounding territory, regardless of profession or station in life, the opportunity of self-expression in the art of acting, or its kindred fields, and to provide an organization in which all crafts and arts may pool their resources for the creation of beauty."

Charleston, South Carolina. WPA Reconstructs America's Oldest Theatre.

1938—The most publicized community theatre of the year.
1940—The most important theatre of the Atlantic Seaboard? ?

A group of players now known as the Footlight Players of Charleston, are, in cooperation with the Carolina Art Association, housed in the historic Dock Street Theatre. The story of the cooperation between the Art Association and the Footlight Players and the erection of the Dock Street Theatre is a unique tale of the development of a cultural idea in an old American city.

Charleston, South Carolina, is not a city built over night. Charleston is not a rich city when figured by the income per capita. But Charleston is wealthy in tradition, in glamor, in history, and in beauty of locale. Charleston does not readily take to new ideas or new ventures. So the success of the Footlight Players is even more phenomenal in view of the fact that they were established as recently as 1932, when a group of enthusiastic theatre lovers conspired to present several one-act plays at the Officers Club in the Navy Yard. The surprising success of this initial evening at the Club encouraged them to organize and maintain their identity under the title of the Footlight Players.

The first directorship of this embryo group was under Robert Memminger who guided the Players through five productions of which "The Royal Family" and "The First Mrs. Fraser" proved to be most profitable and successful.

At first membership in the Footlight Players was an exclusive privilege, although the performances were open to the public. From the beginning a policy was established that no soliciting should ever be made for general donations to support the group activities. It was determined that "the plays themselves had to pay and keep the Players out of the red."

The succeeding two seasons saw a general growth of the Footlight Players, and in the fall of 1933 the membership was thrown open to the community. Dues were set at $5.00 a season, which entitled the member to attend six performances and to participate in the extra-curricular activities that were constantly being enlarged upon by the Board of Directors.

A high point of the second season was the production of "Interference," which was taken to Columbia, South Carolina, and there presented under the auspices of the Town Theatre. The Footlight Players hope to establish such trips as a regular feature of their season.

Two years later they set up a community group composed of representatives of all dramatic organizations in Charleston and nearby, and for the past few years they have extended any advice and assistance the groups might need. The Players are charter members of the state-wide Theatre Institute of South Carolina, which was created to correlate the various dramatic groups of South Carolina and to offer mutual assistance.

In the spring of 1935, Emmett Robinson was engaged as the director and the next three seasons show remarkable development. Under his guidance the activities of the Players expanded to include workshop productions, special study classes, dancing classes and a program of cooperation with the local activities of the Federal Theatre.

Through an appropriation from the government, the WPA had been working for many months to reconstruct a theatre in the shell of the Planters Hotel, which stood on the site of the first commercial theatre building in America. In November, 1937, the Footlight Players, on invitation of the city, presented a production of "The Recruiting Officer," a restoration comedy by Farquhar. This was the first play presented in the original theatre and was, of course, a natural choice for the restoration opening. This production attracted nation-wide attention and served to bring the activities of the Footlight Players to the attention of the Rockefeller Foundation. After the opening of the Dock Street Theatre, its management was turned over to the Carolina Art Association, and in January, 1938, a conference was held to suggest a plan for the development and use of this building. The Footlight Players were approached in an effort to merge the interests of the Art Association and their own. The idea was in the main to combine the managerial efforts of the former with the producing and dramatic activities of the latter. In May a satisfactory agreement was reached and the two organizations joined hands, and soon after announcement was made of a generous gift from the Rockefeller Foundation.

Mr. Robinson has accepted a Rockefeller Foundation grant for several years of study in the north and, in his absence, Charles Meredith, formerly of the Dallas Little Theatre, is taking over the direction of the Footlight Players.

The success of the visit of the Cleveland Playhouse Association with two productions in Charleston has raised a problem for the Footlight Players. Rumors have begun to float that a professional repertory company would be in order and that the Players should move in that direction. Yet it is questionable whether or not Charleston would respond to purely professional players. The city is essentially self-sufficient. The Footlight Players include entirely capable actors and actresses whose performances under able directors equal those of professional casts. The city supports them—rightly. If the change to a repertory company were made it might mean the death of the Footlight Players, who today are, thanks to Robinson, one of the healthiest Community Theatres in the country. Cleveland and Charleston are widely different cities.

If, however, this rumor turns out to be idle, there is every reason to expect that Mr. Meredith's regime will see the development of the Footlight Players into one of the most substantial contributing theatres in the field. They are at the place now where they would dare to undertake experiments in play production and have a sufficient audience to attempt productions of new plays. There is an exciting future to be developed with this group, who have in the past few years made themselves so conspicuous that the eyes of the American theatre are watching every step they take.

Charleston, West Virginia. Their Theatre Burns Down, but the Players Carry on.

In 1922 the Kanawha Players made their first bow to Charleston audiences. These players were originally identified with the Drama League of America. The first venture was the production of one-act plays in the high school auditorium under the direction of Rose Fortier. The group was small and plays had to be chosen that would fit the limited number of performers, but the quality of the presentations brought immediate acclaim.

For three years, under the direction of Miss Fortier and her successor, Perceval Renier, a series of well-acted plays was produced and the Players prospered. During this period a workshop was organized and scenes and settings worthy of professionals were turned out.

At the beginning of the 1925-26 season they acquired their own playhouse, a remodeled church. Freed from the limitations of hired auditoriums, a new standard of excellence was apparent in their productions.

In 1927 they engaged their first professional director, Ramon Savich, as the Players felt that their work had outgrown the scope of amateur supervision. Under his direction the Players progressed steadily until 1933, when curtailed revenues made it once more necessary for the Players to turn again to local direction.

But the officers, counting on public support, made preparations for an outstanding season in 1934. As a first essential step, another professional director was engaged, Edward Crowley. During his regime the auditorium of their playhouse, seating three hundred twenty-five, was packed on every evening of the four nights of play production.

In 1935 Richard Gage succeeded Mr. Crowley. Besides his regular duties as play director, Mr. Gage also tried an experiment in Charleston. For fifteen years a professional company hadn't played in Charleston, and so the Kanawha Players stood sponsor for the Theatre Guild production of "Call It a Day," then on tour.

The contract called for a guarantee of $2000, and Mr. Gage has confessed that after the signing of the contract he didn't sleep for days. Two thousand dollars, and also the stage hands must be paid. The company arrived, and Mr. Gage held his breath.

But Charleston turned out in full regalia for the play, and after the count was made at the box office, there was $2400 in the till. The guarantee was paid and the stage hands collected $400, and the harassed director of the Kanawha Players gave a huge sigh of relief.

Then the business manager of the company said to Mr. Gage, "As you know, this is our closing performance, and the Theatre Guild wants to know if the Kanawha Players would be interested in having the eight sets, as the Guild doesn't want them now?"

The value of this scenery was around $1800, and Mr. Gage lost no time in accepting such a bounteous gift. So that's the story of how the Kanawha Players and their director, Richard Gage, stuck their necks out, and instead of having them chopped off, received eight complete sets of scenery.

Encouraged by this success, Mr. Gage the next season tried a unique experiment. He imported professional actors, guest stars from New York, to play the leading roles in two productions.

Having watched carefully the reactions of his local casts and audiences he came to these conclusions: namely, that the Charleston boys and girls want to be in a play where there is a professional acting the leading role. Instead of resenting an outsider, the actors work a bit harder, give an added zest to the performance. Also, he finds his audiences like to see a new face. And he finds it a good publicity stunt.

Mr. Gage has also concluded that a good amateur can hold his own with a good professional, and that there isn't, after all, too great a gap between the two. He finds, too, that it gives the professional who cannot get big parts in New York a chance to regain self-confidence. While in Charleston the guests are royally entertained and given every opportunity to do their best. "It does something fine to the actor's morale," said Mr. Gage, "to be a big shot, no matter how small the puddle."

The next spring, 1936, when "Louder, Please" was in the throes of production, two weeks before the opening night Mr. Gage was aroused from his early morning slumber by a frantic telephone call. The playhouse was on fire!

"I don't remember much of my drive down," so Mr. Gage has said, "except such silly things as I wished I had taken my paint clothes home, and so forth. I arrived at the theatre, and my complete backstage and set were ruined by fire and water. Everyone was running around frantically, and crying, 'What are we going to do now?'

"My one thought was that the show must go on, and on time! This is where I think we are the first community theatre group to go on a showboat. But that's what we did. Billy Bryant's Showboat was in town for six weeks. Because we thought it a good publicity stunt we rented the showboat for three nights and reblocked and remade the set. The curtain went up on the night we said it would!

"About 1500 people saw the play, and it was lots of fun doing it. A number of priceless things happened. The young juvenile of the showboat made us realize that he was professional. And we were not able to forget it. In fact, he told me that he would go backstage to help me get the actors on and off, and to keep them quiet, because, 'You know how easily amateurs get scared.' He thought it rather silly that we had a dress rehearsal, as after all, the showboat people never did. They knew their audience, and had worn their costumes before, so why a dress rehearsal?"

But in spite of the loss of their theatre, the old spirit in Charleston has carried on. When the theatre burned they had only four hundred and fifty members. But during the 1937-38 season they had twenty-five hundred members, and Mr. Gage is inclined to believe that losing their playhouse was the best thing that could have happened. It stirred the group and the community to action.

They made plans, however, to get another theatre of their own in the 1938-39 season.

In the meantime Mr. Gage has a dream that he would like to put into effect. Being an enterprising young man, he'd like to present twelve shows each season in Charleston; six done by the townspeople, as the theatre should never lose the community touch, and six by a group of young people who could devote all their time to the theatre. Eventually this group might work into a repertory company. These young actors would be paid, be given the opportunity to make a living at the thing they want to do, and the hazards and risks of Broadway would be avoided.

"It's only a dream," says Mr. Gage, "but it's a nice one!"

Charlotte, North Carolina. The Little Theatre Goes Touring.

Thomas B. Humble came to this group as director in 1930 when it was called the Charlotte Drama League. It had been in existence for two years, producing plays spasmodically. Upon Mr. Humble's arrival the name was changed to the Little Theatre and immediately plans were made for the building of their own playhouse, which was completed in 1934.

Six plays a year is their production schedule, but sometimes they find it necessary to give another play to satisfy all the demands of the actors and the patrons. Usually this play comes at the end of the season, and is conducted on a cash basis. That is, the members all pay for tickets in addition to their yearly dues. One year when they gave "Little Woman," they netted nearly $1000 on this extra production.

Their playhouse is never dark, as the workshop carries on informally with three one-act plays every few weeks. To date they have given seventy full-length plays and over two hundred one-acters.

Plays run according to popularity, and this varies from three to five performances. Also each season they take a play on tour to other towns and cities in the Carolinas. Many of their players are from surrounding towns, and the Charlotte Little Theatre has been instrumental in helping other theatres start.

Their membership roll is one thousand, and outside of an occasional rental of their theatre and patron memberships, the yearly dues are their only source of revenue.

One feature of this membership is the fact that the attorneys of the town take great interest in the Little Theatre. Usually attorneys act as president, and they have even had a judge appear upon their stage.

Mr. Humble, besides directing the plays, designs and constructs all the settings. He has even confessed that there are times when he has swept the stage before a performance.

Chattanooga, Tennessee. Torch of Thespis Burns Brightly in a Fire House.

It was a group of business and professional men of Chattanooga, together with a smaller number of equally able and prominent women leaders in the community, who started this Little Theatre in 1923.

The theatre, as it happens, is an old fire-engine house. On the payment of $2500, the group received a deed of trust from the city which included lot and building. There is a clause, however, stipulating that should the building cease to be used as a Little Theatre, it will revert to the city. The members themselves, through subscriptions and gifts from individuals, raised some $14,000 which was spent in remodeling the fire house into a theatre.

One of their young artists in Chattanooga, Hubert Black, has painted a series of murals around the upper walls of the auditorium, depicting the history of the stage from early times down to and including the motion pictures.

Two original plays by a Chattanooga writer, Adelaide Rowell, have been presented in this playhouse.

The casts for their productions have been notable, according to John E. Gilbreath, of this group, for the fact that nearly each one has been representative of every walk of life in Chattanooga. Lawyers and physicians, manufacturers and executives, capitalists and newspaper editors, social and philanthropic leaders, all play parts on the stage of their theatre.

And while Mrs. Alfred H. Thatcher says that although the Chattanooga audiences are not interested in the experimental or even the unusual, and what they want is entertainment, still she is hoping that in the future they may be able to give more plays with thought-provoking content.

"But I am convinced," she adds, "that a community theatre must 'make haste slowly'—and that it should try to give the community what that particular community wants. Slowly, we may be able—I think we shall be able —to improve the level of their wants. Certainly our proposed program for next season is the best yet. It contains nothing trivial, and yet is, we feel, reasonably sure of getting over."

Columbia, South Carolina. The Townspeople Build Their Own Town Theatre.

During the World War there had been an interchange of entertainment programs between Columbia and nearby Camp Jackson, an army cantonment. These relations had been cordial and rich, and exceptional effort had been devoted to their fulfilment and success by a group of ardent Columbians inspired by the talent they had discovered.

The war came to an end. The townspeople still had lots of enthusiasm, but no place to go. So, quite naturally, they began to look about for some means of continuing their activities. Their first thought was the establishment of a Little Theatre in Columbia.

There was at that time a play-reading group known as the Columbia Drama League (now the Columbia Drama Club). To them went Martha P. Dwight, then Society Editor on *The State*, the morning newspaper. She took with her Daniel A. Reed, a sergeant at Camp Jackson, who had participated in the various productions. At a meeting of the Drama League on April 10, 1919, at which "Lord Dunsany and His Plays" was the subject of discussion, Mr. Reed was presented and read "Gods of the Mountain."

Plans for the establishment of a Little Theatre were made. Twenty members pledged themselves to work toward the desired goal. A circular letter was sent out inviting interested people in the community to join. On July 2 the first meeting was held. Officers were elected and the enterprise was named The Columbia Stage Society. Daniel Reed, who in the meantime had been mustered out of the army, was invited to become director.

During the first year plays were given in various auditoriums about the city. In 1920 a campaign was launched to raise money for the purchase of a theatre property. Citizens throughout the community, and even in neighboring towns, sent in checks and pledges. The "brave little band of twenty" which had started the movement now expanded to several hundred and suddenly found itself able to incorporate the Columbia Stage Company.

While the producing group was still called the Columbia Stage Society, a holding company was chartered to make ownership of property more sound and practical, and to give assurance to the public that subscriptions, to be represented by stock certificates, would go into the tangible asset of a permanent theatre. The building project was thus removed from the status of a rather loosely organized producing society: the monies subscribed for a playhouse were guaranteed protection in a separate corporation, the Columbia Stage Company, and were placed out of reach of the Columbia Stage Society, which, having its own canoe to paddle, would have to survive on merit, without subsidy from the theatre holding company.

This step has proved itself to be one of eminent wisdom, as the Stage Society throughout its nineteen years has been forced to do what it probably would not otherwise have done: carry itself financially without undermining the home furnished to it by the generous subscriptions of the stockholders of the Columbia Stage Company, owners of the theatre property.

From the subscriptions of the 1920 campaign, which aggregated some

$27,000, only about $15,000 was realized before the first post-war depression stopped all collections. This amount, however, was sufficient to purchase an old residence and convert it into a temporary playhouse. This crude make-shift, with an auditorium and balcony seating two hundred and fifty, was used until 1924, when it was condemned as a fire risk by the city authorities.

Here was crisis. What could the group do without a place in which to work? It could not go back to the high school auditoriums and dismantled soldier shacks in which it had spent its first year. What could be done to satisfy its now large membership and also its growing public? Should it close its doors for all time? Or could some means be found of wrecking the old converted residence and building on the same site a new and adequate theatre?

After much lost effort and delay, a new building campaign was launched in April, 1924, with W. Bedford Moore, Jr., as General Chairman. This whirlwind campaign, with daily publicity followed up by intensive effort, was remarkable in that it was given a theatrical vehicle, in three parts. The first, "A Prologue to a Wedding Pageant," was Mr. Moore's opening speech launching the campaign in the old theatre. The second, "A Wedding Pageant," was a symbolic phantasy, representing the "wedding of Columbia to the drama as its special phase of artistic expression," and proved to be a beautiful piece of pageantry by Director Reed. It was given as the last per-formance on the stage of the old playhouse, upon the announcement that the campaign for the new theatre had been successful and the new theatre assured.

Then the third was "An Epilogue," and that was the turning over of the completed new theatre in December, 1924, by the General Chairman, Mr. Moore, to the Columbia Stage Society for its use and benefit, so long as it might survive.

Although most of the money for the new theatre was subscribed and paid in cash, the participation of the merchants and manufacturers of Columbia was solicited by taking subscriptions in goods and materials: lumber, brick, hardware, and so forth. Further participation, in cases where the materials sold or manufactured were not usable in the construction of the building then going up, was by issuance of trade coupons to members of the Town Theatre group, who bought the coupon books for cash and then traded them out in purchases at the establishments so subscribing; hat shops, clothing stores, drug stores, filling stations, and so forth. Subscribers in coupons and in goods and materials, in addition to stock certificates, got special advertising, which the generous newspapers in turn (*The State* and *The Columbia Record*) contributed to the Stage Company without cost. Moreover, the merchants and manufacturers invited to subscribe in this way were carefully selected so that they would receive the greatest possible advantage from their specially advertised cooperation in a community enterprise in which the best element of the city was interested. And throughout the publicity the theme of "The Wedding Pageant" was so employed as to give special news value and lend colorful news interest to the progress of the campaign.

The result of Mr. Moore's theatrical campaign vehicle as propelled by an intensive drive, his original scheme of reaching the commercial people of the community, and the magnificent cooperation of the newspapers and the citizens of Columbia generally, was that within a month from the time the campaign opened the money necessary for the new theatre building was fully subscribed.

The new Town Theatre was built on the site of the old, the total cost of the property as it stands today, clear of debt, being about $42,000.

In the annals of Community Theatre building, the achievement of the townspeople of Columbia stands unique. Shoulder to shoulder they worked, and by unstinted cooperation under inspired leadership they built their own playhouse. They did not seek nor ask, in any way, for outside funds or help. And their theatre is rightly named—The Town Theatre.

Although more than five hundred people contributed to the new and artistic Town Theatre on Sumter Street, which one newspaper aptly described as "idealism in brick and mortar," no account of the project would be complete without the mention of a few special contributors to its realization. Among them were Dr. Robert Gibbes, chairman of the building plans committee; the late Arthur W. Hamby, architect; the late Morton Visanska, who back in 1920 had sufficient faith in the enterprise to take over in his own name the original deed to the property and whose enthusiasm and support never flagged till his death in 1929; the late Ambroze E. Gonzales, president and publisher of *The State*, who from the start gave unstinting support and encouragement to the movement and who through the columns of his paper conducted for several years a state-wide playwriting contest, with prizes of $300 for the best three-act, and $100 and two $50 prizes for the three best one-act plays submitted to a committee of judges of the Town Theatre, for which production rights were reserved; and the late William D. Melton, president of the University of South Carolina, who upon completion of the new Town Theatre, gave the organization an anchorage in the state university, which continued for several years.

The materials used all came from South Carolina. The exterior is of Sumter brick, and this same pastel brick furnishes a charming and restful interior. The wrought iron chandeliers of Russian cartwheel design were made in a Columbia foundry, as were the artistic sconces over the door. The theatre seats four hundred and thirty persons. There is included in the building also a business office, a box office, and a studio and Green Room overlooking the auditorium.

Just ten years after the Columbia Stage Society was launched, the Players' Club was formally organized under the aegis of the Stage Society's then president, Mrs. Julius H. Taylor. From the start it has been both an enjoyable playground for workers in the theatre and a useful auxiliary branch. This Players' Club carries on the theatre's workshop, producing for its monthly meetings one-act plays, both original and imported, and frequently burlesques the big productions just given by the Stage Society. A good illustration of the latter was the burlesque of "Hamlet" following the Stage Society's ambitious and amazingly successful production of the great tragedy, the farce being called "A New Wing to Elsinore."

In addition to these monthly meetings, which go a long way toward keeping up vital interest and enthusiasm, the Players' Club gives each year a grand costume ball, which has come to be looked forward to generally by the people of Columbia, whether or not they are members of the Town Theatre.

In the past nineteen years the Columbia Stage Society has presented one hundred and twenty-eight plays.* And over one thousand Columbians have, at one time or another, trod the boards of its stage. And, of course, an even greater number have helped with the backstage work, and the business arrangement.

In an editorial in the program at the time this group gave "Hamlet" W. Bedford Moore, Jr., had this to say concerning the purpose and function of a Community Theatre:

"If a community can afford but one purely idealistic institution, it can do no better than a Community Theatre. This is true because the theatre is the broadest of all the arts in its scope. It touches, employs, almost all the so-called specialized arts and crafts—the drama, the spoken word, the plastic effects of the stage, appreciation of the varied aspects of life itself, music of every kind, dancing, painting, sculpture, and, most important of all, playwriting, which is the primary self-expression of all cultured peoples.

"Just as philosophy is a sort of crossroads for the sciences, so the theatre furnishes a meeting-place where all the arts may join to produce a composite effect, to hold the mirror up to nature.

"How valuable to a community then is a successful experimental theatre, one such as our own Town Theatre? The answer is obvious. Its value may be measured precisely by the community's appreciation of it. Such a theatre is a very storehouse of living opportunities, all under one roof. And the opportunities it affords, available to every citizen, are at once the Town Theatre's *raison d'être* and gift to Columbia—a gift that has been widely heralded throughout the nation and beyond the American borders."

* See Appendix H.

To mention all the distinguished visitors who from time to time have dropped in at this playhouse would make a long list. Hatcher Hughes, the playwright, attended the opening of the new theatre. At the premiere performance of Dorothy Heyward's "The Lighted House" was George Pierce Baker with Dorothy and DuBose Heyward. Visits of Richard Burton, Carl Sandburg, Burton Holmes, Mrs. Edward MacDowell, Padraic Colum, Barrett H. Clark, Vachel Lindsey, and others have become part of its tradition. And on the stage of the Town Theatre Julia Peterkin, the novelist, has often played parts.

From this Town Theatre several of its players and directors have gone forth. Fay Ball Alexander played in New York with the Theatre Guild and with Madge Kennedy. Bobby Woods was also with the Theatre Guild. Frank Durham became the Director of the Little Theatre of Macon, Georgia. Harry Davis, for two years Director of the Town Theatre, is now on the staff of the Carolina Playmakers at the University of North Carolina. Daniel Reed, the first director of the Town Theatre, was for a time with the Shuberts in New York and also has been to Hollywood in several capacities. The late Belford Forrest, another of its directors, was also a playwright; his "Lost Sheep" was done on Broadway, and another of his plays, "Sing, Sweet Angel," was presented during the Shakespearean Festival at the Pasadena Community Playhouse. Lonnie Goodkind now lives in New York and is story scout for the moving pictures. Frank Woodruff is also in New York on the radio. And there have been many others. The present director is Carl Glick.

Now in its twentieth year, the basic spirit of this group is its sincerity. Having hitched its wagon to a star, it labors on toward a high and distant prospect with a faith that has pervaded its every struggle and that has sustained it through all the long years of its continuous and progressive growth.

Dallas, Texas. The Child Grows Up.

Nineteen years ago a weak, faintly whispering, almost unwanted orphan was tossed onto the basement steps of the Dallas Unitarian Church, and was christened "The Little Theatre of Dallas." Its parentage was obscure; no one would admit having conceived the idea. What kept it alive and who supplied nourishment and incentive for it to live is not known, but to those who shall be nameless the organization today is greatly indebted.

The first director was Talbot Pearson. During his regime there was difficulty in keeping up with the agile infant, which sprinted from one place to another without warning.   Some of its temporary homes were various high school auditoriums, a more or less swanky restaurant, and the Scottish Rite Cathedral.

The Little Theatre became what it was supposed to be in 1922, when Alexander Dean, now of the Yale University faculty, took a whirl at it.   He moved the group to a small auditorium in a downtown store—neat but somewhat cramped quarters.   At the close of his first season, Yale called Mr. Dean and he left the theatre to Oliver Hinsdell, who was brought from Le Petit Théâtre du Vieux Carré in New Orleans.   Hinsdell reigned from 1923 to 1931, building and occupying first a barn-like theatre in Olive Street, and then in 1928 the $125,000 edifice on Maple Avenue.   Hinsdell departed in 1931 to become talent coach for Metro-Goldwyn-Mayer in Culver City and shifted in 1936 to Paramount in Hollywood.   Hinsdell gave the Little Theatre two homes of its own, three David Belasco Cups on Broadway, a sizable membership and an enormous vogue.   The Dallas Little Theatre won permanent possession of the Belasco trophy, and with one of its prize-winning plays, "The No 'Count Boy," introduced to the American theatre North Carolina's Paul Green.   In 1929, with "They Knew What They Wanted," the Dallas organization walked away with the first ribbon and a substantial cash award in the Texas Little Theatre Tournament.

Hinsdell's successor was Charles H. Meredith, once of the Lobero and New Orleans groups, whose resignation in July, 1938, to direct the Dock Theatre, in Charleston, S. C., came after seven seasons, during which the theatre was given a greater seriousness of purpose, a successful school for the training of young actors, and a thoughtful repertoire.   In 1934, Meredith brought the theater front page notices in London, New York, and elsewhere with his world's premiere of George Bernard Shaw's "A Village Wooing."

The Board of Directors founded the theatre's school more or less at the request of its membership.   For a period of ten or twelve years no courses of instruction were given.   Vaguely organized groups would meet and the director would conduct classes in diction, acting, and various phases of stagecraft.   In 1933 the theatre formed an alliance with Southern Methodist University in Dallas to give courses at the theatre for which credits would be given on degrees at the university.   Some of these classes were conducted by members of the university faculty and others by the theatre's director.   The arrangement proved unsatisfactory.   The university is a church-supported institution and necessarily could not sponsor some courses which were necessary to maintain a complete school of the theatre; therefore, two seasons later, the alliance was terminated and the theatre started its independent school.   The enrolment has varied from sixty to seventy for each session since.

The theatre regularly produces six subscription plays during the season, with three additional student productions. The director is responsible for all of these, and he is likewise the administrative head of the institution.

During the lush days before Depression I, the Little Theatre of Dallas had an annual income of around $35,000. Its annual expenses were usually from $3000 to $5000 more than the income and the deficit was made up annually by passing the hat around the Board of Directors. During the depths of the depression, the income dropped one year to $10,000, but with economies here and there and by reworking old sets until they hung by threads, the theatre struggled through the lean years. Meanwhile, all obligations, all interest charges and substantial reductions on the capital debt of the theatre were met. In 1937-38 the income rose to above $25,000, and early indications for the next season pointed to a still higher figure.

The theatre originally had three paid employees: a director, an executive secretary, and a porter. The permanent staff, other than the school faculty, is now four.

On Charles Meredith's resignation, in July, 1938, the Board of Directors was confronted again with the problem of selecting a suitable successor. It has been history that directors of the Little Theatre have used the Dallas group as a stepping-stone into larger and more responsible positions. That the Dallas Little Theatre is a leading civic group in the country was evinced again when more than fifty top professional men from the Atlantic to the Pacific applied for the vacant post as soon as Meredith's resignation became known.

In his place came Edward J. Crowley, who, for the past three seasons, had been at the helm of the Grand Rapids Civic Theatre. On leaving the School of Speech at Northwestern University, Mr. Crowley founded and for six years directed the Chicago Little Theatre Guild, afterwards going to the Kanawha Players in Charleston, West Virginia, the post he occupied before taking over the Grand Rapids directorship.

Associate director of the Dallas Little Theatre, and dean of its school, is Amy Goodhue Loomis, and Kenneth Slaybaugh from the Lobero Theatre in Santa Barbara and the Pasadena Community Playhouse is technical director. Executive secretary is Bertrand Heflin.

Del Rio, Texas. From the Mexican Border.

One hundred and fifty-six miles west of San Antonio and only two miles from the Rio Grande River is Del Rio. Situated in the heart of the wool and mohair producing district of Texas, Del Rio derives its income principally from the sale and shipping of these products. And across the Rio Grande is romantic old Mexico. Del Rio is the cross-road of two nations.

Into the lives of the people—more than one-half of whom are of Mexican descent—has come an institution that has borne much cultural fruit: the Little Theatre, which so pervades the schools, churches, clubs, and business organizations that mingled with the routine conversations about daily lessons, missionary societies, and the latest news from the ranches, are discussions of the plans of the Theatre.

The population of Del Rio is 14,864. Of these 5783 are whites, 8755 are Mexicans and 306 are negroes. In these figures lies the major problem of the Del Rio Little Theatre, for this group is supported entirely by the white population. Other (film) theatres in this section draw upon the Mexican population, but not so the Little Theatre. Above everything, there rises the general civic attitude of Southwest Texas.

With much bustling about, many aims and ideals, effective publicity, an existing hope, and tremendous physical activity on the part of the City Federation of Women's Clubs who sponsored the movement, the Del Rio Little Theatre came into being on August 28, 1929.

Mrs. Brian Montague, wife of the present State District Judge, was one of the guiding forces of this movement and was elected its first producing director. Mrs. Walter F. Jones was president for that first season; Mr. R. T. Hunnicutt was elected treasurer and has continued in this position. A meeting for all interested in the Little Theatre was called in August. All who thereafter bought season tickets were recognized as members of the parent body of the Little Theatre. This group then elected a Board of Directors, who in turn elected their own officers. This procedure of general election of Board members has continued to date. The Board of Directors incorporated the Del Rio Little Theatre on a non-profit basis and work on the first production started immediately.

"Green Stockings," "Dulcie," "Her Husband's Wife," and three one-act plays constituted an active first year. The following season of 1930-31 saw the production of only two plays: "Buried Treasure," and a production for the school children of the city of "Snow White and the Seven Dwarfs." In presenting "Buried Treasure," the Little Theatre showed their courage by venturing into the field of originals and gave their townspeople a play of local color written by one of their own—Edith Long Mordfield.

Then came the depression. The Del Rio Little Theatre had to suspend production for two seasons, but the fall of 1934 saw the group active again doing "Ladies of the Jury," "Polly with a Past," and "One Hundred Years of Love Making."

During the 1935-36 season, "The Haunted House" and "The Torchbearers" were the only productions. The next season, the Little Theatre was able to do only one play, which was directed by Maud Stevenson. But in

1937, an uprising of the young people in the theatre created a burst of enthusiasm and energy, and a director was brought from Fort Worth, Texas, under whose direction "The Night of January 16th," "Private Lives," and "The Drunkard" were presented.

Jene Crotty, the new director, aided in bringing the membership campaign to a new high of three hundred and thirty-six members. The coming seasons are being planned and guided by the president, Mrs. Jo Sander, and Mr. Crotty with hopes of a series of plays more valued and more ambitious than has been undertaken to date.

The Little Theatre of Del Rio does not have a home of its own. Ordinarily the plays are presented in the new high school auditorium, a well-equipped modern edifice that serves the needs of this community handsomely. The Del Rio Little Theatre operates without sustaining members or patrons and all expenses are met directly by income from ticket sales. This necessitates a tight check on expenses, but it has in no way hampered productions. Ingenuity is one of the keywords in the Little Theatre movement in Del Rio and there they meet obstacles with anticipation rather than fretfulness.

When the Little Theatre was first organized, there was a whole generation of young people in Del Rio who had seen nothing but movies. Of course, the older members of the community had enjoyed stock companies and road shows, but a dearth of these for many years had denied them all pleasures in legitimate productions. The Little Theater started at bed-rock to create a new interest in the theatre. It now has its own library, which includes not only plays and books, but the current magazines on many phases of the theatre. For each production there are many applicants who wish to work on research, stage design, make-up, publicity and back stage. Since the inception of the Little Theatre, a number of young people who have majored in dramatic work in college, children, and adults alike have shown a desire to learn by studying each year with the director and other drama teachers in Del Rio.

Mr. Crotty outlines the responsibilities of the community theatre by saying that "Here in Del Rio, we have attempted to give as many people as possible an opportunity to work some place in the Little Theatre each year. It is the director's duty to give the community the best shows possible, using and coordinating the work of as many helpers as he possibly can employ . . . From the border of Texas that touches the colorful nation of Mexico, we send forth greetings to our fellow builders across the world who serve and love the theatre, and we say in the language of our neighbors—'Salud!' "

El Paso, Texas. The President Makes a Yearly Report.

This Little Theatre got its start in 1928. It was an outgrowth of the Drama Study Club, an auxiliary of the Woman's Club. Mrs. Warren D. Small, Chairman of the Drama Study Club, found that this group was inadequate to satisfy the dramatic inclinations of "Young El Paso." So they added the actual production of modern dramas to their program of reading and discussion. The success was so outstanding that Mrs. Small in April of 1928 gathered together a few brave spirits and the Little Theatre of El Paso was started. The results of the past few years have more than justified its existence.

The organization and its work can be studied in the following report of the president, Mrs. Sam Watkins, for the season of 1937-38.

To the Board of Governors, Advisory Committee, and members of the Little
    Theatre:
Your President begs to submit the following report of activities for the year 1937-1938.
The Little Theatre has made definite progress this year.
I wish to express gratitude to the Board of Directors. This group comprises the hub of the activity of the Little Theatre, for the whole body is actively interested and from this group the results are achieved in year by year bettering the Little Theatre.
The Advisory Committee, with Mrs. J. W. Lorentzen, chairman, gave many recommendations. Since this group comprises Past Presidents of the organization, I fully recommend the cooperation from the Advisory Committee as they have had the actual experience and each new President can benefit by their results.
A new committee was introduced into the year's work. Namely, Ways and Means Committee. Mrs. R. K. Evans was chairman of this committee, and much credit is due her and her efficient committees in raising the money to redecorate the Little Theatre building. $358.62 was made through a Spanish Fiesta given on the lawn at the home of Mr. and Mrs. Sam Watkins.

.   .   .   .   .   .

One of the highlights of the year was again returning to "open membership." This entitles a member to a book containing coupons that any number of coupons may be used for one play and the member is privileged to buy a second coupon book.
All members of casts in major productions must buy full membership or coupon book. Single seats are sold at $1.10.
Through this means we interested new members from time to time and in single seat sales we added greatly to our finances, allowing further interest in El Paso of Little Theatre activity.
Up to date, 331 members are full paid Senior and 31 are Junior memberships.

Four major productions have been efficiently cast and presented to full houses. The fifth and last play of the season will be given in May.

Miss Chella Maloney, Chairman of Casting, with her efficient committee very cleverly selected fine casts.

Great approval and interest was expressed throughout the membership over the selection of plays. Much credit is due Mrs. Charles Goetting and her committee for their untiring efforts in selecting plays appealing to the general membership.

At the beginning of the season ballots were given members to select five plays from the five groups of plays listed. This gave the membership opportunity to select plays and in turn gave the Committee an idea as to the kind of plays most popular to our Little Theatre audiences.

The Social Committee, under the Chairmanship of Mrs. Rosalie Walz, later Mrs. Camille Craig, added much enjoyment, as the committee endeavored to get about and see that all were introduced, adding an interesting touch to the evening's entertainment. Coffee was served between acts and a general get-together atmosphere enjoyed.

Miss Esther Brown, Chairman, selected ushers for the plays.

Miss Florence Cathcart (Mrs. Melbey) did fine work as Publicity Chairman, later followed by Mrs. Bernard Krupp and Mrs. Walter Stephenson.

.   .   .   .   .   .

Mr. Carl Glick gave us fine publicity in the Eastern papers and your President enjoyed the publicity of the El Paso Little Theatre given in various cities by those expressing much interest in our outstanding activity through the various branches.

The Spanish Play under the Chairmanship of Mr. H. G. Parteoroyo, always adds glamor to the year's work. This, being an extra play, adds to our financial success. This, a special privilege of enjoying our Sister Country's language and customs in the beautifully directed plays, an annual presentation, your President feels a great addition to the year's program.

This year we will enjoy a musical comedy titled *La Marcha de Cadiz*, directed by Pedro Meneses, to be presented May 8 and 9. ($600 was cleared on this.)

Production for our major plays was beautifully accomplished and well scheduled under the fine direction of Milton Dennis. Much credit is due him for the presentation of the attractive sets for our fine plays.

Your President recommends adding equipment enabling this committee to function under less trying conditions.

The Workshop plays were well rendered. Added interest from the membership is noticed from time to time.

This is a fine school for those interested in acting and greater cooperation should be given by the full membership in attending these plays.

Much credit is due Miss Prather for her fine work in curtailing expenses by printing her own programs and using only the cyclorama for stage scenes.

The Children's Theatre plays were very lovely under the efficient direction of Mrs. Frank Hughes. They were well chosen and splendidly cast. This group is sponsored by the various Service Clubs, giving pleasure to underprivileged children in providing means for their attendance to the children's plays. The Little Theatre heartily appreciates the response of this gracious gesture by the following: Rotary, Lions, Kiwanis, Altrusa, Junior League and Young Matrons of the Woman's Club. Mrs. Hughes and Committee with your President took the first children's play to Hot Springs, New Mexico, and presented an afternoon's entertainment for the crippled children at the Tingly Hospital.

.   .   .   .   .   .

El Paso's Little Theatre candidate, Miss Charlene Watkins, was elected Queen of the Southwestern Sun Carnival with a majority of 55,000 votes. This, El Paso's outstanding community achievement, again put our Little Theatre at the head, and much publicity was given our wide-awake organization. Mrs. T. W. Lanier, as business manager, was given praise for her untiring efforts in promoting the Little Theatre candidate.

The Little Theatre presented her Queen with a beautiful scepter matching the official Queen's Crown. The Officers, Board of Directors, and Committee Chairmen were included in an open house honoring the Queen and her Court and out-of-town officials attending the Carnival New Year's Day in the home of your President and Mr. Watkins, as also the Past Presidents were honor guests at the Coronation and Ball for the Queen.

.   .   .   .   .   .

We are ever grateful to Major R. F. Burges for his continued interest and professional advice at our Directors' meetings and greatly appreciate his gracious hospitality, with Mr. and Mrs. Preston Perrinot in opening their beautiful grounds to the Little Theatre for the annual garden party. Mr. Ed Heid will be chairman for this year's party, to be given in June.

Our scrap book, compiled by Mrs. R. G. Hosea, is very interesting and most complete.

.   .   .   .   .   .

The box office, under the direction of Mrs. Dave Price, has been handled efficiently. This is a responsible position, with long hours in preparation. Your President recommends a paid box office Chairman by two or more Senior memberships.

The Little Theatre has been well kept and warm due to the fine management of the House Committee, W. T. Shannon, Chairman. Ralph Sanders, House Committee Chairman, has taken care of all necessary repair work on our Little Theatre building.

The cooperative spirit of G. H. Krakauer is noted throughout the year in handling committees such as programs, properties, and others when chairmen have been unable to act.

The same cooperation has been enjoyed through Mrs. Erma Berliner, Telephone Chairman, and Mr. Don Knoblaugh, Make-up Chairman.

Our financial report has been kept most satisfactorily and all bills paid by the month. It is the wish of your President to turn over the year's report owing nothing and money in the bank.

We are most appreciative to the following bondholders in releasing their bonds to the Little Theatre: Major R. F. Burges, Mr. C. M. Irvin, Mrs. K. D. Olivir, Mr. Luis Zork, Mrs. Warren Small, Mrs. Julius Lorentzen, Mr. Allen Grambling.

Special mention goes to our Director, Miss Lucia Hutchins, for her splendid direction and presentation of our plays this year. This is the only paid position in the Little Theatre organization and much appreciation goes to the full organization comprising busy active patrons. It has been splendid to note the enthusiastic and sympathetic audiences, and I take this opportunity to thank all from the membership who have helped in any way the success of the year's work.

. . . . . .

Your President, feeling that the Little Theatre offers the most in combination of education and enjoyment in El Paso, recommends open membership as most beneficial.

The Little Theatre enjoys a distinct place in the cultural and recreational development of El Paso.

With added enthusiasm, the incoming officers of the Little Theatre, with the splendid Board of Governors, will experience a most interesting year's activity. I want to welcome all to a happy year's endeavor.

We want all of El Paso to become interested in our Little Theatre.

Respectfully submitted,

FLORENCE WATKINS.

Gainesville, Florida.   Scholarship Fund Stimulates Town and Town Relationship.

For several years prior to 1927, a small group of adults in the city of Gainesville had been vitally interested in dramatics. Their interest had been expended mostly in sponsoring school plays and in attempting to promote a few children's plays in connection with school celebrations and affairs. After several years of unorganized effort, a group met at the home of Mrs. F. W. Buchholz on June 8, 1927, for the purpose of effecting an association to sponsor an organized Children's Theatre Group.

At this meeting it was suggested that the association appoint a committee to study the rapidly spreading Little Theatre Movement, and report on the possibility of an adult dramatic society. The committee was not slow with their report, and on June 17, 1927, a much larger and more enthusiastic group of citizens met, elected officers, adopted by-laws and a constitution, appointed standing committees, and began real work.

The plans at first provided for three groups: the Children's Guild, the Junior League, and the Adult Membership Group. The emphasis was first placed upon the younger groups, and thus it was that in September, 1927, the

Children's Guild and the Junior League collaborated to produce "The Pied Piper of Hamlin," the first play produced under the Gainesville Little Theatre sponsorship and direction.

Gainesville welcomed the new organization, enthusiastically applauded the first play, directed by a professional director from the University of Florida, and offered the Little Theatre sound financial support by purchasing a large number of season tickets.   For the first few years the policy of the Little Theatre was to hire professional directors, but recently directors for the various productions have been drawn from local talent, many of them from the University of Florida faculty.   This later policy has seen the production of many successful plays.   The organization is financed by membership dues and door receipts, and these have proved to be ample for the needs of the group, as the organization has never shown a deficit since its inception and for several years has closed each season with a surplus in the treasury.

Gainesville is the home of the state university, and thus the citizenry is composed of people of widely different tastes and talents, yet the problems of the theatre are not unlike those elsewhere.   The first problem presented was that of convincing the community of the value and worth of a Little Theatre, that the organization was definitely a community asset.   Fortunately, the community was not hard to convince, so that today that old shawl of grandmother's, or the mahogany sofa of Mrs. Brown's, or membership dues all come easily.   The second problem was that of appealing to the widely varying likes of its members.   This was done by producing widely varying types of plays.   The third problem was gaining the cooperation of both "town and gown"—that is, getting the university community as interested in the Little Theatre as were the townspeople (not always an easy task).   This was accomplished by applying the surplus funds in the treasury to a Scholarship Loan Fund, which has increased in amount each year.

Studio nights, receptions, and from three to five plays a year have attracted and pleased the members and the public.   It has been very gratifying to the Little Theatre that very excellent cooperation and assistance has been given it by the Florida Players, the university group, and by the various public school groups.

The great need of the Gainesville Little Theatre at the present time is a playhouse of its own.   In the past the organization has utilized the public school auditoriums, and that of the University of Florida.   More recently it has been able to use the model stage and auditorium of the P. K. Yonge Laboratory School, the university's experimental school.   As satisfactory as these places have been, they cannot offer the advantages that the Theatre's own stage would.   Through the efforts of several prominent business men of the city and the work of a former president of the Theatre, Dr. Sigismond deR. Diettrich, the Little Theatre has hopes of erecting its own building in the near future.

In September, 1938, the Gainesville Little Theatre began its eleventh year of productions. With new stage equipment and much new scenery, the organization was ready for another successful season, under the presidency of Professor Kenneth G. Skaggs of the University of Florida English Department.

Jacksonville, Florida.   By-product of the World War.

During the World War, an organization to provide entertainment for soldiers, called the "War Camp Community Service," was created in Jacksonville. It existed for some time after the war as "Community Service." Then, in the autumn of 1920, at the suggestion of its president, Leed Guest, a branch was formed called "The Community Players." Captain Basil Stephenson was its first president and Miss Maude Francis was brought to Jacksonville to direct its presentations.

The first presentation of the Community Players was "A Marriage Has Been Arranged," by Alfred Sutro, given at the Mason Hotel in December, 1920. During their first season of productions, and in the years following, a score or more people gave much of their time and energy in creating a theatre for Jacksonville.

From 1920 to 1926, The Community Players went through the ordinary good times and bad that Community Theatres experienced during this postwar period. In 1926, however, the name of the group was changed to The Little Theatre of Jacksonville, and a state charter as a non-profit organization was secured. In the years to follow, the Little Theatre was so fortunate as to have a number of highly skilled professional directors.

For several years after the Little Theatre's inception, productions were given in the Women's Club Building on Duval Street. Then came a period in which the Little Theatre found itself bouncing from the Metropolitan Club to the Playhouse, to the auditorium of the Chamber of Commerce, the Morocco Temple, the Arcade Theatre, and then back to the Women's Club.

In 1927-28, when the membership had reached a high mark of six hundred subscriptions, hopes of building the theatre ran high. A lot was purchased and plans were drawn. But the succeeding years proved so progressively disappointing that the idea was abandoned and the lot was sold. Recession in membership kept pace with the general depression (there had also been a Florida depression before 1930) and had reached a point in the fall of 1936 when two attempts to bring together the necessary quorum for an election of officers failed. It became apparent that the organization would collapse unless some new stimulus could be found. A few of the die-hards made a personal canvass of those most interested, and assembled a small but determined group which elected officers, revamped policies, and sent the organization hopefully forward under the capable leadership of its president, Martin Sack. At the suggestion of the new Chairman of the Membership Committee, Carl S. Swisher, the inauguration of a limited seasonal membership of three hundred and fifty was adopted.

This plan proved so successful that for the 1937-38 season the membership limitation was raised to seven hundred, which was fully subscribed long before the first production.

Under the leadership of Sack and Swisher, thoughts of a new home revived. With membership of seven hundred and possibilities of more, it did not seem impossible that the Little Theatre might acquire a permanent home. At that time Carl Swisher, Chairman of the Membership Committee, advanced a proposal to finance personally a new Community Theatre building, providing the Little Theatre could increase its membership by a respectable number. The ticket selling committee plunged enthusiastically into the work and secured a total of nine hundred and sixteen 1937-38 subscriptions. This surge of energy so impressed Mr. Swisher that he gave the word to go, and estimates for a new theatre building were considered. The original estimate was only $15,000, but development of a complete building plan satisfactory to the organization revealed need for an investment of more than $40,000. Then Mr. Swisher made another notable civic gesture: first a gift of $20,000 outright, and further a loan of $20,000 secured by mortgage without interest.

This theatre is of modern design and built in a new and attractive suburb. The main entrance, on the most prominent boulevard of the community, leads into a large semi-circular foyer with an arc-shaped dome. The auditorium seats three hundred and thirty-two people and the sight lines are perfect. The acoustics, scientifically worked out, and the intimacy of the entire house incite the actors to their best work. The stage is fifty-one feet across, with a proscenium opening of forty feet. The front of the stage consists of three different floats permitting rapid scene changes; all that is necessary is to move each set secured on one of the floats into the desired position. Moving time is less than twenty seconds. On the second floor, reached by a graceful winding staircase, is a large lounge, beautifully decorated, where all assemblies of the organization are held.

The theatre was opened January 18, 1938, with the dedication of a plaque in honor of Mr. Swisher, and nine plays were produced in the space of less than nine months, an extraordinary record for any community theatre in theatrical activity and interest.

Mr. Swisher, elected president at the end of the season, soon afterward held his first board meeting to plan for 1938-39. A strenuous campaign for membership was undertaken and set a new record of fourteen hundred and fifty paid memberships.

A summer school sponsored by the Little Theatre was opened in 1938. One hundred and forty students enrolled, and classes running three nights a week for four weeks were held in diction, fencing, stage craft, acting and make-up. Short plays, including "Back From Reno," written by the director, Huron L. Blyden, were given as a final presentation of the season.

The Jacksonville Little Theatre has contributed its bit toward American literature by sponsoring playwriting contests from time to time. Among some of the entries that have received production as rewards for excellence in these contests are "Garden Varieties" and "Ten Years Old," by Elaine Ingersoll Minick; "The Green Eyes of Eros" and "Slender Strings," by Miss Isabelle Williams; "The Conqueror," by Mrs. Willis M. Ball; "Raw Meat," by Miss Birsa Shepard; "The Shenstone Emeralds," by Mrs. Irene C. Tippett; "The Woman of Magdala," by Phillip Devlin (adapted from the story by George Creel).

Jacksonville is extremely fortunate that Carl Swisher happened to be just a little stagestruck, for without his love of the theatre it would have missed the opportunity it has now of developing one of the finest and most important Community Theatres in America.

During an interview with Mr. Swisher in the office of the large corporation of which he is president, we had a shining example of the essential democracy of the American Community Theatre. During the questioning, Mr. Swisher suddenly reached for the telephone and said: "Get me Jack." A few minutes later a young man in short sleeves, obviously from the stock room, walked into the office and took his place in a heated discussion of the policies and future ambitions of the Jacksonville Little Theatre. Here was the president of a large business corporation and his stock room clerk spiritedly seeking a solution to the artistic problems that faced their mutual avocation—The Jacksonville Little Theatre.

Johnson City, Tennessee. Undaunted by Problems.

Less than five hours from New York by plane, overnight by train, a day and a half by car, lies Johnson City, beautifully situated in the mountains of Tennessee. A city of some thirty-five thousand, it has small opportunity of seeing legitimate productions except those presented by its Little Theatre

Players. However, they have the advantage of little competition, there being only two or three small movie houses and no very near cities offering anything more enticing.

The Players were organized in 1920 by a very small group motivated by a love of drama and a desire to produce it. This love and desire were the only two assets of the group, but they have proved to be adequate, for today they have around sixty active members, no debts, some money in the bank and an accumulation of stage properties.

The founders of the group were Mary Gump, Louise Barton, Charles Broyles, Robert Lyle, A. T. Earnest, Sarah Cook Barton, Emma Lee Barton, Ben Everett, and possibly one or two others. At any rate, the membership was limited, and at the first meeting, held at the home of Louise Barton, there were so few present that everyone held an office! Mary Gump was the first president, and has been most active in the Players ever since and one of its ablest directors, making a "pilgrimage" to New York every year to study the latest stage productions on Broadway. Incidentally, all of the "charter members" have continued to be the backbone of the Players through the years of its existence.

In 1925 they gave their first open performance, and since that time plays have been produced each season. Of course in the beginning the audiences were rather small, but each year has shown an increase until at the present time the Players are always sure of a representative audience at any of their plays.

Miss Carrie Pace, the present president, writes: "The greatest element showing growth is the fact that the group has never disbanded, and has carried on all during the depression, when practically all other clubs in this community ceased, and during its entire existence has been self-supporting, although at times there wasn't much support."

It has been the ambition of the group to have its own theatre, and for several years its home was in the basement of the Mayne William Public Library, where the Players built a stage, hung a curtain, and stored properties. This was finally relinquished because the WPA needed a place for a sewing, book binding, or some other project and no other place could be found. It is, in fact, characteristic of the group not to mind being moved about, and the members seem to enjoy going from house to house and from storeroom to storeroom, collecting props the day before a production is scheduled, or even the afternoon before—a sort of treasure hunt.

At the present time, through the kindness of one of the members, they have a large room on the second floor of a downtown building which has been dubbed the "Workshop." There is a small stage there and they are contemplating enlarging it. Rehearsals are held at the Workshop and the season is begun with an "Open House" there, refreshments being served. A one-act play is also presented at this time to which friends are invited.

Before the workshop was acquired, properties had been stored wherever most convenient, and evidently no inventory was ever taken. For when they started collecting various props accumulated through the years, it was discovered that they were the proud owners of eight sets of steps! Every time they produced a play calling for steps, some helpful soul had dashed off and made a new set.

The main objective of the Little Theatre Players has been to lift their standards of production, and of course to make the public play-minded. In furtherance of this idea, they have produced such plays as "Death Takes a Holiday," Ibsen's "Doll House," "Candlelight," and other similar plays.

Four three-act plays are presented each season, beginning usually in January, with one play a month thereafter, using the stage of the Junior High School. For the past two years one of their plays has been presented each year at the East Tennessee State Teachers College as one of their Lyceum numbers.

The most serious problem of the Players seems to be that they do not have a paid director; that they do not have anyone free to devote full time to the furtherance of activities, and there is also a lack of skilled labor for the construction of sets, etc. The members do all the work in connection with the presentation of all plays and, since practically all of them are employed during the day, rehearsals, costuming, construction of sets, painting, assembling of properties, etc., are done at night. And the most surprising thing about it all is that at six o'clock on the evening of a production, any sane person would say it was impossible for a play to be produced, yet at eight-fifteen the drawing of the curtain marks the beginning of another credible performance. It seems to be a mystery to everyone—including members of the cast!

Another problem that a community theatre faces in a very small city or town is the fact that audiences are so enthralled at seeing their next-door neighbors on a stage that they are unable to enter into the realms of make-believe and really enjoy the play for itself. The Players, however, have been able to make their neighbors forget personalities and really feel all the drama that their able members give to them.

The Players do not meet during the summer, but have their first meeting in September, and once a month thereafter. At the meetings there are always interesting programs, sometimes a one-act play, directed by some ambitious soul with no previous experience, and usually using younger and newer members in the cast. The audience, composed of members, is allowed to criticize and a good time is had by all.

Each year the Little Theatre Players give an award for the best play written and produced by a member of the High School Dramatic Club and also an award for the most outstanding performance by a member of that Club. And last, but not least, an "Oscar" and "Oscarette" are awarded to each of the Players' own members who have given the most outstanding performance of the season. To quote Miss Pace: "I still insist that some award should be made to the best Property Chairman of the year, because that would be the only possible way I might have a chance of getting one of the statues, and inasmuch as I am the President for the coming year, this new custom may be inaugurated—but please don't tell any of my members of this plan!"

The Players seem to be able to meet individual problems, including supplying a bodyguard for one of the most loyal members for twenty-four hours before his performance so as to assure his appearance in the "pink of condition" and without the added stimulus of the beverage for which Tennessee is most justly famous. Another member who gave a most memorable and commendable performance as "Death" in "Death Takes a Holiday" faced what seemed to be an unsurmountable obstacle the night before the play. In the pursuance of his various duties he, in some mysterious manner, came up smiling but with a very black eye. However, by matching up the other eye (less painfully, with make-up of course) he appeared as a most appropriate "Death" and for days received compliments on his realistic make-up!

To quote Miss Pace again on the ideals of the Players: "Yes, we do have definite opinions as to what a Community Theatre should be—an organization continually striving to lift the standards of drama, to produce good drama and to do it purely and simply for the love of the drama itself."

None of the Players has become professional—gone on to Broadway or New York, but they have had, and still have, members of the group who were professionals.

The following excerpts from "Who's Who" in the cast of the last play presented ("I Want a Policeman") introduce some of the members of the Players:

J. G. Pitts (Eric)—A veteran of many Little Theatre plays. Will be remembered as hard-boiled "Steve" in "Ladies of the Jury."

Anne Bryant (Fern)—Has played in numerous Little Theatre presentations. Was seen in "Smiling Thru" and "Adam's Evening" last season and played "Mrs. Sharpe" in the pre-season play "The Passing of the Third Floor Back."

Jim Trolinger (Commissioner Baldwin)—Comes to Little Theatre Players from the Little Theatre group in Elizabethton, where he has worked in many plays.

Hugh Millard (Alfaro)—Is well known in Johnson City as actor and director. He has had experience with the stage in New York, and will always be remembered for his portrayal of "Death" in "Death Takes a Holiday."

Jepson—It was just that our director is superstitious. Count the cast and then see if you wouldn't have added one—well, just for luck.

Nowell Pace (Sergeant Lynch)—We were forced to use him because he has a uniform!

Lake Charles, Louisiana. The Inspired Leadership of One Woman Creates a Theatre.

Lake Charles has a population of some sixteen thousand, half of it Negroes. But the story of the accomplishments of its Community Theatre is amazing.

Let them speak for themselves. Here are ten reasons why they feel proud of their theatre in Lake Charles.

1. We are the theatre that is as far South in the United States as the Gulf of Mexico will let us go.

2. We play in the deep South, where (we regret to say) education and culture is at its lowest ebb.

3. We have never been in debt. We have lived within our budget; have never had a drive, campaign, or benefit. We now own three lots on which we plan to build our own theatre, and the lots are paid for. And we have never had so much as an ad on our programs, nor have we cost any member or player anything other than membership dues. We even buy stockings for the cast in non-costume plays. And we have money in the bank, kept through the depression.

4. We are truly a community enterprise, having no paid workers and using a hundred or more people in various capacities on each production.

5. We have a sixteen-piece orchestra that has been with us since our first play. We claim that the theatre is the meeting ground of all the arts: music, literature, acting, painting, everything, and we encourage every department. It may be a "poor thing but our own"!

6. We have never had a professional director. A local person who has directed us for ten years, one who never had instruction or saw any other production directed.

7. We stand alone in the fact that we have never had a quarrel or fuss of any kind in our theatre—and the same people are working together as started in 1927.

8. Lake Charles is the only town of its size in the state that has no educational institution beyond the high school. So the community theatre takes the place of all culture beyond secondary education.

9. We have sent one girl to dramatic school, who played in summer stock immediately. And we have sent one boy to art school, who won two Cresson Scholarships at the Pennsylvania Academy (à la Jo Mielziner), and

is now teaching in art school, having got his start doing crepe paper sets for us at the age of sixteen.

10. We choose our casts much more from people who need us than from those we need. If people are unhappy or have particular problems or need outlets, social, spiritual, emotional or physical, we invite them to work or act. We have had excellent plays. Mothers thank us for giving their young sons cultural and educational and happy work. Wives thank us for helping husbands over bad periods of depression. Sick and nervous people thank us for putting them on their feet again.

And that's the Community Theatre of Lake Charles; a theatre that has been in existence for the past eleven years. They present each season five major long plays, one junior long play, and four drawing room or readings and discussions. They don't know exactly how many people they have had tread the boards and work backstage in that time; but they do know they have some three hundred and fifty members who pay $5.00 a year which takes care of everything. There is no other source of revenue; there are no individual admissions to the plays except the guest privileges of membership. These tickets are $1.50 each.

"We think this is too much for our plays," says the Board of Directors, then adds, resignedly, "but they pay it, and like it!"

Their Board of Directors of ten, five officers and five members at large, is truly representative: a sewer pipe manufacturer, an oil well supply salesman, a rice broker, a civil engineer, a timber company executive, housewives, working girls, a school teacher, an oil leaser, an insurance man, an author, a typist and an ice cream manufacturer. There are twelve committee chairmen.

The Director is Rosa Hart.

Her story is worth telling, and Mary Louise Dunn tells it. "She is from our home town (no professional importation). She has been torch bearing against the great odds of indifference and ignorance for more than ten years. She has been offered the position of director in other places but declares she does not know the job well enough since she has never had any training, and besides that she feels that her place is with her own folks. However wrong or right she may be about knowing her job, she has directed plays locally that are equal to if not better than many other community theatres I have seen.

"Here are a few facts about her. She was the first woman cheerleader in the country, and the first given the right to wear the athletic letter from a man's university—Tulane in 1920. She works in an insurance office from 8 to 5; teaches boys for Annapolis (none of her candidates has ever failed) from 5 to 7:30; directs the plays for the community theatre from 7:30 to 10:30, and then conducts her 'Very Idea Studio' (doing anything for anybody from writing a letter in Polish to roasting a chicken) on into the night, and then starts all over the next day. On the side she promotes an orange-pecan business, and conducts the local culture club (the slogan being, 'You pays your quarter and you takes your culture'). She has the distinction of having won a trip to Europe by making a mistake on the typewriter. She promotes everything in the town from Community Concerts to Hart-Open-Air-Academy which she runs on her front porch on summer afternoons.

"But that is not what she has done in the theatre. She believes that a theatre should be a volunteer institution for the community. She started by being president, scenic designer, and director. Her first men actors she swears that she pleaded with on bended knees to be in the plays. They didn't, at first, want to get mixed up in any Ladies' Aid Stunts. She has given courses on the drama and has, *single handed,* built the Lake Charles Community Theatre into one of the finest organizations of its size and kind.

"She has a spirit that she has put into the whole town. She asks that the casting committee do *not* give her actors. She wants people who need the community theatre more than the community theatre needs actors. She has taken a switchman who could not read or write and literally 'learned' him his lines and his part. He is now one of the most faithful workers in the theatre. She gets her players from all the highways and byways of the town and the surrounding country. She did 'The Trial of Mary Dugan' with the leading lady from a town fifty-six miles away, and did double re-hearsing and then put the two parts together. She feels that the best part of the community theatres is the name 'Amateurs'—meaning lovers of the theatre. She gives all her spare time, and will take no pay for her services. And these services and the good she has done for our city cannot be over-estimated. She spends her money getting local boys and girls to school and has developed more talents than many college professors.

"She is thirty-six years old and unmarried, with a grand spirit and a fine sense of humor. She is worthy of your attention!"

She certainly is.

It was Deems Taylor, we believe, who said that the drama is in the safe hands of the "amateurs."

Certainly with such courageous, self-sacrificing, vital, and civic-minded persons as Miss Rosa Hart guiding the destinies of the Community Theatres, the future of the theatre in this country is indeed in safe hands!

Louisville, Kentucky.   Town and Gown Join Hands Across the Footlights.

2 clubs joined on Campus

The theatre of yesterday and the theatre of tomorrow are side by side at the Playhouse in Louisville, Kentucky.

On one side of the footlights the community players in sock and buskin, grease paint and wig, keep alive in their own way the traditions of the living drama.   On the walls of the Playhouse hang playbills and portraits of the stars of yesterday—the famous players of a by-gone day—the good old troopers who took to the road and played a one-night stand in Louisville.

This is the famous collection of Colonel John T. Macauley.   When the Macauley Opera House was torn down in 1925, Boyd Martin salvaged these playbills and theatrical photographs, some three thousand of them.   Many of the glasses were broken and some of the frames damaged.   But Mr. Martin had all the pictures reset in the quaint old frames and they now hang on the walls of the Playhouse auditorium and foyer.

The playbills include one of the City Theatre, built in 1810, the first Louisville theatre.   The original playbill announcing the opening of the Macauley Theatre hangs by the box office, and one wall of the Playhouse is hung exactly as the pictures hung in Macauley's foyer.

And as the youthful players of today troupe in the Playhouse, the players of yesterday smile down upon them and almost seem to say: "We, too, loved the theatre.   The road is no more in Louisville.   But you are keeping the theatre alive.   Thank you—and good luck!"

In 1911 Dr. John L. Patterson, whose death not long ago robbed the Players of their greatest admirer, organized a dramatic club at the College of Liberal Arts of the University of Louisville.   In the early fall of 1914 he secured Boyd Martin, on the dramatic desk of *The Courier-Journal,* to direct his little club.   At that time the policy was to give experimental plays during the year, and a final play, in which the more able students could appear, at Macauley's Theatre in the spring after the regular theatrical season.

Mr. Martin continued this policy, until one day to his surprise he found a balance of $300 in the treasury.   This he spent on building a stage in one end of a room on the second floor of a two-room building at the rear of the College of Liberal Arts.

Borrowing $125 from a wealthy faculty member—an amazing feat in itself—Mr. Martin put the finishing touch to the tiny second floor theatre which seated two hundred and two, with a wine-colored velvet curtain and opened what he christened The Dramatic Work Shop in the spring of 1919 with "Green Stockings" by A. E. W. Mason.

But the policy of going to Macauley's for one production each spring continued until the University of Louisville moved to a campus. Upon these grounds stood a little wooden Gothic chapel. It was turned over to Mr. Martin for a theatre.

The chancel was raised and a stage added. Mr. Martin's plan was to have a gridiron floor fifty-eight feet above the stage floor. The president of the University of Louisville on an inspection trip discovered steel columns supporting the gridiron rising in the air. He thought they resembled a grain elevator.

"Cut them down!" he ordered, and despite protests from Mr. Martin they were hacksawed to thirty-six feet, to annoy stage crews and provide additional problems in rigging and shifting scenery ever since.

But the old chapel, remodeled at the cost of $14,000, opened November 13, 1925, with "The Swan," which had never been played professionally in Louisville. The same year Macauley's Opera House came down. The old gave way to the new!

The success of the University of Louisville Players, composed entirely of undergraduates, aroused a few older members of Louisville society to consciousness of the Little Theatre Movement. Many Louisville citizens had been members of "The Dramatic Club" which functioned for many years before 1911, when it was dissolved.

In 1918 these citizens had formed the Players Club of Louisville and had presented many interesting plays. Frequently the club had been able to secure professional direction; George Somes, directing the Little Theatre Society of Indiana, and William Sams, directing stock in Louisville, were able to assist immeasurably.

But the Players Club of Louisville had no permanent home; no permanent director. An offer to Mr. Martin was rejected because of University policy.

In ten years of production the University of Louisville Players, whose personnel changed every four years, had graduated many experienced players. One or two joined the Players Club of Louisville upon invitation. But many, seeming to lack the necessary social background, were never invited to become members of the organization. Mr. Martin urged them to organize a graduate group.

This was done and during the season of 1927-28 the Alumni Players of the University inaugurated a season of five productions. For the next four seasons the Alumni Players drew more and more Louisville theatregoers to their plays. During the last two seasons Mr. Martin has been permitted to direct also the Players Club of Louisville.

Dr. Raymond A. Kent, the university president, apparently saw the advantage of building toward a real community theatre with the campus as a center of operations. Younger men and women in the meantime had joined the ranks of the Players Club of Louisville—sons and daughters of former members—graduates of out of town colleges who were returning to Louisville to take their place in the community, young people who wanted to act in the Playhouse. They also wanted the Playhouse director.

So Mrs. Charles M. Garth, one of the most experienced of the Players Club members and William Hoke Camp, a Players Club founder and manager of the Louisville's Memorial Auditorium, effected amalgamation of the Players Club of Louisville with the Alumni Players. And under the title "Little Theatre Company" graduate work in dramatics has been going on as a community enterprise since 1932; thirty-one major productions had been given by 1938.

The Little Theatre Company when formed obligated itself to improve the Playhouse—a large foyer where the audience might meet between acts; paint and electrical rooms and back stage toilet rooms for the players. Mrs. Garth gave a covered walk from the drive to the main entrance door to protect patrons in inclement weather. And last season a private office was built, decorated and furnished for the director and board members.

Neither the University of Louisville Players nor the Little Theatre Company operate for profit; all box office receipts are spent upon productions. Students of the College of Liberal Arts are assessed $1 a semester for their tickets to undergraduate productions, but there is no compulsion put upon them to attend performances of the Little Theatre Company. However, students actively interested in the University of Louisville Players, which is open to all students in the college, are generous in their support of the Little Theatre Company, admission to whose performances they may purchase at a reduced price.

Membership in the Little Theatre Company is divided into two groups; active and associate. The membership for either is $4.00, or $7.50. The latter entitles the member to two seats to one performance of each production given during the season. Five productions are guaranteed each year. When the flood of 1937 made it impossible to follow the proposed schedule of the Little Theatre Company, only four productions were offered; however, six were given the following year to make up for the loss.

A building program at the University, known as the Larson Plan, sponsored by President Kent and Trustees of the University, calls for a Music and Drama building which will provide better working conditions for the young men and women without whose aid there would be no community theatre in Louisville.

Yet, members of the Little Theatre Company, the majority of whom first saw theatre in the Playhouse, say that they do not want a new building even though the Playhouse, in terms of modern theatre architecture and community centers, is primitive.

It seats five hundred thirty-three; its stage is twenty-four feet deep; fifty-six feet wide between dressing rooms and its proscenium opening is twenty-eight feet. There are eight dressing rooms with running water; one property room, a similar space used as a Green Room; an orchestra room and space in the basement for the storage of scenery. It is provided with an efficient but simple switchboard, fool-proof for obvious reasons. And, though the stage has to be used as a carpenter shop and paint bridge when a production is being constructed, the players love it. It's their theatre!

At least ten young men who had their first feeling for entertainment aroused while undergraduates of the University have created places for themselves in Louisville's two major radio stations as actors, announcers, or continuity writers.

Rollo Wayne, after working with the players, where he was initiated in the art of scenic design, went to Harvard to study with Professor George Pierce Baker. Later he joined the Shubert forces in New York and at one time was the most prolific scenic designer on Broadway. Tom Douglas, who appeared upon the old Workshop stage as an undergraduate, went from this theatre to the screen, vaudeville, the London stage where he played in "Merton of the Movies," "Fata Morgana," and other plays; then to the movies.

Playhouse performers used to augment Louisville's stock companies, and play with Stuart Walker in Indianapolis, Cincinnati, and other mid-western cities. One is with the Theatre Guild.

More than five thousand young people have experienced the thrill of facing audiences for the first time in the Playhouse, Louisville's Community Theatre. And in 1938–39, its twenty-fifth season, the hundredth production was given by this combination of town and gown.

No wonder the old troupers, the stars of yesterday, smile down from their portraits on the walls of the Playhouse and wish these young people joy in their work and success in their undertakings!

Lynchburg, Virginia. A Tobacco Warehouse Becomes a Theatre.

The Lynchburg Little Theatre was "of a piece" with that movement which germinated simultaneously over the country in the early 1920's. Its growth was rapid because the seed was dropped on fertile ground, enriched through a century's civilization by the efforts of three other dramatic groups keenly interested in the non-professional theatre.

The idea of forming a Little Theatre in Lynchburg was conceived by a small group in the spring of 1920. Impetus and encouragement were given to the project when, during the season of 1920–21, the Woman's Club of Lynchburg included in its program a series of four dramatic readings by the late Robert Dempster, playwright, actor, director, and, at that time, professor at Sweet Briar College. Preceding Mr. Dempster's readings the organization of a Little Theatre League was discussed. He created the interest and enthusiasm necessary to form such an organization. In September, 1921, a meeting was held in the rooms of the Woman's Club to perfect plans for a Lynchburg Little Theatre. Before the meeting adjourned Mr. Dempster had agreed to direct a production provided those interested would secure a suitable place in which to present it, and an audience to witness it. In November, 1921, a bill of three one-act plays, "The Good Bargain" by Dunsany; "Suppressed Desires" by Susan Glaspell and "Sham" by Frank G. Tompkins, was presented in the Masonic Hall before an enthusiastic audience totaling over five hundred people.

For a year and a half this building continued to be the only home the Little Theatre knew. For each performance this hall had to be converted into the semblance of a playhouse. Proscenium arch, apron, foot troughs, and all necessary contrivances had to be erected but not a nail could be driven or any mark put on the woodwork or walls. In two tiny anterooms the fifteen or more members of the casts were made up and costumed. When the performance was over, all the appurtenances were taken down, passed in sections through the windows to the second floor of an automobile establishment where they were stored until needed again—a trying experience that would have discouraged a less determined group of dramatic enthusiasts.

Late in the spring of 1922, the Little Theatre moved to new quarters in an old tobacco warehouse, remade into a theatre under the direction of one of the members. This old building, known as The Sign of the Lamp, hung halfway up a hillside so steep that to reach it one had either to scramble up or roll down. Although the improvised building possessed none of the luxuries and few of the comforts of a well-appointed playhouse, yet it did contain good lighting facilities for making rapid changes of scenery and an auditorium making up in picturesqueness what it lacked in modern appointments.

In January, 1928, a lot was purchased with a view of erecting, at an early date, a permanent home. This step was taken reluctantly for everybody was deeply attached to the old quarters. Visitors to The Sign of the Lamp had enjoyed the suggestion of possible adventure lurking in the dimly lit alley leading to the door of the theatre; a sense of homely cheer was in the smell of the smoking stoves combined with the odor of paint from the shop overhead; the chilly air seeping through the windows, and the stiff chairs were more than made up for by the charm of the picturesque brick walls and the mellow beams browned by the curing of tobacco during many decades. It was realized, however, that a point had been reached where there could be no standing still. Accordingly, two years after the purchase of the lot, ground was broken for a new building and in December, 1930, it was opened with the production of Arnold Bennett's "Milestones."

This building, opposite the Public Library, is of grey concrete-brick, unpainted without and unplastered within. It has an entrance lobby, retiring rooms for members of the audience, an auditorium seating three hundred, and an orchestra pit. About one third of the structure is taken up by the two-story stage, with its trap-door, its cycloramas and its bewildering medley of lines and battens. Beneath the stage are dressing rooms, make-up rooms, wardrobes, and facilities for making and painting sets. The decorations of the building are simple throughout. On the lobby walls are two murals done by members. One of these depicts tragedy, done in an amusing manner to show early American melodrama; the other, a scene from "Twelfth Night," represents comedy. Hanging in the auditorium are rare tapestries (executed in cold water paint) and portraits that have been painted by members for the sets of past plays. The seats are of Spanish red leather, and the draperies at the windows are flowered chintz on a Chinese red background. The drop curtain is gray velvet, several tones darker than the walls.

The Lynchburg Little Theatre is a Community Theatre in the broadest sense of the word. Anyone interested is welcome, either as a worker or as a member of the audience. Active work is not obligatory for members. The business of carrying on the details of play production is, however, in the hands of numerous committees working with the director and every effort is made to give "working opportunities" to those members desiring them. The annual dues for membership are kept within the reach of the average pocketbook so that the theatre in reality may be open to the many rather than to the few.

Chiefly, perhaps, because this Little Theatre has been of the inclusive type, it is rich in those incidents which warm the heart and cheer the "inward eye." There is, for instance, the Italian, Tony, who spent his days at a loom and his evenings in one small room equipped with the barest essentials. Needing for a play a man who spoke Italian, the casting chairman sought the Catholic priest who suggested Tony with his broken English and his violin and his starving soul. To Tony the Little Theatre offered a bit of that beauty which his Italy had provided. When Tony came in to be made up for dress rehearsal the curtain was up on the set which had just been completed. Those responsible for the Neapolitan scene felt that the supreme compliment had been paid them when Tony's face lit up and he said in his hesitating English with a trace of nostalgia, "It eez Italy! How beautiful!" Tony was an actor—and thorough—every inch of his five feet five. In the "Bad Man" he was playing Pedro, the lieutenant who failed to carry out an order. For this he was due to receive a slap—administered gently during the five weeks of rehearsal. But this wasn't good enough for Tony. As dress rehearsal began Tony marched himself up to the Bad Man and said to him, "Meester Bad Man—when you slap, slap *hard!* I can take eet!" So, acting on instructions received, "Meester Bad Man" walloped Tony, and Tony's remark when the act was over was made with an appreciative grin: "It weel be red tomorrow, but it was good!" The Little Theatre has proved, not only to Tony, but to dozens of others, an outlet for their creative abilities and an opportunity for recreation that is all-absorbing and all-rewarding, a ticket of entrance to the land of make-believe and reality that is the theatre.

The Lynchburg Little Theatre has engaged, too, in other forms of dramatic activity, not limited to the regular productions of the season. It has sponsored playwriting contests and has produced original plays. An extension committee has assisted other groups both within and without the city in organization, play selection and other problems of play production. From its library the theatre lends plays without charge for reading purposes to groups and individuals; costumes and scenery are lent to organizations within the city, and advice is freely given to all who ask. On two occasions series of forums have been held, one on the organization and functions of the committees, another on the history of the theatre and the technique of producing. For the past two years a group of the younger members of the theatre have been producing one-act plays which are open to the public. These plays are chosen and produced entirely by the young group. Plans for the coming years include collaboration with the Junior League in establishing a Children's Theatre Institute conducted by Miss Gloria Chandler, Field Secretary of the Association of Junior Leagues of America. In these diversified undertakings the Lynchburg Little Theatre sustains its claims as a community theatre with educational and cultural aims.

In the early days of the theatre's existence only one-act plays were given, but as casts and workers grew in experience three-act plays were introduced frequently so that now the one-act play is the occasional offering. During the eighteen consecutive years of the Lynchburg's theatre's existence more than one hundred plays have been produced, representing the best of foreign and American authors. With the exception of a year and a half the work has been done under the guidance of a professional director. Following Mr.

Dempster came Miss Margaret Fawcett (daughter of George Fawcett) who in turn was succeeded by Harry Rogers Pratt of the University of Virginia, Miss Edith Mack of Maplewood, New Jersey, director for nine years, and Mr. Robert Warfield of Washington, D. C.

Macon, Georgia. A Community Theatre Is Wrung from a Laundry.

It must be very nice to live in Macon and belong to the Community Theatre, for if you happen to be ill, get married, or have a baby, the Board of Directors sends you a greeting card of congratulations, sympathy, or good wishes—depending, of course, upon the event. We like that friendly gesture and the good will behind it. It's neighborly! No wonder the whole town turns out when the Macon Little Theatre gives a play.

Certainly here is a theatre group which enjoys exceptional community participation.

In the spring of 1938 Mrs. Piercy Chestney, president of this group, wrote: "In our twenty-three major productions since our organization on January 14, 1934, two hundred sixty-eight different persons have acted on our stage. Thirteen hundred eighty-five others have helped with costumes, scenery, make-up, lighting, sound, loans of properties and so forth, making sixteen hundred fifty-three different people who have taken part in the various activities in the five seasons, and after our next play there will be others. And then there are those who have worked in the lobby this year, serving coffee, doing publicity, ushering, taking tickets, distributing programs. Also must be counted the fifteen members of the committee who judge the work of our players, making in all one thousand seven hundred and three citizens of Macon who have taken an active part in the affairs of our theatre. Of course some twenty of us work on *everything* that goes on down there!"

This group held its first meeting on January 14, 1934. The organizer was Rei Terry, who had just closed an engagement as leading lady of the Peruchi Players. In response to a call from Miss Terry, there were forty-five charter members: lawyers, artists, musicians, the registrar of Mercer University, head of the music department and head of the dramatic department of Wesleyan Conservatory, manager of the Chamber of Commerce, the Mayor of Macon, politicians, librarians, Red Cross heads, newspaper people, motion picture and theatre managers, members of the Junior League, Beth Israel Sisterhood members, several ministers, young men and young women interested in the theatre, housewives and their tired business men husbands. It was a cross section of the whole city. They started off on the right foot in Macon.

The temporary organization meeting was held in the studio of the head of the music department of Wesleyan Conservatory; the permanent organization meeting in the assembly rooms of the Washington Memorial Library. Since then the theatre has served the city as a genuine community enterprise.

The group has its own theatre. Formerly a laundry, which had been unoccupied for twelve years, the building was loaned to the players for four years by Mr. and Mrs. W. D. Lamar, two of Macon's most generous citizens. In the spring of 1938 when the players were presenting Ibsen's "A Doll's House" it was announced on the opening night that Mr. Lamar was presenting this laundry, now made over into a theatre, to the community players.

"The applause," says Mrs. Chestney, "would never end it seemed. I then announced that the seats the Lamar party were occupying were to be marked with engraved brass plates and were to be theirs forever. Then we presented them with a basket of flowers. Great was the excitement."

It is a large stone building—three stories—a great gift! But let Frank Durham, the director of this group, describe the theatre in his own words.

"It is a rambling concrete brick affair on the banks of the muddy Ocmulgee River and is nestled close to a railway track. At ten-thirty each evening of performance the actors automatically start shouting to drown out the passing night express. On one corner of the building is a cast iron sign proclaiming it to be the 'Sanitary Dairy,' while on the front in letters two feet high are the words, IDEAL LAUNDRY. Cows, cleaning, and now drama—and the last has all the earmarks of being a permanent tenant."

The theatre seats two hundred thirty-eight, but two hundred seventy can be and usually are crowded in. The first night is full dress; the second evening what might be called family night; and the last evening a general mixture of clothes: some arrive in evening dress, and other as they wish. The people in the lobby and the ushers wear evening clothes each night.

Just below the auditorium ceiling is a border of masks, made by the Sketch Club, all members of the Community Theatre. Similar masks, placed on the walls of the theatre, are marked with the names of the best actor and actress of the year, the plays and roles they have appeared in. A secret committee of fifteen attends all plays and at the end of the season announces its selection of the two players. Then, at a gala theatre evening the masks are unveiled. So far there have been no hard feelings and the contest is generally stimulating. The rules of this contest are presented in the Appendix.

The group is on a membership basis. This is $5.00 with two tickets for each play and $1.00 a ticket for out-of-town guests. Only the final play of the season and the workshop plays are open to the general public. However, non-members have the privilege of trying out, without invitation, for parts in the plays. The membership appeal is made to the entire community. The membership consists of artists, agents, physicians, ministers, club members, bankers, store clerks, stenographers, secretaries, dentists, nurses, opticians, playground directors, mill workers from clerks to owners, librarians, lawyers, musicians; men's clothing stores, loan societies, book shops, beauty shops, paper hangers, morticians; shoe, dress, drug stores, brick, paint, laundry, ice, coal companies, and so forth; students of four colleges, teachers, all men's civic clubs, officers and members of the Parent Teachers Association, the D.A.R., the U.D.C., the B. and P., the Y.W.C.A., the Woman's Club, and—three memberships are held by the City of Macon itself!

There is a Board of fourteen managing the theatre. Each has a specific job. One is the casting director who makes appointments and introduces applicants to the play director, who makes final selections. Another board member is in charge of production: arranges for some person to do the set and, with his committee, secures the necessary properties.

One of their settings is described by Mrs. Chestney: "The walls were— well I suppose Pomeranian Red comes nearest the shade. Nearly all the furniture was white with some pieces trimmed in moss fringe. For accent there was a gorgeous blue chair. The center exit rear had two steps leading up to a balcony at the back of which was an iron railing painted white. The railing was borrowed from a construction firm salvaging one of the fine old Macon buildings. At each side of this exit were windows hung with Venetian blinds. Draperies of white, with swatches of red with white dots was the treatment given the two windows and exits. The cocktail glasses were the blue of the chair. In front of each Venetian blind was a pedestal with an indirect lighting urn of blue and white. All around the openings was a six-inch border of red, gold and white paper that gave the effect of a metal tracery which carried out the balcony railing, the delicate metal of the white metal furniture, the wall shelves and so on. Loops of red cord were used in the room effect left back and straight lines of red cord paneled the doors which had small red knobs. The set, done by Delmar Warren, counting everything including drayage, cost well within $10.00!"

The production chairman is always a woman for women know where interesting pieces of furniture are. Another duty is making appeals to Macon residents for everything from Victrola records to riding boots, size eleven.

Another board member directs the stage crew, making an effort to get different people each time, to let as many as possible learn the ropes. The hostess chairman secures ushers, ticket takers, people to serve coffee between the acts and last, but not least, someone to list the first night patrons and costumes so that the newspapers get ample society notes. One board member is librarian, listing and taking care of the play copies and scripts, making them available to all colleges and dramatic groups of the state at a cost of twenty-five cents. Other committees are: play reading, membership, publicity, business management, playwriting contest, music, and so on through the entire list of activities. A distinctive feature is the annual award to the outstanding worker of each season.

In addition to five major productions each year, they have workshop plays, concerts, children's entertainments, exhibitions of local artists, both on the walls of the lobby of their theatre and in the plays. So a great part of the artistic life of Macon centers around the Community Theatre.

The teachers of dramatic art in Macon give all their programs in the theatre, being charged only actual expenses. The artists in Macon paint the scenery and plan the settings. The musicians are given the theatre for concerts on Sunday afternoon following each production. These may be church choirs, music clubs, individual instrumentalists, or soloists. Also these groups supporting the theatre have play readings.

Five radio playlets written by the members have been presented over the local station. There are classes in diction, make-up, fencing (a public exhibition was given recently), and other phases of theatre work: scene building; directing; lighting; etc.

They also conduct an annual playwriting contest, giving a small prize ($5.00) for the best one-act play submitted, and honorable mention to three, with promised productions. These activities give opportunity to everybody in the city to do the thing he likes best.

"We feel that the theatre has been worth while, aside from productions," says Mrs. Chestney, "because it has brought together people who otherwise would never have known each other. It has established enduring friendships, I feel certain. It has given many of us an understanding of others whom we did not care for, proving the old adage that the only people one does not like are the ones one does not know."

Two marriages have resulted among young people meeting for the first time at rehearsals. From love scenes on the stage to love in the homes—that's the spirit back of the Community Theatre of Macon!

Memphis, Tennessee. Memphis Little Theatre.

Scattered activity in dramatics in Memphis crystallized by organization of the Memphis Little Theatre in 1921. The first productions were bills of one-act plays presented in school halls and in the women's Nineteenth Century Club.

The first organized productions were full-length plays under the direction of Mrs. Beverly Bruce in the season of 1924–25.

For the following season the Little Theatre acquired its own home, a converted old carriage house and stable behind a large private home which had become the Memphis Academy of Arts Building. The theatre seated less than one hundred, on uncomfortable benches acquired from a Billy Sunday tabernacle, and was affectionately known as the Stable Playhouse. Scenery was changed by hoisting everything not used in the next scene into the hayloft over the heads of the audience. Mrs. Minor Coburn, their first professional director, was employed at this time. The Stable Playhouse "caught on" and the Little Theatre has had an uninterrupted schedule of plays produced by professional directors.

Colin Clements, who has since become well-known as a movie writer, was the director for the season 1926–27. The outstanding event of his season was the winning by a Memphis delegation of a prize in the Belasco Cup Tournament, held in New York.

In 1927 Mr. Alexander Wyckoff came as director and produced for two seasons in the Stable Playhouse. For his third season Mr. Wyckoff moved into Clarence (Piggly Wiggly) Saunders' famed Pink Palace which had been taken over by the city and was being converted into a museum. The marble mansion became a Little Theatre, and the space cleared of his private power plant and shop became a parking lot. The Little Theatre with its two hundred seventy-five seating capacity is still in this location, about seven miles from and on the opposite side of the town from the business district.

Mr. Wyckoff stayed one season in the new playhouse and then turned it over to Mr. Blanchard McKee who watched the depression clamp down on Memphis.

In the fall of '32, Eugart Yerian came rattling over the roads from Pasadena, Hollywood and points west in his old Dodge coupe. He is now in his seventh season, having just finished a production of three of the plays from "Tonight at 8:30." The leads in this production were Doris Patston and Jack Sheehan imported from New York for the purpose. On two other occasions the Little Theatre has imported professional guest stars. Regis Toomey came from Hollywood to do Hildy in "The Front Page," and Mrs. Richard Mansfield came to do "The Goose Hangs High." All of these guest star performances, and other occasional productions besides, were played in a large downtown auditorium.

The Little Theatre program presents "Tonight at 8:30" as the eighty-seventh regular production of the Memphis Little Theatre, but says nothing of the dozens of one-act plays that have been presented as extra-curricular activity since establishing the policy of producing only full-length plays in the subscription season.

The most exciting month in recent Little Theatre history was the rehearsal period for "Idiot's Delight" when the Italian society set out to heckle members of the cast. A number of the parts had to be cast three or four times before the play finally got on the boards, and the actors who stuck did it despite the chance of being fired from jobs, losing business deals, having all night arguments with family and sweethearts, and being involved in fist fights. Amateur actors at best are hard to keep on the job, but during re-hearsals of "Idiot's Delight" they stayed away from the theatre in droves. The newspapers took up the fight on their editorial pages, which boosted busi-ness to one extra performance. The management never suffered any anxiety over possible physical violence, however, because they had an ace in the hole; they could always escape through the trap-doors in the stage and take refuge in Mr. Saunders' very substantial swimming pool.

Mobile, Alabama. A Sailor's Bethel Turns into a Theatre.

Eighteen years ago, a small group of enthusiastic folk met for the purpose of creating a Community Theatre in the City of Mobile. The desire to act, as rampant in Mobile as in Chicago or New York, created a unity of pur-pose among these people. They also felt that they were advancing the suc-cessful arguments that the Provincetown Theatre had made against the worn-out formalities of the early Twentieth Century theatre. That little group created something that night which has survived adversity and has given to Mobile much that is truly worth while.

After the organization of the Mobile Little Theatre, a constitution and by-laws were adopted and Hammond B. Gayfer was appointed chairman of a committee to find a home for the new group. There must have been realiza-tion of wearying work ahead, for Gayfer was made a committee of one.

The first show was chosen, rehearsals began, and the time of their initial performance grew near with no suitable location yet discovered. Fortunately a friend of Gayfer's remembered that in the old part of the city was a run-down sailors' bethel (a sailors' bethel, to those not familiar with nautical ways, is a church, not a misspelling) which was ideal for remodeling into a Little Theatre. The location was just a short distance from the river and ships, and across the street from an armory, a fish market and a fire station. It soon became a sort of small Covent Garden. The night life was furtive, interesting and probably undesirable. For a long time after the occupation of the building, the sailors used to come in for dress rehearsals. Honest in their remarks, they probably made very excellent critics, because a story goes that once their ridicule saved a play. The Little Theatre was in the final rehearsal of "A Night in an Inn," and the Idol, instead of being sinister and menacing, was grotesque and absurd. Loud sneering and cat-calls changed all that, and by the opening performance, the Idol was all that Lord Dunsany meant it to be.

From the small group of sixteen people who started the Mobile Little Theatre under the guidance of Maria Sheip, it grew to an organization of eight hundred subscription members. There was a gradual decline during the depression; but Mrs. Muriel King and Mr. Gayfer carried on and today there is promise of strenuous activity in the near future. The Mobile Little Theatre has contributed its share of talent to the professional theatre: Gavin Gordon (now in Hollywood), Francis Palmer, who worked with the Theatre Guild afterward with the national radio networks, and Frank Crenshaw who has been active in various of the younger professional groups.

The thing that makes the Mobile Little Theatre distinctive, besides its romantic and atmospheric home, is the personality of Mr. Gayfer, whose generosity symbolizes the entire organization's attitude. He should be commended for his encouragement of young people to participate in the theatre at Mobile. The time will undoubtedly come when his patience and faith in the Mobile Little Theatre will be rewarded by the knowledge that he has established a permanent cultural institution in his city.

Nashville, Tennessee. Community Playhouse Godfather to Other Groups in City.

In the memory of many Nashvillians there is a plaque marked: "Little Theatre of Nashville, Born 1926, Expired 1936." The Little Theatre of Nashville of revered memory is now but definitely that, for the Community Playhouse, which was established in 1935, has taken all the remnants of the parent organization, renamed itself, re-incorporated itself and started out fresh in the world.

During the summer of 1935 a mass meeting was called, and the Nashville community playhouse was born. The few people who had been active in the old Little Theatre, 1926–1936, and a number of younger people, new blood, comprised the temporary officers. In November the Playhouse presented its first production under the direction of Rufus Phillips and has never missed a production since. The season was a financial success for when the books were balanced on the last night there was a profit of $6.95.

The Playhouse is situated in the midst of a residential section about two miles from the main part of the city, within easy driving distance of most of the homes of the city. It occupies an old moving picture theatre, which fortunately was built with an excellent scene loft and wings, and has a very deep stage. The theatre would probably hold about one hundred seats more than the present four hundred, and they will probably be added before long.

Original playhouse,
Columbia Stage
Society, Columbia
South Carolina.

The Society's
present home,
The Town
Theatre, built
in 1924.

Little Theatre of Shreveport, Louisiana (above).

"The Drunkard."

Lake Charles,
Louisiana.

"Kind Lady."

Jacksonville, Florida.

"High Tor."

Nashville Community
Playhouse productions.

Design by Fritz Kleibacker for "Winterset."

The Little Theatre of Birmingham, Alabama, presents "Ah, Wilderness!"

The Footlight Players present "High Tor" at the

Dock Street Theatre, Charleston, South Carolina.

Lynchburg Little Theatre: "Pomander Walk."

Chattanooga,
Tennessee.

"The Night of January 16th."

Dallas Little Theatre.

Herman Bahr's
"The Concert."

(Photographs by Parker-Griffith, Dallas.) "An Enemy of the People."

"On Board Ship," Act 3, Scene 1.

Le Petit Théâtre du Vieux Carré, New Orleans

"The Hall of the Mountain King." (Photo by Leyrer.)

Le Petit Théâtre
du Vieux Carré.

Board of Governors
in session.

(Tribune Rotagravure.)

Costume approval.

"First Lady."

Tyler (Texas) Little Theatre.

Above: "Ceiling Zero." Left: John Boles, whose visits to his Tyler relatives have resulted in excellent advice for Little Theatre moguls, with members of the group.

The Playhouse, Belknap Campus, University of Louisville.

Interior, The Play-
house, Belknap Cam-
pus, University of
Louisville.

The Little Theatre Company, Louisville: "Lucky Sam McCarver."

University of Louisville Players: "Garden of Memory."

Washington (D. C.) Civic Theatre: ". . . one third of a nation . . ." (Jordan photo.)

Washington Civic Theatre: "Yellow Jack." (Jordan photo.)

"The Distaff Side."

Washington Civic Theatre. (Jordan photos.)

"Johnny Johnson."

Amarillo,
Texas.

"Love from a Stranger."

"Good-bye Again" as presented by the San Antonio Little Theatre at

The San Pedro Playhouse in San Pedro Park, San Antonio, Texas.

The second season was highlighted with productions of "Biography," "Winterset," and climaxed with "Boy Meets Girl" which the Nashville Playhouse staged with a Hollywood opening—Kleig lights on arriving patrons, broadcasting and interviewing in the lobby, back stage and after the show. Nashville took warmly to the Hollywood idea and "Boy Meets Girl" set all records for the new Playhouse.

In the season "High Tor" was the critical success of the year, and "Stage Door" broke all box office and attendance records. An experiment was tried by presenting what is called a "cash play" at the end of the regular season of six productions, to make money for new lighting equipment. Another tradition has been started: an annual dinner at which small sculptured figures are presented to the best actor and actress, to the best players in supporting roles, and to the best "bit" performances with additional rewards for the back stage workers. This has made a perceptible impression on the morale of the working group of the theatre, and is a custom which merits the attention of all Community Theatres.

There is a Back Stage Club of people working continuously in the Playhouse. The Back Stage Club is largely social, but has ambitions to be more important to the Playhouse as it grows. A workshop with its own small stage has been created to serve as a training ground for the main stage.

One feature of the Nashville Playhouse is its monthly publication—*The Off-Stage Noise*—which is as pert a theatre publication as may be found in the country. It is half magazine and half program. It contains local gossip, social items, and technical news for everyone with the slightest interest in the activities in the Playhouse. It also serves as an excellent means of publicizing the Playhouse. For more and more the Community Theatres of America are exchanging programs and publications.

An affiliate group is the Children's Theatre sponsored by the Junior League of the city. The purposes of the Children's Theatre as stated by Eleanor Hankins Fort, Chairman of the Junior League, are very high-minded. One suspects that these young women have as much fun as the hundreds of children that they entertain every time they put on a show. The Children's Theatre of Nashville antedates the Community Playhouse by some five years, but they are finding mutual strength in collaboration. An average of fifteen hundred children see each of the four plays given every year, and in the casts are some of the most talented actresses of Nashville.

Also affiliated with the Playhouse are other organizations whose activities can be culled from the *Off-Stage Voice:*

"We are proud to claim as a brand-new affiliate this year the recently organized Vanderbilt Masque Club, which held its first meeting in October of this year and is planning as its first production (some time in February) an original musical review, taking as its theme history as the students see it. Its ambitious program includes original music and skits, a mixed vocal chorus of sixty voices, and a twenty-piece orchestra. Listen for 'Singing a Song About You' and 'Helpless.' Perhaps we'll all be singing them next spring. With by-laws and constitution duly drawn, John Durrett was elected president; Margaret Johnston, vice-president; George Bentley, secretary; and Joe Burke, Jr., treasurer. (More about this in the next issue.)

"The Junior League Children's Theatre presented its first play in a series of four on November 5, 6 and 7 at the Playhouse, and judging by the sounds the audience made, it was a howling success from start to finish. The settings were most effective and were designed by Barbour Pilcher, and Mrs. Inez Basset Alder directed.

"Peabody College Dramatic Club has just elected officers for the first quarter. Their first play, to be presented the second week in December, will be that old comedy farce by John Emerson and Anita Loos—'The Whole Town's Talking.'

"The Stagecrafters held their first meeting of the season on November 1, among their business being a decision to hold all future meetings of the club in the Green Room at the Playhouse (it's on the balcony, in case you haven't heard.) Our own director, Mr. Kleibacker, discussed most interestingly the subject of playwriting. By the way, Stagecrafters are thirty years old this month, and plan as an anniversary celebration to present a play from the period of their first performance thirty years ago come May, with all the costumes and settings of that time. It bids fair to be a gala occasion, of which we will tell more in the spring.

"When school opened the Hume-Fogg Dramatic Club began in earnest with rehearsals of the first play, 'The Cat and the Canary,' given October 2 and 3, in the Hume-Fogg Auditorium. The club has had several interesting programs at their meetings. Mr. Kliebacker, director of the Community Playhouse, spoke on modern training in the schools of dramatics. The purpose of the Dramatic Club this year is to develop student directors. Every play that has been produced has had one student directing the cast."

Recently the Nashville Little Theatre presented interesting figures showing the increase of interest in their activities:

	Subscriptions	Box Office
First Season	$2200	$500
Second Season	$2600	$927
Third Season	$4200	$1102

Recapitulating, they say:

WE portrayed 269 characters, ranging in age from 65 days to 65 years, and including a couple of pups (woof, woof!).

WE appeared in *The Offstage Noise,* under the heading of "Technical Staff," 282 times, some once, some twice, some ten times.

WE gathered six or more per evening, to usher the rest of us to our seats.

WE wrote *The Offstage Noise* 17 times and made offstage noises much oftener.

WE begged, borrowed, or built furniture and gadgets for 'props.'

WE're not only GOING TO WIN, WE'RE ALMOST THERE.

WHO ARE WE?

WE who saw the plays this year are 1 per cent of the population of Nashville.

The Nashville Playhouse is one of the few theatres that makes public its annual budget; one which all theatres throughout the country will find most interesting to peruse and compare with their own.*   It is too bad that other theatres do not follow the same policy.

The ambition of the Nashville Community Theatre is, of course, to create an organization that will allow more and more Nashvillians to participate in theatre activity to further justify their claim to the title "The Nashville Community Playhouse."

New Orleans, Louisiana. One of the Few Bilingual Theatres in the United States.

Prior to 1916, in New Orleans, the Drawing Room Players, an organization with an extraordinarily healthy growth, had been staging plays in the living rooms of its members.   As these players gradually achieved more experience, they became aware of the Little Theatre Movement in America which was crystallizing that time and, though they disclaim that their ambitions were prompted by propaganda in behalf of this movement, it must have played some part in their decision in 1919 to establish Le Petit Théâtre du Vieux Carré.   For while their organization had always been almost belligerently independent, undoubtedly their later growth was aided by the similar development in all parts of the country of the so-called Little Theatre Movement.

The first step taken by the new group was to lease apartments in the Pontalba Building on Jackson Square, an ideal location in the heart of the old French Quarter of New Orleans.   The outlook on the beautiful park from their second story balcony was enchanting.   By their own labor they transformed the dingy hall into a charming theatre with an auditorium seating a hundred and eighty-four persons, and a small but adequate stage. Every function from ticket-taking to directing, including the construction and decoration of scenery and the designing and making of costumes, was carried on by the members.   There were no paid employees.

Despite the fear of a few of the oldsters that boredom would overtake and dissipate the membership, the demand for admittance to the group in-

* See Appendix G.

creased and the limit was extended first to six hundred and then to one thousand. An experiment with a waiting list resulted in six hundred more persons promptly applying, and after three years, Le Petit Théâtre du Vieux Carré found itself again compelled to seek larger quarters.

In 1922, a location at 616 St. Peter Street was purchased and an auditorium with a seating capacity of four hundred and sixty-eight was built. The membership was extended to two thousand and plays were given six nights a week, once a month, from October to May.

Still the membership increased, until it now has reached the maximum the auditorium can hold in seven nights of production.

Le Petit Théâtre du Vieux Carré is a corporation chartered under the laws of Louisiana. As provided in its constitution and by-laws, it has two classes of members, active and sustaining. The active members are those who carry on the work of producing plays. All others are sustaining members from whose ranks active members are being constantly recruited. The latter usually number about two hundred with an equal number on probation. Only fully accredited, active members have the right to vote at elections. The general management of the theatre is conducted by a Board of Governors, five of whom are elected annually to replace the five whose terms expire. From its own membership the Board of Governors elects a president, a chairman of the board, a treasurer, a secretary and the chairmen of dramatic, production, and membership committees.

Customarily it hires a professional director each May to serve the following season. Novices are trained by volunteer directors in the workshop which gives a number of productions throughout the year.

In the spring of 1938, Le Petit Théâtre du Vieux Carré achieved a ten year ambition by purchasing the adjoining property which will enable them to complete a building program that has been their goal. They will now acquire a very complete and beautifully equipped little workshop with much additional rehearsal space and room for various production activities.

As this is one of the most beautiful theatres in America, it is entirely appropriate to give some idea of the charm and atmosphere found there.

"The theatre is entered by the loggia, whose doorway is an adaptation of the old carriage entrances to the courtyards of the Quarter. The loggia serves as a passageway between the old and the new buildings and also as entrance to the courtyard or patio. The loggia floor is of flagstones taken from an adjoining building and the ceiling is of dark stained pine such as may be found in any ancient town of Spain. There is a large crystal chandelier from one of the old houses in the Quarter. The walls are of plain plaster with replica tapestries and at one end is an old chest from Verona.

"Adjoining the loggia is the coffee room, originally a small restaurant in the old building, the end walls of which were cut through to form an archway with wooden gates marking the juncture with the new structure.   The present beamed ceiling of the coffee room was found when some boards were removed by electricians during the renovation.

"Next to the coffee room and forming the Chartres Street corner is the rehearsal room or workshop, originally a room in the governor's palace and later the famous café, Le Veau Qui Tete.   The paneling is old and is an interesting adaptation of a French room.   Back of the rehearsal room are the men's dressing rooms with entrances from the patio, and the stage.

"The lobby of the theatre is off the opposite side of the loggia from the coffee room and acts as a buffer for the auditorium from the noise of the street and as an exit.   Two small iron stairways lead to the auditorium.   This is a very simple room of tinted plaster walls, whose lines are broken on either side by doorways, in front by the rectangular proscenium and in the rear by the iron rail of the balcony.   The walls are hung with Cluny tapestry replicas and brocatelles.   Four antique Italian chandeliers throw a soft amber light over the audience.

"The stage is twenty-nine feet wide by twenty-four feet deep and adjoins a large stock room on one side and the ladies' dressing rooms, a green room and workrooms on the other, with a passageway connecting to the men's dressing rooms.

"In the center of this elaborate setting is the gem of the ensemble, the courtyard.   At night when the audience overflows into it between acts from the foyer, loggia and coffee room, it becomes a glamorous garden in the blue flood moonlight which plays from a balustrade upon a sparkling fountain in the center and spreads its soft glow unevenly over rich semi-tropical shrubbery, vines and flowers which grow profusely in all space not occupied by the flagstone walks leading to various departments of the theatre.

"The site and form of the courtyard were suggested by the roof lines of the old building.   This had been totally wrecked and the ground was covered by small sheds but enough remained to suggest on one side the brick arches of the arcade with spindled columns on the gallery above, such as may be seen in many preserved courtyards of the Quarter.

"The climate is such that the patio also forms a practical means of circulation.   The walls are covered with jasmine and blue morning glory, and the beds are filled with banana, myrtle, sweet olive and orange trees; and with spider lilies and other plants associated with Creole gardens."

Bernard Szold, who came to the New Orleans Theatre from Omaha, has brought with him theatrical integrity and a spirit of adventure that has made the past few seasons at Le Petit Théâtre du Vieux Carré one of the most venturesome and exciting in the entire community theatre field.   There is a story which has prompted many a chuckle among the workers in the Community Theatres.   It seems that Le Petit Théâtre du Vieux Carré has a very charming French secretary with an entrancing accent who often functions as a guide to the various tourist parties that are constantly dropping in to visit the theatre.   One day after taking a group of gentlemen from Iowa through the entire building and explaining at great length the historic background of the theatre and its locale, she received the thanks of the various guests and as the last one shook her hand, he said: "I'm going right back to the hotel and write my wife that at last I have met a real French Madame."

This is the only bilingual theatre in the United States. Productions in French are frequently given and every effort is made to keep alive the French classics.

No one has epitomized Le Petit Théâtre de Vieux Carré more aptly than the beloved Minnie Maddern Fiske who said after a visit in the early 20's: "Your Little Theatre is compendious New Orleans. It has the complexion of a rich and florid past, and charm in sequence from the Spanish era to this day of a vital, thriving, but unique modern community. The Little Theatre here memorializes and perpetuates and instigates."

Orlando, Florida. *A Saga of Struggle.*

Larry George and Mrs. A. H. Smith, Jr., have in their own way summed up the relationship of Broadway and the Community Theatres by saying: "Hits may come and as quickly go, leaving Broadway's wide streets gloomy with shadows; producers flame into popularity and sink into oblivion; authors sky-rocket to Pulitzer and die vicariously in drawing rooms. Through it all, the Community Theatres go on jabbing hypodermic needles into lackadaisical audiences, eking out their meagre financial existences and subsisting merely on curtain calls!"

In 1927, a group of Orlando citizens pledged themselves to an attempt to "elevate the souls of the Florida crackers for these, blighted by movies, hardened by tourists, these souls resisted."

This group of actors found that "The Pay-Off" and "The Patsy" were merely "pearly jewels cast on a sea of indifference." Still the group struggled along, presenting first one play, then another . . . meeting first here and then there . . . hoping for a break . . . day-dreaming of a home of their own. Came 1929, the year of debacles, and Orlando, located on the shores of its thirty-three lakes, felt the heavy hand of national disaster. Dues came hard—audiences came harder—and the Orlando Little Theatre valiantly but hopelessly tried to swim against the tide of depression. The bank holiday, from which some banks never recovered, took their savings, and the group went into hibernation for a few years—all but their dreams and hopes.

In 1932, revival, rebirth swept the country. A new organization sponsored by the Orlando Art Association appeared and grew slowly. It commanded respect through its affiliation. It directed, acted and produced worthwhile plays. It built up a small dependable clientele. This required work and more work, but a new spirit, Phoenix-like, had risen from the ashes of the first Orlando Little Theatre. Slowly the membership increased until the group felt that it could afford to assert its independence by breaking its ties with the Art Association and venture forth under its own heading. In 1934 the Orlando Little Theatre became an actuality.

A number of the productions during this season were received with enthusiasm by growing audiences. Studio and workshop activity blossomed out. Local radio fans were surprised listeners to three radio dramas presented by the Orlando Little Theatre Players, and as the year drew to a close, satisfaction was registered by the increasing memberships, newspaper recognition and other portents. But the purse was still lean and a home of its own for the Orlando Little Theatre was still merely a dream. The season of 1935–36 was highlighted by productions of "The First Year," "Murray Hill," and "The Shining Hour." Eleven one-act plays were prepared, cast with newcomers and sold to organizations needing entertainment features; thereby increasing good will toward the Little Theatre, and definitely aiding its coffers. Radio dramas were continued. Monthly meetings featured discussions of theatrical issues, one-act play productions and round tables.

A summer program was drawn up to interest prospective members. The Little Theatre held picnics to which new friends were invited, where, besides the usual sports, the Little Theatre presented skits, scenes from plays, and burlesque. These picnics proved increasingly popular and succeeded in increasing the membership to its present number. The 1936–37 season saw an increased membership attending the four major productions. And the season 1937–38 is conceded to be the most successful of the Orlando Little Theatre's history.

While Orlando has a normal population of some 35,000, the Little Theatre finds many friends among the 25,000 tourists who visit during the winter. The Little Theatre also notes that this reacts favorably upon their own local business men who are beginning to realize that the Little Theatre is definitely attractive to tourists. During the past season the Chamber of Commerce bought some of their plays for entertainment.

The Orlando Little Theatre has no limitation on membership, for they are still trying to build their parent organization. Anyone who has talent is eligible to join, and a constant search for amateur directors, costume and stage technicians is carried on. They try to give every member a chance to work in the job for which he is best fitted and to train himself for the job that he hopes to hold.

They have a little money in a building fund and hope to save a great deal more. Their ultimate goal is "a beautiful small theatre of our own, with adequate club rooms for social and business meetings, and a membership which takes pride in presenting the finest plays for our friends the public."

Mr. George and Mrs. Smith, in summing up the activities of their theatre, say that "our idea of the purpose of a Little Theatre in the community is that it should foster talent and encourage creative effort. Other organizations preach of their plans to give young America handsome recreation buildings for making finer citizens, and it is our firm belief that nothing so fills this need as the Community Theatre. It acquaints one with the writing of the leading dramatists of our own and other days, it teaches discipline and improves the memory; it provides an outlet for artistic and creative endeavor and the associations formed there are zestful and inspiring."

Whatever the eventual result, the record to date in the Orlando Little Theatre is one of courage and painstaking, conscientious work. The City of Orlando, in setting aside a lot for the Little Theatre in a very desirable location, has advanced it a step toward permanency, and the exciting possibility of a home looms larger.

San Antonio, Texas. A City-built and City-owned Community Theatre.

It was in April of 1927 that the newly organized Little Theatre of San Antonio was ready to present its first play. This was Milne's "The Dover Road," and the director was Lily Cahill, a star from Broadway, who was visiting relatives in San Antonio at that time.

But where to play was a problem. The only available playhouse was the Teatro Nacional, a theatre in the Mexican quarter of picturesque San Antonio. And here the play was given. Across the street once stood a famous landmark, the old Market House, which had been torn down. This was considered one of the finest pieces of Doric architecture in America, and at the time the building was razed the stone pillars of the front were stored in Brackenridge Park at the request of the San Antonio Conservation Society. Some day, it was hoped, they could be used again for one of San Antonio's public buildings. They were, as will be told.

Previous to this first play by the Little Theatre, amateur groups had struggled along in San Antonio in inadequate quarters, doing interesting work with limited resources. The time had come, civic and social leaders felt, for these various groups to combine their efforts. And so a number of theatre-lovers, under the leadership of Mrs. John Bennett, banded together and formed the Little Theatre of San Antonio. Representative men and women of the community were chosen to act as officers and on the Board of

Directors. Because of her tireless efforts in the past for community drama, Mrs. W. E. Wilson was made honorary president. The active president was Mrs. John Bennett, who served faithfully in this capacity for the first four years. Assisted by Mrs. Lane Taylor, the vice president, Mrs. Atlee B. Ayres, chairman of the first membership campaign, and other interested founders of this group, Mrs. Bennett worked all during that hot summer of 1925 for members. When fall came they had the promised support of some five hundred at $5.00 each and some twenty-five patrons who subscribed $25.00.

With this working capital safely on deposit in the bank they engaged Carl Glick as their first director. That first year they batted around from pillar to post, giving their plays in school auditoriums, at old Beethoven Hall, and under any roof that would shelter them.

In the meantime Mrs. Bennett and Mrs. Taylor and others of the group were not idle. Meetings were held, plans were made, and rumors spread of something in the wind. Then on May 23, 1928, one year after its founding, the newspaper came out with the announcement that Mayor Chambers had approved the plans of a small auditorium to be erected in San Pedro Park by the city. It was to be used as a production center of the Little Theatre and available to other civic organizations of San Antonio. The plans for the new structure, drawn by Bartlett Cocke and Marvin Eichenrodt, architects, called for the use of the front of the old Market House. San Antonians were pleased. The old Doric columns were to be restored.

The next season, while the new theatre was being built, plays were given in what was affectionately called, "The Green Gate Theatre." Due to the efforts of Frank Drought, this building was obtained; it was located on grounds of St. Mary's Academy. The entrance was through a green door in a high stone wall. There was a small stage and a seating capacity of about two hundred ninety. And here the players held forth, painting their own scenery, freezing in cold weather and stifling in hot. But the theatre had a new coat of paint, the membership had doubled over the first season, and interest in community drama ran high.

It wasn't until the January of 1930 that the new theatre in San Pedro Park, called the San Pedro Playhouse, was ready for occupancy. The formal opening was set for January 22. The play was Molnar's "The Swan." Everything was in readiness. The house was sold out; San Antonio society would be on hand the opening night in its best bib and tucker, and the army in dress uniforms. The dress rehearsal had gone well the night before; and the players and the backstage crew had gone home very late, promising the director to take things easy the next day in preparation for the opening night. The director was sound asleep in bed the next morning when the telephone rang. He was told the theatre couldn't open. The fire chief had neglected to make his inspection and give his approval. Frantic telephone calls followed. A committee from the Little Theatre appeared at the Mayor's office. A compromise was reached.

The curtain did go up the night of January 22. But outside the theatre was not only a fire engine, but a hook and ladder—even though there was no second story to the building. And on the stage in the wings stood a dozen firemen each hugging to his bosom a baby fire extinguisher.

Mayor Chambers, in dedicating this theatre, said: "The San Pedro Playhouse has been constructed by the City of San Antonio to meet the urgent need for a small auditorium wherein the fine arts, the culture and educational programs as well as other community activities may find inspiration and expression. The officers of the Little Theatre and other civic clubs, who so ably and convincingly presented the need for this edifice, deserve not only the credit but also the thanks of the citizenry, for this accomplishment. In presenting the San Pedro Playhouse to the people of San Antonio, the Commissioners feel that a service has been rendered for the good of all our people. 'The House Is Yours'—may it help all of us toward happiness and contentment."

In the entrance to this beautiful playhouse is a bronze plaque on which is inscribed: "A little theatre for the pleasures of all people and the interest of all arts. The facade of this building is a reproduction of the old Market House, and is a monument to the genius of a pioneer architect who gave us this masterpiece. May this building inspire the people of San Antonio to give to their city those things which for their simplicity and truth shall endure forever."

Aside from the main auditorium which seats about seven hundred and a stage which is equipped as well as any Broadway theatre, there are four dressing rooms backstage, as well as a workroom for properties and a scenic artist. In the front of the theatre is a lounge, where exhibitions of local artists are often held, a box office and a kitchenette for the preparation of refreshments for social events. The total cost was $104,000, and ever since 1930 this theatre has served the people of San Antonio.

At the time of the opening telegrams and letters were received from people prominent in the world of the theatre. Otto H. Kahn, in the longest telegram the director of this group had ever seen, said in part: "I look upon the stage, if rightly conceived and utilized, as a potent social and cultural force and valuable asset for the community. I believe it of the essence of its greatest usefulness that the theatre should not be represented by occasional visits of traveling companies, but that it should be rooted in the soil of many cities throughout the land and find substance in the active interest and spirit of many communities. I felicitate the art-loving people of your city on the part they are taking in the national service of upholding and fostering the cause of the theatre in America."

Even David Belasco, that same David Belasco who once had spoken harshly of Little Theatres, said: "I understand you have a very beautiful and complete theatre and I am glad to know that. The splendid, earnest and able acting that your group has been doing entitles you all to the best. The Little Theatre Movement is priceless and invaluable and a community which has one is fortunate indeed."

Among others who wrote their good wishes and felicitations were Roland Holt, Frederick H. Koch, Alice Fischer, Stuart Walker, Edith J. R. Isaacs, Clarence Stratton, Stark Young, Constance D'Arcy Mackay, and Sue Ann Wilson.

It was in this theatre that same year of 1930 that the first performance on any stage of "Gold in the Hills, or the Dead Sister's Secret" by J. Frank Davis was given. Mr. Davis, for long a resident of San Antonio, granted permission for the play to be done. There was no thought in his mind, or in the minds of the actors and directors of this production, that this play would become one of the most popular plays to be given during the next few years by Community Theatres throughout the country. Probably of all the plays having a premiere in a community playhouse and not a Broadway production, "Gold in the Hills" has to date the greatest number of productions to its credit. In the cast of this premiere was Julie Benell, who has since gone on to leading roles on Broadway and the West coast. Cast as "Tony the Tout" in this production was Maury Maverick, who went to Washington as Representative Maverick from Texas.

During the first four years of this group, Jack Allensworth was the technical director in charge of the work backstage, and while other volunteer workers came and went, he never missed a single dress rehearsal nor a performance of the Little Theatre.

In the spring of 1931, Carl Glick resigned as director. In succession came other directors, Coates Gwynn, Harry Griffith, Jack Edwards, Milton Ling, John Binney, Rita Connally, Frank Beckwith, who left in 1937 to go to Warner Brothers in Hollywood as director of their young starlets, and Joe Clay Roberts, the present director.

In 1936, while Frank Beckwith was director, a two-storied building, not far from the San Pedro Playhouse, was obtained for a workshop. Here the scenery is designed and executed, rehearsals held, the properties assembled, and the stage lighting and decoration arranged. When a play is ready for production it is moved intact to the playhouse in the park. Also in this workshop are the casting files, the executive offices, the library and the cos-

tume rooms.   Thus the workshop is the creative home of this Community
Theatre.

During the ten years of its existence with four to five productions annually, it has given to San Antonio every type of play, from the sophisticated
comedies of Noel Coward to the plays of Ibsen, Shaw, and Galsworthy.

Financially successful since its conception, this community theatre group
remained strong and solvent through the depression years, because it ful-
filled the requirements of a community which appreciated its work.

Sarasota, Florida.   From Country Club to Furniture Store and Dance Hall.

The first production of the Players of Sarasota, Florida, was given during
the holidays in 1930 in a little golf club house on Siesta Key.   It was
Dunsany's "A Night at an Inn," together with two other one-acters.

The founders of this group were Fanneal Harrison, director of the nationally known Out-of-Door School, Katherine Gavin, and Adelaide Bean,
who was the play's director.   Three years later Miss Bean was Broadway
bound, and appeared not only in the original production of "The Late Christopher Bean" but also with the Theatre Guild.

Next an empty furniture store became the theatre for this group.   A
stage was built at one end—benches, gradually rising to the rear, were put in.
But the Players had found only a temporary home.

For six years they presented at least four major productions yearly in this
theatre, with monthly workshop programs, including play readings and play
discussions.

Then in 1936, at the close of a successful season, they made plans for a
permanent home.   The auditorium, belonging to the Mira-Mar Hotel, was
offered for sale.   This building had been used not only as a dance hall, but
had housed the Flower Show and other similar affairs.   Its price was five
thousand dollars.   And the Players estimated that another five thousand was
needed to remodel the building.

The Players felt justified in undertaking the ownership and operation of
this auditorium.   During the first three years of the Players' existence there
were small deficits which were covered by members' contributions.   However, permanent property far in excess of the amount of the deficit was accumulated, so that the operations of the Players had been self-supporting.
Since that time all expenses have been met, some permanent property acquired each year, and in spite of increased budget expenses, the 1936 season

found the organization with a considerable accumulation of theatrical property and a small cash surplus.

So they called upon members for subscriptions and the needed money was raised. Their first season in their own theatre proved successful. The landscaping was done by Prentiss French under the auspices of the Garden Club, and another beautiful Community Theatre came into being.

This group is unique in that most of the members are visitors to this charming winter resort. They come from all parts of the country. Many of them, of course, belong to the Community Theatre back home, and through their advice and counsel the group learns how things are done in other sections; this is one city where you can be a member of two Community Theatres at once. Others come from the metropolitan centers, and after having seen all the plays on Broadway during the previous fall and spring, have in mind the roles they want to interpret.

Often visitors with a background of Broadway appear in this playhouse: Paul Allen, brother of Viola Allen, and Mrs. MacKinlay Kantor, wife of the author of "Arouse and Beware," who did the leading role in "Another Language."

During the 1937–38 season they had six hundred seventy members at $5.00 each. An extra $5.00 is charged for first choice of seats, and $2.50 for teacher and junior members.

For several years the president of this group was Mrs. W. H. Donaldson, whose husband was formerly owner and publisher of *The Billboard*.

Savannah, Georgia. *A Welcome to a New College and Theatre.*

From time to time throughout the country, we come on an outstanding example of cooperation between a community and the dramatic organization of a local educational institution. A "town and gown" association is always profitable to both sides, and it often exists in a city that would otherwise lack the benefit of a permanent theatrical organization, and it always supplies a realistic background to the activities of the college dramatic courses.

A good example of this is at the Armstrong Junior College of Savannah, Georgia. There Stacey Keach has been attempting to build a real community playhouse under the sponsorship of the Junior College. To date this has proved immensely successful and gives strong evidence of continued service to the community in the most altruistic manner.

In a new and exceptionally well-equipped theatre built especially for the Junior College, the Savannah Playhouse has been presenting five plays a season. The shows usually run two nights to a maximum audience of twelve hundred. These shows are cast from a general reading open to anybody in Savannah. However, most of the backstage work, such as scenic design, painting, construction, is done by members of Mr. Keach's production courses.

The response from the public has been the surprising thing in the short history of the Savannah Playhouse. The community has, obviously, taken this theatre to its heart. Performances are looked forward to from month to month. The Playhouse, to show further its civic interest, has established a library service containing at present more than three thousand plays which are loaned free to any group in Georgia that cares to ask for them. Free theatrical advice is also given, and in just two months more than one thousand requests for such information came in from all parts of the state.

Stacey Keach remembers the legends of the Town and Gown Workshop at Northwestern University which, in its few and all too brief years of success, became the outstanding example of the relationship that can exist in a community between its local college and its theatre institution.

Mr. Keach is very wisely following these traditions and Savannah will therefore enjoy a permanent, ambitious, and substantial Community Theatre.

Shreveport, Louisiana. Sixteen Seasons of Consistent Growth.

On the night of December 5, 1922, the Little Theatre of Shreveport gave first public evidence of its birth with the presentation of a program of one-acters on the stage of the City Hall auditorium. Julia Rogers, founder and guiding spirit, was chiefly assisted by Olivia Allen, Opal Woodley Parten, and Duncan Allen Brown. The eleven one-act plays presented under Miss Rogers' direction during the first season began to crystallize the dreams of the sincere little group.

A change of location to the basement of the Jewish synagogue and the production of several long plays brought to Shreveport the first professional director, Harry A. Huguenot, and a highly successful production of "The Whole Town's Talking" at the Grand Opera House in the spring of 1925. And the town did begin to talk of this new kind of theatre which used sincerity and devotion as amazing substitutes for the magnitude and commercialism of the professional theatre.

The season of 1925–26 was housed in the auditorium of the Woman's Department Club and consisted of five long plays and a single one-act. The particular one-act play, however, was destined to have a more lasting effect on the Little Theatre of Shreveport than all the five long plays together. The short play was "The Cajun" by Ada Jack Carver and was selected, in a playwriting contest, as the Little Theatre's entry in the Belasco Contest. Although the total membership of the Theatre was barely two hundred, enthusiasm was abundant and "The Cajun" came back from New York with second place in the contest and prestige for their theatre that was to carry the organization well along its road.

From 1926–27 through 1930–31, Arthur Maitland was director and carried it through the important period of acquiring a permanent home. On March 14, 1927, the Playhouse on Margaret Place was opened with a production of "The Yellow Jacket." During Dr. Maitland's five years as director, the membership neared the six hundred mark and developed in the lovely theatre building a home that has much charm and beauty.

From 1931-32 through 1935-36, Mr. Talbot Pearson was Director of the Theatre. Among his productions were "Sun-Up," "The Swan," "Candida," "Three-Cornered Moon," "Yellow Jack," and "The Cradle Song." Through these five years constant attention was given to the training of players and audience toward the day when the Little Theatre would be "little" in name only.

In the fall of 1936, John Wray Young became director and brought to the theatre a rich background achieved in an exceptional career in the professional and Community Theatres of America. In his first season the membership reached a new high point of twelve hundred. Attendance for such productions as "Winterset," "Call It a Day," and "Ceiling Zero" averaged more than fifteen hundred. In Mr. Young's second season membership soared to eighteen hundred and fifty and average attendance for the seven major productions was at the two thousand mark. His belief that the modern Little Theatre must stand upon a foundation that is community wide has found proof in Shreveport. In the season of 1937–38, Mr. Young used one hundred and sixty different players and Mary Margaret Young directed the talents of more than a hundred and fifty technical workers.

The Shreveport Playhouse has had important additions to the physical plant during the past year with the building of additional dressing rooms, a scene storage room, a shop, and the installation of a ventilating system. Adjoining real estate has been acquired so that if continued growth makes further expansion necessary there will be space.

Today the Little Theatre of Shreveport looks back on sixteen seasons of consistent growth. At the moment it stands as the dramatic center of an area a hundred miles in diameter. Its plant, worth more than thirty thousand dollars, is entirely paid for and its business is administered by the fifteen members of the Board of Directors with the same care and sanity that is given to the affairs of a great financial institution. Its players and audiences are capable of experiencing "High Tor" or "Tonight at 8:30" with equal enjoyment.

Ahead the Little Theatre of Shreveport looks to ever increasing usefulness to its community.   Pledged to doing the best of drama in the best possible way, this playhouse has only one gospel—good theatre.

Tyler, Texas.   *A Growing Theatre Marks a Growing City.*

Very often the democratic purposes of the American Community Theatre are expressed best in the words of some active participant.   North Callahan, the Theatre Editor of the *Tyler Daily Courier Times,* says in a recent announcement:

"The best community theatre is one which is comprehensive enough to appeal actively to persons from all walks of life and strong enough to interest the leading citizens in its welfare.   Although there should be a definite aim toward a professional standard, never should the organization be confined to the few actors in the community who have had some professional experience . . . No one should be allowed to feel frightened when he appears for the reading of a play . . . Local color should be used for all of its original value."

The Tyler Little Theatre, centered in one of the richest and fastest growing cities in the lusty east Texas area, is now twelve years old and has averaged five productions a year, which at the close of the 1937–38 season totaled sixty-five.   An average of at least ten people in each cast indicates over six hundred chances for people to get the benefit of theatre experience.

The Tyler Little Theatre has produced two local playwrights' efforts. The first was "Cotton Country," by Theresa Lindsey, and the other "Flamule," by Jan Fortun, both produced during the past two years.   Not only have they made this gesture, but they are interested in receiving, and will give serious consideration to, any new plays that may be sent to them.   Their director, Juan Villasana, along with the president of the Theatre, C. J. Lauden, has been reelected for the third season, and under their guardianship the Tyler Little Theatre is making a deliberate attempt to acquire and own a home.

An extra production, outside of the regular subscription season this year, was presented with the entire proceeds going to establish a building fund, and they sincerely believe that soon ground may be broken for a model theatre which will serve the needs of this enterprising group, heretofore limited to a stage of seventeen by twenty-seven feet, and hampered by inadequate lighting equipment, lack of off-stage space, and no dressing rooms.

In *The Playbill,* which is the program for all the professional theatres of New York City, there is a cast listing printed separately wherein the theatrical experience of each individual in the show is given a short résumé. An idea of how healthy the American Community Theatre is may be gained from the program of the Tyler Little Theatre which contains a cast listing as follows:

Mrs. Reagan Caraway, President of the Tyler Little Theatre Guild in 1935, Vice President of the Little Theatre last season. Appeared in Dallas Little Theatre, two years professionally in Dallas and New York. Tyler's Little Theatre in "The Curtain Rises."

North Callahan has appeared in "The Dover Road," "Dulcy," "The Valiant," and Gilbert and Sullivan operas. Formerly president of Cleveland, Tennessee, Little Theatre.

Klyde Yarbrough Feder appeared in Theatre Mart, Hollywood, and Tyler Little Theatre in "Enter Madame."

Ruth Rucker, instructor in Speech and Dramatic Department at Tyler Junior College. Appeared in A. & M. College Little Theatre, "A Servant in the House," and "Twelfth Night." M.A. in Speech from Northwestern.

Charles J. Eastman, 25 years amateur dramatics with Uptown Players, North Shore Circuit Players, in and around Chicago, Ill.

John R. Strother played in "Winterset" and "Libel" in Shreveport Little Theatre, and "Up Pops the Devil" with Monroe Little Theatre. Appeared in "First Lady" with Tyler Little Theatre.

Harry Rubbright appeared in "Ceiling Zero," "The Wedding Night," "The Chocolate Soldier," for San Antonio Little Theatre. Won second best actor in State High School Plays in 1930.

S. A. Peters has appeared in "The Drunkard," "Life of Sam Houston," "She Stoops to Conquer," and "The Perfect Fool."

Katherine Downs has played in "The Silver Cord," "The Constant Wife," "Beyond the Horizon," "The Thirteenth Chair."

L. C. Foster has played with Grant F. Owens Dramatic Co., last year "Night of January 16th" with Tyler Little Theatre.

When "amateur theatres" can list actors with so rich and varied a background as this, the charge of provincialism can scarcely be leveled at the Community Theatre Movement.

Washington, D. C. The Washington Civic Theatre.

The Washington Civic Theatre was organized in 1936. The Columbia Players and the Drama Guild, with some members of a summer theatre group, The Roadside Players, worked all summer toward a merger into a real civic theatre. In September, The Washington Civic Theatre began activities with the assistance of the Junior Board of Trade.

The membership was divided into two groups—the regular Subscribing Membership and the Production Group. An active interest in the theatre and a desire to work were the only requirements for admission to the latter group.

Mr. Day Tuttle, chosen as director, came to the Civic Theatre from the Westchester Playhouse at Mount Kisco. He was formerly with Boleslavsky, the Lobero Theatre in Santa Barbara, California, the American Laboratory Theatre, and the Yale Drama School. Mr. Richard Skinner, associated with Mr. Tuttle at Mount Kisco, was the business manager of the group. The technical director chosen was Mr. William M. Girvan of the Lobero Theatre and the Yale Drama School.

Plays for the season were announced: "Caesar and Cleopatra," "Kind Lady," "Front Page," "Lysistrata," "The Petrified Forest," "It Can't Happen Here," "Girls in Uniform," and "Fly Away Home."

Work began on the season's opener. Society girls, sons of Supreme Court judges, diplomats, government clerks, and college students put on slacks and old clothes and built a "Nile Dynasty" on the Wardman Park Stage. The opening night was a great success and the Washington Civic Theatre was launched.

The drama critic of the *Washington Post* said that the Washington Civic Theatre "completely vindicated its judgment in selecting so pretentious a vehicle for its debut by giving the handsomely staged work an extraordinarily good production."

The *Washington Herald* said "William Girvan deserves endless words of praise for his imaginative backgrounds and the effectiveness of the lighting and costumes." Mary Woodward Davis of the Production Group designed the costumes.

The next play was "Kind Lady" by Hugh Walpole, followed by "The Petrified Forest." The January play was "It Can't Happen Here," by Sinclair Lewis, which was also being produced by the WPA in New York. "It Can't Happen Here" was so successful it ran into the second week. "Lysistrata" followed and the critics objected to it as too "risky" and then the fun began. "Lysistrata" was beautifully staged and received the award of the Palm from *Stage* magazine. "Girls in Uniform," "Front Page," and "Fly Away Home" completed the year's work.

The second season began with a new director, Mr. F. Cowles Strickland, of Stockbridge and the St. Louis Civic Theatre. Mr. Girvan remained as technical director. "Excursion" was the first play, followed by "Yellow Jack." "Noah," planned for the year before, was directed by Charles Dillon of the Dallas Little Theatre. "The Distaff Side" was the drawing room comedy chosen, the type of play all theatre groups feel is a "must." Then came "George and Margaret," with Director Strickland playing the father. "George and Margaret" was not a regular subscription play and was called a "Benefit for Ourselves." "Johnny Johnson" by Paul Green was by far the best production of the Civic Theatre. The setting was a simple platform used at different levels and the entire play was interestingly produced. After "Johnny Johnson" it was very hard to choose a fitting play, but the Board decided to produce ". . . one third of a nation . . .", the WPA play. Washington, the home of the main divisions of the Housing Bureaus, became immediately "housing conscious," and all the bureaus backed the production. A Washington scene was written in by two members of the production group, using Washington figures and facts. The play ran for eleven performances, the last five of which were S.R.O.

The success of "It Can't Happen Here," "Johnny Johnson," and ". . . one third of a nation . . ." proves that the Washington audience is interested in plays of current problems. Certainly the people working in these productions believe firmly in the message they are acting. During "Johnny Johnson" the dressing rooms hummed with peace propaganda, and in ". . . one third of a nation . . ." everyone was alive with interest on the national housing question.

No other theatre in this country has so great a chance of assuming leadership in the Community Theatre field as has the Washington Civic Theatre. This was aptly illustrated when at the beginning of the second season Mr. Strickland was waited upon by several members of the local stagehand's union who put forth definite and excessive demands accompanied by the threat of a general strike among the six hundred employees of the hotel where the Civic Theatre gives its productions. Instead of fighting, arguing or capitulating, Mr. Strickland sensibly sought out a lawyer who was well known for his connections with the labor organization in the Capital City. The story goes that within twenty-four hours this friendly intermediary was able to reach the ear of someone who passed down the word "lay off the Washington Civic Theatre." Needless to say no further difficulty was experienced that year from the stagehands. There will come a time when the Community Theatre will need a friend in Washington and it may well fall upon the Civic Theatre to assume the role.

A number of the members of the Washington Civic Theatre have gone on Broadway. Harry Bratsburg, who was in "The Petrified Forest," played in "Golden Boy." Jimmy Rawls worked with the Mohawk Players in the summer of 1938. A number of the active members are professional radio actors. Mr. Marvin Beers, a member of the Board for two years, is Radio Director of the Farm and Home Hour of the Forest Service. Marvin Beers, Don Sisler, Virginia Rand, and Pat Davis are working in the motion picture division of the Forest Service. Pat Davis is on a National Radio Program.

Waycross, Georgia. "Long Live the Theatre" Their Motto.

The idea of a Little Theatre in Waycross was conceived and consummated in 1934. The founders were Julian Lines, who had been a member of the Little Theatre of Savannah, and Fred Youngblood, now of the Federal Bureau of Investigation of Washington, D. C. They were aided in the beginning by Virginia Knight.

The growth was spasmodic. The first year the players took a fling at one-act plays. Then they decided to do "A Murder Has Been Arranged." However, there was some dissension about the ability of the group to present the play, so it was postponed. And the players still have $9.00 worth of books but as yet no "murder."

Their greatest problem was finding a place to present their plays. At first they used the Employees Club of the A.C.L. Railway Shops, until the club passed a rule that it could be used by employees only, for their own functions. Some of the members worked for the railroad, but since they couldn't all become employees, this place had to be given up.

They next considered the auditorium of the high school. But the WPA had built a magnificent auditorium which has to be taken care of in an exacting fashion, with a fee of $5.00 charged for its use each evening, including rehearsal, and the players simply couldn't afford this fee.

However, one of the members has a large recreation room with a stage. And this they put to use during the 1938–39 season.

So far no one has gone from this group to either Hollywood or Broadway. But they do boast among their membership Caroline Miller, Pulitzer prize winner for the best novel of 1934, and her one-act plays are often given by this group.

"We want to continue to present plays," says Jack Williams, Jr., president of this group, and son of the editor and publisher of the *Waycross Journal-Herald*. But he also fears that the meetings may become too social unless they determine to present a certain number of plays each season and do just that.

" 'Long live the Little Theatre' is our motto," he says, "and we hope our group will come to have more and more part in this great movement, because if 'all the world's a stage' some of us should most certainly become better actors."

And Other Theatres of the South

Algiers, Louisiana.

1929 may have been the year of the crash, but it also saw the beginning of the Algiers Little Theatre. Mr. and Mrs. F. A. Fox direct the productions and have expressed themselves as being interested in doing plays by new playwrights. This group sponsors a junior division which presents three children's pageants each year. The Little Theatre membership totals about five hundred each season.

Amarillo, Texas.

Dr. R. P. Parcells frankly admits that in the ten years of the Black Mask Players' existence, they have mainly attempted to bring Broadway to Amarillo. The doctor writes that: "Our organization is not a money-making project as no one receives any salary, neither do we feel that we have been selected to uplift the 'drayma.'"

Austin, Texas.

This group started as the Community Players. Back in 1925 they had their theatre in a firehall. But during the performances if a fire alarm was turned in, the firemen below responded all too noisily. In 1929 they incorporated as the Austin Little Theatre and moved first to a Labor Temple, then to a hall near a bowling alley adjoining a beer garden. Here, too, noises disturbed the finer nuances of the spoken drama. But in 1933 they took possession of the theatre in the Hogg Memorial Auditorium, where there is one of the finest stages in this part of the country. They make an effort to include plays concerning the great Southwest. It is with no little pride that the Austin Little Theatre points to its past seasons, all of which have been self-sustaining. The organization has never solicited funds, and one season they had over one thousand members.

Bluefield, West Virginia.

In 1937 the Little Theatre here was organized by Martha Jane Williams. They have some fifty members, but are planning an intensive campaign to increase interest and bring more potential thespians into the fold. Miss Williams also serves as director, and their first productions proved most successful.

Clearwater, Florida.

The Francis Wilson Little Theatre of Clearwater is housed in a delightful auditorium seating two hundred persons. The building is entered through a beautiful lobby and there is ample and convenient off-stage space with adjacent property rooms and storage space for scenery. A Green Room and generous dressing room space are also supplied. A long screened porch overlooking Clearwater Bay is ideal for promenading between the acts, an established custom that is definitely part of the atmosphere and tradition of the Little Theatre. This theatre and its equipment were donated by Mrs. Edward Bok as a tribute to the late Francis Wilson. The Little Theatre has been in operation since 1930 and annually sells approximately seventy-five subscription seats with an additional two thousand admissions at the door. They have signified that they are interested in producing plays by local playwrights and are even looking for original scripts from outside sources.

Corpus Christi, Texas.

After three years of struggle this group, known formerly as the Corpus Christi Players, reorganized and renamed themselves the Civic Little Theatre. Their aim is to establish a home of their own, a theatre that belongs entirely to the members. They have secured the backing and support of the local civic clubs, and the future looms rosy. The director of this enterprising group, Marie Marion Barnett, is the daughter of George Marion, the famous actor, and the original Old Chris in "Anna Christie." With her background and skill, the Civic Little Theatre is assured of an experienced leader.

Fort Belvoir, Virginia.

The Essayons Club's first performance was during the winter of 1863–64, and the actors were officers of the Engineer Corps detachments operating with General Grant's army. And this club has been giving plays ever since. It is a self-supporting group of army officers and their wives. Season tickets, priced at $1.50, admit the holder to three productions each season. Mrs. Harry Woodring, wife of the Secretary of War, is one of their distinguished sponsors.

Greenville, South Carolina.

Here Arthur Coe Gray divides his activities as director between the Drama Department of Furman University and the Greenville Community Players. Acting as his assistant is Harold Shaw. Besides producing seven plays a year, they aid and encourage groups of aspiring players in nearby towns.

Houston, Texas.

Henning Nelms has been directing this very active group for the past two seasons in their large and handsome Playhouse on Chelsea Boulevard. The

Little Theatre sponsors a workshop which gives everything from Gilbert and Sullivan to melodramas. The Little Theatre in Houston should look forward to assuming leadership of all other groups in its section of the country for it is the most substantial and the best equipped group in the district.

Jackson, Tennessee.

Mrs. George H. Brandau, the president of the Little Theatre of Jackson, writes that her organization would be extremely interested in doing original plays, either full length or one-act. As they operate on a very limited budget of about one hundred season tickets and depend upon the box office to show a profit, the royalty question has always been a delicate one with the Jackson Little Theatre.

Littlefield, Texas.

One of the lusty infants among the Community Theatres, this Little Theatre started production of plays in the fall of 1938. The director and organizer, David Shein, was formerly one of the outstanding players of the Little Theatre of San Antonio, Texas. For their first season they gave three productions, and have already made a name for themselves and aroused interest in their part of Texas.

Miami, Florida.

Once this Little Theatre gave "The Pursuit of Happiness" by Mr. and Mrs. Lawrence Langner at the same time the play was running on Broadway. An unusual procedure. We don't know a case where it has been done before. Usually Community Theatres have to wait until the New York production goes to the storehouse. But since in this instance Mr. and Mrs. Langner were spending the winter in Miami, and also helped direct the play, which pleased everybody, the mystery is explained.

Montgomery, Alabama.

Twelve years ago this group started. In addition to six productions a year, the ticket holders are offered four Sunday afternoon concerts by the Alabama Chamber Music society, and also two children's productions.

Norfolk, Virginia.

1938–39 was the eleventh season of the Little Theatre of Norfolk, with a membership of about two hundred and fifty. Each production is given three nights. This group of Players is extremely proud of the fact that once upon a time, before fame and fortune overtook her, Margaret Sullavan was among their leading players on the Little Theatre stage.

Plain View, Texas.

The Plain View Players have been active in this Texas city since 1923, giving in that span of years more than eighty major productions. Mr. E. B. Miller is the director of this group and T. H. Duff is the scenic designer. Productions are staged in the municipal auditorium and nearly ten years ago a Little Theatre Orchestra was organized which has grown and expanded until it has become one of the most popular dance bands in West Texas.

Richmond, Virginia.

The Theatre Guild of Richmond (founded in 1934) has as its director Bertram Yarborough. This group has the active support of the Mayor of Richmond and is a genuine Community Theatre. Like most groups in a formative period, classes are conducted and training is given in theatrical experience to the beginners as well as those who have already established themselves as capable players. The membership is a large one, and interest in Richmond in community drama is growing by leaps and bounds.

Tampa, Florida.

Started in 1927, the Tampa Little Theatre has given more than one hundred productions to date. Subscription seats are sold at $6.00 and season tickets are sold for $2.50 each. A professional director, Miss Dorothy Meadows, is assisted by W. J. Hodges, Jr., as scenic designer. This group has expressed itself as being anxious to do original plays if suitable ones are submitted for their consideration.

Wheeling, West Virginia.

Mr. A. Bates Butler, Jr., estimates that approximately one hundred productions have been given in the thirteen years of the Little Theatre's existence. Prices of subscription seats in Wheeling are $5.00 each and about four hundred and fifty are sold each year. The Little Theatre would like to do good original plays if any were submitted, but thus far they have not had much luck in turning up any that they deemed worthy of production.

Wilmington, North Carolina.

Founded in 1790, this group of players, known as the Thalian Association, is probably the oldest in America to have had a continuous existence. At first it was a dramatic club with only men for members. In 1814 incorporation papers were drawn up. And in 1856 they obtained their own theatre. Quietly and without ostentation each year they present their program of plays, and like father like son, grandfather and grandson, the "good old days" are as inspiring as the present.

IV. COMMUNITY THEATRES OF THE MIDDLE WEST

Akron, Ohio
Burlington, Iowa
Chicago, Illinois
Cincinnati, Ohio
Cleveland, Ohio   / 89.
Columbus, Ohio
Des Moines, Iowa
Duluth, Minnesota
Fargo, North Dakota
Fort Wayne, Indiana
Glidden, Wisconsin
Grand Rapids, Michigan   Censorship   212
Hutchinson, Kansas
Indianapolis, Indiana
Kalamazoo, Michigan
Kansas City, Missouri
Marshalltown, Iowa
Mason City, Iowa
Omaha, Nebraska
Peoria, Illinois
Quincy, Illinois
St. Louis, Missouri
Sandusky, Ohio
Shaker Heights, Ohio
Sheboygan, Wisconsin
Springfield, Ohio
Toledo, Ohio
Western Springs, Illinois
And Other Theatres of the Middle West

Akron, Ohio. The Inspiration of a Weathervane on a Barn.

"Look! It has a weathervane on top of the cupola. We'll call it 'The Weathervane Playhouse'!" And that is how Mrs. Laurine Wanamaker Schwan happened to name the Community Theatre in Akron, Ohio, although Mrs. Schwan says that Mr. Kyle Crichton of Collier's is really responsible for Akron having a community playhouse at all. For while talking to him in New York, they got on the subject of the stage. Very brashly Mrs. Schwan sniffed about a current Broadway production: "If our Community Theatre in Akron ever put on a show as bad as that, we would be run out of town."

"Community Theatre in Akron?" asked Mr. Crichton with interest. "Never heard of it. Have you your own playhouse?"

"No," she faltered, chagrin overcoming her. "No, we're in the Women's Civic Club." Mr. Crichton laughed, very brazenly, very patronizingly. Stung to the quick, Mrs. Schwan left . . . but the damage was done. The point was driven home.

The Community Theatre Movement in Akron had begun fifteen years earlier under the impetus of two eastern women, formerly members of Baker's 47 Workshop: Mrs. J. B. Dickson and Mrs. J. S. Spear. Living in Akron for a short time, they interested the College Club in sponsoring a Community Theatre and it started on a magnificent scale, with more than a thousand members, to found the Civic Drama Association.

Its first production was a huge pageant, put on by an out-of-town director who taught them "tying and dyeing" of costumes, how to twirl mournfully like a dying leaf, and the proper pantomime to express a stricken heart. It was all most illuminating and the result was a gorgeous spectacle, surprisingly a thorough success. Following this was an outdoor production of "As You Like It" (naturally, what Little Theatre could be launched without it?) and then a street carnival. This ambitious season ended with a lot of money.

Then an old movie theatre was rented for a playhouse—and the movement languished. For a year or two, there were two or three productions that were successful financially, but the organization was too loose, its original guiding forces were gone; perhaps Akron was not ready to support it. So the old Civic Drama died.

The remnants, two years later, began gathering under the auspices of the Woman's City Club, where they held forth for several years not as a Little Theatre, but as a dramatic group putting on three or four plays a year. Here they were principally under the direction of Florence Lahrmer, a local teacher and director who put on plays with finish. They were thoroughly drilled, letter and property perfect. They kept gaining ground.

But no Community Theatre group can live long under anybody else's roof. Not if it's essentially community theatre, or worth its salt. To develop, to expand, it must be on its own. For years most of the members had scolded and done little else about their own quarters. The Civic Drama still shook its bones at most of them. They hadn't been able to swing it then, how could a new group do it now—still in the great depression?

But in July, 1935, smarting under the laughter of Mr. Crichton, Mrs. Schwan went to a meeting of the group—and she heard—"We must have a place of our own!"

"Fine!" she answered. "We'll go right over to the old Dick barn, and see what we can get it for."

The old Dick barn was brick, exceptionally well built, in the right part of town, and close to transportation. They found they could rent the first floor for $25 a month. It faced a side street with a nice lawn in front.

Said Mrs. Schwan, "We can put on a carnival here on the green and make enough money to pay our rent for a few months."

"It's easy!" said Helen Toesch. "We'll borrow some bleachers from the Board of Education for seats."

"We'll get some second-hand timber to build the stage!" said Grace Crawford.

"We'll start producing right away, and run as long as the public will come!" said Muriel Maclachlan.

They felt certain that if they went slowly, not taking on any expense that they were not sure they could handle, the group could not fall into disaster.

Their group dissatisfaction with club restrictions had grown so that no one could be found who would accept the presidency for the following year. So then and there Mrs. Schwan was pressed into being president pro tem of the new Weathervane Playhouse. Her discussion of the experience follows:

"Oh, I little knew what I had let myself in for! It's a heart-breaking job to found a new theatre. To go slowly and test each step requires unremitting toil. It means watching every penny, every activity. We had no organization able to cope with such a problem. At the Club we had had almost nothing to manage. We could have invited in people more experienced in organizing, but we were jealous of our freedom. We had an aim . . . to produce fine plays, and lots of them. The more people we took into conference, the more compromises we would have to make in that aim. I should advise all groups who want to produce good plays, and can produce good plays (of course you must have varied specific abilities in your group to do this) to step out and do it! Don't listen to skeptics . . . or to anybody who doesn't love the stage first. You'll find enough audience to support you if your needs are modest.

"We have our playhouse now. During three years of successful operation, beginning from scratch without capital of any kind, we have produced over forty plays, equipped our barn, and have six hundred dollars in the bank. And of all this, we're proudest of our productions. They've been grand.

"The barn, as I said, was of brick, three stories high, with a cupola and a weathervane. Inside it was merely a square open room thirty-five feet by forty feet, a shape by no means to be recommended for a stage and auditorium. But we were keyed up and nothing daunted us.

"It was decided to set the stage at a slight angle across one corner which would give us a little back-stage space at one side. . . . But in the center of the place reserved for the audience was a nice ten-inch square post! Mr. John Crawford now came to the fore and replaced this with a four-inch iron pipe which, while requiring some neck-stretching of course, was not too bad.

"We came in at once with workmen, scrub buckets (and how hard it was to get that automobile grease off the cement floor) and pails of white-wash. Clean and sanitary, we went ahead with our carnival.

"Our troubles began. Our carnival netted us only $60. We were new at it, the lighting was pretty expensive . . . and it rained! Oh, how it rained! We were perhaps the sickest people in Akron when that thunderstorm hit us at six o'clock in the evening. Some superstitious ones feared it was a dark omen. Telephones rang and rang. I wanted to postpone the affair, but the two chairwomen in charge of the carnival vetoed that and it went on. The rain stopped about eight-thirty, some people attracted by the lights did come, and we cleared $60, for which we were sufficiently grateful.

"So with this $60 capital we began producing. Our first offering was to be an evening of one-acts which we could assemble in a hurry, while getting ready for our chef d'oeuvre, 'The Merchant of Venice' (a classic at last!) set for two weeks later.

"The Board of Education did loan us the bleachers which we set up. The stage was built, a mere wooden platform about eight inches high. The diagonal wall toward the north was fashioned from an old flat. Painted the same color as the brick walls it looked, and still looks, marvelously substantial! The sides of the proscenium arch were strips of celotex; we had some worn black curtains we had used at the City Club which we put up for a proscenium curtain, and had enough left over for a cyclorama for the stage itself. One of our former Civic Drama members, Paul Strough, had gone into the decorating business, and he made those curtains for us—bless him!

"We sold membership cards for the summer at $1, good for three admissions (to be punched at the door), and single admission was fifty cents. The first night of the one-acts brought out a nice crowd. They liked our shows . . . as well as Akron ever likes one-acts, they were intrigued with our venture, and afterward we served hot dogs and coffee on the green to those who wanted them, and everybody was happy. We played three nights."

The production of "The Merchant of Venice" opened the eyes of many. It was a fresh, rapid-paced play. Their next production was another series of one-acts—plays were following each other a week or two weeks apart— and they were already at work on "The Adding Machine." Here let Elderkin take up his saga again:

"In the meantime there were mutterings . . . skepticism . . . alarm. Shakespeare! Goodby to plays like 'The Adding Machine'! Tsk! Tsk! Our former director, Mrs. Lahrmer, remained mysteriously aloof, waiting to see how the wind would blow. We wanted a lot of production! The literature of the stage is of infinite variety. Why confine ourselves to any one kind? To arty plays, or costume plays, or to the kind of cheery fast-moving play 'the men will like' which had been practically all we had produced of late at the Club. Why not do them all? We had good directors in our own group. It seemed reasonable to give each of them a chance to do the kind of play they liked best to work with . . . a scheme we have followed ever since with most satisfying results.

"However, Mrs. Lahrmer had now made up her mind to join us. The Weathervane was getting the support of a lot of Akron people who had never been interested in us before. . . They knew we were trying to give something to the community . . . a place open to everyone interested in the stage . . . not just to people able to pay dues in a social club. So the real theatre people were united."

It is always amusing to listen to the tale of someone else's hardships, but Mrs. Schwan's recital of the difficulties that faced the Weathervane Theatre the first winter is one which cannot be read without sympathizing as with an old friend, for she says:

"In the first place we needed the second floor. It was all very well to put actors and even properties outside during the summer, winter would soon put a stop to that . . . and they hadn't been able to get the second floor. The rental manager, a queer duck evasive as water, had foiled all efforts. He wanted to keep wall paper and paint on that second floor, and keep it he would, with a padlock on the stairway door. Also the roof leaked and somebody had told them it would cost $150 to repair. Of course there was no heat and no water in the barn, and if we couldn't get a lease (we couldn't) it was absurd to consider putting such conveniences in. So our new men members were all set to get us out of the barn at once.

"You'd think any sane person would quit now. Everybody was in a stalemate. Bad news spreads quickly. Predictions of failure flew far and wide, and the City Club smirked.

"Well, we did'nt want to get out of that barn! We loved the barn!

And we knew, because we had looked, that there was no other location in the city suitable to either our needs or our funds. So I went to Columbus to see the president of the holding company who owned the property and got the second floor released to us for $5 more a month. At last! A Red Room for membership meeting, after-theatre coffee, dressing rooms and props . . . a grand high-ceilinged room with a balcony for storing flats! And one of our members offered to repair the roof himself for $15.

"Meantime the men were scouring the town for a new location. They were firm in their insistence on the absurdity of putting money into a place without a lease. One of them wanted us to take an abandoned hospital building, full of partitions and with all windows broken. Another thought we should rent a store room for rehearsals, and then rent somebody's comfortable auditorium for our plays. Nobody could agree on anything. Any possible quarters had a prohibitive rental. When they finally conceded this we came forth, Muriel Maclachlan, Helen Troesch, and I, with our pencils and papers and told our story. Suppose we could find a place for $150 a month, which is what the Civic Drama had paid, after ten months we would have paid out $1,500. If we stayed in the barn we would pay out only $300. For the difference between those two sums we could put in everything we needed (second-hand prices) and it would be ours. We could take it away if we had to move. So at last we decided to stay. With a breath of relief we started plans for the winter.

"While Mr. Pearce busily got to work on blueprints for heating, for plumbing, and for a vestibule with a ticket window, we sent back the bleachers (they were too uncomfortable) and when wooden platforms were built one of our stores loaned us comfortable auditorium chairs to use until after Christmas. The only disadvantage to this was that whereas our bleachers would seat a hundred and thirty, the chairs cut this down to eighty-six.

"We were now set for our winter season. We sold books of tickets, eight admissions for $5, and sustaining memberships at $15 or over. These memberships entitled one to two books of tickets, and one's name on the back of programs. We had thirty sustaining members very quickly. Active membership was set at $2 a year, student membership at $1, student members being anyone still attending school or university. We began a School of the Stage, under the direction of Muriel Maclachlan, where neophytes were taught English diction, the rudiments of French and German diction, pantomime, posture, some ballet work, and fencing. All instructors donated their services for this and it was free to members!

"We opened with 'Paris Bound,' a revival, directed by Mrs. Lahrmer, a charming comedy that was well received. The second show was a pretentious one, which had been in the making all summer—Schiller's 'Mary, Queen of Scots,' which was a costume affair played behind an illusion curtain. It was a great drawing card, and we couldn't take care of all the people who wanted to see it. Although the script is a loosely connected series of historical episodes, Mrs. Maclachlan, who directed it, introduced narrators between the scenes to bridge gaps in continuity. Besides directing, Mrs. Maclachlan also played the lead, an heroic taxing role, performed admirably. The whole production was as colorful as a tapestry.

"Other plays included Alfred Savoir's 'He,' a satiric fantasy we had long pined to do. It was produced by another talented director, Burton Garlinghouse, most successfully. Mr. Garlinghouse, a musician, now puts on Gilbert and Sullivan each year. These adored plays he does with a special flair, with simple harmonious costuming and much verve. They are very popular.

"Helen Troesch produced Shaw's 'Pygmalion,' long a favorite of hers. It was rib-tickling and thoroughly enjoyable, and the rain and fog for our opening scene was the joy of our hearts . . . the illusion curtain again, with a perforated pipe dripping water into a gutter which we took off and swished out the stage door between acts—to mention only a few.

"But we were not yet out of the woods! Opening night of our third winter production brought an injunction from our neighbors against us as a nuisance, claiming we had violated the zoning law! Their street had been so peaceful before we came! They wanted us out. The papers simply loved this, and came out with flashlights and feature stories and a great to-do. As a matter of fact, we had been warned of this some time before and had already handled the zoning thing. Finally the ridicule of the entire town suppressed the injunction by popular demand. And our last hurdle seemed cleared.

"We play each play at least a week, which is far better training for an actor than one or two performances. Some of our members have gone on to other theatres. Richard Burdette is playing in stock; Sylvia Page and Oscar Miller went to the Cleveland Playhouse; Frank Dodge is traveling with a marionette show. Several others have been asked to go to the Cleveland Playhouse, but business or family ties have kept them here.

"We are developing several capable new directors from our own membership. Mrs. Lahrmer is now back with the club, where the group puts on one dinner party a month and two or three plays a year. Peace reigns again.

"We are still in the barn. Soon perhaps we can have bigger quarters. Our pocket handkerchief stage with its irritating jog of stairway has perforce kindled our ingenuity and produced many interesting sets. But we begin to be impatient for a larger one."

Burlington, Iowa. *Community Success through Radio Production.*

"We shall keep our group representative and democratic at all costs! We would rather struggle along on the meagre proceeds of our own efforts than accept endowments with the penalty of dictation attached," said Walter Stone of the Players Workshop of Burlington, Iowa.

Entirely free of debt and unshackled by endowment! That, after eight years, is the result of hard work and a carefully planned organization, the achievement of Burlington.

This Players Workshop was the product of the depression. It was a hot summer in 1930; many people were idle. So John Dunn Martin, Drama Instructor at the High School, decided to hold some classes to help while away the time. For a course of study he obviously turned to things theatrical.

Some of his students who had appeared in high school plays, now vacationing from various colleges, were eager for something to do. There were other people, too, out of jobs; clerks, teachers, young professional people, and two or three railway clerks.

Many of the charter members of this group, which emerged from these summer classes, were forced to participate in this activity because of the boredom of leisure thrust upon them. The finances of the organization were limited. Dues were twenty-five cents and were paid only by the more affluent.

Meetings were held in the ballroom of the Hotel Burlington by courtesy of the hotel management, and programs consisted of such one-act plays as could be presented in a corner of the hall.

During the first four years there were about twenty-five members, mostly women—mostly school teachers. It was difficult to interest the men of the community. And then something happened that is unique in the growth and development of a Community Theatre.

The group began producing radio plays. Its membership expanded and attracted men to its activities. Mr. Stone firmly believes that the Players Workshop would not exist today had it not been that they thought of the radio as a medium of self-expression. The novelty of this means of dramatic entertainment brought people to them who had not been attracted by the corner-of-the-ballroom plays. Radio production did more for them than increase their membership. It awakened the community to their existence and possibilities. "I urge any group to try radio production if for no other reason than to gain publicity."

The alert Burlington Chamber of Commerce saw a means of getting publicity for the town. It started paying the group for its radio shows and has been doing so ever since. And in the space of three years they have given forty-six half-hour radio plays, all from original scripts authored by members of the Players Workshop.

Slowly a clientele was built upon the publicity gained through the radio plays, and when they gave their first major play it was not difficult to obtain both a sponsor and an audience. The play was "Tommy," by Howard Lindsey and Bert Robinson; the sponsor was the local lodge of Elks. This was in the winter of 1935.

In the fall of 1936 they produced an outdoor pageant for the Kiwanis Club. This was based on local events and written by one of the members, Marianne Prugh. Over three hundred people took part, and many of the participants became interested in the Players Workshop and later joined it. Again that season the Kiwanis Club paid the group for a three-act play which they sponsored for the benefit of under-privileged children.

By this time the Players Workshop was serving the community in three ways: first, by lending their assistance in benefit performances; second, by advertising Burlington through radio plays; and third, by interesting and combining the forces of local writers, directors, performers, and craftsmen in a group where cooperative service provided opportunity for cultural development.

The Chamber of Commerce and the various service clubs were not ungrateful, neither was the city administration. As a reward for the fine community spirit fostered by the Players Workshop, the Board of Education gave them their theatre rent free.

This theatre is situated in the center of a park, seats about a hundred and fifty, and has an adequately equipped stage, with a twenty-two foot opening and a depth of eighteen feet. There is also a shop for the craftsmen with motor-driven lathes, saws, and so forth. In 1938 a radio studio was installed, with full facilities for rehearsing and auditioning radio plays. While broadcasting regularly for WTAD, they also give programs for KWK and KRNT. This Community Theatre group is therefore unique in carrying a full radio production program.

Burlington is very much interested in original plays and has discovered several good scripts among those offered by their members. And if it were entirely feasible, they'd like to do nothing but original plays in their theatre. They have been encouraged by winning several awards at the Iowa Play Festival, held yearly at the State University of Iowa.

In 1935 Walter Stone received second place for his play, "It's a Trick." In 1936 he received first place for "Below the Bridge." In 1937 Robert Glenn was given a superior rating for his work, "The Patricide." They wish there were more authors in Burlington. Four of their writers sell to national markets.

Besides authors the membership of this group consists of grocery delivery boys and chain grocery executives, dentists, telephone girls, office assistants, teachers, mail men, railway mail clerks, music teachers, commercial artists, housewives, and people from other vocations.

The organization is governed by a board of ten, presided over by the president. Elections to membership on the board are held only as a vacancy occurs. The board elects the president, the plan being to keep a well-informed group at the helm rather than "names," who might seek to dictate policies although ignorant of actual problems of backstage.

They have no involved system of government. On the other hand, all routine is taken care of most informally. "We blunder along on the trial-and-error system," says Mr. Stone, "leaving a few enemies and some hard feeling in our trail, but it has been fairly successful in building a well-knit and agreeable group."

They do not have a paid professional director in Burlington. The voluntary directors are persons busy by day at their vocations.

So here is a true Community Theatre—democratic and representative—with the backing and sponsorship of the Chamber of Commerce, the Board of Education, and other civic groups!

Chicago, Illinois. A Mobile Theatre.

In the spring of 1934, the Chicago Repertory Group first saw the light of arc-lamps, foots, floods, spots, etc.—only there weren't any foots, spots, etc. The group of six persons was fired with the enthusiasm which accompanies the building of a new theatre. These young actors were discontented with the Little Theatre and professional stage, its static fare and restricted audience. By performing as a mobile theatre, they sought to bring theatre directly to the great masses of people, many of whom had never been in a position to attend plays.

These young people did not find the going easy. Early rehearsals were conducted in a loft; when script was not available they wrote their own; if a director was needed and there was none to be had, one of the actors turned director and the show went on. Says Lloyd Lewis of the Chicago *Daily News*: "This particular brand of young-people-mad-about-the-stage started three years ago, rehearsing in dingy lofts. Cooperative, very much in earnest, deeply excited about a new program for making the drama grip the problems of the day . . . they may be pioneers in a renaissance of the drama itself. One thing makes them different . . . they have kept their sense of humor, they have satirized themselves as they have grown, which is, of course, the way to growth."

The early part of 1935 witnessed some interesting productions. The Group established its policy of building an audience by taking the theatre to the people before asking the people to come to the theatre: "If the mountain will not come to Mahomet, then Mahomet must go to the mountain." About this time "Waiting for Lefty" appeared on the American theatre horizon, and when the Group obtained the rights of production, many actors of professional calibre were attracted to the theatre.

The Chicago Repertory Group in furthering the cultural and artistic developments of new talent conducts a studio, which furnishes extensive training in all branches of the theatre. It also conducts lecture series and symposiums.

The Chicago Repertory Group consists of some fifty members. It is a collective enterprise, self-sustaining and non-profit making. The organization is democratically governed by "the group council"—at present fourteen actors, directors, and technicians chosen for their ability from the membership. There are no honorary members of "the group council." Each is a functionary with specific responsibilities. Artistry, creative initiative, and the adequacy with which one fulfills responsibilities are the criteria upon which membership in "the group council" is based.

Charles De Sheim, the permanent director of the Group, has this to say about the methods which he uses in achieving outstanding results:

"The group conceives of the theatre as a collective art, and its primary aim is to make each of its productions a synthesis of the creative contributions of directors, actors, designers, and technicians. The permanent ensemble develops together towards constantly improved craftsmanship and fuller realization of theatrical 'truth,' with complete honesty of artistic method. From forty to sixty hours are devoted to study of a script before casting and rehearsals begin; actors, playwrights, and technicians exchange values and experiences in open seminar sessions. Through this round-table method of work, each actor becomes a responsible artistic contributor to the entire production, instead of a director's puppet, or the 'star' of a single part. This is the collective approach to a script, founded on the system developed by Stanislavsky at the Moscow Art Theatre, and followed in one form or another by the leading theatres of the world."

Perhaps one of the most interesting things about this group is the suggestion printed on the back of one of their programs, which reads as follows:

A SUGGESTION

"The Chicago Repertory Group is a mobile theatre and will bring its programs to any trade union, peace organization, or other group that wants an evening of good entertainment with an educational value. Its repertory includes 'Waiting for Lefty,' the famous play by Clifford Odets; 'Hymn to the Rising Sun,' a picture of a chain gang by Paul Green; 'The Young Go First,' 'Black Pit,' and a great number of short sketches dealing with headline topics of the day. Many of these are song-and-dance sketches ('If This Be Reason,' 'Hearsterical Revue,' 'International Hookup,' 'Anti-War Cycle'), serious and comic. A group can obtain any one of these sketches individually, or a full evening's well-planned entertainment at moderate fees, covering production expenses. The Chicago Repertory Group will not only provide the program, but will help in the promotion and organization of the affair. If you are looking for something to make your club social, union meeting, or group affair attractive and interesting, get in touch with the Chicago Repertory Group for a program."

The Chicago Repertory Group has played before tens of thousands in its brief four years of existence. They have appeared at the Civic Theatre, the Stevens Hotel, Keith's Orpheum (Indianapolis), Auditorium (Indiana Harbor), and International House (University of Chicago).

Cincinnati, Ohio. Railway Terminal Houses Civic Theatre.

"All aboard!"

"All aboard for Chicago."

"Track 16, lady."

"What time is the train due from Indianapolis?"

"How much is a ticket to New York City?"

"How much cheaper is a round-trip ticket to Kansas City than . . .?"

"What time does the Actors Guild show begin tonight?"

This last is one of the oddest questions asked at a railroad information booth, but it is a frequent inquiry from hundreds of Cincinnatians as they inquire about the curtain time of their new Civic Theatre. For the Actors Guild of Cincinnati is comfortably and luxuriously housed in a theatre located on the concourse of the Union Terminal Railroad Station, one of the most pretentious railroad terminals in the country. The Terminal Theatre is a modern intimate playhouse originally intended for the showing of news reels. The seating capacity was slightly over one hundred, the theatre was air conditioned and offered all the advantages of the most modern playhouse except for the fact that when the Actors Guild leased it, they found that it had no stage whatsoever. But since that time a stage eighteen feet long and eight feet deep has been built into it, and on this limited stage interesting and exciting productions are being offered.

To tell fully the story of the Actors Guild and their history, which has accumulated in the Terminal Theatre, we should go back to records submitted us by Ray McGoldrick, who explains that when Stuart Walker disbanded his company in Cincinnati to accept a position with Paramount Pictures, he left a group of young actors who were so anxious to continue their work that, under the guidance of Owen Phillips, they formed the Cincinnati Actors Guild. The purpose of the Actors Guild was to make a tour of the smaller towns near Cincinnati where they had formerly appeared under the Stuart Walker banner. Prominent in the original group were Margaret Callahan and Gertrude Michael, both of whom have achieved success on the stage and screen. After a successful season, the Actors Guild was disbanded, and the actors, answering the call of Broadway and Hollywood, left Cincinnati.

But Owen Phillips did not forget the Actors Guild. He had organized the company, directed the productions, and also handled the entire business management. In the Guild young Phillips saw the beginning of a civic theatre for Cincinnati. While serving an apprenticeship as an actor on

Broadway and on the road, he was making plans for returning to Cincinnati, and for carrying on the work of the Actors Guild.

In the fall of 1934, Owen Phillips returned to Cincinnati to become head of the drama department of the Cincinnati Conservatory of Music. Every time he mentioned the reorganization of the Guild as Cincinnati's civic theatre, he met with discouragement. Other civic theatres had failed in Cincinnati, and few people were willing to be associated with what might be just another failure. But Owen Phillips continued his plans. He had directed a very successful production of Euripides' "Iphigenia in Tauris" for the Cincinnati Women's Club, so they offered the use of their auditorium for the venture. Several influential citizens offered endorsement and support. All that was needed was an unusual play for the opening bill.

In the summer of 1935 Owen Phillips, directing at the famous Barter Theatre in Abingdon, Virginia, found the play for which he had been searching—"Storm Child." When he returned to Cincinnati in the fall he brought with him several young professional actors who had appeared in the play's initial performance in Virginia. It was an outstanding success. ("Storm Child" was later produced professionally by Mary Young in Boston.)

Following "Storm Child" the Guild presented "The Pursuit of Happiness," "The Goose Hangs High," and a new play by a local author, "Mixed Doubles." The first season closed with a profit. There had been no patron list, no solicited advertising, no subsidy of any kind. The new Civic Theatre in Cincinnati had survived!

The second season opened with "Mrs. Moonlight." Owen Phillips had been associated with Lulu Vollmer at the Barter Theatre, and Miss Vollmer was anxious to have him present the try-out performance of her new mountain play, "The Hill Between." Earle Larimore of the New York Theatre Guild, who had received his early training as a member of the Stuart Walker Company, was engaged to play the leading role. Ann Dunnigan, Therese Wittler, and Ray McGoldrick, all Miss Vollmer's choices, were the other principals. "The Hill Between" was presented at the Cox Theatre in June, 1937. With this production the Actors Guild was recognized as an outstanding Civic Theatre. ("The Hill Between" was presented on Broadway during the late 1937–38 season.)

At the beginning of the third season the Guild was faced with the problem of finding a new home. The Cincinnati Women's Clubhouse was so far from downtown Cincinnati that the patronage was limited. The group was still too young and the budget too small to consider building a theatre. Finally, the Terminal Theatre was decided upon.

The Guild opened its third season with a production of Irwin Shaw's "Bury the Dead." This played to capacity houses, and was finally closed while orders for reservations were still being received. The stage was enlarged; the absence of dressing room space was solved by building rectangular dressing rooms against one of the side walls of the theatre. "Bury the Dead" had been presented without a curtain, but realizing that a curtain would be needed in the future, brown flannel was purchased at a cost of twelve dollars, and was sewn by the costume department. The result was a serviceable curtain professional in appearance.

Early in the summer of 1938, the Guild announced its first summer schedule. The opening bill was a revival of "Bury the Dead," followed by "Kind Lady" and three original one-act plays. After three successful productions, the summer season was closed to enable members of the company to fill previous engagements with other summer stock companies. The summer season had proved even more popular than the winter season, and had made possible the future of a permanent summer theatre for Cincinnati.

Membership in the Guild is open to anyone in Cincinnati or the surrounding area. (Numerous members of the Guild from nearby towns commute for meetings and rehearsals, arriving and departing from Cincinnati without leaving the railroad terminal!) There are no dues or fees of any kind. A dramatic workshop with classes in voice and diction, acting, commedia dell'arte, make-up, and directing is open to all members. A One-Act Play Group with accent on original plays serves as a try-out basis for new members. These plays are directed by student directors and are presented at invitation performances.

Membership is most representative. While the majority of the actors are amateur or semi-professional, each year the Guild features one or more young professional actors. This list included Frank Lovejoy, Louise Dunn, Richard Ellington, and Ray McGoldrick.

Cincinnati offers excellent advantages for radio appearances, and over fifty per cent of the members of the Actors Guild have been heard on one of the numerous stations. The Peacewaves Program, a permanent program sponsored by the Cincinnati Peace League, presents original plays and adaptations of famous short stories and plays under the direction of Owen Phillips; the casts are recruited from the Actors Guild.

While the Guild is still almost too young to have many of its alumni successfully launched in the theatre or in the movies, already a number of former Guild players are making a name for themselves in the professional field. Frank Lovejoy appeared in prominent roles on Broadway. Mary Jane Croft is leading lady on the dramatic staff of Station WLW. Jean Benedict is a contract player at Warner's. Richard Ellington appeared on Broadway in "Dead End." Several Guild players have been featured in professional summer stock companies.

Besides acting as managing director of the Actors Guild, Owen Phillips has also directed the Muncie Civic Theatre in Muncie, Ind., The Playhouse Group in Dayton, Ohio, The Lyceum Players in Glendale, Ohio, the Cincinnati Junior League Children's Theatre, and the Barter Theatre in Abingdon, Virginia. His experience in the professional theatre includes prominent roles with the Stuart Walker Stock Company, in vaudeville, movie shorts, and the road company of "Twisting the Law" with Harry Green. For three years Mr. Phillips was head of the drama department of the Cincinnati Conservatory of Music.

Cincinnati under the Stuart Walker regime was recognized as one of the country's leading drama centers. It remained for Owen Phillips to carry on the work which Stuart Walker had so successfully begun. In three brief seasons—against almost overwhelming opposition and with no capital—he built a small amateur group into a nationally known civic theatre, a self-supporting, integral part of Cincinnati's community life.

Cleveland, Ohio. An Incorporated Theatre Not for Profit.

The Play House of Cleveland began when the Little Theatre Movement was epidemic; when most of the "little theatres" began. Since then all those "little theatres" have died or evolved into something else, in some direction not anticipated by their founders.

The late Charles S. Brooks, first president of The Play House, effectively sketched its history:

"It was, I think, in the early fall of 1914 that the possibilities of establishing a little theatre in Cleveland were discussed.

"Mr. Raymond O'Neil, who became the theatre's first director, serving from 1916 to 1921, at that time was a newspaper critic of music and drama and had been in Europe, where he had become much interested in the work of Gordon Craig and the continental modernists.

"So, one Sunday evening, a group of eight guests gathered in my drawing room to watch a performance on a tiny stage created by Mr. O'Neil."

Sunday meetings continued at which guests "sat fascinated, seeing a spark that will contribute to a flame of great feeling."

"It pleased our Bohemianism," said Mr. Brooks, "to sit on the floor in a great ring around a plate of sandwiches and a tray of beer bottles. Our desire was to establish a theatre to experiment primarily in the newer forms of stagecraft, and to present plays which might not be expected to have commercial success on the professional stage. Our policy, secondly, was to give an opportunity to the members of the organization and to persons in the community to act in plays and to participate in the different activities of the stage."

Interestingly the group was composed primarily of painters, cartoonists and illustrators and those whose interest was directed toward community service in providing others with coveted opportunities for acting in which they, personally, did not share.

Next came new supporters and the growth of the original group of eight to forty. The comfortably informal meetings in the homes of the members became impossible and larger quarters were needed to carry on a program of reading, discussing and experimenting with plays.

"About this time," Mr. Brooks reported, "a committee was appointed to look up possible quarters for a theatre. And several of us . . . journeyed up and down town looking for an abandoned stable that might be refitted at little cost."

At this point names enter The Play House history that, like Mr. Brooks', are threaded through its development: Francis E. Drury, now deceased, and Mrs. Drury. The first of many generous offers the Drurys were to make was the use of an old empty house on their property for the weekly meetings.

"Our practice of sitting on the floor," says Mr. Brooks' history, "was of some profit, for there were no chairs or any furniture whatsoever in the new building."

Until the time of their moving the group had produced only one play: a shadowgraph in the home of one of the members. Shortly after going into the new building the group produced Maeterlinck's "The Death of Tintagiles." The stage was in the dining room of the house and a hallway gave room for an audience of thirty or forty.

The next move was into the attic of the house, where a temporary stage was erected and where The Play House gave its first stage play—"Mother Love," in which the late Clare Eames took part.

A barn and a ballroom became the next auditoriums for the constantly enlarging group.

Where, how, or why The Play House took its name is not known. The first official record of it is in a 1916 report:

"The Play House was formed to establish an art theatre; to encourage native artists and native art in all its forms; and to cultivate folk art possessed by the cosmopolitan population."

The search for a permanent new building to fill the needs of this rapidly developing group ended when a church building was found and its purchase was made possible by a gift from the Drurys. This gift plus the theatre's small fund, plus a building fund raised by Cleveland citizens, made it possible to take title in 1917 to the church building, which served for a decade of Play House history.

The stage was made on the altar platform and the auditorium seated an audience of two hundred.

"All hint of holy living except four rows of pews was covered with gaudy paint."

At first the office was an alcove with the telephone silenced by a rubber band. The cellar beneath the stage served all purposes for dressing rooms, paint and carpenter shops and storage, until an addition was built of five dressing rooms, a Green Room, a work room and an office.

During this period there were three or four productions a season with three or four performances of each.

In 1921 O'Neill, who had been founder and director of the group, resigned and in his place came a director with many new theories and policies. He was Frederic McConnell.

To quote William F. McDermott's history of The Play House, written in 1930—years after McConnell had assumed direction:

"It has been under the guidance of this shrewd and able Scotsman, who combines a good executive head with an understanding of the theatre as an art and a quiet tactfulness with a faculty of getting done what he wants done, that The Play House has developed from an amateur organization giving three performances a week to a predominantly professional group with performances every night in the week for a season of eight months in an elaborate theatrical plant.

"In these nine years The Play House has grown from an essentially amateur institution, comparatively limited in audiences, and tentative in direction, to an organization with a paid staff of twenty-five, an audience that is a cross section of all Cleveland, a settled assurance in its aims, and of recognized civic importance.

"Without exception everybody in Cleveland interested in the theatre as an art or as adult entertainment goes to The Play House. It is the one theatre in town, under its present scheme of things theatrical, in which the playgoer can be sure, week after week, of a certain quality of play, reasonably good acting, of a maximum and invariable ticket price of one dollar."

In 1938 *Stage* magazine awarded to McConnell its "palm" for the most distinguished theatrical service of the season.

"To Frederic McConnell," *Stage* said in offering the palm, "who has guided The Play House to its position of high importance in the world of the Community Theatre. Who, by patience, diplomacy and keen sense of showmanship, has made The Play House not merely an institution of isolated artistic merit but an integral part of Cleveland's community life. Who has assured its permanency in this community scheme by fostering an elastic policy, capable of shifting to accommodate the public taste."

All this takes us ahead of our history.

McConnell had come to Cleveland with a background of training at the Carnegie Institute of Technology, College of Fine Arts, followed by assistant directorship of the Arts and Crafts Theatre of Detroit, assistant directorship of the Greek Theatre of the University of California, and at Carnegie Tech; and associate directorship of the Guild Players in Pittsburgh.

He brought with him from Pittsburgh, whence he came to The Play House, K. Elmo Lowe, who since has become associate director, and Max Eisenstat, now assistant director.

The coming of McConnell marked the transition of The Play House from little theatre objectives to the rationale of a civic repertory company with a standard program and professional technique and a range of productions wide enough for the diversified taste of a modern multi-cultural urban theatre.

It was an astonished group that learned that the new director planned a season of eight plays plus a number of revivals. Growth of the number of productions and the number of performances of each play was gradual but definite. The theatre, increasing its scope and reaching out into larger and larger audience circles, felt a constantly pressing need for more adequate quarters.

The building had been enlarged to its limit, a balcony added, and still was not able to accommodate its constantly increasing permanent clientele. Once more, about 1926, The Play House leaders set out in search of a more adequate building. Once again the Drurys stepped forward, this time with a gift of land. This was on East Eighty-sixth Street in a section of the city between downtown business and uptown residential sections. It was midway between two important traffic arteries.

By a quiet public campaign for funds, once more led by Charles Brooks, and by a loan from Cleveland banks, enough money was raised to erect a building.

In The Play House scrap-books, a sheet of stationery written in longhand by McConnell is testimony to the first activity in the new building. "This theatre was unofficially but actually dedicated and put to use this day, January 8, 1927, the proceedings taking place in the Rehearsal Room, where several acts of 'In a Garden,' by Philip Barry, were rehearsed. Those participating in and witness to the above conduct subscribe their names"—and the names follow.

To quote McDermott, again: "For some years now, the local Play House on Cedar Avenue has probably had the distinction of giving more first-class plays in an uncomfortable and inadequate building than any theatrical or-

ganization in America. Beginning in April, the group will present its repertory in what is perhaps the most complete theatre building this side of
Moscow."

Black-edged notices to Play House subscribers bore the notice of the end
of the historic Cedar Avenue theatre building.

"Died April 3, 10:30 P.M.," the notices read. " 'The Old Play House'
at the Late Address. Sittin' Up and Obsequies Monday, April 4, 9
o'clock P.M."

These crossed in the mail the formal invitations to "attend the dedication of the New Theatre for The Play House on Saturday Evening, the
Ninth of April—for the opening performance of 'The Jest,' by Sem Benelli."

"One wishes them luck," said McDermott in his *Plain Dealer* column.
"They have done excellent things with most meager and uncomfortable
equipment. They have asked for little except honest appreciation—they
have worked earnestly, honestly, tirelessly, intelligently, and their theatre has
become a model of perfection for dozens of similar groups scattered throughout the country."

Charles Brooks formally dedicated the building Saturday evening, April
9, 1927.

Physically the new establishment was ideal. Unique among the country's
theatres, it housed two stages and two auditoriums under one roof. These
were appropriately named for the two men who had figured so prominently
in the birth and existence of the theatre—the Francis E. Drury Theatre and
the Charles S. Brooks Theatre. Tall stage towers provided for great depths
of fly gallery in both theatres. Proscenium steps connecting the Drury stage
with the auditorium, flanked by high portals, permitted eighteenth century
or Elizabethan mise-en-scene or heroic height to modern symbolic perspec-
tives. Conveniently and economically ordered were the integral production
shops, offices, library, social and dressing rooms for the acting and technical
staffs.

The Drury Theatre, seating five hundred and twenty-two, was planned
originally to house the major productions of a repertory which would attract
a large public. The Brooks Theatre, seating one hundred and sixty, was to
serve for experimental or short-run production of manuscript plays or pieces
of special artistic interest or originality, and not of wide popular appeal.

In practice, however, the two theatres are used alike according to the
needs of production and the convenience of schedule.

In these two theatres as many as twenty plays have been given in a
season. With the increasing audiences it becomes necessary to extend the
length of run of each play, so that in turn it becomes possible to give fewer
plays. An average season is about fourteen plays, from tragedy to comedy,

European or American, new or old. An average run, which used to be three weeks, is now six or even seven weeks of nightly performances and Saturday matinees.

Open to the general public during an eight-month season of constant playing, it attracts annually an audience of more than a hundred and ten thousand people. Of this number many are subscribers, who receive reduction in ticket prices and other privileges.

The production program of The Play House is professionally organized with a company of thirty members. The staff is supplemented from time to time by the employment of guest actors, by using amateurs who through long association with the theatre have become part of The Play House ensemble, and by assimilation of apprentice students who do resident study in the theatre.

Probably foremost among its educational activities is its own School of Theatre. Qualified apprentice students selected by the director are afforded one or two years of laboratory training in every branch of theatre work. Tuition is free in exchange for the students' time and services.

The foundation of the school is McConnell's belief that the "student of the theatre should have contact, intimate and personal, with the living process of the theatre; that technique is not so much a matter of matured and reasoned theory and specific application thereof, but rather a free experience and association with the steps and moods that evolve in the production of a play from the early stages of preliminary reading to the conclusive reception and response of an audience which has paid money to see a performance."

The school, which began about ten years ago with three students, numbers fifty now. For the time being it is limited to that number.

A further educational activity is affiliation with Western Reserve University and Bennington College, Bennington, Vermont. Play House staff members serve as staff instructors in the graduate work of the drama department of the local university and students of both Reserve and Bennington may fulfill their field work requirements by work in the theatre.

The Play House distributes through the school systems of Greater Cleveland specially priced student tickets which enable the young people to follow the season's dramatic program. At the close of each season a Shakespearean production is given and a series of about a dozen specially priced student matinees brings five thousand students to the theatre.

Continuing downward in the age range, The Play House attracts some five hundred children from seven to fourteen years of age to its Children's Theatre: The Curtain Pullers. Organized, first experimentally, in 1933, the group has grown from one hundred to five hundred, from three performances a season to seven, and from an annual attendance of five hundred to five thousand. The Curtain Pullers pay no tuition but receive weekly lessons in theatre practice and get actual stage experience in productions presented to the public once a month. In addition to providing enjoyment and training to the children participating in the group, the public performances provide a worth-while type of children's entertainment usually lacking in a community. During the past season The Play House extended activity of the Children's Theatre to include engagements in one of Cleveland's suburbs— imitating on a very small scale the traveling activities of the Adult Theatre.

Part of The Play House regular theatre program are guest performances in suburbs and adjacent cities. The theatre also provides the company for a summer theatre group at Chautauqua, N. Y., each season. The farthest point to which The Play House has carried its banner is the Dock Street Theatre of Charleston, South Carolina, where it was invited in the spring of 1938.

One of The Play House's closest contacts with its community is a Women's Committee of five hundred members which supports all branches of the theatre's activity and serves as the liaison unit between the larger public and the theatre. It promotes cooperation especially between the theatre and schools and clubs, furthers contact with regional and social groups, and acts as spokesman and representative in matters of mutual interest.

Fund raising has occurred only a few times in The Play House history. The theatre's income, like that of any other practical theatre enterprise, rests upon its door admissions and seasonal subscription sales, and the theatre must live within that income.

Outside of the gift of land and building subsidies, The Play House has no endowments. In 1937 the organization, then clear of all operating deficits and with a remaining mortgage indebtedness of $76,000, was offered a gift of $38,000 for educational use by the Rockefeller Foundation on condition that an equal sum be raised in the community, which friends and patrons of The Play House did.

Holding that artistic freedom and financial self-sufficiency are inseparable, The Play House strives consistently to promote the ideal of an independent repertory theatre, deriving from distinguished European examples; to keep alive the genius of every epoch of the world's dramatic literature; to recognize new creative forces in the current drama, thus to build toward the theatre of tomorrow.

Columbus, Ohio. First Nights—Club Nights—and You Get an Invitation.

It was a gala night in February, 1937, in Columbus, the capital of Ohio—where the University of Ohio as well as the State Penitentiary is located. So they've everything there—students, crooks, senators, and actors. And on the night in question they had unearthed something else—a home-town boy and girl turned playwrights. And this was the premiere performance of their first opus.

Floodlights, huge electric signs, a radio hookup which announced the arrival of local celebrities, and music by the Continental Trio made the first production by the Players Club in their own theatre of a full-length play written by Columbus authors something to be long remembered. Besides the members of the Players Club in full evening regalia with the news photographers taking candid camera shots, there were some Broadway and Hollywood scouts as well as the city's newspaper dramatic critics, looking stern and chewing their stubs of pencils. The play was "Fools Rush In," by Mildred Henry Merrill, the wife of Theodore Merrill, and John S. Truesdell, a Columbus candy manufacturer and aviation patron.

One of the critics the next morning—Mary Jose in the *Columbus Citizen* —said: "A lusty brainchild romped on the Players Club stage last night while the godfathers and godmothers of the club sat around and admired the brat. An appreciative audience offered the play and the authors the fine encouragement of a fond family."

Another critic, Samuel T. Wilson, in the *Columbus Dispatch*, wrote: "It is zestfully presented by the club's most audible and understanding cast of the year."

The play was a big hit. Its success encouraged other local scribes to dust off typewriters, and more premieres may be expected in Columbus.

The moral is: it isn't necessary any more to go to Times Square for first nights with all the glamor and all the trimmings.

While this was the first original full-length play offered by the Columbus Players Club, it wasn't by any means the first original play. For several years they have had a Playwriting Seminar in connection with the work of this theatre group. It meets once every month under the leadership of Mrs. H. C. Nolan—and at least once a year a program of one-act plays, written by the members, is produced. Two of these plays, following tryouts by the Players Club, have been published. This Playwriting Seminar is another evidence that the Community Theatres throughout the country are becoming interested in developing latent talent.

In one season at Columbus they proudly listed among their productions
—which included several plays that had proved successful on the New York
stage—one experimental major production and the first production of four
one-act plays written by their members. In fact, they were prouder of having
done these plays than in presenting the Broadway successes. "Of course,"
they said, "any group wants to do tried and successful plays, but there is no
use in being just an amateur stock company all the time, is there?"

So an eager spirit and willingness to experiment is one of the characteristics of this group.

They once did Balfe's "Bohemian Girl" in Columbus by taking the entire
score and writing a modern book with gangsters and "new dealers," but
with new lyrics except for the three old favorites. The three sets for this
opera showed interesting digressions also. The first, the governor's mansion, was done in white oil cloth; the second, a swamp scene, with black oil
cloth, tree trunks and moss done in silver Christmas tinsel; and the third, a
futuristic reception room, with soft, orange duvetine drapes painted in red
and blue bold designs. The production was received in Columbus with
mixed feelings, some thinking it too great a jar, and others considering it
very amusing. But all agreed it was an experiment worth trying.

This group was started in May, 1923, when Mrs. Frederick Shedd called
a formal meeting of people interested in the theatre to discuss plans for producing their own plays. Their first thought was for a playhouse of some
sort. The summer was spent by enthusiastic members scouting alleys for an
old barn.

In October a barn was found, and a scheme of operation laid down which
has needed surprisingly few changes. In December the barn was ready and
a program of one-act plays was given. There was a tiny stage, and the auditorium seated only two hundred and twelve jammed together. But the
members sportingly laughed off the dirt from the two large coal stoves,
drank water between the acts from the one lone hydrant, and on cold nights
roasted when they sat too near the stoves and froze when they sat too far
away from them.

Yet for five years this barn was the home of the Players Club, with a
membership between seven and eight hundred. Mrs. Shedd generously supplied many items in the equipment and for two years paid the rent. The
dues were made $7.50 a season with the hopes of being able to meet pay-
ment of rent by the organization. This was accomplished and the club has
been self-supporting ever since.

The members realized the first year that a paid director would be needed
if the club was to grow and be permanent. Stokes McCune at that time was
assistant director of one of Stuart Walker's companies in Dayton. He was

sent for and engaged for the second season. He has been in charge ever since. He now has an assistant director, Darrel Yoakam. These two and a janitor are the only paid employees.

In the fourth season a full-length play was tried. It was feared at first that the members would not rehearse or learn lines for a long play. But they did, and the production was so successful that—save for original one-acters—full-length plays have been given ever since.

But the tiny stage of the barn was so small (it had a proscenium of only eight feet and made the actors appear like giants) that the members began talking of having their own theatre—building one, in fact.

Mrs. Shedd generously offered to double all contributions. An architect's drawing for a $70,000 theatre was obtained and a campaign for sales of stock in the building started. Fortunately, they feel in Columbus, this did not go through, for such an elaborate theatre would have been a burden and probably a millstone in the troubled times of the depression ahead.

But the two-year discussion resulted in the plan of a simpler theatre. An option was obtained on a suitable lot with an old brick house upon it. Again a stock subscription was enthusiastically promoted under the leadership of John X. Farrar, president of the club at that time. With Mrs. Shedd's duplication of subscriptions, enough money was obtained to justify building. The theatre was built back of the old house, so the house itself could be used for workshop and dressing rooms.

Herbert Baumer was the architect, and, with the handicap of an old house in front, accomplished wonders with a small but adequate stage, an auditorium seating two hundred and sixty-four, but with excellent sight lines and rough brick exterior and smooth brick interior, which has been greatly admired by visitors. One experienced theatre man remarked that it pleased him much more than the endowed and completely equipped Little Theatres because there was so much to do. An attractive lobby was built three years ago (there was none at first) ; footlights have recently been installed, and before many seasons and before the old house falls down, the club hopes to build a new front for the workshop and dressing rooms. The value of this property as it stands today, owned by the theatre-minded citizens of Columbus, is $35,000.

There is one unique feature of this playhouse. The actors enter from the street. The audience finds its way into the theatre from the alley at the rear of the building. At times this may seem inconvenient—but it lends charm and novelty to the Columbus theatre.

The organization of this group is somewhat different from that found in most communities. It is operated on a strict club basis. People must be invited to join. New members are proposed by old members and voted upon by the Board of Directors. At the peak of its membership there was a total of one thousand and fifty, with applicants waiting. Yet this membership is representative of the entire town.

On a few occasions they have opened their productions to the general public, but there was little response. So this was given up, as they feel the real support of the players comes from the membership.

This club idea had been maintained in spite of objections from some newspapers and seems to have been the salvation of the players in a financial way, since the theatrical gamble is somewhat reduced because dues may be estimated and budgeted better than ticket sales. There is still a gamble and a variation in receipts, but not the disastrous spin of the wheel which has wiped out many a Little Theatre.

And while this club organization is not recommended for all cities, it has worked well in Columbus. Perhaps one reason is due to the democratic spirit of the leaders, for membership applications of talented and interested persons are always received with favor.

One interesting feature of the Players Club is its "Club Nights," whereat members who wish to experiment do so. Suggestions for new methods of production, staging, lighting, the vigorous discussion of plays, any idea for informal entertainment, are welcomed. These Club Nights bring the members together for an evening of serious consideration of the various problems as well as some lighthearted frivolity. So all difficulties are ironed out and solved in a friendly club spirit.

The Players Club values highly the services of its director, Stokes McCune. When the tenth season a few years ago came to a close one of the newspapers the next morning said, in part, "And surely there is no better time to applaud in print the energy, the talent and ability of the man chiefly responsible for the consistently high quality of the Players Club offerings. That man is Stokes McCune, director of the club."

The old problem of what to do with the "swear words" in a play reared its ugly head in Columbus when they produced "Merrily We Roll Along," the Kaufman and Hart opus. There was a storm. Then Mr. McCune, in *The Callboard*, the publication that this group brings out monthly during the year, amusingly stated his case. He wrote:

"In our first announcement of 'Merrily We Roll Along' you may remember we said, 'You'll laugh at it, you'll get mad at it, too, maybe.' Then in the first issue of *The Callboard* we repeated, 'It will undoubtedly strike some of our members as too rough.' So we were not surprised when some members objected to the swearing.

"Turning personal, several members asked me why I did not cut out the profanity. I could say, 'I did cut four of the most sacrilegious oaths.' But their answer would be obvious and proper, 'Why not cut more?' Two of the women in the cast who had 'swearing roles' wanted to cut it all, so we don't blame them. Well, here's my reason.

"If you cut out most of the swearing, cut out the play. If you do the play at all, do it! The point of the play to me is the picture of a successful crowd in New York (and maybe not just New York), cynical and profane and more or less immoral, and, then tracing sketchily back to their start, so that you may realize how merrily they rolled along. Someone mentioned the profanity not being excused by the lesson in the speech at the end and the lesson that speech taught. That isn't a noble speech teaching a lesson. It is the bitterest thing in the play when you realize how Richard started and how he finished. The lesson is in the whole play.

"The language is not pleasant (we quoted a critic who called the play savage and disillusioned), but it is an essential part of one of the ten best plays of last season, if you agree with Burns Mantle. And it is not just for laughs, as in so many plays I could name, and you could, too. To those who didn't like it, a minority, but a worth-while one, I sing my old refrain, 'Hope you'll like the next.' It's 'Mrs. Moonlight'—has one mild damn and is also a fine play."

So it seems the rights of free speech having been questioned and answered in Columbus, the air is now purged.

The fall of 1938—the sixteenth season—opened with their seventy-third major production. That means, with six plays a year on their schedule, it won't be long before the Players Club has a celebration of great importance when it reaches the century mark of play production.

Des Moines, Iowa. Former Governor of State Presents Playhouse to Community.

They say in Des Moines that when one of their directors, a very handsome young man, sent out calls for public tryouts for that practically all-girl show, "Stage Door," exactly two hundred and forty-five young ladies answered the call. And undaunted when "First Lady" was announced, a hundred and twenty-seven appeared to try their luck.

This group was started in 1919 and survived its first ten years under the name of "The Des Moines Dramatic Society." The first president was J. B. Weaver, prominent attorney. In 1931 the late Governor Kendall gave Des Moines its present Community Theatre in memory of his wife, Belle Kendall. Since that time the theatre has been known to all Des Moines theatregoers as the Kendall Playhouse.

In this same year the organization was incorporated under the name "Des Moines Community Drama Association." However, as with most of the theatres in the country, it is now referred to as the Community Theatre.

The Kendall Theatre was formerly the Congregational Church and was unusually adapted to a theatre plan. A remodeled stage and auditorium gives Des Moines a theatre with a seating capacity of three hundred and fifty and a stage twenty-eight by nineteen feet. Also on the ground floor are two offices, a box office, a store room, and a lobby. In the basement can be found the Green Room, the Children's Theatre, the kitchen, the technician's office, four dressing rooms, a prop and costume room, light storage, and the workshop.

They do seven plays a year, with an average of fifty persons participating in each. Their total membership is close to the seven hundred mark, with dues of $5.00 for adults and $2.50 for students. Individual admission to the plays can be had for 50 cents and $1.00.

Outside of the director the only paid employee is the technical director. The Board of Directors is composed of eighteen persons, of whom two thirds are selected because of their active participation in the activities of the Playhouse.

One thing they stress in Des Moines is classes in theatre training. Selecting carefully a group of mature and earnest theatre-lovers and workers, they meet twice a week for a period of nine or ten weeks before Christmas. The group is limited to ten persons and admission is granted only to those who make personal application and show that they have sufficient background, experience, or interest to be worthy of a place in the group. During the term the students are thoroughly trained in the fundamentals of play production: the selection of plays; the systems of casting; revising and rewriting the manuscripts when necessary; rehearsing the play; staging the play, which includes designing, construction, and painting; lighting the play; sound effects; and, finally, theatre management. The aim is to make this a training school for serious workers, and to supplement experience with knowledge of the goals to be reached in Community Theatre activities.

As a novel means of publicity for its fall campaign one year the Playhouse gave a series of broadcasts over Station KSO. These plays were dramatizations of historic and interesting happenings in the development of the Playhouse from its obscure beginnings to the present. Many of the names mentioned, many of the personalities lived again in Des Moines dramatic circles over the radio waves, and came as a pleasant surprise to everyone interested in the Playhouse. Bits of dialogue from some of the early productions, displays of temperament during rehearsals, realization of the ideals on the part of earnest board members, disagreements, squabbles, engagements, and even marriages were woven into a strictly authentic, yet highly romantic series of dramas which were broadcast weekly for a month.

Of interest is the fact that two of their former directors have turned to radio professionally. Gordon Hughes is a production man for NBC in Chicago, and Gregory Foley holds down the same sort of position for CBS in New York.

Others who have gone into professional work from the Des Moines Community Theatre include MacKinlay Kantor and Tom Duncan, both now well-known authors; Donald "Dutch" Regan, who is with Paramount Pictures; and Joy Hodges, who was a featured singing and dancing player of "I'd Rather Be Right" on Broadway.

John Ross Winnie, an Iowa boy himself, and present director of this theatre, says: "A Community Theatre must have a multiplicity of purpose. To be artistic is fine, but we find in the middle west that it must be a very substantial form of art. There is no place in the middle-western theatre for affectation or the long-haired artist. People here live pretty close to the soil, whether it be the city or the farm, and actors must, whether they wish it or not, be pretty 'homespun.' Our theatre must be primarily a place of entertainment, where the very people who make it possible for us to survive, our membership, can enjoy themselves.

"It is our duty and our purpose to make this entertainment both cultural and educational. Secondly, we must, in some small way, provide adequate training for those who wish to go into the movie and radio fields. Therefore, it is obvious that a mere production program would be entirely insufficient. A training school is the answer to this problem, one that really functions and aims to train the actor. Thirdly, our theatre must be a place where people can spend their leisure time, find wholesome recreation, either renewing old interests or learning new means of profitably spending idle time. A theatre survives on activity and interest—directed into constructive channels."

Their membership and box office last season under Mr. Winnie's direction increased forty per cent, and with the Community Theatre firmly established they are now entering their twentieth season—a progressive and vital group in the cultural life of Des Moines.

Duluth, Minnesota. A Dream Theatre Materializes.

Early in the year 1911 the Little Theatre of Duluth became destined for reality. Mrs. S. R. Holden, founder of the theatre, then began to dream of what a Community Theatre could mean to the city. In a few short months the Drama League of Duluth took the first definite step toward securing funds for the purchase of a building.

On the night of January 22, 1912, the curtain of the old Lyceum Theatre rose on "The Adventurer," by Alfred Capus, under the direction of Benedict Papot. The play was a great success and the "dream theatre" began to materialize.

On October 13, 1914, Mrs. Holden announced the purchase of the building formerly occupied by the First Church of Christ, Scientist. In a few breathless weeks the charming little colonial building became a theatre and the opening of the first regular season was at hand.

The event drew national attention as eastern newspapers and magazines carried stories of Duluth's contribution to American culture. The climax of the first program was the initial American production of Bernard Shaw's "The Dark Lady of the Sonnets."

Activities increased in the new theatre. Thomas H. Dickinson and Lady Gregory came to lecture. In honor of the grand old lady of the theatre, Duluth's new playhouse housed "The Workhouse Ward." The season came to an exciting close when William Webster, of Minneapolis, its first professional director, produced "Her Husband's Wife," by A. E. Thomas.

The second season saw productions of plays by Barrie, Chekov, and Margaret Culkin Banning, a city resident who won the Drama League prize of $50.00 with "Her Sacred Duty," one of many submitted by native playwrights. Granville Barker visited the theatre in the spring of 1916, and expressed great enthusiasm over the work being done. The Little Theatre gained new friends each season and went into the war years doing its share to raise funds for the Red Cross and kindred organizations.

But as the crushing effects of the war began to be felt in Duluth, people became too busy for the theatre. Late in 1919 the group came to a decision to sell the building and decrease activities. An auction was held and the building sold. All bills were paid and the balance of more than $1200 was invested in Liberty Bonds against the day when another building would be needed.

In 1926 the tide of the Little Theatre turned again and Clyde Fitch's "The Truth" ushered in a new era for Duluth playgoers. J. Hooker Wright, well-known professional actor, directed until the summer of 1927. The Little Theatre then moved into its present building at Twelfth and Superior Streets. Duluth has had a long succession of interesting and important directors, including, among those already mentioned, Mrs. F. A. Patrick, Maurice Gnesin, Allan Wallace, John Wray Young, Gordon Giffen, and its present director, Gregory Foley.

The membership of this group has varied from time to time, the low ebb being four hundred and the maximum eleven hundred. Five to six plays are produced each year and run six nights each. While their theatre accommodates three hundred comfortably, it is often necessary to give additional performances on the second week to take care of the many who wish to see some particularly outstanding play.

When they celebrated their twentieth anniversary, a note of hope for the future was struck when they said on their program: "The dream theatre of 1911 has been a reality for twenty years. Today Mrs. Holden and the many, many others who have worked with unselfish devotion through the years believe the time has come when the theatre must again move ahead to greater things. The new philosophy of living demands it. The second third of the Twentieth Century has brought a new axiom to social planning. It is, 'The sound life provides for work well done and leisure well spent.' Thus the one art which combines all arts logically provides the greatest medium of expression for the greatest number. The new American Theatre is rising in the land. From coast to coast great new theatres are building. In them a mighty nation is finding joy for their hearts and enrichment for their souls. And so the reward due to hardy pioneers and a truthful prophet draws nearer for your theatre. Already those who have looked forward so accurately through the years can see it. On a rugged, northland hill by Lake Superior, there will stand a building of beauty, a house of magic, Duluth's own Civic Theatre."

Fargo, North Dakota. The Little Country Theatre Spreads Its Wings.

The year 1939 promises to be a big one in North Dakota. It will mark the twenty-fifth anniversary of the beginning of rural community drama in that state.

In 1914 a rural school teacher wrote to Alfred G. Arvold, then an instructor in public speaking at the North Dakota Agricultural College, for suggestions for a play she wished to present. Mr. Arvold had some copies of comedies he had once acted in. He sent her the plays. She produced one of them. Somebody from a nearby town saw the production, and it was not long after that he, too, sent in an inquiry. Letter after letter followed asking for material. From these requests, which necessitated the establishment of a package library system designed to supply material for various kinds of programs, the idea of the Little Country Theatre was conceived by Mr. Arvold.

Twenty years ago at the Agricultural College there was an old, dingy, dull-gray chapel in Old Main. Mr. Arvold made this into a theatre. Here he planned to try out the various plays he was suggesting. Today this theatre is a Mecca for country folk and city folk alike meeting to discuss and suggest ways and means to make life in the open country or the town in which they live more attractive, more interesting, and more human.

One might call it a humanizing agency whose sole aim is to stimulate an interest in good, wholesome drama among the village people, in order to help them find themselves, that they may not only become better satisfied with the community in which they live but also make their neighborhoods inviting so that other people will want to live there. In short, its real purpose is to use the drama and all that goes with the drama as a force in getting people acquainted with one another. Instead of making the theatre a luxury for the classes, its aim is to make it an instrument for the enlightenment and enjoyment of the masses.

The influence of the Little Country Theatre is far-reaching. It penetrates into practically every corner of the state. Scarcely a school house is erected in the state today without a stage that can be used for plays. Frequently suggestions are sent out on how to build a new hall or remodel an old one. Not long ago a project was started sending graduate students to various sections of the state to make a social analysis of different neighborhoods and communities in order to find out the possible talents residing in these out-of-the-way places.

Very few of Mr. Arvold's students have become professional, but the number of young men and women who are now recreational leaders and directors of Community Theatres is enormous.

Don C. Jones of Fargo says: "Here is a man who has given twenty-five years of his life in an attempt to teach the farmer, the small-town butcher, the president of the Ladies' Aid, that they can knock ten years from their age by entering in an avid way into the building of a Community Theatre. And that, to me, is the important thing that the Community Theatres in North Dakota are doing. They are bringing art back to the people, back where it belongs, and where it will do the most good."

So in practically every town and city, and in the outlying rural districts of North Dakota, community drama flourishes.

And somehow, the world has gone to Mr. Arvold's door. George Bernard Shaw inscribed a copy of one of his plays to Mr. Arvold, saying, "In grateful acknowledgment of his services to dramatic art in virgin fields in the United States of America."

Charles Coburn, Hollywood screen actor and Director of the Mohawk Drama Festival, said in a letter: "Its (the Little Country Theatre's) influence is felt all over the world . . . It is a real and enduring masterpiece you have built. As long as such artistic integrity is devoted to the drama, it cannot fail in this country."

Sidney Howard once spent three days with Mr. Arvold to get his interpretation of life in the rural neighborhoods. Ethel Barrymore's distant "Humpf" turned to one of wonder as she relaxed in the homey atmosphere of the theatre, and Walter Hampden turned playful as he sat at the head of a long supper table and became an honorary member of the Little Country Theatre.

The great and the small find their way to this Little Country Theatre, the center of Community Drama in North Dakota, and the truly observant take away a lesson in simplicity.

Fort Wayne, Indiana. The Old Fort Players.

But for the Old Fort Players, the Majestic Theatre—across whose boards have trod David Warfield, Mme. Modjeska, Bernhardt, Mrs. Fiske, John Drew, the Barrymores, William Gillette, William Collier, and George M. Cohan—would have been in the hands of wreckers in 1930. It was a Community Theatre that came to the rescue of this old traditional theatre. For on a December afternoon in 1931 a dozen courageous souls gathered together to organize the Old Fort Players.

On that day William J. Grass was named provisional president and the *News Sentinel* (January, 1934) quotes him as saying: "We shall, of course, expect each performance to stand on its own merits without the practice of any endowments, subsidies, or 'shake downs,' and we feel very certain that after the public has had an opportunity to see our work, the decision as to the length of our organization's life will be fairly determined."

On that afternoon each person present paid $1.00 and books from play publishers were ordered. Mr. A. J. Arnold, an ex-professional, was selected to direct the first production. After hectic rehearsals over a period of a few weeks, and a never-to-be-forgotten dress rehearsal when everything went wrong, and with mad moments when the newly organized casting committee tried to direct the play, the director, the lights and even the musicians, the curtain finally did manage to ascend on a fairly well-presented play.

At that time the Old Fort Players had no equipment, no props of their own and no set, but they were an ambitious lot—eager and idealistic. A grand heritage bequeathed to all the Old Fort Players for all time to come.

It is amusing to look over the first program and see the complete lack of long lists of committees' names which these last few years have made the programs of the Old Fort Players conspicuous. However, there were a hundred and nineteen names under the words "Charter Members," and a board of governors, imposing and large enough to sit and ponder at The Hague. The success of this initial experiment may be recorded in the first signs of a small triumph on the part of the Old Fort Players, for they were able to give

$50 in gold to their director as a birthday present. This gift was presented at a cast party after the show. Such a party after the closing performance has become an established custom of the Civic Theatre—it would take a major catastrophe to prevent the words, "Going to the cast party?" from being the most frequently heard during make-up periods preceding the last performance of every production.

After the first performance began a long thrilling chaotic barnstorming period for the Old Fort Players. They literally brought the theatre to the people, in churches, halls, schools, giving a long list from "Holiday" and "Pygmalion" to "Death Takes a Holiday." Having gained many friends, the Players began looking for a permanent home, and a breath-taking decision was made. The executive committee signed a contract whereby the Majestic Theatre, grand old show place of Fort Wayne, was to become the home of the Old Fort Players and to be renamed the Civic Theatre.

The Civic Theatre is acoustically perfect, rich in the glories and tradition of yesterday. Like other legitimate houses, it had come upon bad days, falling so low as to house cheap circle burlesque, movies of doubtful aesthetics, and now and then a political rally or revival. In July, 1933, the Old Fort Players took over the Majestic; their 1938–39 season found them firmly entrenched, though they had one scare a year or so ago when they noticed a piece in the paper saying that the Civic Theatre was to be sold for a parking lot. However, possibly due to the combined prayers of all the players, this deal fell through and the building remains the Civic Theatre of Fort Wayne. However, the players realize that sooner or later they must face the necessity of acquiring a new home. Carl W. Rothert, president of this group, has this to say about what he considers their biggest problem:

"The largest problem confronting the Old Fort Players is to build up public acceptance and support of the right kind.

"Operating as we do without an endowment, we must constantly have an eye to the box office. Our problem, however, is not confined merely to selling enough season tickets and individual admissions to finance our season. That part of it we have solved pretty successfully for the past two seasons at least. We have had enough paid patronage to wipe out a deficit which had built up gradually through several seasons and to give us a small cash surplus at the close of the 1937–38 season.

"Our problem is rather to convince the more substantial business interests of the community that we are worthy of their continued and greater future support. We realize that it is a question of only a very few years until we must obtain other quarters and we are building toward the time when we can ask the citizens of the community to support a new Civic Theatre building ($100,000).

"We have a peculiarly conservative population with which to deal and they must be convinced that we are genuinely substantial before they will hazard any large sums of money toward such a building for us.

"With this in mind, we have been gradually changing the personnel of our directors and officers to include a number of outstanding business men; we are planning our seasons to include a large number of box-office plays, principally of the Broadway success type; we have made use of every opportunity to increase our income and reduce our expenses, and in general are shaping all of our activities in the direction of proving to the people of our city that we are a substantial organization, occupying a necessary part in the local scheme of things."

The period from 1933 to 1938 saw a succession of directors, including Bessie Baldwin, Herbert Butterfield, Merrill Mathews, Volvey Hampson, William C. Hodapp, and the present director, L. Newell Tarrant, Jr.

A subsidiary group and workshop was organized in 1933 by ten people who foresaw the need of a training school for newcomers into the group, both in the acting arts and in production. Every Monday night many youngsters and oldsters trek down Berry Street to the Civic Theatre where they take part in class work: voice and diction, rehearsal technique, lighting and scenic design, make-up, etc. The workshop does not function as a separate unit entirely, but as a stepping stone to the main stage. The Old Fort Players also have a children's theatre so that their democratic penetration of the community is complete.

Mary E. Ebersole says: "The Community Theatre which received its impetus as a result of the debacle of the road furnishes a splendid outlet for the desire of self-expression."

Undoubtedly many people will smile with understanding and sympathy at Mary E. Ebersole's recounting of impressions from eight years of work and experience with the Old Fort Players and the Civic Theatre of Fort Wayne, Indiana.

"These wierd sounds heard in the theatre in the daytime or in the wee small hours—probably the wraiths of Madame Modjeska, Barrymore or mayhap William Collier or John Drew, protesting our histrionic efforts. The hush of that moment felt by all when the stage manager calls 'Places!' The scare Mrs. Telfer of the Trelawney cast threw into all of us when prior to the final performance she contracted scarlet fever—another rushed in the part and almost through the costume—but we carried on unvaccinated and unscathed and our audiences unsuspecting. The hoopskirts of Trelawney and the bats swooping low over us, whilst their pals chittered from above somewhere in the house. The God-awful suspense when, on a sultry spring evening, a member of 'The Green Beetle' cast took a stroll and a smoke on a roof-top adjoining the hall—and overstayed his leave. The squeaky chairs and rickety stairs of some of the halls. The lovable jolly barrister who was discovered comfortably seated out front just prior to his entrance in 'Stage Door.' Dashing in the rain for the last street car after rehearsal. The tedious, interminable waits at dress rehearsals. The hysteria of the 'Alison's House' cast after five weeks' work, at their dress rehearsal. The balky second act curtain in 'Icebound' with the two lovers finally unclinching and strolling off. Such nonchalance! The time the lead in 'Saturday's Children' made a quick change from office frock to a formal and got the deep décolletage in front—changed while those on stage were ad-libbing madly. When she did enter aeons late, the dress was all right but the high neck of the slip was in reverse! Howard's splendid comedy was a bit too risqué for our audience as it was—and this one has always wanted to do 'They Knew What They Wanted'! The town eccentric dressed in black, who owned much downtown property, and who had been the belle of the ball in her day, and who always bought a seat in the balcony. The frantic moment in the horror play 'Double Door' when we made our exit to get our coat—to find that we hadn't hung it on its customary nail. Pitch dark—nary a soul near—tense drama with Victoria staring holes in the morbid set and probably vowing she really would lock me in that vault if I didn't return soon. I did—minus the coat. Oh, the shame of it all!! The terrific strain the boy felt who played the lead in 'Danger' just as his mother passed away. The suicide of the 'Out of the Night' cast member. The joys of creating a character—a part to set one's teeth into. Playing 'The Distaff Side' before a WPA crowd—the laughs when the perfectly attired gentleman wearing tails entered. Playing 'Post Road' before CCC boys. The unfortunate lad who rehearsed 'Death Takes a Holiday' and who a week before the show, lost his mind. Dress rehearsal of 'Death' which listed until after 2 A.M. a bitter cold night. Scouting around for a stone bench for the same play and finally getting it from a stone monument firm. What could be more true to type!"

Doesn't this sound as if it might have been written by any actor of Boston, Omaha, Seattle, or El Paso?

Glidden, Wisconsin. Blizzard or No Blizzard—the Play Goes On.

"This is a small community," says Mrs. F. W. Altenburg, of Glidden, Wisconsin, "and really, nothing very unusual has happened to us since we organized."

But they have a Community Theatre in Glidden—and that's something! Mrs. Altenburg was the organizer of this group. Formerly an actress, known on the professional stage as Patricia Dunphy, this is the second theatre group she has established. When the depression hit the country in general in 1929 and the theatre in particular in 1930, her husband, also an actor, decided to leave the theatre and enter the teaching profession. Naturally that left Mrs. Altenburg with nothing to do, and with her love of the theatre and plenty of time on her hands, what was more natural than that she should organize a community theatre group? This was in Hazel Green, Wisconsin, and the group grew and prospered for six years. Then the Altenburgs moved to Glidden, a lumbering town in the northern part of the state. This meant a new school for Mr. Altenburg and a new Community Theatre for Mrs. Altenburg.

She hadn't been in town a month until she inserted a little notice in the paper, asking all who were living in the vicinity and interested in the theatre, in any capacity whatsoever, to come to a first meeting to be held in the high school. She prepared written forms for each person to fill in, stating whether they would act, work back-stage, or in the front of the house, learn art work for the making of posters, handle publicity, or take care of the properties. She was delighted to find that all were not interested in acting alone but in doing many of the other necessary things which contribute to a finished performance.

She also wisely organized the married women of the community, those who had families and could not take part otherwise, into a Study Club. The purpose of this group was to read plays, and from them select the plays to be produced during the season. This met with instant favor, and the fact that they felt it was their selection being produced helped everyone to realize Glidden really had a Community Theatre.

Between plays, this group studied the current Broadway productions and the lives of the playwrights. Much of this material was obtained from the University of Wisconsin Extension Division under the direction of Ethel Rockwell, who cooperated with them whole-heartedly.

"I believe that a great deal of the success of every Community Theatre group depends upon the selection of the proper play for that particular community," says Mrs. Altenburg. "I have found that people in different parts of the country like different types of plays. The most popular here is the homey type of comedy drama."

This group did not sell subscriptions in the regular way. Mrs. Altenburg felt that if the first play was good people would come to the succeeding ones without having to buy tickets in advance. This proved a good plan; getting the audiences into the theatre was the least of their troubles.

Her plan was to produce plays appropriate to the season. In the spring a farce comedy, in Lent a Biblical play, in the summer a comedy drama, in the fall a tragedy, and in the winter a mystery play.

One of the outstanding problems of the Glidden Community Theatre is getting enough men to take part. The business men in this town do not feel they can give enough time to learn parts and be present at all rehearsals. The young men work in the woods all day, and unless theatrically inclined, are not interested. However, there was one exception. A young man from a nearby town became so interested in taking part in a play that he walked five miles to rehearsal one night when his car was snowed in.

A girl who had taken part in several of the plays lived in the village of Peeksville. On nights that her car would not start she thought nothing of putting on high-top boots and a snow suit, and "hiking in," as she called it—a matter of three miles in the cold. However, Glidden is accustomed to the wintry blasts, and it does not affect attendance at the plays. It was twenty-five degrees below zero one night, and yet all the seats were filled. Once, when the first rehearsal was called for a new play, the weather man had scheduled a blizzard; none of the players could even reach the school house. So the rehearsals had to be postponed a week. However, the play was presented on schedule, for everyone worked harder to make up for the lost week.

The plays are produced in the high school gymnasium, which is equipped with a stage and seats. All money taken in is used to pay royalty on the next play, publicity, make-up and to buy any equipment needed. At first rehearsals were held in the homes. The home which had the largest living room was the one selected. Later the school board kindly consented to let them have the music room in the school for their rehearsals.

The organization is non-profitmaking, and everyone donates his services. It is their idea in Glidden that the theatre should be made accessible to everybody, and for that reason admission prices are scaled as low as possible: ten and twenty cents! Yet they find this sufficient to cover the cost of the average $25.00 royalty play.

"My idea as to what a Community Theatre should be," says Mrs. Altenburg, "is that everyone in the community who cares to should be allowed to take part in some way in what they seem best fitted to do. They should be made to feel, by the director, or head of the organization, that it is their theatre and success depends on their cooperation and enthusiasm. I believe Community Drama is the self-expression of the entire group which participates, not a part of that group. At first I was inclined to use my best people over and over again, then I realized that I was not helping the community in the way I had set out to do."

Service to the community—and community participation—no matter what the thermometer says—is the way they keep the theatre alive in Glidden.

Grand Rapids, Michigan. Chilean Bond Proves Unprofitable.

The Civic Players of Grand Rapids had a season so successful that a $1000 profit was realized, and on the advice of a banker friend, converted into a Chilean bond. It grieves us to report that Chilean bonds are not a good investment for Community Theatres. Spot lights, extra curtains, revolving stages, yes; but Chilean bonds, no! So say the Civic Players.

It was in the halcyon days of 1926 that the Civic Players began thier organization under the guidance of Mrs. Myrtle Koon Cherryman. Starting with the usual small membership, the Players produced where they could, were directed by various local people, and at the end of the first year felt that they had established themselves well enough to hire a professional director, Paul Stephenson. One of his first duties was to help the House Committee find a permanent home for the Players. The customary search for a barn proved unfruitful, but the committee did uncover Old Germania, an old German meeting place. It was an unpretentious brick structure with the orchestra floor heated by two conspicuous coal-burning stoves which supplied heat only fitfully during the winter. There was a small stage which practically compelled a cameo stage technique and there was a pretense of a balcony. A coat of paint helped a little. Old Germania with a capacity of three hundred was home for the Civic Players from 1928 to 1931.

The second season the Board of Directors were not sure of being able to raise the money to pay Mr. Stephenson but they were sturdy souls and set out to accomplish this by selling season tickets. They hoped to raise an additional $2000 for current expenses by obtaining patron memberships and, should there be a deficit, the amount was to be underwritten.

From its unsure and small beginning, the Civic Players grew to a membership of one thousand, and except for an interlude during the depression years, the Civic Players have had no difficulty in financing themselves. For by 1932 the Players had moved into more pretentious quarters, renting part of an attractive building owned by the Ladies' Literary Club. During the depression, by asking creditors to be indulgent and by tightening the purse strings, the Players were able to keep solvent. When the depression lifted, increased membership and box-office receipts enabled them to pay off their debts and end the season with a bank balance.

The present quarters are adequate, but not luxurious. The stage is comfortable, dressing rooms are available, there is space for a workshop and a property room, but it is a haunting dream that some wealthy devotee of the Players will dig down for enough money to start the Civic Players on the road to owning their own home.

Grand Rapids is one of the few theatres that has had real difficulties with local censoring boards. The local committee which concerns itself with keeping the movies "clean" has also tried to clean up the Players. The height of this insidious influence was reached when complaint was made that "Yellow Jack" was too filthy to be accepted. With some forethought and cautious use of the blue pencil, a quick-witted director managed to arrange a suitable script.

Every theatre has its problems. In Grand Rapids, the problem at the box office is whether they should aim at being a stock company, a commercial theatre, or an artistic theatre. Undoubtedly, as the years go by, a happy medium will be found.

Off the beaten track of road companies, Grand Rapids has in recent years become a one night stand and even in this undignified position there are infrequent visits from the Eastern theatre. Those inhabitants who ache for "big time" theatre manage to get to New York, Chicago, or Los Angeles for their theatrical binges. When they return, the prospect of seeing the same play done in the Little Theatre seems dull. On the other hand, the people who cannot or do not travel this far for the sake of a play want to see the plays that make Broadway glitter. A problem is born. Although the Civic Players are no stock company, they are considered by Samuel French as being in one of the old-fashioned stock company zones. As a consequence they are unable at times to obtain releases on plays just off Broadway and all too often the movies are able to present them before the Community Theatre. How often it has been noticed that Community Theatres report: "In the minds of some of our customers there is no point in seeing the Civic Players' production of a movie presentation."

During the years of their existence, the Civic Players have had a slow turnover of directors, and as a result, the men who have been there have left definite impressions. In addition to Paul Stephenson, they have had Rufus S. Phillips, Murray Tucker, Drew Montgomery, Edward J. Crowley, and Thomas Stephenson.

The Players are proud of their contribution to the professional stage. This includes Josephine Bender, Earl Gunn, Richard Kendrick, Don De Jaeger, Dean Jaggar, Harry Young, and David Hauman.

One of the best stories of the Grand Rapids Players is that concerned with an interview that Paul Lukas of the movies was kind enough to grant to a group who had made a pilgrimage to a nearby city to see his performance in "A Doll's House." Mr. Lukas was grumbling about the monotony of playing endless performances of the same character. Laughingly one of the members of the Civic Players told him that he ought to come to Grand Rapids where he would have ample opportunity to do a variety of parts in the Civic

Players' repertory. Mr. Lukas was enchanted. "Where is Grand Rapids?" he asked. "I will be happy to go there for half my present salary." They told him that the actors with the Civic Players not only did not get half his salary but got no pay at all. After a look of wild astonishment, Mr. Lukas dropped the subject. In Europe, actors usually are paid to act!

Hutchinson, Kansas. *The Chamber of Commerce Offers Its Helping Hand.*

Early in the history of Hutchinson its citizens expressed the urge for dramatics and in 1873 the Dramatic Society of Hutchinson was formed.

This organization leased a building which had previously been occupied by a billiard hall and erected a stage. They were soon in rehearsal, and it wasn't long until they had ready for public performance "The Lady of Lyons" by Bulwer-Lytton.

The play had a run of two days, and on the morning of March 14, 1873, what was probably the first dramatic review to appear in the *Hutchinson News* said in part: "We attended both performances of 'The Lady of Lyons' and must confess that we were surprised at the success of the entertainment; considering that nearly all of the troupe are amateurs too much praise cannot be bestowed upon them for the zeal and ability they have shown in their undertakings. On next Wednesday the public will be treated to two laughable farces, 'Toodles' and 'The Two Buzzards.' "

This first dramatic effort may well be considered the forerunner of the present Community Theatre of Hutchinson, which got its start in 1922.

But in the intervening years two young men, who were destined to play an important part in the Community Theatre Movement, walked the streets of Hutchinson, and there have been rumors that their first attempts at play directing were done in this city. One was Gilmor Brown, now Supervising Director of the Pasadena Community Playhouse, and certainly one of the best known directors in the country. The other was John Wray Young, who has made a name for himself at Sioux City, Iowa, at Duluth, Minnesota, and now guides the destinies of the theatre at Shreveport, Louisiana.

The present organization started when seven teachers of speech arts formed a club with a brief constitution stating: "The purpose of this club shall be to study the speech arts, and to foster movements toward better drama in the community."

Originally the club did not plan to give any full-length plays, but immediately embarked on a program of presenting short plays to a membership audience of not over fifteen. These plays were given in the various homes.

Henry Pegues, the president of the Hutchinson Community Theatre, says: "I have done some mighty heavy acting in my time in front of a screen in a dining room for an audience of fifteen—or less. Imagine doing 'The Giant Stair' under those circumstances. But, brother, the club had their necks bowed and they went ahead, month after month, with always a new program."

Then in 1925, W. V. O'Connell, speech instructor in the high school, volunteered to direct a full-length play. The cast was selected from the club, so were the stage hands—some of the actors had to double in props, and tickets were sold during their spare time. But the play was a success.

Today the Hutchinson Community Theatre stands firmly. Thirteen consecutive years of producing plays without ever a season's deficit is the record of which this group is proud. They present four major plays a season. To date they have given thirty-six full-length plays, an average of about fifteen one-acters each year, and for the workshop, cuttings and single acts from longer plays. Many of their productions have been repeated for civic organizations, rural schools, churches, and all types of organizations, particularly at holiday time. Such performances have been produced either without charge, or for part of the cost of moving stage properties and scenery where necessary.

The organization is a dual one. The original group, organized in 1922, "The Hutchinson Dramatic Arts Club," today is the inner circle of working membership in the larger Community Theatre Group. Membership in the Arts Club is by election upon application by members in the Community Theatre Group, and implies a willingness to work in any capacity to forward the work of community drama in Hutchinson. This willingness to work means selling season tickets to the major plays, keeping up the membership in the larger group, painting and shifting scenery, collecting properties, and all the other jobs that naturally fall to the real workers in Community Theatres. In short, only genuine enthusiasts are allowed in the Inner Circle.

But the activities of the Community Theatre are open to the public. Many, outside the club members, find much to do and are welcome, but the members have always felt the obligation to work when volunteers were few.

An executive committee formulates the policies of the club subject to the approval of the entire sponsoring body, the Hutchinson Dramatic Arts Club. This body enters into all discussions with great interest, and no secret plans are ever put into effect. This has always insured interest throughout the year. Four of the original members still belong, and most of the membership has been active for more than five years.

Dues have been kept low—$1.00 for membership first of all for the Dramatic Arts Club, and an additional $1.00 for membership in the Community Theatre. All members of the Community Theatre, of course, pay their dollar. Then season tickets are extra. Admission to the four major plays are sold for $1.50, $2.25, and $2.75, but the yearly membership dues pay for admission to all other performances.

The Dramatic Arts Club membership is approximately fifty at this time. This was first limited to thirty, but the limit was raised to fifty in 1936. Consequently, membership in this club is a goal for all the Community Theatre workers.

In this latter group are a hundred and fifty persons who pay yearly dues, and the advance sale of tickets to the public averages eight hundred.

The present status of the Hutchinson Community Theatre is a working bank balance of more than $1000 with all bills paid. Lighting equipment and other properties are valued at well over a like amount, and above all there is the good will of the community.

The director holds the only paid job in the organization, and the season is operated on a budget of approximately $2200. A room is rented where the one-act plays and play cuttings are given, and this room is in use practically every night and many days throughout a season, which runs from the middle of September until the middle of May.

At the beginning of the 1937–38 season they were badly in need of good lighting equipment and a piano, and a few members of the community, including Governor Walter Huxman, were asked for $25 each to help in these extra expenses. The response was surprising, for the sum of $700 was raised, and wisely spent, so for the first time in their history they have a good, but not by any means complete, selection of spots and flood lights, and a second-hand piano for community singing and entertainment.

The organization has discovered by dearly bought experience that only through their own efforts can they keep going. Early they tried having their tickets sold on a split basis by other civic organizations, and while one season it worked splendidly, the next season was very unsatisfactory, and almost a complete reorganization was necessary to sell enough tickets to pay expenses.

They also brought in professional companies to augment two early seasons, but such experiences were equally dear. The only basis of operation that has been profitable is the one hundred per cent local operation within their own group, knowing what they faced when they started. Their record of many years without a deficit is due to planning and budgeting. Their profits have come from additional single ticket sales not figured in the budget.

The organization has always been a cross section of the entire community: "The Colonel's Lady and Judy O'Grady" meeting in community of spirit and desire to work and gain self expression through the theatre. No plan of taking in any social group has ever been considered, and in only a few cases are husbands and wives both included in the Dramatic Arts Club. Semi-annual Dutch treat picnics and box suppers make up the entire family social activities of the club. "Treats" for club members after each major performance are the only other social activities, and these are with a purpose: to make sure everyone stays for striking the set and to see that properties are promptly returned and carefully handled.

There is no adequate stage in any sense of the word in Hutchinson. The old "Home Theatre" was torn down twenty or more years ago, the Municipal Auditorium seats thirty-five hundred and a big sloping stage makes play presentation almost out of the question. The acoustics are bad, and years ago road shows gave up the idea of trying to use it. About once in two years one of the local movie houses brings in a musical comedy—and once "Green Pastures," the only Broadway production in many years.

So what theatre they have in Hutchinson must be created by the Community Theatre Group.

Since the beginning their major plays have been given in the school auditorium—pitifully inadequate for plays of more than one set as in no case is there any room back-stage after the scenery is put up. In fact, many plays have been staged with realistic effect by utilizing a center entrance through the backstage door, which was an afterthought of the architect in making an entrance through which scenery might be carried.

Once when they were giving "Dover Road," in which the actors are supposed to come in out of a storm, this back-stage door was opened and in a "Way Down East" fashion real snow blew in. That's realism! But it doesn't work so well when the play is a lighthearted comedy and the players in sport clothes and white flannels, taking a stroll into the garden for an off-stage love scene, get hit by a chunk of ice!

Another handicap to using this stage is that everything is done at once when dress rehearsals are in progress.

One actor relates: "Our director was a perfect—what do you call a guy who is always concentrating? He had to have every activity from carpenters to furniture movers and actors under his gaze—nothing perturbed him. I wanted to take him out and show him to the Indians. I was trying to rehearse the difficult scenes in 'Libel' with a rip-saw going behind stage—three hammers in front building a jury box—the property committee discussing with the director some odd detail—the costume committee waiting—and me trying to wring out a few lines of pathos. Boy, howdy!"

The group has had many types of directors. After Mr. O'Connell came Mrs. Alice Campbell Wrigley, who commuted from Wichita when a play was in rehearsal. Finished diction and styling were the qualities demanded by Mrs. Wrigley.

When she went to England in 1931 they sought a new director and found Mr. C. E. Oelrich, a newspaper man and an old trouper, in a little town thirty-five miles away. For two years he drove to Hutchinson each night for rehearsals and then drove back. "Jack" was a stage technician of the old school. Stage setting, stage positions, actions, walking, grouping, were paramount in his work. And from him the players felt they learned that thing called technique.

Mr. O'Connell came back and directed some plays, and then in 1934 they got their first full-time professional director, Roland Mabie. He remained with the group for two years and was the first professional director in the state of Kansas. Finesse and a modern college outlook were his contributions to the group.

From their next director, Theodore Little, they learned tempo. While he was in Hutchinson curtains rose promptly at eight-fifteen and descended at ten-thirty or very near to it.

Their present director is Robert Prettyman, a graduate of Yale, and under his guidance the group is forging steadily ahead.

They are facing the future with great hope in Hutchinson. Last year when they asked for sponsorships to buy additional equipment, the Chamber of Commerce offered to raise part of the funds for a Community Theatre, which offer still holds when a workable plan is presented. They have been deeded by the city—rather an ordinance has been passed—giving them the title to a plot 180 × 200 in the city park near the center of town. The deed will be recorded as soon as papers of incorporation which have been applied for are issued by the State Corporation Committee. Some day soon they'll be having their own Community Playhouse in Hutchinson!

Indianapolis, Indiana. A Little Theatre Becomes a Civic Theatre.

Shells screamed over battlefields in Flanders.
Henry Ford's Peace Ship was earning plaudits and puns.
Preparedness agitation was gathering force here in America,
    and all over the world a serious throb of life and death could
    be felt as history was made in February of 1915.

For the cultural life of Indianapolis, history was being made by a small meeting of theatre lovers who, on the fifteenth day of February, 1915, gathered to create the Little Theatre Society of Indianapolis. The first membership rolls show one hundred and thirty names and the first director was Samuel Eliot, grandson of Charles W. Eliot of Harvard University.

The first productions of this group were given in the John Harron Institute, and the following year Murat Temple was leased as a permanent location for the activities of the Little Theatre Society. This "permanence" changed in 1925 when the Society, after ten years of hard work, careful budgeting and civic initiative, secured its own Playhouse at 1447 North Alabama Street. A handsome, adequate building was erected at the cost of $40,000 and today it is completely and efficiently equipped with almost everything a theatre building could require.

The Civic Theatre of Indianapolis, as it is now known, has had a long succession of excellent directors, including Carl Bernhardt, George Sommes, Hale McKean, Frederick Burleigh, Alfred Etcheverry, and Edward Steinmetz, formerly of the Omaha Playhouse. Under the presidency of Mr. Frank Hoke, the membership in the theatre for the 1937–38 season was fifteen hundred.

In 1936 Frederick Burleigh inaugurated a tradition that the Civic Theatre recommends to all sister groups: an annual musical review, collecting the talent exclusively from the membership of the theatre, but never hesitating to get the best professional help necessary in the way of musical arrangements and sketches. Burleigh brought James Baynor from New York to arrange the numbers and write the sketches, and Louise Spillman Sparks was engaged to do the musical arrangements. This musical review has proved to be a great budget balancer for the Civic Theatre and brings the enthusiasm of the spring season to a climax.

Another feature of the Civic Theatre is its Children's Theatre, which department is now in its twelfth season. Four productions are usually presented each year and the presentations are quite often adapted from original stories by members of the Children's Civic Theatre. These plays are presented with adult casts.

One of the high points of the activities in the Civic Theatre of Indianapolis is their $500 prize play contest. This is particularly interesting in that they are so anxious to encourage the indigenous Hoosier playwrights that they are restricting this contest to entrants who either are native-born or present residents of Indiana. Production of the winning play is scheduled by the Civic Theatre and the results of such a tournament should interest all theatres throughout the country as this method of encouraging the local playwright has proved many times to be the only effective means of securing superior manuscripts before they are sent to Broadway.

A clever publicity scheme was employed by the subscription campaign chairman several seasons ago, when he persuaded Mary Pickford and Buddy Rogers to stop off in Indianapolis and lend their support to the beginning of their membership drive. They were very gracious and enabled the Civic

Theatre to gain hundreds of column inches of publicity for the subscription campaign.

To aid various members of the subscription teams, a speaker's outline of the history and background of the Civic Theatre is prepared in mimeographed form for study. It is amusing to read that in 1927, almost belligerently, the Board of Directors of the former Little Theatre of Indianapolis announced that henceforth they would be known by the title of The Civic Theatre of Indianapolis, inasmuch as they were no longer a "little theatre," which term meant to many people an "arty, social and amateur group." The Board of Directors also felt that they had been serving as a civic institution long enough to assume that title.

An editorial criticism in *The Indianapolis Star* speaks with such fervent enthusiasm of the work of the Civic Theatre that we feel justified in closing this brief sketch with a quotation from it:

AMATEURS ARE GOOD TOO

"There ought to be a word other than amateur to use in reference to such splendid play-acting groups as the Civic Theatre, whose members, while they are in it for the fun of it, really maintain a standard which compares most favorably with that we call 'professional.'

"Why is it that in sports, such as golf and tennis, we grant the glory boys recognition equal to that of those who play for gold, but when it comes to acting, we popularly suppose a fellow isn't much account unless he makes a living at it? Not only are there many people with fine talents who have never had the inclination or opportunity to make capital of them, but there are others who, having left the stage for business or domestic life, keep their skill sharp and their interest in the theatre alive by participating in the activities of play houses like the Civic Theatre."

Corbin Patrick in *The Indianapolis Star.*

Kalamazoo, Michigan. One Hundred Plays in Ten Years.

Dr. William E. Upjohn of Kalamazoo has set an example as a civic-minded individual that should be warmly recommended. For Dr. Upjohn very wisely and very kindly saw fit to erect and donate to his city a community center built around a civic auditorium. The Civic Auditorium of Kalamazoo, one of the most completely and beautifully equipped Community Theatres in America, was designed both by its donor and an architect as a building flexible enough to meet the ever-varying needs of a community. An art exhibit, a musicale, or a dance may be held there, or it may serve as the home of the Civic Players of Kalamazoo.

Possibly the Civic Players of Kalamazoo are to be commended most, inasmuch as their earnest activities first brought this idea to the mind of Dr. Upjohn and convinced him that he was endowing a worth-while project. For in July, 1929, Howard Chenery, Arthur Kohl, and Frances Hall, all of whom had been associated with the professional stage, conceived the idea of combining their talents as directors and actors with those of experienced amateurs and undertook to demonstrate the possibility of creating for Kalamazoo a theatre of its own. Despite the fact that it was midsummer, with the courage of their convictions and the cooperation of a few interested citizens they launched the venture which in the first nine weeks produced nine plays in a local high school auditorium.

It was hard, discouraging work at times. Expense was always a limiting factor; equipment was meagre or lacking; there was neither stage room nor scenery enough for a change of scene. Aside from a faithful few, audiences came spasmodically. Weird things happened during the action of the under-rehearsed plays; safe doors that should open stayed obstinately shut; scenes were played out of sequence; and the curtain was apt to go up or come down in the most peculiar circumstances. Fortunately, these were infrequent incidents and out of this experiment something seemed to be emerging which proved that Kalamazoo really wanted this venture and would support it.

At the end of the ninth play, a representative group of citizens became interested enough to form an organization around the venture, and so created their first Board of Directors, headed by their beloved Dr. Allan Hoben, to whose guidance in those formative years the Players are still indebted. Someone should have recorded for posterity a picture of this Board, as night after night they sat for hours in the tiny chairs of the school's kindergarten room, drafting and redrafting the constitution and by-laws preparatory to incorporation and to launching a new series of six plays between October and Christmas.

The seats may have been small, but the problems were big. One of the biggest was to sell $1000 worth of stock, but it was accomplished in less than a week. With Arthur Kohl and Frances Hall continuing as directors, and the new schedule of a play every other week in effect, rehearsals were begun with a new confidence. Interest was growing. Still to be faced was the problem of augmenting and stabilizing the audiences and enlarging the acting personnel. A membership committee was formed with Alice Louise McDuffee as chairman. The idea of "good drama, well presented" spread through the community and the prestige of the Civic Theatre grew with each succeeding production.

Doubt remained, but belief, courage, and loyalty carried the day and there were many friends, known and unknown, to whom they feel they owe a lasting debt of gratitude for their support during those early days.

The response that fall was gratifying; yet owing to the limitations that time, theatre location, and facilities placed on the standard of productions, the Board felt that it would be wise to move to the Central High School Auditorium for the presentation of the next series of plays after the New Year.

Meanwhile, before Christmas, Dr. William E. Upjohn purchased an old brick house which stood facing Bronson Park, which is the present site of the Civic Auditorium. Under the supervision of Mrs. Dorothy DeLano, this old house was remodeled with a tiny stage and auditorium. Offices, kitchen, and dining room were made available to the Civic Theatre for its headquarters.

The presentation of plays at the Central High School Auditorium and the added stimulus of a permanent home for the members lent fiber and stamina to the organization. Five hundred and fifty members were secured by the membership committee in December and January. Six more plays were offered at intervals of three weeks for the balance of the season, making twenty-one plays the first year. The Players prospered at Central High School, gained the respect of the community, and the membership went to six hundred and twenty-five before the first annual meeting in June closed one of the most gruelling of dramatic seasons.

The Players were thrilled and delighted that summer when Dr. Upjohn told them that he planned to erect a Civic Auditorium that would be devoted to social and cultural purposes, and that he thought they, among others, might find it adapted to their needs. They were honored to be one of the inspirations for such a building and were quick to grasp its potential importance to the community.

While the Civic Auditorium was under construction during the following year, 1930–31, the Civic Players continued to present their plays at Central High School Auditorium, and their neighbors, the Ladies' Library Association, made offices and rehearsal space in its building available.

That fall the response to the Players' membership campaign was in itself an inspiration and an endorsement by the community. With the prospect of headquarters in the new auditorium, a new feeling of stability permeated the organization. A more normal schedule of only ten plays permitted greater attention to the details of production. More and more actors became available, offering wider selection in casting. Audiences grew to flattering proportions.

This second season is counted as one of the most important, for it was now possible to relax a bit from the struggle for existence and to devote time and thought to laying the firm foundations of organization.

Dedicated to "the happy use of leisure," the beautiful Civic Auditorium was formally opened in the fall of 1931. Here, for a nominal rental fee, the Civic Players had at hand all the facilities for play production: workshop, wardrobe space, rehearsal room, offices, property room, dressing rooms, a magnificent stage and, for the comfort of the audience, a beautiful auditorium of intimate proportions.

Now it was possible to expand the scope of the Civic Players still further: Frances Hall organized the Children's Theatre; the Green Room, lounge, and kitchen offered opportunity for more frequent social activities; outside dramatic attractions could be sponsored.

Naturally the third season met with instant response from the community and the first play opened with eleven hundred and fifty members and standing-room-only houses. At last the Players felt they had arrived!

In spite of the business depression, which was soon upon them, the Civic Players for the next few years progressively raised the standard of productions. They not only became an important influence in Kalamazoo, but were receiving an increasing measure of recognition abroad.

During this period finances were of critical concern. But long ago the Players had established two policies which now proved their soundness. One, that the affairs of the Civic Players should be run on a business basis; the other, that they should stand on their own financial feet with their endowment, the support of the community, and hence not be a burden to individuals. In this respect the business manager, Norman Carver, has been an important member of the Players staff ever since its organization. Through him and the finance committee, a careful check of income, expenditure, economy, budgeting and long-range planning contributed a great deal toward surviving critical periods in their history.

In some respects, therefore, the fourth, fifth, and sixth seasons might be called "the lean years." However, during this time there was no retrenchment. That there was no compromise in the matter of production standards was a great tribute to the resourcefulness of the director, the committees, and the technicians. The latter, especially, under the wise counsel of Howard Bush, created settings practically out of thin air. Mr. Bush's talent as stage carpenter has always been most valuable, but never more so than at this time.

Emergence from the depression in 1935 seemed to offer opportunity for expanding their activities. A new phase in their development became evident under the direction of Paul Stephenson, whose background and experience proved invaluable in enlarging their dramatic appreciation. During this and the succeeding season, the Players attained a new and higher reputation for excellence.

The Kalamazoo Civic Players were headed during the season of 1938-39 by Lester Lang, whose work at the Experimental Theatre at Vassar established him as one of the most interesting scene designers of the times.

The Civic Players are to be commended for their integrity in serving their own community and fulfilling so adequately the dream that Dr. Upjohn must have had when he saw fit to give to the city of Kalamazoo such a splendid living monument that will be proof of his good taste, discretion, and love of the theatre for generations to come.

Kansas City, Missouri. Upon the Ashes of Failures a New Theatre Is Founded.

From 1927 to 1932 there was no Community Theatre in Kansas City. In the early '20's the Kansas City Theatre was one of the country's outstanding organizations, but due to internal bickering, bad management, lack of objective, and uncertain leadership, which was reflected in the productions, the doors were finally closed with a deficit in the neighborhood of $40,000. This cooled the most ardent Little Theatre enthusiasm with the result that communal theatrics were neatly bundled and put to bed. Kansas City was theatrically dormant.

From the death of the Kansas City Theatre to the birth of Kansas City's Resident Theatre, the Little Theatre was kept alive by several cliques of actors and authors who organized in as many groups as there were leaders, with only one purpose or objective—to "act"—forgetting that a Community Theatre is basically organized for "audiences." These many groups lacked serious intent and professional supervision and were too diversified to make any impression on the cultural life of the city.

It was about this time, too, that the middle west began to feel the pangs of the depression and New York retrenched, keeping the road companies away from the so-called "backwoods." Stock failed, tent shows couldn't find lot space; not even a "borscht circuit" to keep the interested few interested! The theatre was not only dead; it was buried.

During this period Mr. Max Bretton, Executive Director of the Jewish Community Center Association of Kansas City, saw the need of the spoken drama and began to encourage his organization to foster a Little Theatre. Kansas City was becoming the cultural center of the middle west. The beautiful Rockhill Nelson Art Gallery was under construction, the Kansas City Philharmonic Orchestra was being established, the Art Institute was flourishing, the new Kansas City University was about to open; but no one had attempted to unite the thousands vitally interested in the theatre.

A farsighted program was immediately introduced. A professional director, W. Zolley Lerner, was engaged, and Jay Doten as technician. The auditorium of the Center Building, with its suitable stage, began to resemble a theatre with the installation of a switchboard, spots, x-ray, scenery, platforms and, moreover, actors and rehearsals. Soon the smaller groups which were scattered throughout the city found their way to this new organization, aligning themselves with its purpose to bring the drama to Kansas City. Thus, the Jewish Community Center Association began the sponsorship of a civic theatre to become one of the links of cultural Kansas City—it was called Kansas City's Resident Theatre.

A Board of Directors was immediately invited to take over the management of the Resident Theatre, and under the leadership of Mr. Harry Schwimmer, this autonomous group immediately began to professionalize the idea of a Community Theatre, actively began to publicize the functions of this institution, and permitted all the devotees to join in its advancement. Patronage as well as intimate theatrical activity became available to all those who desired to participate. The spontaneous growth of this organization is shown by the growth from seven hundred in the 1932 season to thirty-two hundred patrons in 1937. This, of course, is directly due to the efforts of Mr. Bretton, Mr. Schwimmer, and the various members of the Board of Directors as well as the new Board of Trustees, which constitutes some of Kansas City's outstanding citizens.

The story of the growth and struggle of the Resident Theatre is that of every little organization. At the outset it was seen that too many Little Theatres without organization had spoiled the broth for the Resident Theatre which was to follow. Many times patrons had been deceived by the work of Little Theatre organizations. As in every other city, Little Theatres had become open houses for personal exploitation, amateurish productions, and dilettantes.

The Resident Theatre problem, then, was acute. Productions had to compete with what few road shows or stock companies there were during this period. Also the audiences had to be convinced once again of the sincerity, the professional and artistic integrity of the Resident Theatre. The thing that finally won wholehearted communal support was not the good publicity, the enthusiastic Board, the fine leadership, the close cooperation (though these helped immeasurably), but outstanding productions done in a professional, artistic manner.

It was evident to the Board and the director that further success was dependent on the physical plant of the theatre. With a great deal of effort the one-time auditorium of the Center, which had been used for dances, lectures, parties, games, and all imaginable social functions, was converted into a comfortable, beautiful theatre. Money was scarce, patronage was not yet assured; but the Board finally procured enough funds to begin the renovation of this auditorium into one of the most complete and beautiful Little Theatres in the middle west with five hundred comfortable seats and a stage equipped with exceptional effects.

There are many problems that confront a director of any Little Theatre in a large urban community. In Kansas City they have found that the only way to enjoy continued patronage and approval is outright competition with cheap traveling road companies rather than presentation of typical noncommercial productions. The Resident Theatre, located in the gateway to the west, has found this aspect of its problems most harrowing, for New York producers have the habit of reserving Kansas City for stock rights whether they intend playing there or not.

Productions of the Kansas City Resident Theatre equal to or better than many New York productions depend perforce upon a strong gate to make expenses. This puts them into competition for early releases since they can do more business with "Ah, Wilderness," "Parnell," "Idiot's Delight," and "High Tor" if these plays come to them immediately after the New York run, before pictures are made. Efforts to use plays ten to twenty months old or to follow movie releases are failures. Many "artistic" successes merely help to create a yearly deficit.

Perhaps this is too commercial for a Little Theatre. Perhaps the Little Theatre should devote itself entirely to untried plays, revivals, foreign importations, closet classics. Such a theatre would have to open its doors to a guest audience and work under benevolent patronage. But in Kansas City success demands commercial theatre in an artistic, enthusiastic, non-profit manner. Their plays are chosen for their demonstrated drawing power, actors are chosen for their histrionic ability, and the audience is invited to pay and to scoff or to praise. Within these limits the director and his staff have free rein.

It is because their patronage includes people from all social levels that they are able to do "Winterset" one month and follow it successfully with "Paola and Francesca"; or to stir with Odet's leftist play "Awake and Sing" and then soothe with Kansas City's own Elsie Shaffler's "Parnell"; or to offer the dynamic "Bury the Dead" and "Idiot's Delight" and then their own modern version of "Caesar . . . the Death of a Dictator."

They believe definitely that their productions need the enthusiasm of an amateur approach, but the finish and smoothness of the professional. It is because of this, too, that they have won plaudits from all their newspapers and the hearty recommendation of Mr. Burns Mantle of the New York *Daily News*; and have received excellent notices from the *New York Times*, *Variety*, *Billboard* and other professional organs.

Mr. Lerner, the director, says: "The Community Theatre in the larger cities, to continue, faces many vital problems: it must procure from play-brokers good plays—early; not dish out mild, unwanted semi-hits. It must continue to attract audiences at the box office to make it self-supporting, not beg for patronage from stage-struck dilettantes. It must continue its high professional, commercial, competitive standing. It is essential to build up a repertoire company. This is important and difficult because the talented people available in each community are limited. The Community Theatre, therefore, must become self-supporting to the point where the nucleus of an acting company may be hired. These people may well be men and women of the community. Talented artists are willing to appear once or twice without pay, but cannot afford to do it continuously. With such a group augmented by other local talent, which would not want money, and by new-comers to the field, an acting company of real importance can be maintained in every live mid-western city." *

Patrons witnessing local talent, regardless of how much pleasure they derive from the production, regardless of how expertly they feel the presentation had been accomplished, somehow or other are always dubious as to the true merit of what they have seen. To get an audience to forget that they are witnessing a Community Theatre production is undoubtedly the ideal of any director. The best method of achieving this is to present prominent guest stars with the repertory company. Only then will the untutored, midwestern audiences realize the deftness of their own performers' work. The Resident Theatre is, therefore, making every effort to build an outstanding repertory company out of which may easily come a substantial number of adequate players. They feel they will reach their objective quicker by hiring a nucleus of professionals.

They have already inaugurated the guest star system by using Lenore Ulric in "Idiot's Delight," Hart Jenks in "Othello," and Rose Keane in "Awake and Sing." This has been exceptionally valuable to the people in the various casts and to the box-office receipts.

For the training of newcomers to the acting company there is a workshop which presents several productions that otherwise would not appear. Since organizing the Resident Theatre has run a Children's Resident Theatre, casting both adults and children. Next they hope to establish a school of the theatre to fill a definite need in this heart of the middle west.

The Resident Theatre has progressed steadily and the future looks bright. They feel they are aiding in a steady development of the taste of their community and raising the standard of dramatic appreciation.

* The editors of this book do not subscribe wholly to this doctrine and wish to point out the failure of this procedure in Pittsburgh.—Ed.

Although only five years old, it has already contributed to New York and Hollywood. Carl Rogers, David Friedkin, Jerome Mayer, Harry Coultoff, and Betty Lou Kalis, all comparatively young people, are just beginning to advance in the professional world. Almost every radio station in Kansas City and surrounding territory has Resident Theatre players.

Marshalltown, Iowa. The Largest Membership Per Capita in the Country.

Over thirty years ago Billy Sunday descended upon Marshalltown and held one of his typical revivals. He was a home-town boy, so to speak, having started his baseball career from this Iowa city. The revival was a success, resulting in the building of several new and beautiful churches. But how Billy Sunday thundered against that "hot-bed of vice called the theatre." It even looked for a time as though the senior class play of the high school would not be given. The play was "The Lady of Lyons," with Esse Hathaway directing. But the play did go on, despite Billy Sunday.

Thirty years have passed since then. Today Marshalltown for its population has one of the largest Community Theatres in the country. Practically one out of every ten residents belongs—and community participation is the keynote of this theatre.

"It is a community enterprise," they say on every program. "It was conceived by, and dedicated to, our interest in the combined arts of the theatre. It will live only as our interest in these things endures. It is first, last, and foremost—OUR Community Theatre."

It had its beginning in September of 1932. Alice Van Law, Edward Wright, teachers in the high school, and Evelyn Bowman, librarian in the public library, were the pioneers. They called a meeting of interested people at the public library, at which a board of directors was chosen. A play was selected; tickets were sold in advance; books for the play were bought. At the tryouts more people attended than could be cast. So two one-act plays were also announced and then given in the attic of the D. W. Norris home. No admission was charged. This was simply to further interest in the Community Theatre and to explain to more people what it was all about.

Then the first full-length play, Sherwood's "The Queen's Husband," was given to the public. The group made $35, enough to start a second production. The profit on the second was $75, so they gave a third. The season closed with $150 in the bank and two hundred and fifty pledge cards signed for membership for the second season.

The next year they had five hundred; the third year seven hundred and fifty members. Then one thousand, twelve hundred and fifty, fourteen hundred, and for the 1938–39 season over fifteen hundred memberships.

Season membership, open to everybody in town, is priced at $1.00. There is no social restriction or recommended membership. Everyone participates to the extent he wishes. Many merely attend the plays, of course, but some two hundred and fifty persons work each season on the technical staff, and one hundred is the average number of actors used each year.

Eight or nine monthly productions and numerous one-act plays are given during the winter. Plays are presented in the auditorium of the senior high school, although they have their workshop above a downtown garage. They have their own twenty-piece orchestra, too, composed of theatre members.

Besides producing plays they often bring professional companies to Marshalltown. The Globe Players have appeared twice, Marionettes also, and Ethel Barrymore Colt in "Accent on Youth."

Miss Colt's booking was on a day when there was a coal shortage due to the extremely cold weather. Schools were closed, and most people stayed in their homes hugging the fire. But the play went on. Theatre members brought coal in sacks from their own cellars to provide fuel to heat the auditorium. (It was thirty years ago that Billy Sunday warned Marshalltown of the "hell-fire of the theatre." It didn't take—praise be!)

"We haven't the funds most theatres have," says Alice Van Law, one of the play directors of this group, "and yet we manage to have new sets for each performance. This is possible because no one gets paid for his work. not even the directors. It has made a feeling of good will as nothing else could do. We've never had a faction. Everyone glories in the success of others. Many work in obscure places willingly with little recognition. Because of this we feel we have a real Community Theatre—in function as well as name."

Margaret Barnum, the president, echoes these sentiments, as do Carol Houghton and Frances Tankersley, play directors.

"Our theatre is a factor in community life," Miss Van Law goes on to say, "and the whole town is acutely aware of it. Play nights are red-letter nights. Many of our players work in the mills and factories by day. Others come from the business and professional world. We are truly democratic!"

Mason City, Iowa. Twenty Years of Pioneering.

Among the pioneers who have struggled valiantly in their communities for the establishment of a theatre, Mrs. Ina K. Trissel of Mason City must be prominently placed. For over twenty years she has worked to establish a Community Theatre in this city.

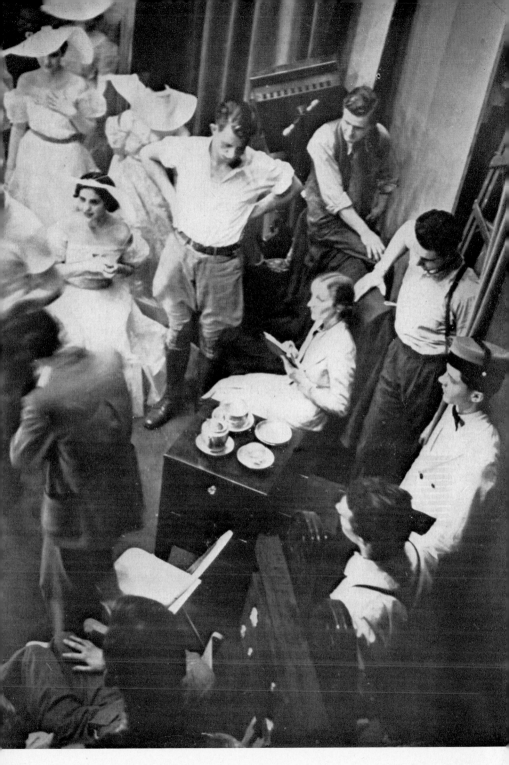

"Trifles make perfection. . ."

Chicago Mummers Theatre.

"Chicago."

Chicago Mummers Theatre.

"Night Must Fall."

The Mummers of St. Louis present "High Tor."

The Kalamazoo Players: "Bury the Dead."

Repertoire Little Theatre, Toledo: "Mrs. Moonlight."

Terminal Theatre, Cincinnati: Home of the Actors Guild.

"Petticoat Fever."

Sets designed by John R. Winnie for the Des Moines Community Theatre.

"Night Must Fall."

"The Swan" and "Bury the Dead" as presented by the Springfield Community
Players in Ohio.

Hutchinson, Kansas.

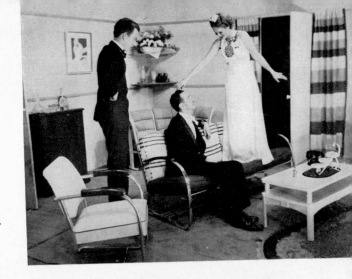

"Candle Light."

Workshop.

"Ceiling Zero."

The auditorium seats three hundred and twenty.

"If This Be Treason" as presented in Indianapolis.

The Civic Theatre of Indianapolis offers variety in "The Late Christopher Bean" and "Mary Tudor."

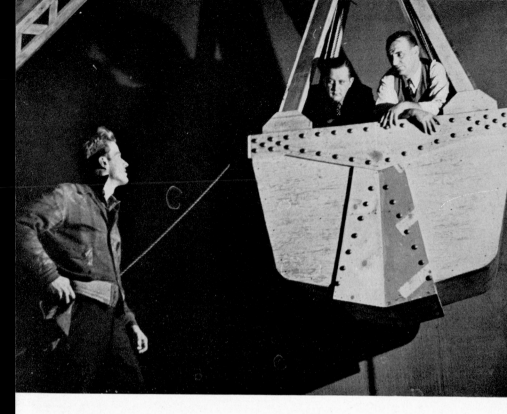

The Omaha Little Theatre offers "High Tor" and rehearses "Excursion."

The Shaker Players of Shaker Heights, Ohio, present "First Lady."

Scenes from "Youth in Command." Sets by Arne Nybak.

The Duluth Little Theatre, Minnesota.

"The Shining Hour." Set designed by William Baumgarten.

"Hay Fever."

"The Tavern."

Weathervane Playhouse, Akron, Ohio.

"First Lady" at the Players Guild, Joplin, Missouri.
(Action photos by Tom Korn.)

"Awake and Sing."

Kansas City Resident
Theatre.

Scenes from "Parnell."

At Glencoe, Illinois, the Threshold Theatre says: "The public still likes *East Lynne!*"

"The world's worst critics."

Lady Isabel: "I hope you'll be happy here at East Lynne."

There was very little interest in the drama in Mason City when she arrived in 1918. Mrs. Trissel formerly had been an active member of the Community Theatre of Waterloo, Iowa, where she had acted in the plays, helped with the properties, and even had helped shift scenery.

But in Mason City she found that the Declamatory Contest, the Senior Class Play, the Elks' Minstrels, possibly a musical comedy and one or two road shows were the extent of things dramatic. Musical talent and interest there was, and still is, in abundance. The records of many years revealed to her that practically all of the "home talent" entertainments were musical rather than dramatic.

The Woman's Club, one of the oldest and largest in Iowa, had many departments: art, civic, history, music, and nature study, but no drama. She was asked to organize such a department and act as chairman. For four years she held that position, and during this time organized and directed the Drama League for three years of its existence.

Speakers were brought in from places where groups were already under way: Iowa City, Grinnell, Waterloo, Centerville, and Des Moines. Mrs. A. Starr Best, one of the originators of the Drama League, visited them twice, and gave much assistance.

The Des Moines Community Players, with Professor J. B. Gifford as director, were brought to Mason City in 1921 and presented two one-act plays. A talk by Professor Gifford at that time resulted in a decision to form a Drama League. The League had a membership of about three hundred and fifty, with yearly membership tickets priced at $5.00, admitting the holder to classes and to all plays. Once the organization got under way, an unusual amount of talent and ability was discovered. The greatest obstacle to the successful production of plays, which still exists, was the lack of an adequate auditorium and stage. The high school auditorium, seating about twelve hundred, was the only available place, and was in constant demand.

About this time the Iowa Little Theatre Circuit, an association of groups of community players, representing several towns and cities of the state, began. Each group prepared a play to be sent to other towns. This interchange of entertainment was an innovation at the time. Mason City's offering was "Her Husband's Wife," by A. E. Thomas. The leading man was Merle A. Potter, now dramatic critic on the *Minneapolis Journal.*

The work of the Drama League continued with unabated interest until the spring of 1924, when it closed for the summer. Mrs. Trissel had decided to open a Drama Shop in Mason City, handling plays for various groups throughout the state. So she resigned from leadership of the Drama League. To her great surprise and disappointment, no one was found to take up the work in the fall, and the Drama League was no more. But interest in the movement did not die, and the Drama Department of the Woman's Club still carried on.

During the next two years, Mrs. Trissel was too busy with her Drama Shop to give much attention to outside interests. But because of continued demands, she helped organize a number of small groups in connection with clubs, churches, and schools. In 1926 many of these groups were again united, under the name of the Drama Shop Players, with Mrs. Trissel as director. This was a smaller organization than the old Drama League; membership was by invitation only.

The Players met once a week at the Drama Shop for study and rehearsals. Besides their own productions they presented many plays for the benefit of clubs, churches, and other civic organizations. One of the most popular programs was that given at the close of a season, known as "Studio Nights." The five numbers on this program were a satire, a fantasy, a comedy, a drama, and a mystery play, illustrative of the work done by the Players.

Members of the Drama Shop Players represented Mason City in the Iowa Play Tournaments at Iowa City many seasons and never failed to bring back either a "First place" or a "Superior" trophy.

Special groups of entertainers, known as the Drama Shop Gypsy Story Tellers, the Drama Shop Fun Makers, and the Drama Shop Masquers, were trained and made available for programs at any time or place where entertainment was in demand. Their popularity aided the cause of dramatics generally.

A large group, mostly older people, known as the Drama Shop Play Readers, met twice a month. At each meeting there was a review of a current play, a reading rehearsal, a question box, and a discussion of some phase of dramatic work.

Because of her interest in children and her former experience in Junior Chautauqua, Mrs. Trissel in 1928 organized the first Rural School One-act Play Tournament. She went first with her plan to the county superintendent, who was interested but skeptical. Some of the best material from various schools was offered, but Mrs. Trissel preferred to work with the pupils of only one rural school. So eight children: the entire enrolment of one school, were brought to Mrs. Trissel and rehearsals started. The results amazed the teachers who witnessed the play.

The following February the first county drama tournament was held in Mason City. Only seven schools entered, but the idea flourished, and in 1929 forty-three schools entered plays in the tournament. This meant holding preliminary contests, so the county was divided into four districts. Two schools from each district were selected for the finals. In 1930 sixty-three schools entered, and when the finals were held the auditorium of the high school was packed from the time the first play started at nine o'clock in the morning until the last was finished late in the afternoon. The tournament was a delight to the merchants of Mason City, who said that not even the circus brought as many people to town.

The enthusiasm spread far beyond the little group of children at school. Whole neighborhoods now get together to help the teacher and the children. One year a group of fathers went to the Mason City library to read up on Colonial times and manners before making stage settings for their children's historical play. And so Mrs. Trissel has laid the foundations for community drama in the rural districts of Iowa.

The tournament brought instant and countless inquiries from county superintendents in all parts of the United States. Mrs. Trissel has received letters from Tampa, Florida; Tacoma, Washington; Dallas, Texas; and Portland, Maine, on the same day. Now, not only have these tournaments been instituted in nearly every state, but they have led to the introduction of one-act play contests in both public schools and high schools of hundreds of towns and cities.

The result of this cannot, of course, be told today. But in twenty years, when these boys and girls have grown to maturity, they should step into the Community Theatres of America and, theatre-minded, carry on the movement already so gloriously started. Mrs. Ina K. Trissel deserves an honored place among the Community Theatre pioneers of this country.

During 1936 there was a gradual disintegration of the Drama Shop Players, and save for the yearly play presented by the Drama Department of the Woman's Club, there was a lull in things dramatic in Mason City. But during the early fall of 1937 there was a renewal of interest, and in November the Mason City Little Theatre was organized with a membership at the start of about five hundred. Dues were $1.00 a year, and membership tickets admitted the holder to three productions and any classes that were being held.

At present they are making plans for a permanent home, a professional director, and all the other luxuries of a flourishing Community Theatre group.

Charles L. Groman, president, says of these players: "We aim to create social centers where not only the workers but the audience may meet on a common level with a resulting enrichment of everyday life and experience."

The prospects are very bright for one of the outstanding Community Theatres in the country in Mason City. Hats off to Mrs. Trissel.

Omaha, Nebraska.   Henry Fonda—Omaha's Quota to Hollywood.

At the end of a long history of the Omaha Playhouse, a casual sentence leapt out and caught our interest: ". . . there is ample room for additions or even an additional building." This sentence has been the keynote of the policy of the Omaha Community Playhouse since 1924; for in the fall of that year a group of citizens interested in the theatre met to discuss the possible organization of a Community Theatre. The result, a non-profit corporation, was registered under the Nebraska laws. Stock at $10 a share was sold to about ninety persons and a temporary Board of Directors was elected to serve until the first annual meeting, to be held in January of 1925.

As a starting gun in their campaign, to interest the general public in the possibilities of a local theatre, a vaudeville performance was given in a high school auditorium in February, 1925. The reaction to this night's entertainment was so favorable that a permanent director was sought, and Gregory Foley, of Evanston, Illinois, was employed. His first production was "The Enchanted Cottage," all parts being taken by Omaha amateurs, all sets and production work being done by volunteers. Mr. Foley was engaged for the following season of eight plays, and five hundred season tickets at $5.00 each were sold—the single ticket sales of $1.00 each at the box office helped to make the total of the season's income equal $7000, which miraculously was the budget expenditure to a penny.

The Omaha Playhouse found that extra-curricular activities such as workshop performances, public rehearsals, and cabaret dinner dances did a great deal to arouse interest and satisfy those who wished to enter into group participation in theatre craft. This second season was carried on in cooperation with the Omaha Drama League, which was then in its twelfth year of bringing outstanding productions of the professional theatre to Omaha. A combination season ticket was offered which admitted a person to eight Playhouse productions and also to the Drama League season. Among the highlights of that second year was Henry Fonda's performance in "Merton of the Movies," his initial appearance on any stage and in a title role which was almost symbolic of his future career.

The second production that season, "Anna Christie," was attended by the late Otto H. Kahn. That evening was an exciting experience for all members of the cast, as there was not one who did not respect and hanker for the approbation of this prince of the arts.

Foley's third season with the Playhouse saw one thousand thirty-five season tickets and twenty-eight hundred single admissions sold. However, in the middle of the season the need for a new place to play resulted in a debt of $2600, which considerably discouraged the more practical and business-minded members of the Board. Undaunted, the Board of Trustees worried and worked all summer, and in September of the following year they were able to purchase a desirable piece of ground in a residential neighborhood by the grace of a $15,000 second mortgage, secured through the kindness of an interested friend of the Playhouse, Mrs. George A. Joslyn. The Play-house then was able to secure a first mortgage of $12,000 from a local build-ing and loan association, with which money they erected a playhouse and fully equipped it: sets, curtain, switchboard, and all. At this time the exist-ing stock corporation, under which the Playhouse had been operated, was liquidated. A new non-profit corporation was organized to take its place along with a property holding corporation. These organizations were held by the district court to be exempt from local and state taxes, and the federal government exempts them from all federal taxes, the brief being held that the Playhouse serves as an educational and cultural function to the com-munity. This item should be called to the attention of any Community Theatre in the United States that has been paying taxes, either local or fed-eral, because they are entitled to exemption.

The theatre building in Omaha is a structure of brick and stucco with a fireproof roof, a stage fifty by twenty-five feet, adequate dressing and make-up rooms, reasonably large property rooms, offices, etc. The seating capacity is two hundred and fifty-two, and the entire structure is set on one side of a large piece of property, a hundred and eleven by two hundred and fourteen feet, which, as we have mentioned before, will allow for the addition of any construction program the Playhouse undertakes in the future.

The fourth season was opened in the new building with Bernard Szold as director. The combination of a new building and a new director raised the number of season tickets to eleven hundred and eighteen, and single ad-missions to four thousand, three hundred and ninety-three. Mr. Szold re-mained in Omaha as the director for seven seasons, during which time season ticket holders increased to sixteen hundred and twenty-eight, along with good cash box-office receipts for every play. The Omaha Playhouse attracted na-tional attention when it gave a world premiere of "Brigham Young," and productions of "They Knew What They Wanted," "Elizabeth the Queen," and "The Devil Passes" served to enhance their prestige and spread the word of the great surge of theatrical activity that was taking place in Omaha.

In September of 1935, Ted Steinmetz succeeded Mr. Szold, who became the director in New Orleans. At this time, the Playhouse discontinued the sale of single tickets, restricting audiences to season ticket holders, out-of-town guests, and single tickets (not over two each) purchased by cast members only. This arrangement assured revenue at the beginning of each season and justifiably removed the constant worry about weather, epidemics, and possible choice of play.

Steinmetz finished the season of 1938 with the announcement that he was to move on to the Indianapolis Civic Theatre and that Gordon Griffin would take his place in Omaha.

The original Board of Trustees has been increased gradually from nine members to twenty-one as the interest in the Playhouse has spread to various civic groups throughout the city. The Board meets once a month regularly, and on call. An executive committee, composed of the four officers and one additional Board member, meets on call and is empowered to act for the Board on all matters when it is not convenient nor practical for calling together a large body.

The Omaha Playhouse estimates that it can operate satisfactorily on fifteen hundred season tickets. To secure the balance needed, a rather strenuous campaign is carried on each fall with subscription teams captained by each of the Board members. Team members receive a free season ticket for each ten season tickets sold. This plan is always successful when a campaign chairman of ability can be found to undertake this very tough job. Evidently the Omaha Playhouse has been consistently successful in finding the right man for this thankless job.

The Playhouse notes that plays are rehearsed three to four weeks and presented six nights. Occasionally repeat performances are necessary when a show is extremely successful. Surprising and worth noting is the tradition that no Board member is ever permitted to play during his incumbency and seldom does a person appear on the stage more than once a season.

The Omaha Playhouse has contributed its quota to the professional stage without making any definite effort toward giving training with that ultimate goal in view. The list includes Henry Fonda, Damien O'Flynn, Hudson Shotwell, Dorothy Maguire, and Louise Fitch.

Half way between Chicago and Los Angeles lies the Omaha Community Playhouse, with a theatrical season as active as that of either of these two cities.

Peoria, Illinois. Twenty Years of Play Production Culminates in an Engine House.

In May, 1919, the suggestion of a Community Theatre in Peoria came from Charles Gouvier of Jacksonville, Illinois, a college friend of George Barrette, on the editorial staff of the *Peoria Journal*. They had acted in plays while at Illinois College and later in stock company productions. And now, away from the theatre, both felt something should be done about it.

Mr. Barrette got in touch with a number of interested people in Peoria. The idea appealed to many, some of whom had been active in the Peoria Women's Club and other dramatic organizations. Among these people was William Hawley Smith, well-known author and lecturer. A meeting was called for early in June. It was held on Mr. Smith's beautiful lawn and was attended by about seventy-five. Enthusiasm was high. Organization proceeded immediately.

From the beginning it was determined that the Peoria Players should be a democratic group. It was felt that a limited clique or society club Little Theatre would have trouble surviving. Later, but in time, it was also realized that many groups fail through offering too much "highbrow" drama or financial ineptitude. Fortunately the Peoria Players have avoided these pitfalls.

When the Players started there were not many similar groups in the country, and although the Peorians were anxious to learn how others were proceeding, it was almost impossible to get information. Letters brought no replies. They went on alone up to the time they prepared to build their own theatre. "We didn't get nothing from nobody" is their comment when questioned as to procedure.

The opening play was given in October, 1919. Originally, only one-act plays were produced, in what they now consider a very crude manner, and at slight expense. The Peoria Women's Club Auditorium, seating over four hundred, but with shallow slanting floored stage and very simple much-used scenery, was rented to them for a nominal fee. Several productions were attempted unsuccessfully, in downtown commercial theatres, bringing a realization that Community Theatre ideals are apt to be submerged in such endeavors.

Also they realized that theatre ownership was essential if they were to become a permanent institution. For years this ownership was but a hope of the faithful and a jest of the others. But finally, in 1928, it was decided, despite considerable opposition from doubters and their wives, to raise funds for a building.

They started with over $2000 earned on their own productions. The first attempt to raise funds fell short; they planned and conducted a second campaign in 1930 under the direction of an out-of-town professional which failed to realize on his roseate promises. A bank closing tied up funds, plans submitted were impossibly extravagant; delay followed delay. But steadfast purpose blew away such clouds; costs of building dropped; plans were simplified and improved, and in the fall of 1932 the theatre was built.

Four hundred and fifty-four people or concerns contributed gifts ranging from fifty cents to $5000. Gifts of $500 or more were rewarded with life memberships. The theatre opened formally in April, 1933.

Remodeled from an engine house abandoned by the city, fifty-one by one hundred feet, two stories high, only the front and side walls were used. A stage twenty-five by fifty-one feet, with a scene dock thirteen by thirty-five feet and a workshop, ample dressing and make-up rooms, clubrooms, kitchen, costume and property rooms for men and women, and an office, together with an auditorium seating three hundred and fifty-six comprise the interior. The dressing rooms, three for men and three for women, are in the basement, as is the make-up room, which is large enough for rehearsals. The scene dock is connected with the stage by a wide door and affords additional depth if needed. The property is valued at $55,000, with an indebtedness of $2300, which is being reduced yearly. Each of the nineteen seasons of operation has ended with a favorable bank balance.

The deed from the city provides that the property, if not sold for the benefit of the subscribers (a remote possibility) should the Peoria Players cease to operate, shall revert to the city. The Players are not obligated to pay interest or dividends or repay principal to the subscribers.

Two hundred members paid $3.00 annual dues the first year. During the 1937-38 season there were fourteen hundred and fifty members paying $5.00 for senior and $3.00 for junior membership. The junior department has a membership of about three hundred, mostly college and high school students under twenty-two years of age. It has a separate director who is responsible for one play each season. This involves a large number of young people with acting talent and management ability who, in time, will become the mainstays of the Peoria Players. A well-organized membership campaign is conducted each year.

When membership was smaller, opening and closing season dinners were held. These were very enjoyable and profitable and are now being resumed. To buy additional equipment and reduce indebtedness, the Peoria Players for the past two years have given a "grand ball"; in 1938 it netted $667.

There were three play directors the first season. In 1937-38 they presented eight plays with eight directors serving without pay. This development of a number of competent directors has been the outstanding work of the Players, contributing much to both financial and artistic success.

"There are several good reasons why our plan of having many directors is a good one," says William Wittick. "Very seldom has one director had charge of more than one production a season. Of course, all directors are not equally capable. Many minds, many ideas, many plans. With different directors more acting and production talent is developed and used. No burden is imposed on any one. The tendency of only one director is to use the same competent people continually."

In the early days they presented plays after three weeks' work. Now, six weeks' work goes into a play and more finished productions result. Each play is presented four or five times, depending upon circumstances. With an official board of thirteen meeting monthly, the affairs of the Players are conducted in business-like fashion.

Each season more than two hundred members have some part in the activities of the Peoria Players. Frequently more than one hundred actors appear in the plays in a season.

During their nineteen years of existence more than a hundred and fifty plays have been presented, running the whole gamut of taste. They have found that audiences become more exacting as the quality of productions rises, and with their wealth of experienced actors they are able to approach, if not excel, the best professional work.

The Peoria Players have done some work in playwriting but, William Wittick says, "Far too little. This is a problem that most theatres face. They must originate if they would justify their existence."

So here is a Community Theatre where the citizens put their shoulder to the wheel, built their own theatre, and are now entering the twentieth year of successful play production!

Quincy, Illinois. Interested in Original Plays.

To the people of Quincy undoubtedly the history of their Community Little Theatre is as glamorous and involved as some of the plots of their successfully staged plays. Also to an insider the fact that their theatre began a year before the crash and valiantly outwitted all villains such as Old Man Depression and his bad companions Lack of Funds and Lowered Membership is not so important as the problems of the coming season. But to the outsider the Quincy Community Little Theatre is the essence of a well-ordered typical Community Theatre.

The Community Little Theatre actually was christened in November, 1928. Since the first year, which had only three productions, the players have attempted to give not less than four major plays and an extensive studio program each season. From the first the Board of Directors realized that Quincy could afford and should have the benefit of professional directors. Albert Morrison, Henry B. House, Charles T. Dazey, Edward Avison, Allen York, and William Vance have been among the professionals who have guided Community Little Theatre activities.

During the first ten years of the theatre's life more than forty-three major productions were given with an average cast of twelve and with approximately twenty-four technicians for each production. It is clear from these figures how many people have received benefit from participation in this enterprise. The Little Theatre is proud of the fact that from time to time it has given its membership opportunity to work in experimental groups for the workshop, classes in playwriting, make-up, and other phases of production.

In recent years the membership has totaled about four hundred and twenty season subscriptions a year, with approximately one hundred and fifty individual tickets sold from time to time.

Among the forty-some plays given in the past years, Mr. Dazey's famous "In Old Kentucky" stands out. This play was very cleverly staged in Baldwin Park with an actual horse race run around the track as a climax. Of such widespread interest was this event that all metropolitan newspapers in Illinois sent reporters, and practically the entire countryside witnessed the production.

The Little Theatre has sponsored many card parties, cabarets, and for the last few years has been giving a Little Theatre Ball on New Year's Eve which has become an established part of the social life of Quincy.

The organization is also responsible for bringing "Green Pastures" to Quincy in December, 1934, and at one time the Little Theatre sponsored a children's theatre.

The Little Theatre maintains headquarters in a workshop which was formerly an old Baptist Church. The building has become, through tireless effort on the part of active members, an attractive setting with a workable plant. The second floor auditorium is cleverly furnished and equipped, while underneath there are office rooms, dressing rooms, etc., which are the scenes of much activity the greater part of the year. It is understood, however, that the main stage productions are given at the Empire Theatre in downtown Quincy.

Of interest to any prospective playwright is the fact that the Quincy Community Little Theatre would welcome an opportunity to read new manuscripts that would be suitable for production in their city, and it is interesting to note that they have spent approximately $4000 on royalties in the past ten years. If every town the size of Quincy contributed $4000 to American playwrights every ten years, it would be a much more lucrative profession than it is at present. Therefore, any playwright with a new script that needs to be tested and is actually worth being done should take advantage of this generous proposal from the Quincy Community Little Theatre.

St. Louis, Missouri. Combine Amateur and Professional Theatres.

The Little Theatre of St. Louis, as now organized, started its twelfth consecutive season in the fall of 1938. However, it grew out of two organizations: the Players, which still produces several plays each season, and the Artists' Guild, a group of painters, writers, musicians, sculptors, and others interested in the arts, who have been together for more than fifty years. Clark McAdams, an editor of the *St. Louis Post-Dispatch* and an influential patron of the arts, was the leading spirit in making the development of the Little Theatre possible. He was active in both the Players and the Artists' Guild. Theirs is a distinguished heritage. During the early years Irving Pichel, Stark Young, Melville Burke, Maurice Browne, David Carb, and Sam Hume severally guided the destinies of the local amateur theatre and established the high standards which have been maintained.

The present home of the Little Theatre of St. Louis is a building owned by the Artists' Guild. When the theatre in this building was erected no one dreamed that it would be such a center of activity. The theatre has grown in every way and now suffers seriously in the overcrowded building. The stage is too small and has no wing space. The auditorium, seating two hundred seventy-six, is too small and much of it has a flat floor. Plays must run for two weeks to meet the public demand. And while so long a run gives actors and staff excellent experience, it is too much of a grind for those who have jobs to keep and other social and family obligations. The attitude of the workers is professional; they accept the long grind and the lack of proper facilities, and turn out production after production of professional calibre. But many good actors cannot work at the theatre because they cannot give the time: almost three weeks of dress rehearsals and performances after the usual four weeks of rehearsal.

The theatre has outgrown its present plant because many complex auxiliary and subsidiary activities have grown up in and about it.

Each year five plays are presented for two weeks each, in the regular subscription season. One and sometimes two "extra" plays are presented for a week.

The Cryptic Club, an organization of men and women who have worked at the theatre, is dedicated to serve the theatre and foster its welfare. In recent years the laboratory has been its outstanding enterprise. Each year three or four plays are presented by the laboratory theatre, directed by volun-

teer workers. They are usually experimental and each plays two performances, providing a chance for new actors to be seen, for other actors to gain
additional experience, and opportunities for young directors.

For several years classes in theatre arts have been offered by members of
the staff, and the demands for these classes have grown apace. Last year
there were more than a hundred enrolled in classes in acting, voice and diction, ballet and design. In the first ten days of the season two hundred
seventy-four people applied for class work. To help meet the demand for
acting training, a series of rehearsal groups, inspired by the American Theatre
Council, is being formed to rehearse under volunteer directors and give occasional informal demonstration performances for invited audiences.

A woman's committee, with a membership of more than three hundred,
was formed last year to study the Little Theatre and its work and will become
increasingly active in the organization.

The theatre operates on an annual budget of $10,000 and, even in the
darkest days of the depression, succeeded in staying out of debt. Salaries,
royalties, and rent are the principal items of expense.

Subscriptions provide the chief source of income. Each fall a spectacular
subscription campaign occurs. Originally managed by a professional, it has
now come under the direction of Mildred Carpenter, the theatre's press representative. Under her leadership two hundred workers annually sell between fifteen hundred and two thousand subscriptions. The campaign is a
thrilling project for the workers: a series of meetings at which reports and
plans are made and strategies discussed in an air of tense excitement. Dozens
of prizes are given to the most successful workers; everyone selling a dozen
season tickets gets a pair for himself. Zeal for prizes combines with devotion to the theatre.

Because of the theatre's heritage and standing in private organizations,
the general ticket-buying public has never been approached, and only one
tenth of the audience each year buys tickets at the box office for individual
plays. This year the Cryptic Club is creating a special promotion department to spread a knowledge of the theatre and of its plays to a greater
public. About ten thousand people in St. Louis know intimately about the
work of the theatre and support it more or less regularly. But Greater St.
Louis has a population of nearly a million and the theatre has come to
realize that many thousands more of the population need and want what the
theatre has to offer.

Behind all these activities is the Board of Directors: a strong, wise, conservative, forceful group which never interferes with the actual working of
the theatre. Several members of this board, headed by William G. B. Carson,
have served since the theatre was started. They have seen it through the

rigors of depression and have motivated quietly the high standards which characterize the activities.

Because good training in theatrical work is not available elsewhere in the city, nor within a radius of several hundred miles, and because the demand for that training is so great, the Little Theatre of St. Louis must inevitably develop a much more extensive educational program. This is felt to be a civic responsibility which will also demonstrate to the city the civic value of the theatre. Even now it serves as an answer to the social and cultural problems of hundreds of workers.

It is important to the theatre and to the city that these functions be expanded. The theatre needs a new building to house adequately its productions, its classes, and its services as a community center. A building campaign, started in 1938, appealed for contributions of a dime or thousands of dollars.

Frederick Cowley was the first director of the Little Theatre and under his leadership much of the present system was initiated. In his first season a policy of giving a carefully planned series of plays originated; beginnings were made at building up a list of subscribers for this annual series; workman-like methods and professional standards were established.

After four seasons Frederick Cowley died and his place was taken by Thomas Wood Stevens. Mr. Stevens was also the leader in another theatrical enterprise in St. Louis: The Garden Theatre, an outdoor Shakespearean theatre which still is fondly remembered. As a scholar, a gentleman, an inspiring idealist, and a brilliant director he is still idolized in St. Louis.

Neil Caldwell was Mr. Stevens' assistant. For a time he directed the theatre and the plays, and in the autumn of 1932 he did a production of Georg Kaiser's "Gas" in a spectacularly experimental style which is considered one of the outstanding accomplishments of the playhouse. A few weeks after this production Mr. Caldwell died suddenly. His loss, not only to St. Louis but to the theatre at large, is still deeply mourned there.

In the fall of 1933 F. Cowles Strickland became the director. He had been eminently successful as director of the Berkshire Playhouse in Stockbridge, Massachusetts, and had directed on Broadway. He brought to the theatre a wise, professional point of view and was able to provide its workers with knowledge, high standards, and wide contacts.

During a four years' regime as director, which he combined with summer directing of the Berkshire Playhouse, he took Mary Wickes, now an established Broadway comedienne, from the Little Theatre of St. Louis to Stockbridge for her first professional experience.

Harold Bassage succeeded Mr. Strickland in the fall of 1937. Mr. Bassage likewise had had professional experience on Broadway and in summer stock. He had also taught drama for seven years in schools and colleges, and came to St. Louis after three years as director of Bard Theatre and head of the drama department of Bard College, where he had established and developed the policy of trying out new plays with casts made up partly of Broadway actors.

During Mr. Stevens' and Mr. Caldwell's regime, Gordon Carter, resident of St. Louis, became designer and technical director of the Little Theatre. He still serves in those capacities, although by reason of his increased scope his title has been expanded to associate director. He has been a designer in summer stock and the Berkshire Playhouse and in Colorado, and also with the Federal Theatre in Chicago.

Thus, through its leaders and the calibre of the work they have done and inspired in others, the Little Theatre is gradually melting the icy barrier which has stood between the amateur and professional theatres.

Sandusky, Ohio. The Harlequins.

In 1938 the Harlequins of Sandusky, Ohio, celebrated their tenth anniversary with a revival of their first production, "Outward Bound." This play, which had been eminently successful and directly responsible for the birth of the Harlequins, was originally produced in a high school auditorium. Since that time, however, the Harlequins have occupied several different homes until now they are lodged in Sidley Memorial Hall, which is an adequate, if not completely ideal, home for the players.

The Harlequins have had the usual hectic times forming the background and backbone of their Community Theatre. They started off in high hopes before the depression and were able to weather the most bitter effects of adversity and difficulty during the past few years. They now seem to be on their feet and will be going places as soon as they can overcome their foremost problem, securing a permanent home.

Donald Wonders in the tenth anniversary program sums up efficiently the entire background and hopes for the future of the Harlequins:

"Ten years! Calvary Parish House, winding stairs, bad ventilation, queer but attractive mural decorations on the walls, folding chairs borrowed from the local undertakers to sit upon, uncertainty in the air as to whether the curtain would go up straight or crooked—all these things made up the atmosphere of the opening nights of the first production of the Harlequins. The hard work, the planning, the trying to fit, and the failures which had to be overcome are the elements which the people who bought the first tickets and memberships will never know.

"This was the beginning of a venture of faith of the original members of the Harlequins that there was a place for a Community Theatre in Sandusky. That this venture of faith was well founded, a glance at the past ten years will amply prove. From the very first meeting enthusiasm has been manifest. People have come and people have gone, which has caused the membership to change rapidly at all times, but the same fine spirit has always been in evidence. During all these years there has been a faithful handful of people who have been in the membership from the very beginning. To these must go the credit of keeping the lamp burning and the ideals high. Too much cannot be said of the sacrifice and the hard work which this little group has poured into the work. Midnight oil has burned often that scenery could be completed and rough places be ironed out of parts so that the production could go on as nearly perfect as possible.

"The next ten years will not contain the elements of the first ten years, for better equipment has been obtained and work is easier. Experience alone is a great asset. New members coming into the organization will find standards already set to which they can aspire. Perhaps the greatest boon to this second decade's record would be the securing of a permanent home for the Harlequins. The establishing of a real Little Theatre in Sandusky will come in the acquirement of a building which will afford a proper working place for the members. The difficulties which have had to be overcome, because there was no place in which to work, have been greater than most people have imagined. The making and painting of scenery in a room with insufficient height and with no heat in the winter time has demanded a heroism which is not demonstrated in these modern days when comfort is held at such a premium. The lack of a place in which to hold rehearsals has had to be met by meeting in one place tonight and in another place tomorrow night. Homes have been disorganized, office furniture has been made to serve as living room simply because any place with a little space and proper heating facilities had to do.

"No greater boon could come to the Harlequins than a place in which to do their work. This is the opportunity of the next ten years.

"Let our thanks go out to the faithful membership of the Harlequins for the fine work they have done, and let our thanks go out to a fine public which has responded to the efforts of Sandusky's Little Theatre. These are the elements which must go into any effort for civic betterment, and the record of the Harlequins and people of our city in their response shows that this community is on the forward march."

Shaker Heights, Ohio.   All Ages Participate—Nineteen to Seventy.

To help raise money for the building of a church—that's the way the Shaker Players of Shaker Heights started. In the spring of 1919, when only the chapel of the newly organized Plymouth Church had been partly constructed, Mrs. William S. Cochran inspired a group of young people who called themselves "The Plymouth Players" to present a play which netted $90. This was turned into the building fund.

But the success of the venture led to the organization in 1920 of the Shaker Village Players with eleven members, who met in the homes. In 1921 a club of thirty-three members began meeting regularly in the parlors of the then completed Plymouth Church.

But the audiences grew more rapidly than the membership, and when they gave their first production in the auditorium of the high school, which seated about seven hundred fifty, a packed house greeted them.

Since that time the Shaker Players have missed but one season in producing three, sometimes four, public performances each season, and for many years have met once a month for an evening of short plays, readings, study, or social affairs.   All meetings are now held in the Shaker Heights public schools.

The group incorporated under the laws of the State of Ohio in 1934 and is now managed by a Board of nine trustees, three elected each year, who in turn elect their own officers.

Membership has remained small, limited in general to active participants, although they have associate members and patrons.   There was a period when membership was limited to one hundred, but they found that more members were needed for wider choice in casting.   But it has never exceeded a hundred and fifty.

The single tickets are seventy-five cents or a book of six for $3.00, good for any show during the season.   Each single member buys five books of tickets at $3.00 each.   However, he may sell all these tickets and get back all he paid for the books.   Each married couple buys eight books for $24 at $3.00 each.   So, as in Ashland, Kentucky, matrimony is encouraged in Shaker Heights.

Associate members pay $5.00 a year and do not participate, but may attend plays free.   Patrons pay $10.00 and may bring six friends to any or all shows.

"Incidentally," writes Alice Bruce, secretary of this group, "we have more women members than men, and more married couples than single people. We range in age from nineteen to seventy. We've had half a dozen inter-mural romances and have worked up an enviable reputation on that score."

Their greatest activity, of course, centers on the public performances. They have had Barclay Leathem and Vandine Miles of the Drama Department of Western Reserve for directors in the past five years. They have also given benefit performances for the Parent-Teachers Association of Shaker Heights, scholarships, and one-act plays for the Community Fund Campaign, readings for the society of the blind, plays at the McGregor Home for the Aged, and one summer two guest performances at the summer theatre on Lake Erie.

In the past they have had an active study group which met for play readings, study of playwrights and their works, and discussion of plays for presentation. That group developed into the play reading committee, which select plays for public performances with the approval of the Board.

At one time they had a playwriting group which produced several original scripts. Outstanding was "Dust," by John French Wilson, poet, and Professor of Poetry at Cleveland College.

Their greatest problem is utilizing available talent. An individual may be an actress of ability and experience in Shaker Heights, but if the plays scheduled provide no role for her, and she does not function well on props or make-up, she feels thwarted. Yet because they don't cater much to "problem children" nor to would-be temperamental players, they have a remarkably cooperative, wholesome, capable group of players, good sports all, willing to give time and energy.

"Of course," says Miss Bruce, "we have to work late every night the last weeks before the show goes on, but I don't know if that's the actor's problem so much as it is the long-suffering family's problem. Some wives complain of being theatrical widows. We try to put them on costumes or props. Or some husbands complain of canned meals and neglected children. We try to put those husbands on the stage crew. There's always someone in the cast who can't cut class in his evening course, or someone who has to go out of town on business the night of dress rehearsal, and sometimes the 'sitter' doesn't come to stay with the baby. In one play a girl broke an ankle the last week, so the director pinch-hit—did a female impersonation—and the show went on!"

Theoretically, the players are residents of Shaker Heights, a suburb of Cleveland, but actually a third of them live in Cleveland Heights, East Cleveland, or Cleveland, which means great distances to cover coming to rehearsals.

At least six members have gone to the Cleveland Playhouse, and one, David Wayne, toured with the Tatterman Marionettes, played Shakespearean roles at the Globe Theatre at the Great Lakes Exposition in Cleveland, and is now headed for Broadway by the summer theatre route.

"We hope eventually," reports Miss Bruce, "to have our own theatre home—a community affair—Lincolnesque (of, for, and by the community)— non-professional, and recreational. We believe people of Shaker Heights are interested in seeing good shows in their own community instead of trekking to the city, with its traffic and parking problems.

"My personal opinion is that participating in a group is good for any individual and will make his life a lot more interesting. Home, garden, and golf are all very well, but they don't give you that feeling of joining in and sharing a part in the community life that a Community Theatre does."

They started the 1938-39 season with all bills paid, and $400 in the bank!

Sheboygan, Wisconsin. Recreation Department and Board of Education Cooperate.

Four years ago membership dues in the Sheboygan Community Players was $1.00 a year. Last season they raised this to $1.50.

This group of players is operated by the Recreation Department of Sheboygan under the auspices of the Board of Education. It has no patron list, and no donations of money have ever been received.

The force which successfully moves the Players is the enthusiasm of the director of recreation, Harry J. Emigh, superintendent of schools of Sheboygan, F. W. Hilgendorf, the dramatic director, and the dramatic executive committee combined with the loyal members of the organization.

The city of Sheboygan has always been intensely interested in amateur theatricals, having many organizations and clubs producing plays. Harry J. Emigh, aware of the situation, appointed an executive committee to conduct a city-wide drama tournament. In selecting this committee it was necessary to have a group of representative people. So he appointed the superintendent of schools, two members of the school board, the president of the American Association of University Women, the president of the Fireside Players, chairman of the drama committee of the Woman's Club, a prominent director of a Catholic drama group, a Methodist leader of play production, the city editor of the local newspaper and a banker, to give the committee balance.

The tournament was so successful that the committee called in Professor Cloak of Lawrence College at Appleton to give a course of lectures on "The Directing of Amateur Plays." This course helped to improve the staging and acting in the one-act plays. The public faithfully attended the lectures and a strong desire sprang up for a Community Theatre, a center for productions.

The great problem was how to organize. There was a small sum of money obtained from the tournaments, but a professional director was needed and overhead expenses had to be taken into account. Luckily Mr. Hulton, at that time superintendent of schools, was deeply interested and took the matter up with the director of recreation. An understanding was reached by the Board of Education and the Recreation Department on a plan, which was adopted.

A director was hired by the school board for part time teaching in the high school and part time direction of plays for the Community Theatre. The major portion of his salary was to be paid by the Board of Education, the balance from the funds of the players. The Board of Education also gave the use of rooms in the schools for rehearsals, tryouts, building of scenery and storing of properties and costumes. The auditoriums were open for lectures, monthly theatre nights, workshop nights, and for staging major productions. F. W. Hilgendorf was engaged as director of this adventurous project.

He confesses that in all his experience he has never had such an enthusiastic group of players. The members are sincere and willing to work hard.

He started by organizing a program for the entire year and issued it in the form of pamphlets. These were sent to a thousand citizens who had once belonged to a Civic Music Organization, and to all the drama groups which were at that time organized.

But he was sadly disappointed at the first monthly theatre night when an audience of only thirty-five attended. However, a free performance filled the auditorium and resulted in a membership of over one hundred.

At the end of the first year there were two hundred eighty-three members. The second year they reached six hundred thirty. The third year they almost made their goal of one thousand, and in 1937 the goal was reached!

About two hundred and fifty of these people express a desire to participate actively in the productions; the rest are content to be audience.

The various phases of theatre work operate as follows: for the major productions the director is in absolute power, having direct supervision over all working committees; a committee of three, the Director of Recreation, the president of the Players and one appointed by the Recreation Board works directly with the director, who is chairman of the committee and directs all procedures. There is no casting committee; the director is the sole judge, just as he has final say in the selection of plays approved by the play reading committee. Public tryouts are held, but private tryouts also are granted by appointment. Rehearsals are private unless the director calls in an audience. There are no repeats in casts the same year unless the director finds it absolutely necessary.

Then there are monthly Theatre Nights. These consist of programs of three one-act plays, which are directed by members with the professional director in the advisory capacity. A social evening follows these plays.

They give their plays at the new senior high school auditorium, which has an elaborate and efficient stage apparatus. This stage was built for "theatre" not for commencement purposes only as are so many auditoriums in school buildings. Three productions are given to the public each season.

A library of books on drama and the theatre is available in the office of the Recreation Department to members who need material for the work they are doing in connection with the Community Players.

"Come and experiment with us," they say in Sheboygan. "We are creating and building our own theatre!"

Springfield, Ohio. Born in the Depression.

Of all the years in which to start a civic enterprise, particularly one often considered as much a luxury as the theatre, 1930 was certainly the low point. However, records show that the Springfield Civic Theatre was organized in 1930 for its first regular season.

In all fairness it should be pointed out that this was really a development of a group formerly called "The Folding Theatre Players," which, under the leadership of Miss Martha Johnson and Miss Jane Molanear, produced a great number of one-act plays for a period of over four years before the start of the real Springfield Civic Theatre. It was during the performance of "The Marriage Proposal" by Chekov that unusual talent was discovered in Franklin Raymond who had left his home in Springfield and, after several seasons of work in New York City, had returned in 1930 to be the first full time director of the new theatre.

An initial season began with plays that included "Icebound," the opening bill, and "The Royal Family." These two plays were presented at the local legitimate house and met with such instant approval that it was decided to conduct at once an extensive subscription campaign. As a result, nine hundred members were signed at a cost of $3.50 for six plays.

The policy of the theatre established at that time has not changed materially. No single admissions are sold and the ticket sale campaign ends on the first day of October, after which no tickets may be bought. This enables the Board of Directors to budget completely the production costs of the year and prevents any shift in the audience from play to play. It is a tribute to the quality of the productions that there have been, after the third year of the theatre's existence, no less than fourteen hundred members, and at one time there were more than eighteen hundred enrolled.

The right to act is granted any resident of Clark County whether a member of the theatre or not. This liberal and most important policy has been responsible for an unusually high quality of acting, for the director can choose his players freely. In Springfield the leading dowagers and the grocery clerk rub shoulders in the same cast. Not infrequently the judge's daughter drives the plumber home from rehearsal. It is in all senses of the word a democratic organization; if any one is more closely associated with the theatre than another, it is purely a matter of service. No one has ever given more than the cost of subscriptions to the maintenance of the Civic Theatre. A few by sheer force of loyal and continued service have identified themselves very closely with its history. Of these the patron saint is undoubtedly Mrs. Carl Fried who, since the beginning, has served in dozens of capacities: as president for a season, and at other times board member, costumer, play reader, back-stage worker, guide, philosopher and friend. The loyalty and help of Mrs. M. N. Sanders, the past president of the Theatre, also has been unwavering.

The Civic Theatre does not have its own building. For some time talk of campaigning for a theatre has been in the air, but the time does not seem right. Instead, the Board rents for a week at a time the auditorium and stage of the best equipped school of the city, where facilities have been improved so that multi-scened productions can be given with ease. The rehearsal rooms and office and scene studios are large and comfortable.

Truly the Civic Theatre is a meeting place for the cultural life of the city, offering an emotional and educational outlet to all classes. The theatre conducts a Players' Club in which experimental productions and, on occasions, original plays are produced. Forums on acting and related problems are conducted, and as many as possible are urged to participate in the actual productions of the year. Anybody who participates backstage or in a play automatically becomes a member of the Players' Club. The number of players last season was one hundred and two of whom several appeared more than once. About fifty different persons helped in gathering costumes, properties, or in preparing sets. Musicians, artists, artisans, and plain people helped variously and well.

Among its fifty-two productions to date, there have been of course landmarks. Most patrons remember an outstanding "Macbeth," in which Franklin Raymond, the director, played his farewell to Springfield friends before becoming director for the Federal Theatre in Ohio.

In 1936, Edmund Wilkes, with a background of training in Eva Le Gallienne's Civic Repertory Theatre and several years' experience of production and playing, was appointed director. By far the outstanding production of recent seasons was "Saint Joan," beautifully staged and unusually well played. Mr. Wilkes resigned in the summer of 1938 to devote himself entirely to the Phoenix Players, a professional company organized by him to play and tour in a standard classic repertory. Parker Mills, who formerly played with Walter Hampden and has been for some time a director for the Children's Theatre, was appointed director with Judge Harry G. Gram as president.

One of the principal problems besetting the Civic Theatre director is the choice of plays. A ballot is given to audiences each year with a suggested list of forty or more plays from which they are asked to select six for the coming season. But there is a dearth of plays suitable for a middle class audience. The traditional star vehicle is usually dangerous. The social document they do not wish to see more than once a season. There is constantly a part of the audience which does not like profanity or dirt, even when it is a vital part of the play. Great strides have been made in educating the audience to classic and poetic plays, but there is always an element which prefers the simple love story or the mystery play.

This difficulty of play choice is not voiced as a complaint, but is only a statement of one of the most difficult problems of a Community Theatre which desires to be truly "representative of all classes, leaning not too much to any taste or type, but serving the city to its utmost." This the Springfield Civic Theatre attempts to do.

Toledo, Ohio. A Church into a Theatre.

In the late spring of 1933 a small group of players with professional and college experience was called together by Fred S. Emmett for the purpose of reviving interest in the legitimate drama in the city of Toledo and environs. To that end the use of a stage and auditorium in the Collingwood Avenue Presbyterian Church was secured and in June of that year the group, under the direction of Gibson Barlow, with Mr. Emmett and Pomeroy Hubbard as technicians, produced one play, Ibsen's "A Doll's House."

The play was so well received that the group embarked on its first full theatrical season in the fall of 1933, operating on a limited budget supplied by some three hundred and fifty subscription members in the theatre. Six plays, revivals and modern dramas, were produced that season under the direction of Arthur P. Hyman, who brought Broadway experience to the group, which resulted in finished productions of high calibre.

The Lakeside, Ohio, Chautauqua engaged the group to repeat a performance of "The Three Wise Fools" during the summer of 1934 in their large auditorium seating some two thousand persons.

During that summer of 1934, the group incorporated "not-for-profit," for the purpose of "promoting and encouraging charitable and educational activities in the advancement of art, literature, and science by furnishing training in acting, stagecraft, and playwriting and by providing facilities for the expression of theatre arts in the community."

The second season of 1934–1935 found the same staff using the same auditorium for six plays. During the season Dorman E. Richardson joined the group as publicity and extension manager in charge of memberships which increased to about four hundred fifty for the season. In the summer of 1935, the Repertoire Players were re-engaged for an appearance at Lakeside, Ohio, where they presented a performance of "The Passing of the Third Floor Back."

In the late summer of 1935, a small abandoned church was secured and remodeled entirely by the members into their present cozy, usable theatre seating two hundred ninety-five persons. The level floor was elevated from the sixth row back to the eighteenth row. The group tore out the class rooms at the back of the large room and used the lumber to build the stage, work room in the basement and dressing rooms. They covered over the old baptistry and made a property room and emergency dressing room out of that space. The lounge, with a check room under the stairs, occupies the front of the basement and the box office is at the top of the stairs leading into the auditorium from the street level. Old movie house seats were secured and wine-colored seat covers were made to match the drapes and rug runners on the floors. Burns Mantle, upon seeing the theatre, said that it had an ideal layout for such a Community Theatre as they were offering the local playgoers.

With the new theatre leased, there came other new responsibilities: doing better productions, securing more season memberships, and placing an enlarged number of players and technicians. So it seemed wise to form an organization with the active members who put on the plays as its constituency, and in the fall of 1935 the Players and Craftsmen's Guild of the Repertoire Little Theatre was formed with Willard Mason as the first president. They took complete charge of all the productions, and financed a campaign for membership, which by this time had reached five hundred fifty. Joe E. Brown, Otto Kruger, and Robert Sinclair, all Toledoans, were elected honorary members of the Guild that year.

Not satisfied with starting a new theatre, a new guild and a new rise in the price of the season memberships, the group opened its third season with a new manuscript play giving a world premiere performance of "Life Begins Tomorrow," under the direction of the author, Dorothy Henry VanAuken, a native Toledoan who returned from New York to direct her brainchild. It was well received and played in the east during the following summer. Five other plays were produced. That summer the Lakeside Ohio Chautauqua asked repetition of two productions, "The Trap," and "Rip Van Winkle," in their large auditorium to capacity houses.

The fourth season opened with a manuscript translation from the German of "Old Heidelberg" by one of the members, Hubert Hendrikx, formerly of the Holland National Players. The summer production for Lakeside Chautauqua was "The Night of January 16th," directed by one of the Guild's members. "Fly Away Home" was by far the biggest hit of this season, and the membership for this year grew to eight hundred and fifty.

Again the Repertoire Players opened their new season with a world premiere performance of a manuscript play: "A Crown on the Hall Tree," written by Allen Saunders, dramatic critic of the *Toledo News-Bee* evening paper, and later published by Samuel French. A post season performance of the revival of "Fly Away Home" was taken to Detroit where a benefit show was done for the Society for the Blind in the beautiful Art Institute Theatre before an audience of nine hundred on June 30. "Mrs. Moonlight" was taken to Lakeside, Ohio, in the summer of 1938 as the second summer production.

The group encourages new players as well as professionals to take part in the plays and so far over sixty players have participated in the thirty-four major productions.

Amateurs are trained through one-act plays, lectures. And last fall dramatic classes for adults and children were conducted by the theatre ending in a public presentation of a program of one-act plays under the direction of Jane Clarken and Jean Wright.

During the first season a downtown storeroom was rented for a workshop where the sets were built and transported to the church auditorium about a mile and a half on rent-a-car trucks. The next season a storeroom with a large garage in the rear was rented only about six blocks away from the church and was used as a combination studio and workshop for the use of players and technicians.

Then the new theatre was remodeled from the old church, the workshop was arranged in the basement with a trap-door in the stage floor through which the flats are hoisted from the shop onto the stage for use in the productions; the paint room and property room adjoin the workshop making a rather complete layout for a non-professional theatre with an entirely voluntary staff.

The technical side of the theatre has been under the direction of Arthur P. Hyman assisted by Fred Emmett, Leon Patterson, Earl Beucler, Jacob Bryan, together with Pomeroy Hubbard, Robert Holding, Daniel Pease, and Ralph Leber, who have since left the group. The major portion of the direction of the productions has been carried by Fred S. Emmett and Arthur P. Hyman, both of whom have served without compensation during the past five seasons. Two other members of the theatre have directed: Paul Chapman did one summer production, and William Dunn, formerly with the Scottish National Players in Edinburgh, directed "The Witching Hour" and has served generously as the make-up master during all five seasons. Gibson Barlow, now a radio dramatic coach, directed the first play in 1933.

The Players and Craftsmen's Guild now numbers about one hundred twenty-five members who look after all the details of putting on the plays, keeping the house in readiness for rehearsals and public performances, and handling the finances through a finance committee serving jointly with such a committee from the holding company, The Toledo Repertoire Company, a non-profit corporation, chartered to hold real and personal property for the benefit of the theatre. Any profits go back into the equipment for the stage and building, there being no salaries or wages paid at the present time. However, a full time office secretary with her office at the theatre is contemplated for the coming seasons to develop memberships and handle the details of administration formerly carried by busy persons after working hours.

Western Springs, Illinois. A Little Theatre in a Suburb.

The Little Theatre of Western Springs has the drawbacks that hamper the work of any group in an exceedingly small community or in a large metropolitan area. Western Springs is so close to Chicago that its members are constantly tempted by diversions found in that metropolis. On the other hand, Western Springs is not large enough to support a Little Theatre except by the indefatigable earnestness of everyone connected with it.

Organized in 1929 by Mary Cattell and a dozen or so individuals who felt that there was a place in any small community for a group theatre, they began by canvassing the town for members—presenting a plan to produce one-act plays during the first season. A circular letter was sent to each family in Western Springs. The response was meagre but in some instances encouraging. Starting with a mere handful in 1929, the Little Theatre of Western Springs by 1938 had two hundred fifty-three double memberships, which means that in the eleven years the word had gradually spread throughout the city that here was a group that meant business, would spare no effort to improve its productions, and would steer a middle course between the "arty" play on the one hand, and the Pollyannish play on the other. Growth within the active membership has been slow but sure. Many husbands and wives are equally interested and many in the "Acting Group" are active as well in backstage activities. No one individual is assured of success as a leading star, but each has the satisfaction of contributing something of value to the group as a whole. So far as we know, Western Springs is the only Little Theatre group in the Chicago area that has enjoyed nine consecutive seasons of growth without discord or upheaval—without jealousies and conflicts.

For the past several years, the Little Theatre has rented the village club house for rehearsals and performances. An exceedingly inadequate and shallow stage has forced the technical crews of the Little Theatre to use every bit of initiative and effort to overcome its handicaps.

One interesting note about the Little Theatre of Western Springs is that they not only have a membership fee of $5.00 for the season ticket, but charge an extra fee of $8.00 for those who wish to participate as an active member of the Acting Group. This, in their words, "eliminates those who are not seriously interested in making a contribution to the group as a whole." Members of this Acting Group receive notice that they have been cast for a play, but do not know what role they are to take. This is learned at the first meeting when the play is read and discussed by the group. At the second meeting a round-table is held at which the play and the characters are thoroughly analyzed, each member of the cast having made a detailed study of the play and of the character he thinks he is best fitted to play. Each production is put into rehearsal for six weeks, three night sessions a week, until the last week, when it is held every night. This "group theatre" method is undoubtedly a result of Mary Cattell's study with Ouspenskaya, Daykarhanoba, and Ivan Lasareff.

Charles Grosse, asked what special problems the Little Theatre of Western Springs faced, replied: "(1) As our membership increases and becomes more 'cosmopolitan,' we have the problem of using new members while at the same time maintaining group unity and intimacy . . . in other words, the problem that confronts any growing organization as it begins to be successful. (2) The price we are willing to pay for our independence is that touched on above, namely that of inadequate staging and equipment, lack of financial and material resources, etc. We are gradually meeting some of these problems by buying a few pieces of more modern lighting equipment one season, building make-up rooms in the basement another season, making our own cyclorama a third season, and so on. While this process is painfully slow and prosaic, we have the satisfaction of knowing that what we achieve is ours wholly, and that in the process of achievement we have all gained experience and knowledge that is invaluable to us. (3) Inasmuch as Western Springs is a small suburb, few of our young people remain here very long. Many young college or post-college men and women, who have been with the Little Theatre for two or three seasons, and who have been a definite asset to the group, settle eventually in other parts of the country. The Little Theatre gains in stability and experience through its predominance of middle-aged members, but would benefit too were there a more stable membership among younger people."

Also Mr. Grosse was asked to define the credo of any typical community theatre and he answered for the Western Springs group as follows:

"(1) It should contribute to the American Theatre. This function ties in rather closely with the other two, in that the formation of public taste and the training of individuals in dramatic values are essential to any healthy growth of the theatre in this country.

"(2) It should bring productions of sound dramatic value to its community, constantly increasing its own standards of production and never losing sight of its obligation to the audience which, after all, is its life blood. In doing this it should strive to raise the cultural level of its audience, to cement the very real but often neglected relationship between actor and audience, producer and consumer.

"(3) It should be of service to the active members in its own group, serving to heighten their dramatic sensibilities, and to enrich their own lives and characters through an increased understanding of life."

And Other *Theatres of the* *Middle West*

Battle Creek, Michigan.

When this group was organized in 1930, they called themselves the Little Theatre. After three years of play production a split in the ranks took place. Half of the original membership continued as the Little Theatre, the other half, calling themselves the Pagan Players, presented only one-act plays. Then in 1934 the two groups made peace, and reuniting again renamed themselves "The Civic Theatre." And as the Civic Theatre they now present five plays each year with Robert Stevens as their director.

Bay Village, Ohio.

This Little Theatre was organized by the Women's Club of Bay Village. At first they gave plays for their own amusement, and the poor husbands didn't have a chance to act. At last the club was offered an old school house in which to present its plays, but it didn't have a stage. The husbands said they would build one but in return they must be allowed to act. The women consented (perhaps they didn't need much urging) and so the Bay Village Little Theatre enlarged its repertory. Encouraged by their success, and realizing that other groups similar to their own had been in existence in and around Cleveland, they decided in 1932 to hold a tournament. Nine groups responded. According to the announcement sent out by Mrs. Louis Ferster, the Chairman: "We want this tournament to foster warm friendships and fine cooperation among the Little Theatre groups and to be so pleasant an experience that we will all be looking forward to it next year." It was, and they did.

Birmingham, Michigan.

Elizabeth P. Hart says that in fifteen years of the existence of the Village Players they have given more than one hundred and ten short plays and more than twenty full-length dramas. The Village Players are a group operating strictly on dues and initiation fees with occasional guest fees for out-of-town visitors. They are interested in reading good one-act plays and as they have spent more than $2000 on royalties during their existence, the Players should definitely be considered a good market for any good playwrights.

Cedar Rapids, Iowa.

The Community Players of Cedar Rapids, organized in 1928, present five productions each season under the competent direction of Mervin Severance. They publish a most attractive little magazine entitled *Theatre News.* They also have a yearly prize play contest.

Chicago, Illinois.

In no community in America do young enterprising theatre groups spring up and die so quickly as in Chicago. So far as Community Theatres are concerned, Chicago has a reputation of having one of the toughest and hardest hearts of any metropolis. Among those who have broken their hearts and backs trying to establish a permanent theatre in Chicago have been Maurice Browne, Thomas Wood Stevens, Kenneth Sawyer Goodman, and many others. All of these men gave of their best time, artistic talents, and energy, and yet today, with the exception of Goodman Memorial Theatre, not a shred remains in Chicago of these gentlemen's work.

So it is with unusual interest that we note the rise of a young man now barely twenty-five, who in a short period of four years has created what looks like a permanent theatrical organization in Chicago.

Sherman Marks, the founder and director of the Chicago Mummers' Theatre, has through years of privation and sacrifice, developed this organization. The Mummers' Theatre is a non-professional theatre that has had exceptional luck in winning the respect and approbation of the newspaper critics of Chicago. Such judges of the theatre as Ashton Stevens, Charles Collins, Lloyd Lewis, and Claude Cassidy, have continually attended the Mummers' presentations and their reviews have not only been favorable, but enthusiastic. It should be pointed out that these critics attend in their professional capacity and judge the Mummers' presentations according to Loop standards.

While the Mummers maintain permanent headquarters in the Auditorium Building on Wabash Avenue, they are forced to give their productions in the Chicago Woman's Club Theatre or at the Goodman Theatre. One outstanding feature of the Mummers is their three years' success with a free training school where almost one hundred students each year are given free instruction in acting, make-up, stage technique, production methods, etc. The castings of the main stage plays are made from this exceptionally well trained group and it is no wonder that the Mummer productions have gradually built a reputation of being more polished and professional than any other organization in Chicago.

Dayton, Ohio.

Here, starting in the fall of 1938, is a unique organization. "The Dayton Civic Theatre" it is called, and it combines both professional actors and amateurs. The professional company, under the direction of Edmond C. Wilkes, and composed of young college people, gives five plays each season. The amateur group presents three plays. So between the two of them Dayton has eight plays each season.

Detroit, Michigan.

Here for five years the Little Theatre produced plays, and then in 1934 the banks of Detroit were closed, and the particular bank where this group kept its funds failed to reopen. Their entire working capital was lost. But they bucked up and made plans for the next season. Leading this group was Maxine Finsterwald, who has written several plays that have been produced from time to time at the Pasadena Community Playhouse and elsewhere. For some time Howard Southgate was director. Then Albert Riebling became director, and after a time radio occupied the chief interests of this group.

Elkhart, Indiana.

This group, known as the Elkhart Little Theatre, has its own playhouse. Their backstage facilities are very good and their lighting equipment is one of the best in Indiana. They direct their own plays, and have done Shakespeare from time to time. Clem Easly, one of the members of this group, is a firm believer in community participation.

Gary, Indiana.

One of the liveliest theatres in the middle west is Gary's Civic Theatre. Kerbert Barnes Earl reports that it is not unusual for them to sell nearly ten thousand tickets at the box office during a season in addition to the two hundred fifty subscription memberships at $5.00 each. The Civic Theatre has its own auditorium and studio and two paid employees. In the eight years of their existence, they have spent almost $7000 on royalties which should certainly encourage playwrights to submit original scripts for consideration by the Gary Civic Theatre. A School of the Drama sponsored by the Civic Theatre is open free to everyone.

Glencoe, Illinois.

Frank J. Morre, President of the Threshold Players, Inc., reports that five hundred season tickets for the three productions that the Players have given each year for the past thirteen were sold this year. This theatre has a definite policy of producing at least one original play each year. Mr. Morre writes that he feels that New York producers would do well to release the manuscripts for experimental productions in the smaller theatres which, he feels, would eliminate costly tryouts.

Hinsdale, Illinois.

The organizer and director of the Hinsdale Little Theatre is Everett Mesenbrink. The aim of this talented director is to make the group into a permanent Community Theatre, with professional standards. The membership is open to anyone interested and is not restricted by residence. Members are drawn from nearby towns as well as from Hinsdale.

Janesville, Wisconsin.

For a long time the members of this dramatic group held their meetings in a large room on the second floor of the public library. The library board couldn't get rid of them, so finally they turned the room over to the group, and gave them permission to do what they liked. A stage was built, and now in the public library this group holds forth.

Joplin, Missouri.

Typical of perhaps many hundreds of loosely organized Community Theatre groups throughout the country, the one in Joplin, Missouri, has functioned sporadically for several years. First as a separate Little Theatre group, under the direction of Albert Newman, then as the drama division of a civic Fine Arts League, such plays as "Craig's Wife," "Romantic Age," "Hell Bent for Heaven," "Trial of Mary Dugan," etc., were presented. The two greatest handicaps were the lack of a full time paid director—Mr. Newman very graciously donated his services—and a place they could call their own. At one time, considerable money was spent in renovating the stage and auditorium of an abandoned high school—only to have the building start to crumble in the middle of "The Admirable Crichton"! For a year or two, disheartened, they did nothing. Then a young teacher of dramatics, Iris Korn, with considerable training and experience, came up from Arkansas, directed a children's theatre for a year or two, and out of that organized another interested group of people, young and old, as the Players' Guild. Under Mrs. Korn's direction, a number of popular Broadway successes have been ably presented during the past year or two: "The Night of January 16th," "Hay Fever," "Post Road," and recently, "First Lady." A major difficulty still remains—the lack of an appropriate place. Renting junior high school auditoriums or local motion picture houses proves both expensive and inadequate. The countryside is now being scoured for a good old barn— sufficiently sturdy not to collapse in the middle of Lord Loam's desert island speech, free from the tentacles of expensive union stage hands, and with good ringing rafters (and an angel or two flapping about them!).

Lake Geneva—Williams Bay, Wisconsin.

Half way between these two towns was an old deserted Mormon Church. So the players combined their efforts, named themselves the Belfry Players, knocked out the pulpit of the church, and put in a stage. From as far off as Elkhorn people come to see the plays presented by this group.

Lansing, Michigan.

The Lansing Civic Players Guild in nine years has grown to such an extent that it may proudly take its place with the Lansing Town Hall, the Lansing Symphony Orchestra and the Community Concert Series as an integral part of the cultural life of the city. Lorna B. Millar writes that in the eight years of existence, they have built their group up to an annual membership of almost one thousand; they pay local directors to produce their shows and are definitely interested in reading good original plays. Their extra activities include sponsoring a city-wide original one-act play writing contest and occasional workshop productions.

Mansfield, Ohio.

The Community Players are entering their twelfth season with approximately six hundred members who have purchased season tickets at $2.50 apiece. This group does not employ a professional director and has always tried to produce at least one original play each season. The director, Mrs. Helen Bacon, would be glad to read original scripts that might be suitable for production in Mansfield.

Rock Island, Illinois.

The policy of this group is to do original plays and the talent is selected from among the best in Rock Island. Their progress was so rapid and the enthusiasm for the work was so keen that the members brought in their first managing director, Dwight Thomas. Besides producing plays they hold classes. They call themselves the Attic Players, and have a tiny playhouse in an office building.

Springfield, Illinois.

Founded in 1921, the Community Players have two hundred fifty subscription members and are able to bolster their box office considerably by selling individual admissions. The director, Henry B. House, directs four productions a year and reports that Springfield audiences are hungry only for Broadway fare and are not interested in attempting productions of new playwrights.

Waukegan, Illinois.

Here the Serio-Comic Players have an active membership of fifty, and a large associate group. Among the honorary members are Dudley Crafts Watson of the Chicago Art Institute and Representative Richard J. Lyons of Illinois. The directors of each play are chosen from a director's staff, composed of members who have had special training in this line.

Waukesha, Wisconsin.

Their theatre in this community is the old town hall. Turning this property over to the Waukesha Players was voted at a town referendum in 1928. A stage was built, a basement was put in, and a theatre blossomed forth. Laura Wright, the founder of this group, teaches dramatics at the Waukesha High School. Fred Strong, who bought an old theatre in the town, gave them two hundred seats, and play production goes on.

Wichita, Kansas.

Incorporated in April, 1938, this Little Theatre has made remarkable progress. They presented their first play in June of that year with Robert Gottschalk as director. Many prominent citizens of Wichita enrolled as charter members. They have a workshop, conducted like a school with classes in play production and experimental work. They are a civic minded group, offering opportunities to all interested persons. Plans for the future include a full-time paid director and a building owned by the Little Theatre to insure permanence.

Winona, Minnesota.

Charles Choate, managing director of the Little Theatre Group, says that approximately three hundred season tickets and six hundred single admissions are sold each year. As this group is more than fourteen years old, they have managed to build up a record of almost fifty major productions and of course, a great number of box-office experiments. They are producing in their own theatre and would be interested in reading original scripts. They sponsor a class in acting once a week that is free and open to anyone.

Youngstown, Ohio.

Hubbard Kirtpatrick notes that in the twelve years in which almost seventy productions have been given, the Little Theatre has built its membership to some nine hundred members. Three paid employees are maintained by the theatre and a public reading room and classes in stage technique are given as extra activities.

V. COMMUNITY THEATRES OF THE WEST

Berkeley, California
Burlingame, California
Claremont, California
Denver, Colorado
Eugene, Oregon
Eureka, Montana
Lewistown, Montana 28B
Logan, Utah
Palo Alto, California
Pasadena, California
Portland, Oregon 296·
Reno, Nevada
San Carlos, California
San Diego, California
San Francisco, California
Scobey, Montana
Seattle, Washington
Taft, California
Tucson, Arizona
Yuma, Arizona
And Other Theatres of the West

Berkeley, California. "The Proof of the Play is in the Production Thereof."

Fifteen years ago several students, as they sauntered out of the classroom at the University of California in which visiting Professor George Pierce Baker had just concluded the last lecture of a series, were tempted to paraphrase the old saying, "The proof of a pudding is in the eating," into "The proof of a play is in the production thereof." Some of these students were playwrights in the germ stage, some had budded. All felt that a play on paper, no matter how readable, was an x quantity until it had passed the test of production. The test of production, they felt, would bring to the surface any faults in structure, characterization, dialogue, or faulty technique not discernible in mere reading. Whereupon these students said to themselves: "We'll form a group of writers, actors, producers and directors, the last three of whom shall present the plays of the writers. By this means the writers shall profit and the others shall gain much pleasure and valuable experience." So came about the Berkeley Playmakers.

Their initial performance of original one-act plays proved so valuable to the authors that it was decided to invite other prospective playwrights to submit one-act plays for experimental production. To encourage the writing of good plays, a yearly playwriting contest was established; anyone was eligible to enter and modest prizes were offered for the best plays. Authors submitting plays retain all title and rights except the privilege to give the play its first production, which right may be exercised by the Berkeley Playmakers within a comparatively short stipulated period.

In the fifteen years of the Berkeley Playmakers' existence, these contests have grown so that out-of-state entries far outnumber local contestants. Most of the entries are sent in from points far from Berkeley. There have been prize winners from North Carolina, Canada, and Georgia.

The Berkeley Playmakers limn their ideals thus: "For us 'growth' consists of the gradual approach to these ends: first, a steadily increasing number of skilfully written plays should be submitted each year; second, the production of the best of these plays should be given in a manner technically and artistically satisfying." The fact that the Berkeley Playmakers have enjoyed a continuous existence since 1923 may not be a proof of artistic growth per se, but certainly indicates tenacity. The growth of the Berkeley Playmakers may be measured by the fact that without elaborate promotion efforts they now have a national and international reputation as a short play experimental theatre. The analyses and criticisms furnished all authors by the Berkeley Playmakers Judging Committee in connection with the annual playwriting contest have brought plays by the same writers year after year, not primarily with the hope of winning a prize or a production, but for these constructive comments. The Playmakers do not encourage the authors to write the type of play that will "sell." On the other hand, such plays are by no means discouraged. If a playwright can construct a play with an appeal to an average audience and at the same time be able to find a market for it, more power to him.

Betty Smith, whose play "So Gracious Is the Time" was a recent winner of the playwriting contest, wrote: "I am thankful that the Berkeley Playmakers were courageous enough to tackle this difficult-to-produce play, else it never would have seen production, and I might have been discouraged from writing anything but plays with an amateur appeal."

The Playmakers' schedule usually consists of four programs produced each season between September and May. Each program contains four one-act plays selected from the previous contest, which means that they hope to receive at least sixteen plays that will qualify for production without too extensive revisions. If they get them they are more than satisfied. With good plays production difficulties are simplified, for it is far easier to obtain good performers and competent directors for a good play than for a mediocre piece.

Of course every theatre has individual major problems, but the minor problems in Community Theatre work are familiar to everyone, often amusingly so. Henry Netherton says that under the heading of "nuisance" problems the Playmakers would class the "local would-be playwright who has written some ghastly concoction which he (or 'she'—it's usually a 'she') insists, for some secret and mystic reason, on describing as a play. This 'play' may have been submitted in the contest and of course turned down, whereupon the author proceeds to make life hideous for any acquaintance of his (pardon me—*hers*) who happens to be a member of the judging or production committee. These people are cornered in public, in private, per telephone, via mail, and bombarded with pleas to 'reconsider,' to make some suggestion as to what changes in the play would be producible, to use their influence toward getting it produced, etc., etc."

Netherton adds that another minor problem which perhaps every Community Theatre group has, is "the 'arty' person who has heard of the organization and drops in with the intention of patronizing us. This person has studied the 'drahmah' in London, Paris or perhaps even Pasadena, and has climaxed her life study in a course for vocal diction under the celebrated

Madame de Fish. Our friend can usually be identified by the use of fluttering gestures with a faint English accent—all the a's broadened (as in 'ham') and who frequently betrays herself by saying 'cahn I take a bath?' "

Netherton says that probably one of the least annoying problems is the Babbitt who arrives in the midst of every Community Theatre at least once in every four years, and who believes that the Community Theatre should go in for civic uplift in a big way. The last uplifter who tried to sell the Playmakers on an uplifting program approached them in this vein: " 'Now that we had grown to be a big group with lots of talent, we could gain enormous prestige if we could put on a big pageant depicting the rise of civilization as exemplified in the growth of the City of Wampum Gulch, California. Transportation, costumes could be provided. A grassy little glade, possibly cleared of poison oak, would be our theatre. The girls would wear pink tights, and the men could have bows and arrows and ride on white horses, furnished by the city.' Grim and flinty-faced we declined the offer. 'It was not meant for us,' we told the uplifter. We learned afterwards that the Campfire Girls and the local Benevolent Order of Yaks had really put over the pageant in a big way."

There is one distinction that the Berkeley Playmakers may claim above all others. They are the one short play theatre whose healthy life of more than fifteen years establishes it as the outstanding example of this type of experimental Community Theatre.

Burlingame, California. A Combine.

Burlingame, San Mateo, and Hillsborough, California, have joined hands in dramatic activities and created the Peninsula Little Theatre, Incorporated, which was first organized as the Community Little Theatre in January, 1934.

In response to an announcement in the local papers a number of enthusiastic theatrical fans met one evening to discuss organizing to carry on their fun in some planned manner. At the meeting the group elected a Board of nine directors, prominent local citizens who selected the necessary officers from among themselves.

Frederick Carlyle, local dramatic coach, was appointed director and plans were made immediately for a season of three plays. "The School for Scandal" and "Smiling Through," the first two, costume plays, proved very expensive for the inexperienced group and were not too well received by the public. "The Swan" as a third play suffered from lack of funds, hence inadequate staging, and though it was well performed it received little audience support from the disillusioned community.

The original enthusiastic subscribers had bought books of tickets for the three plays and willing sponsors had pledged themselves to cover any small deficit at the end of the season. But both subscribers and sponsors were disgusted at the close of the season and refused to repeat. Money had been thrown away on costumes, scenery, and props. Fresh flowers for stage settings had been purchased in the luxuriously gardened community; programs and costumes were all too elaborate and expensive. Dissolution threatened.

However the scheme of organization saved the situation. For the numerous members interested in departments other than acting had set up individual sections headed by experienced persons in which they could continue with their interests in play reading, playwriting, scene design, make-up, costume design, stage lighting and so on. And while they did not contribute to major productions they remained as entities of the larger group.

The following year the organization struggled on. An outside director, Valentine P. Newmark of the Mill Valley Players, was brought in to breathe new life into the almost moribund body. A rather ambitious program of plays was presented, and was well received by the small audience which remained loyal. Newmark also revived interest in the Theatre Workshop which did several one-acts and one ambitious three-act, "Pulling the Curtain," under the aegis of member directors—thus adding interest to the season and keeping the members occupied.

Meanwhile the Board of Directors had been busy straightening numerous difficulties besides effecting a merger with two other local amateur groups, one fourteen years old, which increased available properties, players, and members. The name of the organization was changed from "The Community Little Theatre" to "Peninsula Little Theatre, Inc.," whereat the wisdom of the constitutional provision for a rotating Board of Directors was proved by permitting the infusion of the ideas and enthusiasm of the new groups. An economy program brought the Peninsula Little Theatre, Inc., slowly out of the sea of red ink and started it toward success.

The fall of 1935 found the Little Theatre holding together hopefully with an unused store rented for rehearsal and scene construction and an arrangement made with a local church for the use of its small but well equipped stage and auditorium. This acquisition of a "home" did much to bring the group together. New members joined enthusiastically—enough to give the overworked stage and scene staff a chance to take things easier. That season "The Phantom" was produced by a member-director. Next the services of James Sandoe, then affiliated with the Drama Department of Stanford University, were secured to produce "Home Chat" most successfully.

As it became evident that the Peninsula Little Theatre was going places, still more enthusiasm developed, evidenced by constantly increasing membership. Robert Brauns of Stanford University became the Director and under him the 1938 season was eminently successful. Arrangements were made with the Adult Center division of the San Mateo Junior College to use the excellent stage and auditorium there. The Adult Center has appointed Mr. Braun a member of its faculty with pay.

The group now feels the contentment which comes with a series of successes. An interest has developed in San Francisco and the drama critics there give notices and criticisms. The theatre has been out of the red for some time; has the increasing support of the community; has improved equipment; a place to work, an enthusiastic working membership and—high hopes. A theatre of their own is becoming a possibility.

So much for general history. Even during the darkest days there were interludes: a special show for a motion picture scout, the tryout performance of an original play, "Little Acorns Grow," by North Baker. Again, with but one week of preparation, a highly successful show for the Red Cross was staged for flood victims in 1937.

Because of the suburban location, eighteen miles from San Francisco, many of the potential audience go to that city for their entertainment and show little awareness of the local theatrical fare. But with the aid of excellent cooperation on publicity by the local newspapers, photographic posters, and miniature stage displays interest has spread steadily. During 1937–38 box-office sales were seven times those of the previous season.

All known schemes of ticket selling have been tried: scrip books, reserved seats, subscription sales, personal contact sales (both for season and individual plays), general admission, and others. All have their drawbacks, all require downright drudgery without applause or glory. For the coming season the plan is to offer season books of tickets. Funds realized from the plays themselves are put into a drama fund which finances all major productions and workshop activities.

The present set-up of the organization, which functions suitably, does not differ greatly from the original: nine directors, three of whom are elected at the annual business meeting in May each year, elect the officers from among themselves. Each Board member assumes the chairmanship of some committee—publicity, scenery, and so on—and reports on its activity at monthly meetings. Members may serve on as many committees as they wish.

Anita Fowler, to whom we are indebted for the story of the Peninsula Little Theatre, explains their social activities as follows:

"Our dues have been increased to $2.50 a year (originally $1.00) to make possible more social activities. Our Social Committee is appointed with the other Standing Committees early in the summer so that plans may be formulated for the forthcoming season. This committee is one of the most active as it arranges programs and refreshments for the monthly business meetings and the monthly Drama Teas, which are also open to guests, and are held at the homes of members. It also arranges the reception which is held for the cast after each play, and which we have found that our 'public' likes immensely—it is such fun actually to meet the actors while still in costume! 'Daughters of Atreus' was especially good in this respect. We serve coffee and sheet-cake from a large, beautifully decorated, candle-lighted table in the lovely Guild room of the parish house (our first home) which is next door to the Junior College. Our hostesses for the evening dress formally. In winter, a roaring fire in the fireplace adds attraction to the occasion. The friendly atmosphere has stimulated interest and we have liked it, too. The committee is also responsible for two costume-party-jinks, for members only, during the year as well as a possible card party or get-together."

Claremont, California. Real Estate Boom Gives Birth to Theatre.

"What is the 'native American Theatre'?"

It is true that "native American Theatre" is usually taken to mean such plays as "Rip Van Winkle," "Lightnin' " or "Seven Keys to Baldpate," but there are, in a few isolated places in the United States, examples of a "native American theatre" that in another country would be called a "peasant" theatre or a "people's" theatre. The outstanding example of this type of theatre culture is the Mexican Players of Padua Hills, Claremont, California.

The Mexican Players have had a checkered career, which started in 1925. In that year a syndicate undertook to develop some two thousand acres of land located just outside of Claremont, California, in the Padua Hills. This syndicate, to differentiate itself from most real estate ventures, showed especially good taste and originality by building a theatre and community center in the middle of its development, and in 1930 this theatre, with an adjacent dining room, was opened by a group of amateur players who called themselves the Claremont Community Players. After two years of struggle, the Community Players were forced to call it a day and a group of young Mexicans, who had been engaged at first to wait on tables in the dining room and who had showed exceptional talent at various entertainments given at dinner parties and suppers, took over the theatre and attempted to keep at least a few nights of every week occupied with their productions.

At first in 1933, the Mexican Players shared the week with the Padua Players who were a group of young people from the school of the Pasadena Playhouse. These two groups alternated, with the Mexican Players performing on week-ends. Though the relationship between these groups was entirely amicable, finances did not warrant the continuation of such an undertaking, and in 1935 the Mexican Players took over the full schedule of six performances a week and assumed responsibility for the theatre building development.

The Mexican Players comprise a group of fifteen or twenty young people of Mexican or Spanish-Californian descent.   Some of these were born in Mexico, but most of them have lived in California for the greater part of their lives.   The girls live in the dormitory provided for them in Claremont, while most of the boys live in small cabins near the theatre.

An evening spent with the Mexican Players is something like this:

Claremont lies about forty miles south of Pasadena in the foothills of the Padua mountains.   A long hacienda-like group of buildings comprises the Padua Theatre.   The entrance is a long trellis of brick pillars where during certain times of the year grapes ripen in the sun and may be picked as one walks along the colonnade.

On entering the dining room one is led by a Mexican hostess to a table on a porch overlooking a deep canyon from which the roar of a small cataract accompanies music played by strumming guitarists.

After a delicious Mexican dinner, topped with endless cups of salt-bitter South American chocolate, one is ready to proceed to the theatre.   The gradual rustling of the audience denotes that curtain time is approaching. The theatre is strictly a modern edifice, built of rough red brick with unfinished interior, exposed beams and steeply pitched concrete floor.   The lighting is soft and shadowy; the auditorium itself is large, spacious and pleasantly cool.

Probably the program will call for no formal curtain rising, the stage being set with an ordinary street scene such as might be found in any Mexican village.   However, the set is cleverly modern, for some of the rooms are cut away and both the interior and exterior of the houses can be seen at the same time.   There are people sleeping in the beds, night lamps are burning.   The wail of a child is heard in the distance, awakening for its five o'clock feeding. A mother stirs—a twelve year old boy kicks the covers off—and in the distance a cock crows, so realistic as to awaken a murmur of appreciation from the audience.   Several people stretch—get up—wash—make their simple toilets—go down to the kitchen—stir up the fire—and slowly but surely the hum and surge of life of a small village begins.   The first line of this play, if it may be called a play, is a mother calling to her daughter that "It's time to get up."   Children are shaken and awakened, grandmothers creak down to their places by the stove—tortillas are pounded on kitchen tables, the set is getting lighter—shutters and doors are thrown open—dogs bark— brooms are sweeping—the cat is shooed out—the well chain clanks—

neighbors call to each other—women with black shawls over their heads slip away to early Mass, the murmur of which may be heard in the adjacent church (built cleverly as a superstructure over an exit down right of the stage). Breakfast is over—the children are out playing—the women gather their morning wash, proceed to the village trough (in the orchestra pit), and begin the pounding of their clothes—and the first threads of the play are unfolded.

The whole production is in Mexican patois. It is not memorized and yet it is perfectly rehearsed. The actors speak their lines simply, with natural accents, and no attempt at projection. Native dances, love scenes, fireworks, fights, betting, marketing, and all the other incidents that make up life in this small community are in two hours paraded before the eyes of an American audience.

The Mexican Players of Padua Hills are one of the real theatre surprises in America. For fifty years Americans have been making pilgrimages to Oberammergau, to the pageants of Venice, Salzburg Festivals, etc., but here in America is one outstanding example of a peasant theatre which is as unique as the Grand Canyon itself.

Denver, Colorado. University Breathes Life into Civic Theatre.

Recently the Mayor of Denver said: "Denver considers the University Civic Theatre not only an opportunity and an inspiration for its members, but a very real asset to the cultural life of the community." Here is a tribute from a public official to a theatre that has made a conspicuous success of the "town and gown" relationship which is found so often in the Community Theatre field.

The University Civic Theatre of Denver is also conspicuous because it benefits from Mrs. Verner Z. Reed's generous gift of an auditorium to the University of Denver with a proviso that it should house the Civic Theatre. Elaborate lighting and stage equipment was given to the Civic Theatre by Mr. James H. Causey, making it one of the most modern and complete theatrical plants in the west.

For nine years, Walter Sinclair has been making every effort to integrate the Civic Theatre with the cultural life of Denver. Recently he celebrated his fiftieth production in the theatre which occasioned an almost international celebration on the part of Mr. Sinclair's friends throughout the world of the theatre. In reviewing the fifty productions of the past ten years, one realizes that any citizen of Denver who had conscientiously attended the productions would have a liberal and catholic experience in world drama. Mr. Sinclair's choice of plays has encompassed the whole range of dramatic literature.

Undoubtedly it is from the pen of Mr. Sinclair that the preface of the University Civic Theatre flows:

"The purpose of the University Civic Theatre is to provide pleasurable and educational recreation through the medium of dramatic productions—many forms of which are not always available from other sources.

"The University Civic Theatre is in no way competitive with privately owned commercial theatres, or theatrical producers, nor does it ask its community to support it exclusively. It, however, may be reasonably idealistic since it, and it alone, can accomplish ideals which, for obvious reasons, commercial theatres cannot even attempt. It strives to give its patrons the best in all forms of dramatic work—classics, farce, melodrama, comedy, and tragedy.

"The University Civic Theatre is a civic asset as are the public library, the public art gallery and the symphony orchestra since it, too, affords the community recreational necessities difficult, and often impossible, to obtain from other than civic institutions.

"The University Civic Theatre is not a public or civic institution in the sense of being created or maintained by taxation. It was established and is supported by public-spirited citizens solely for the benefit of the community, with no provision for individual profit. It may, therefore, be truly said to be 'of the people, by the people and for the people.'

"Considering the past history of this institution these facts remain outstanding: notable productions have given joy and stimulation to thousands of our citizens and have reacted to the glory of our city abroad. The University Civic Theatre is accredited with having created and maintained a most commendable civic asset."

The fine relationship that can be established and nurtured by the application of the "town and gown" relationship in a Community Theatre is one that cannot receive too much praise. There is hardly a college town in America that would not profit by such a venture, and any university or college theatre that contemplates venturing into this too little developed field might well consult Walter Sinclair.

Eugene, Oregon. A Very Little Theatre Grows Up.

Nowhere in this country are Community Theatres and the essentially democratic idea that motivates them more firmly established in the people than in the great northwest. From Eugene, Oregon, Sally Elliot Allen has graciously contributed to this book an insider's story of the Very Little Theatre of Eugene.

Eight years ago an insurance man, the wife of a football coach, a newspaper editor, an English professor and his wife who had been interested in "college dramatics," an artist, the wife of a journalism professor, a grocery salesman, an architect's wife who was employed in a book store, and a couple of students met together and in gaiety of heart adopted a constitution and by-laws bringing into being the Very Little Theatre.

Some vital motive quite other than love of gain or fame has held this group together for so long and caused its steady growth. It began as a plaything of a few kindred spirits; but in spite of itself it is rapidly becoming a community enterprise. Movement of dollars between the organization's treasury and its members' pockets has all been from and not to the pockets. And dramatic production is not all play. The members give long hours to rehearsals (frequently in cold buildings), ushering, selling and taking tickets, lugging "props" to and from the theatre, keeping records and accounts, attending lengthy committee meetings, mimeographing programs and typing parts, serving coffee, sweeping floors, and cleaning up dressing rooms. The "guest actors," from whom the membership is largely recruited, dip cautious toes into the chill waters of this unpaid drudgery, discover that "having a fat part" is only an occasional reward of membership, and, according to their individual natures, beat a rapid retreat or else plunge into the invigorating waves to sink or swim with the rest. In spite of all this, the history of the group is a story of constant expansion. The first year's intimate group of a score has more than trebled; and, though for years the constitutional limit was fifty members, the number is now limited only by the necessity of keeping out or getting rid of self-seekers or dead timber. At present, there are sixty-five members "in good standing"; and, of the one hundred and ten members whose names have appeared on the membership rolls during these years, only six have actually resigned. The other withdrawals have all been due to removal from Eugene or death.

The history of the Very Little Theatre began in May, 1929, with the production of "You and I" in the Heilig Theatre of Eugene by a casually formed group of people genuinely interested in plays; the success of this venture led a few days later to the formal organization of the Very Little Theatre. There followed the production of three modern, large-royalty plays, all put on in the Heilig Theatre, two in the season of 1929–30 and one in the autumn of 1930. By this time the great expense of a downtown theatre building, the royalties for recent plays, and the difficulty of filling a large house for amateur performances had plunged the infant group deeply into debt.

Two Eugene business men, Sidney Claypool and Walter Van Atta, came to the rescue and offered the group the use of a small store in a residential district near the University of Oregon. The Very Little Theatre's new quarters became known as the Very Little Studio. The members constructed a tiny stage at one end of the long narrow store, made curtains, brought in packing boxes for seats (neatly draping them with old curtains to prevent splinter casualties), and settled into the cramped and chilly quarters. A large wood stove in a back room gave out heat that was more than ample for actors waiting for their cues or dressing behind shaky screens, but penetrated only casually to the stage and the "auditorium."

Here, avoiding large royalties and a paid staff, keeping the cost of printing and advertising to a minimum, the Very Little Theatre began to produce plays. Some of these plays filled the little house for a week. One hundred spectators could be packed in if people sat (as they frequently did) in and over the windows and over the door and "descent from the highest seats was like climbing down the Alps." There were financial ebbs—at one time the members underwrote personally the expenses of a coming production— but gradually the group paid off its debts. Finally rigid economy and the popularity of the plays made possible the beginning of a precious "building fund" for a real theatre. Seventeen full evening performances were given under these conditions between April, 1931, and April, 1935.

In the spring of 1935 the little store was rented from over the members' reluctant heads, and they were forced to seek other quarters at once. On the Lane County vacated fairgrounds a large frame building was discovered and finally rented by the Very Little Theatre. The place needed everything— stage, seats, ramp for seats, dressing rooms, ticket office, sets for a stage forty by thirty feet, lights, heat, janitor service and an increased budget for rent, heat, and light. It was far from the downtown district and from the homes of the theatre's regular audiences. But its size permitted productions that the miniature stage at the studio had forbidden. The audience could be large and more comfortably seated.

The first performance in the new theatre was "Uncle Tom's Cabin," a venture long yearned for by the group. It was the greatest financial success in the group's history. But all profits and the group's slowly accumulated savings went into increased expenses and construction. Expenses continued to mount, even though all the members turned out to help whenever the current house manager announced a "work day." Yet in the long run the gate receipts and fees have slightly more than covered expenses.

The Very Little Theatre company has a unique record of continuous existence for eight years without subsidy or money contribution from any outside source. It has had no "contributing" or "supporting" members. It has depended entirely on membership fees (at first $5.00 for initiation and $2.00 for yearly dues, and now $2.00 a year with no initiation fee), and on the profits from productions. At times the organization has been several hundred dollars in debt; at the peak of its prosperity it had $625 in the bank. A considerable amount of property has been assembled: sets, lighting fixtures, seats (most of which were bought cheap from an abandoned church building), curtains, furniture, "props," costumes, tools, make-up. Individuals and stores have been very generous in loan of properties and costumes, and other organizations have occasionally sold tickets on a percentage basis. But the Very Little Theatre has never asked for a cent from outsiders. Theirs is a proud but precarious existence.

Week-to-week business is entrusted to a small Board of Governors with power to act between meetings. Board members serve for three years. The number of members at first was five but now is seven elected by the whole group—two each year for two successive years and three the third year. The Board elects the president, the secretary, and the treasurer of the Very Little Theatre from its own members. It appoints committees, directors, production managers, house managers; it decides with the Play Committee on the plays; and it inaugurates constitutional changes and outlines policies for presentation to the full membership for decision. Losses of Board members by resignation or removal from the city are filled by the Board itself. The Board has wrestled earnestly through the years with the knotty problems of the group; some of these it has solved; some are perennial. Three perennial problems were intensified by the move into larger quarters: (1) what plays to produce; (2) how to take in new members; and (3) how to keep out of debt.

It has always been a difficult matter to find plays without prohibitive royalties, and yet which give suitable opportunity for self-expression and development of the performers. With the larger building calling for larger expenditure in apparatus and upkeep, and hence for larger audiences to support it, the complicating question of popular appeal arose; and financial need also demanded presentation of more plays.

The increased number of plays produced in turn created a need for a larger membership, and made the second problem more acute—how to take in new members. Personality has never been a criterion—only ability and a genuine, selfless, almost sacrificial enthusiasm for the thing that was being attempted. But the means of testing these qualities have never been perfected. The selection of new members from nominations from within the group proved slow and savored of a closed corporation rather than a community enterprise. Yet encouragement of free application, with tryouts, is cumbersome in a small body, and offers chances of too many heartaches for a small community. A sort of hit-or-miss compromise is the present experimental method. Outsiders who show interest are asked in as guest actors or helpers. Election to membership follows a long period of probation.

The third problem, "how to keep out of debt," has been solved only by planning and hard work and tricky footwork amidst the conflicting demands of the members for royalty plays, for classic drama, or for adequate settings for productions undertaken, on the one hand, and the need for popular appeal and for economy in expenditures, on the other. It is significant that, whenever this group is called upon to be really commercial-minded, enthusiam begins to flag.

A larger town than Eugene would afford the possibility of larger audiences; a smaller town would offer fewer diversions and less competition. In Eugene, a city of twenty thousand, there are five moving picture theatres; a very successful University Theatre, presenting four or five plays a year; a "Greater Artist" series of music, lectures, and dance recitals brought to the city by the student body of the University; and a continual stream of musical events and lectures sponsored by the University. Moreover, there are more than three hundred and fifty clubs and organizations recorded in newspaper archives. There is not a member of the Very Little Theatre who may be said to be a person of great leisure. Every man and woman is vigorously active in business, profession, and community affairs, and the amount of time they can give to this avocation is extremely limited.

What are the values that have kept the Very Little Theatre alive in spite of all these obstacles? The members are infinitely various in occupation. This infinite variety has been held together because, as one member put it, "We're all a little crazy in the head—and in the same spot." To anyone not bitten by that particular bug it may seem sheer madness to give the hours, energy, and travail of spirit that every single dramatic performance calls for— not to mention all the executive headaches. (Tribute should be paid here to the members' wives and husbands, who are *not* crazy in the head, but who have loyally and uncomplainingly spent long evenings alone at home, or given more strenuous cooperation by selling tickets, holding prompt-books, making costumes, serving food, or to other tasks, as need arose.)

The honest comradeship that all this dramatic effort breeds among folk of such divergent backgrounds is one of its larger rewards. The occasional clash of "artistic temperaments," one of the hazards of any such body, has added to the color and to the earned experience of the years.

Members find satisfaction also in the acquirement of many new techniques connected with the theatre beside those of acting. The increased knowledge and appreciation of things in the world of drama has been another definite gain to the members. For the amateur actor the relaxation gained by portraying vicarious emotions, the satisfaction of old "suppressed desires" through real play, the enrichment of his own personality by the interpretation of another's—all these are parts of a genuinely creative recreation that is to him beyond price.

The very difficulties of meagre endowment have called forth in the members that truly American gift of ingenuity; no curtains have ever given the members the triumphant satisfaction that did the first ones, made from flour sacks from one member's bakery, sewed together on a portable machine in the Very Little Studio, and colored with calcimine.

The theatre also has provided an experimental laboratory and real encouragement for local dramatic writing, as well as for talent in acting and directing. Two of its members who directed their first plays under the Very Little Theatre are now successful professional directors; another member is on his way to the professional stage.

In the eight years of its history, the Very Little Theatre has presented to the public thirty-five full evening performances, and has produced two one-act plays as entertainment at receptions given to help acquaint the public with the organization. This does not count repetitions; the productions have run for from one to seven times. Of these productions, twenty-two were three-act plays, one was a so-called "amateur night," seven were groups of one-acts, and four were fantasies given by children. The type of plays has ranged: revivals, "Ten Nights in a Barroom," "East Lynne," "The Streets of New York," "Uncle Tom's Cabin," and "Rip Van Winkle"; high-brow drama represented by Molière, Ibsen, Strindberg, Schnitzler, Chekov, Dunsany, Shaw, the Quinteros; more popular plays by Oscar Wilde, Moeller, Maugham, St. John Ervine, Barrie, Arlen, Moody, Rhinehart, Reed; an occasional one-act farce; two three-act mystery plays and five one-acts, all written by local authors; and fantasies for children.

Besides these public productions, twenty-three one-act plays or single acts from longer plays and four evenings of dramatic "stunts" have been given for the private delectation of the membership only, mostly at the regular one-a-month Sunday evening meetings where business, drama, food, and informality make a savory blend. From these private productions one-act plays have been chosen for public repetition at so-called "studio nights." One year, papers and discussions of the history of the drama were the profitable entertainment of the Sunday meetings. Now and again one-act plays (and once "East Lynn") were taken to outlying communities. A group of one-act plays was put on at the University Guild Theatre, under the sponsorship of the American Association of University Women.

Prices for performances began at fifty or seventy-five cents in the downtown theatre, but admission is now a flat thirty cents.

It has proved desirable to avoid attempts at a "professional" atmosphere. Amateur plays given in an atmosphere of unpretentiousness and unconventionality have a glamor helpfully flattering to the performer. Coffee usually has been served between the acts to help this mood of informality.

It goes without saying that the Very Little Theatre and its individual members have passed through numerous periods of disheartenment and disenchantment; but the years have bred, too, the spirit of the "trouper." Like the proverbial response of the war horse to the smell of powder or of the one-time newspaper man to the smell of printer's ink, so the odor of grease paint drags Eugene's amateur players back to rally once more to the cry, "The play must go on!"

Eureka, Montana. "Since Broadway Has a Theatre—So Shall We."

Broadway is many miles from Eureka, but the members of the Eureka Community Theatre are conversationally familiar with the work of the Theatre Guild, the current successes on the Great White Way, familiar with the plays of Eugene O'Neill, Susan Glaspell, Maxwell Anderson, James Sherwood, and others. They know what is going on in the world of the professional theatre, and reading of these things—since they have no actual contact—they are stimulated to creative impulses which need expression.

When Kay Fetterly came west in 1931, fresh from Randolph-Macon Woman's College, and prior to that the inspiring classes of Alfred Arvold of the North Dakota Agricultural College, she little dreamed that she would turn director and producer of plays for an eager group of theatre-conscious people.

She came to spend a year or so teaching English and dramatics in the high school and then graduate into a larger community. She stayed. She had found something real and vital in the urge of rural people to express themselves. And so she organized this urge into something tangible for the amusement and satisfaction of the townspeople of Eureka.

There were twenty-five members in the beginning of this Little Theatre Club, whom fate and the depression had left jobless at home. They organized in order to afford a worth-while activity for themselves and to stimulate a greater interest in drama in the community.

Eligibility for membership in the group is based on an interest in dramatics and a willingness to cooperate with the other members of the group. Absence from three consecutive business meetings without an excuse acceptable to the Executive Board forfeits a membership.

"Naturally many problems confront us," says Miss Fetterly. "A few of us have had college dramatics—most of us lack experience of any kind in actual theatre work, but we have enthusiasm and an eagerness to 'do anything to help' and so we have managed to survive and be of service to the community.

"We have been too generous in extending membership in the club. Wanting to stimulate community interest in us, we have allowed too many drones to become members. They refuse to assume responsibility and only sit back and bask in the reflected glory of what the club accomplishes through the efforts of a few. We need help and advice as to how to solve this, our greatest problem at present. We want to welcome those who are sufficiently interested enough to help in all fields. And while doing this we do not want to appear snobbish or too exclusive.

"Last but not least we need a community hall. So far we have given our productions in the local movie house and on the high school stage. But we are working toward the goal of a community building. So we may find this problem solved in the not too distant future."

A struggling, adventuresome group, creating their own theatre—unknown to glittering Broadway, but finding inspiration to carry on from the example of its triumphs: the theatre-lovers of Eureka, Montana.

Lewistown, Montana. A Pioneer in the Theatre Carries On.

Lewistown, Montana, is a long way from New York City; as a matter of fact, it is a long way from New Orleans, Los Angeles, and Chicago; and yet through the strength of a single personality, Lewistown has been able to capture a certain urbanity which gives it a definite link with every city in America. For Lewistown, Montana, has a theatre. And the Little Theatre of Lewistown, Montana, has a director—who by sheer grit, force of personality and an unbelievable determination has created for her town a cultural theatre comparable to any in this country.

In 1934 Virginia Vogt arrived in Lewistown equipped with only a sound theatrical background, a burning love of the theatre and a divine ignorance of the vicissitudes besetting anyone who starts out to create a Community Theatre. She, by the grace of non-union hours and the blessings of the citizenry of Lewistown, operates today after four years of strenuous work, a Community Theatre that has already a tradition behind it and very definitely a future before it!

Miss Vogt gives, with so much more sincerity than could ever be captured by a second person, a story that is an episode in Americana:

"September 1934—the first step after my arrival was to canvass the town, seeking out those who had some previous training or experience and would be interested in forming the nucleus of the organization. While this hunt-the-needle-in-the-hay-stack business went on, I was also trying to stir up the interest of the community at large—through talks to service clubs, society matrons, the local press, and street corner chats with anyone who would listen. No political campaign was ever carried on with more fervor—or less money.

"By November, the town (about eight thousand population, but with some eight smaller towns near by) had begun to be—curious. I had found a group of twelve people who had had definite experience, and wanted to help organize a theatre in Lewistown. All but one were primarily interested in acting! A general plan for formal organization was drawn up, ideals and aims marshalled for presentation, possible methods of operations formulated, and a general meeting called—open to anyone in town who was interested enough to walk over to the auditorium. All plans were presented. The floor was open for discussion—and we tried to satisfy everyone's curiosity. Following that meeting a membership committee got busy. Membership fee was set at $3.00. Two weeks later we met, with a scant twenty-five people holding 'dues paid' slips showing up. We organized with a Board of Directors consisting of director, president, secretary and treasurer. A committee drew up the constitution, which after acceptance went to the state capital and to Washington, D. C., so that we could operate tax exempt. Rightly or wrongly, we did not wish to be 'sponsored' by any previously organized service group—since Rotary is jealous of Kiwanis, and the Chamber of Commerce looks doubtfully at the Outlook Club. We wanted to be liked by everyone.

"So the next step was to sell them, by means of a play—having talked ourselves hoarse, and organized as completely as the Mormons.

"We had practically no money—no theatre—no equipment. I only knew my actors by what they said they could do. The town hadn't seen anything except a few worse than bad stock company shows for ten years. The natives were interested, but skeptical. Maybe plays were all right for the city slickers—but it all seemed pretty silly to them. Our one tangible asset was old Doc Ivins, boss of the local press. He was for us—and used up a lot of good space in the paper to tell the public that they should be—free of charge. As a matter of fact, his enthusiasm was greater than his veracity, and I still blush when I recall some of that first publicity.

"I picked the first play in fear. It couldn't be 'high-brow'—I wanted it to be actor-proof—it couldn't be too strenuous a staging problem—it couldn't be too expensive—it had to be popular. Well—it turned out to be 'Three-Cornered Moon,' and I still get green when I write that name. Casting was then no matter of selecting from the many—but of simply getting enough people to fill the cast. They all wanted someone else to earn the first brickbats. I finally rounded out the company by waylaying a likely looking messenger boy in the street, and browbeating him into becoming an actor.

By miracle or the grace of God, I actually got a cast that was better than adequate.

"Cast—then rehearse, so say the books. We had no stage to rehearse on. We had no money to rent a stage—or anything else. I went begging again. No one wanted us for five weeks straight—or even one. So we trailed from one end of the town to the other. A hotel dining room—the police hall— the mayor's office—a dairy barn—amongst the glassy-eyed models of a ladies' ready-to-wear establishment—a warehouse—the fire hall. But we rehearsed. With a vengeance. We could not, however, very handily present our first opus in any of these places. So I went blithely to the movie house. They weren't very happy about our credit standing. Well, neither were we. Finally we got part of the show underwritten, and managed to rent the theatre for one night—with one dress rehearsal at midnight!

"That movie theatre nearly finished us all. We didn't belong to the union—and the idea of constructing our set on their stage was instantly vetoed. We begged and harangued and met defeat. The nearest I ever got to that stage was a tour conducted by two of the union boys to look at the set they'd let us use. It was one of the seven wonders of the world. Replete with lavender willows, painted trellis-work, a golden moon, and a nude in a grotto. They didn't even smile when they assured me that it was the latest and most refined 'parlor number' they had. And I could take it or leave it. However, two days before the play, they broke down and offered to have the set painted—by the union—for us. I tore down with sketches and scale drawings. Little did I know! As soon as my back was turned, they threw my efforts out of the window and went their merry way alone. It was a shock when I saw it—but it was better than those willow trees.

"In spite of all logic, the play was a success. Even on the money side. We paid our bills and took a new lease on life. The town did us proud, and we felt we were destined for great things. Members joined up by the dozens—from society's best who wanted to lend prestige (which God knows we needed), to those from the wrong side of the tracks who were willing to work.

"We finished the year ahead of the red, with an encouraging list of members, and solid organization. More important—we had a lot of good will. There was something for everyone to *do,* and they liked the idea.

"I took the summer off and went back in the fall, crusading for a theatre. We got it. Not very elegant, but we loved it. We rented a store, long vacant, for a nominal sum and did the necessary remodeling ourselves. The auditorium seated about sixty and was novel in that we could have a small platform stage, or, by shifting platforms to the sides of the room and using them for audience tiers, we could give a penthouse production. And a penthouse production, in case you do not know, is something of a god-send to the amateur. . . . Some of the best penthouse plays I have ever worked with are "Three Men on a Horse," "Ladies of the Jury," "First Lady." Such shows are interesting and very popular.

"We got our theatre pretty much on credit and through donation. To our future sorrow let it be said that we were unable to secure a lease. Materials for remodeling were donated, and we did the work ourselves—except for the wiring. The union again! Our backstage was amazingly inadequate. One small room was everything—dressing room, space for props and furniture, place to prepare entr'acte coffee, electrician's booth, and prompter's stall. It was something of an art to make a quick change from riding clothes to evening gown without trailing your chiffon through a pot of coffee, or sitting in a jar of rouge. But when the SRO sign is out you feel pretty good anyway.

"And we finance ourselves. We have never been fortunate enough to have anyone leave us any money—or give us any. Sometimes our royalty problems have us chewing our nails—because we like good plays. We try to balance by doing non-royalty classics which help pay for the others. Costumes are still the problem of the person who wears them, though we do not consider this a good arrangement. Next year, a community-wide board is organizing to help us finance ourselves. It will include members from all service organizations in town. You see, we did sell them all. They will take our finance problem in hand, and some day we hope not to be in that unpleasant position of robbing Peter to pay Paul.

"Our plan we have found helpful—if used fairly sparingly. We sell the play on a given night to a club group. We sell them the tickets at a small discount, they to guarantee us a certain minimum. The club can sell tickets—to members only—at whatever price they can get. In this way we are assured a set sum on a club night, and the club makes some money at the game too.

"We have a mailing list, which has been compiled over a period of time, and cards are sent out to those who miss a production, or to those we want especially to interest. We find that this helps the box office.

"We hope that the new board will get us another theatre. The last went the way of all flesh—almost on the eve of an opening. Our business-man landlord had a chance to rent the place for more than we could afford—so into the street we went. We experienced another period of hiring a hall for one-night stands, and of rehearsing wherever we could. We now have a temporary resting place—well, hardly that—in a union hall! But it is only suited to penthouse productions. Stage shows must go to the high school auditorium—since movie house rent has gone up beyond hope.

"Our problems? Sometimes, I think we have never had anything else.

I don't suppose that they are very distinctive. Lack of money—the necessity of giving instruction so that group members will be of real value—instruction in acting, construction, lighting—the problem of building up a better taste for drama—and we have. The problem of keeping our group democratic. That may sound easy—but in a small town you're always headed for danger in that line. Improving the aesthetic taste—building sets out of ingenuity and packing boxes. The problem of wanting to grow by leaps and bounds, and having to crawl along inch by inch instead.

"Certainly we have definite ideas about Community Theatre. It must be open for any who want to work. If a person hasn't money for our very modest fees, then he can work his way in. The theatre must operate as a business, not as a hobby. It must bring a vision beyond the town boundaries—help to make our town a part of the much larger world. It must stay away from shoddy production. We may not be blessed—or cursed—with any bright stars, but we must make up for that with the best ensemble acting possible. Every play that we open has to be worth the money we ask for it. Every piece of work, from ushering to heading the Board, must be work in which we can take pride—without smugness. We have become a sort of center for social service. Mothers come to us because their daughters and sons need rehabilitation. Many of them can't go to college—have nothing to do but get into trouble. We have something constructive to offer. Older people who have grown dull from routine come to work because it stimulates their sluggish souls. We don't work with high school people because we don't think it fair to the high school dramatic teacher—who is having a bad enough time without our using her actors. The town has come to look upon us with affection, to feel that we are not an experiment, but an established and valuable asset. We may never be great, but praise God, we are keeping a lot of people from stagnation. And that's something—for the hinterlands!"

Logan, Utah. The Mormons Began It.

Dramatic history in Utah almost parallels the state's political history and, without acquaintance with the position of the drama in the life of Utah communities, the trend of the Utah State Little Theatre could not be fully appreciated. Unlike the religious factions which settled New England, the early Mormon settlers of the mountain regions encouraged community recreation and entertainment activities as a means of upholding group morale. Although they had sought the solitude of the isolated desert valleys of the Rockies to escape persecution, they saw fit to create a temple for the drama soon after building their temple for worship. The old Salt Lake Theatre, which served its original purpose until a few years ago, was one of the first public buildings in Salt Lake Valley. In a curtain speech sixty years after its dedication, Henry Miller described it as a "Cathedral in the Desert." Due to Salt Lake's strategic position as a terminal in transcontinental transportation, the city has played host to all the leading producers and players of the east.

As the radius of "Mormon" civilization expanded from Salt Lake City, the interest in drama spread to new territory. Every community provided itself with an edifice which had an amusement hall and recreation center. Dramatic offerings played an important part in the life of each small community.

Even in view of this apparent enthusiasm for the Community Theatre, dramatics were never regarded as an art with commercial or professional possibilities by the settlers. It was not the talented few who entertained the community, but almost every individual participated in performances presented by the church or its auxiliaries at some time in his life. A vital interest in drama, music, public speaking, and church work was regarded essential to an abundant life.

A secular education eventually replaced church activities. However, the church and its auxiliaries still foster plays, operas, cantatas, and pageants, in which they excel particularly. It was with such a local background that the Utah State Little Theatre came into existence.

Three instructors at the Utah State Agricultural College, Mrs. Ruth Moench Bell, Mr. Edward Bok, and Miss Donna Jones, recognized the possibilities of creating in Logan a Community Theatre that would serve not only the college students but also the entire community. Previous to 1925 such an enterprise had been introduced at the University of Utah in Salt Lake City, and its success was applauded although it had later discontinued activities. With no delegated authority from the college, these three enterprising individuals introduced the college-community theatre to their city. The recreation hall of the local Presbyterian Church was engaged to present their offerings to a limited audience. One-act plays were conspicuous on their first programs and the reaction to such an undertaking was so hearty that their public performances were soon transferred to the Lyric Theatre in the business section of town. Mrs. Weston Vernon, a diligent supporter of the Community Theatre Movement, who later became president of the Utah Federation of Women's Clubs, inaugurated the sale of season tickets for the Little Theatre. Presentations were transferred to College Hill the third season in the face of a general protest of the community, for the college is situated a mile east of the business center and at that time there was no bus or street car service. It was also a tedious climb to the summit. Many patrons predicted failure as a result of this new move, but the crowd followed the theatre and gradually increased.

With the spread of enthusiasm the enterprise increased its number of productions per season, and the services of so many capable and experienced directors were available that no one directs more than one play a season at the present time.

During the Utah State Little Theatre's thirteenth season, 1937 and 1938, six full-length dramas were presented three nights each. It has been the tradition that a season's program should include a Shakespearian drama, old classics, and contemporary favorites for variety and comparative study of theatrical tendencies.

For twelve seasons the Theatre operated independently and as a self-sustaining organization. Performers and directors participated without financial compensation, and all proceeds were expended for improving stage facilities. Like the citizens of the early Utah communities, Cache Valley citizens have diligently and unselfishly supported the Community Theatre in making its programs successful. This is particularly true of the college group. Intermission music, dancing, lighting and sound effects, properties, usher service, emergency seating facilities, and even publicity and advertising represent the voluntary service of the community's population.

In the fall of 1937 the college student body organization offering financial support requested representation on the governing board of the Little Theatre and the right to recognize its programs as student activities. The request was granted, and the Little Theatre became a function of the college, although it still remained a community-college enterprise.

The first season Mrs. Bell, Mrs. Jones, and Miss Leora Thatcher directed the Little Theatre's presentations.

At the opening of the Theatre's second season, Dr. N. A. Pedersen, Professor of English and Speech at the college and a Shakespearian authority, showed enthusiasm over the Community Theatre Movement and became president of the board, a position which he still holds. He introduced Shakespearian plays and Greek classics to its season program and participated regularly as director of such plays and actor, his recent portrayal of Lincoln in the John Drinkwater drama being acclaimed as a masterpiece.

Professor Chester J. Myers of the college speech department also contributed his support to the movement that season and has served since as managing director. After the appointment of Dr. Pedersen to the position as Dean of Arts and Sciences at the college, Professor Myers directed the annual Shakespeare classic.

Mrs. Bell has specialized in J. M. Barrie plays, having directed every one suitable for production on the Utah State stage, including "Peter Pan," "A Kiss for Cinderella," "Shall We Join the Ladies," "Quality Street," "Admirable Crichton," and "Dear Brutus."

Others who have been active in directing presentations are Wilford D. Porter, now Professor of Journalism at the college; Ira N. Hayward, Assistant Professor of English and Speech at the college; Dr. Wallace A. Goates, now Professor of Speech at University of Utah; Halbert Greaves and Floyd T. Morgan, instructors of Speech at the state college; and Mrs. Eldora Mc-Laughlin, a Logan resident.

Through the Little Theatre the Cache Valley and college cultural atmosphere has been elevated, and the theatre is generally recognized as an essential institution for education and entertainment.   Its significance to both the participant and the audience can be demonstrated in the following account:

At the time the first old age pension payments were distributed in Cache Valley, an aged lady called for her first check.   Expressing her appreciation to the disbursing clerk she commented— ". . . and they say they have real plays up at the college.   The tickets are fifty cents, and taxi fare is twenty-five cents up and twenty-five cents back.   Now I am not going to miss a one."

*Palo Alto, California.   Triumph—A Community Theatre
Supported by Taxation.*

When Kathleen Norris, the novelist, acted on the stage of the Palo Alto Civic Theatre as Princess Beatrice in Molnar's "The Swan" and as the Widow Cagle in "Sun-up," the whole town turned out to see her.   Packed houses, extra performances, and even then hundreds were turned away.

Making her debut as an actress, Mrs. Norris said: "In my long dramatic career of two parts—it's a great joke to wait almost half a century and then start right in playing leads!   But being in the theatre is good for me!"

Her associates also found it exceedingly good for them.   For they found that being off stage when Kathleen Norris was around was what once would have been called "a barrel of fun."   And one of the members of the Community Players not in the productions has suggested that when Kathleen Norris appears again, they do "Ben Hur" with a cast of several hundred to accommodate those disappointed actors who have failed to get a part in the same play with her.

This group of Community Players was organized in June of 1931 by the Palo Alto Recreation Department, a division of the municipal government. During the first year twenty-five programs of three one-act plays each and ten full-length plays were produced in the old Community House, now turned into a Veterans' Building, upon a most inadequate stage and with makeshift facilities. Deep interest, hard work, and ceaseless activity brought the organization through the next year with money in the bank.

During the 1937–38 season the Palo Alto Community Players engaged in twelve major productions—thirty-eight performances; seven workshop shows—eleven performances; a one-act program of three plays; a vaudeville show; three full-length plays; three play readings by groups. Four hundred individuals participated in these activities: two hundred twelve acting—a hundred women and a hundred twelve men; a hundred eighty-eight technical assistants—eighty-eight men and a hundred and two women. Of that number a hundred and eighty-six were actually participating for the first time. Total paid admissions for the year were twelve thousand three hundred seventy-two, a five hundred thirty-nine increase over the previous year's total despite the fact that three less performances were given.

In July, 1932, the Palo Alto Community Playhouse was presented to the city by Mrs. Louis Stern, a resident who had been interested in the Players since their inception. The auditorium seats four hundred twenty-eight in comfortable upholstered seats, two inches wider and providing three inches more knee space than those of the average commercial theatre. Occupying the complete end wall of the auditorium, the proscenium arch is a rectangle, twenty-six feet wide and thirteen feet high. Beyond the proscenium is a stage thirty-five feet deep and sixty feet wide, larger than most of the commercial stages in San Francisco.

The workshop is a two-story room amply lighted by two enormous windows on the north and east. On two floors adjoining the workshop are found the dressing-rooms. Under an arcade on the south side of the theatre are the Green Room, the director's office, and public rest rooms.

In 1934 another wing was added to the original building which contains a rehearsal hall with a stage large enough so that the "business" from shows can be set and moved to the main stage later without confusion, and the costume rooms. This wing and the opposite wing of the other recreational halls enclose the outdoor patio theatre, where several open-air productions have been given.

Charm and simplicity of style can be found in the foyer of the Playhouse, and over its hand-hewn ceiling are several rooms which can be used for rehearsals and tryouts.

So here in this Playhouse, the Civic Theatre of Palo Alto, the Community Players carry on, with probably the most ideal set-up for community drama in the whole country.

The workshop formerly produced twelve shows a year, which were given free of charge to the membership. This activity was intended to provide new people with additional opportunity for acting, and the plays were experimental in production and talent. However, it was found difficult to maintain the standard of production in the workshop, so that audiences lost interest in the shows. Now four to six special programs are given each year, free to members, with emphasis on excellence of performance.

From a membership of less than one hundred in 1931, the Players' group has grown to between five and six hundred, with approximately twelve hundred different persons having participated during the seven years. The latter figure is based upon an actual count which reveals that two hundred new people participate every year.

In November, 1932, Ralph Emerson Welles, a young man equipped with years of professional and Community Theatre experience, was employed as supervising director. Mr. Welles is still working in that capacity, and his indefatigable efforts in every phase of the Players' activities have been responsible in a large part for the group's continued success.

The other members of the staff are: Carroll Alexander, the technical director, who is a scenic designer with several years of previous experience elsewhere; Waldron Wilson, the part-time stage electrician; and B. Russell Brinley, part-time business assistant and membership secretary, who derives part of his stipend from the membership funds and part from the city budget. In addition to these four, the Players have the services of the general administrative staff of the recreation department, including a secretary, a bookkeeper, a publicity director, desk attendants to sell tickets and give out information, and a janitor.

The Players' group is organized as a distinctly recreational activity, based on the belief that everyone can act, does act, and will act if given an opportunity. Those who have had professional and semi-professional experience act in the same shows with those who have never "spoken a piece" in public before. Starring and featuring vehicles are avoided insofar as it is possible to do so and still provide the audiences with good entertainment.

What makes this group significant is that it is the only completely municipally subsidized Community Theatre in the United States. By complete subsidy is meant that all expenditures, salaries, royalties, expenses in play production, and so forth, are paid for by the city, set up in an estimated budget a year in advance. (And the Community Players stay within it, too.) All income from the box office, costume rentals, equipment, rental, and so forth, goes back into the city till. The city, however, is generous in its relation with the Players; it asks only that they return to it the bare cost of production, which for nineteen productions in 1937–38 was approximately $5000. The total budget ran around $10,000, leaving a difference of about $5000 for salaries, building maintenance, and so forth.

It was not enough that someone gave to the city a theatre; the significance of the above figures lies in the fact that a city has taken on no small obligation in accepting such a donation!

"Now, the Chamber of Commerce optimistically concludes," says Ralph Emerson Welles, "that Palo Alto has a population of eighteen thousand cheerful souls—cheerful because they know they are lucky to live in such a community. And it is a rare thing. Where else on this dizzy globe do so few people support such a program? For the past five years we have produced twenty-four plays each year, and produced them well.

"It's a handful of a job for one paid director and that director has to be young with a vast amount of enthusiasm, idealism, love of the comical animal called man, and no illusions. The director of such an institution must believe implicitly in man and yet he cannot believe him at all; he must remember that man is wholly a selfish fellow, vain, envious and greedy, treacherous and deceitful, and as volatile as the little breeze which creeps out from under the evening star. The director must remember that man does nothing for which he expects no return.

"Therefore, when a Community Theatre is supported by taxes, the taxpayer (man-with-pants) expects something in return. We believe in that. We work toward that end. Sooner or later every person not afflicted with chronic indecency will find some part to play at the Playhouse.

"You may shake your heads, you seekers, you devotees of the perfect Art. That *is* the perfect art. It is art for man, that beastie nearest and dearest to our heart, not the creamy highbrow who sees nothing in his neighbors' eyes but his own image. Not that we are a pot who would tell our kettle-headed friend to wipe off his spout even after we have polished our own. We use them all, the brilliants, dims, rich and poor, the bores, the boors, the haves, the have-nots, the ins, the outs, the four hundred and the baker's dozen.

"The only stipulation is that they play our game while they are here. Simple, isn't it? And yet, not so simple if the city were not behind it. It is that impersonal subsidy that does it. Everything must be done for the good of the most, for we are a PUBLIC SERVICE. I say it's simple if you know how. The standard must be kept up if you expect the neighbors to come in at the front door. It is. Competition is keener for parts, work is harder, lines are learned sooner (if they aren't learned soon enough, they know someone else will be doing it), and I have to learn to teach faster.

"Incidentally, there is no such things as a good director for a Community Theatre. There are good teachers who succeed, but a director would be lost because a director must have 'actors' and there aren't enough actors for him to direct. There are people who want to become (and, of course, think they are) actors, but if the so-called director is up to his job, he will have to spend so much time teaching that he will have no time left for directing. And this all to the good because it is knowledge of this fact which gives people the confidence to join forces with you!"

They come from all over the country to Palo Alto, from Seattle and Los Angeles, New York and San Francisco, to learn something about the theatre. Among the twelve thousand paid admissions last year could be found a season ticket holder of several years' standing who makes monthly jaunts down from Sacramento, puts up at a hotel in Palo Alto, dines, walks a mile across town to the Playhouse, sees his show, chats with a few people who know only that he is a kindly little man of sixty who doesn't hear very well and who seems to live in Sacramento. They don't even know his name *is* Mr. Douglas, but he doesn't care. He says he tried every theatre and group, professional and otherwise, in San Francisco and "all over" but Palo Alto is the only place where he can see and hear everything and be a part of what's going on.

There are times, Mr. Welles feels, when the Palo Alto Community Players most certainly would have gone on the rocks where lie the remains of other earnest little groups were it not for the connection with the city government. He is therefore very much in favor of municipal subsidy—as who isn't?

"City governments (generally speaking) must go on," he says, "and with them their enterprises, whether certain individuals are tired of them or not. Projects dependent upon the good will, the whims, the petty personal desires of ambitious individuals are completely at the mercy of those individuals who, when they become unfriendly, have no mercy. They would rather see a thing go 'bust' than succeed against their advice. They come to feel that the entire success of the organization is due to their efforts and theirs alone.

"There is no business in the world, I think, where the layman feels himself a competent critic with so little justification; where the novice so soon blossoms forth into an artist. Give them two or three parts of importance (or even of no importance) and let them serve on the Board of Directors too long (say three years), and they know so much more than the director who has spent years in the business. Therefore, it is necessary that beyond the director there is a power vested in the hands of the entire Community which must be served, and cannot be made subservient to an individual wish."

Wise words, Mr. Welles, and true.

From this Playhouse several have gone on to success in the world of the professional theatre. The postmaster of Morgan Hill, forty miles south of Palo Alto, made the eighty-mile trip every night for five weeks to play the blind major in "The Enchanted Cottage." He has now gone to Hollywood and is listed as Charles Barnes, Actor. In the same cast were Peggy

Converse, now of Broadway; Waldo Salt, writing screen plays in Hollywood; William Pabst, production manager of radio station KFRC in San Francisco. Pat Gleason is doing all right in Hollywood, too. Olivia De Havilland once played in the Playhouse in "Alice in Wonderland." Aurania Rouverol, the playwright, and her daughter Jean, were both in Palo Alto for several years. Joan Wheeler, Elizabeth Wilbur, Roger Converse, James Corner, Neal Berry, Annalies Morgan, Garret Starmer, are to be found in the professional theatre.

And yet Mr. Welles makes no pretence of training people for the professional stage. He believes in training people for an avocation, not a vocation.

"I have no confidence in the profession I once tried to grace with my loyalty," he says. "It was good to me, too, but I was young then. I know the old ones though and they don't make me happy with the look in their eyes.

"Do you find what I have told you about our Community Theatre disappointing? Does it seem childish or immature to think of a Community Theatre as a social service where people learn to do things together, to understand each other better, to try to be happier, instead of wealthier? Too idealistic? Perhaps, but it works. It works for everybody. So long. Come and see how it works some day!"

And the invitation is for everybody. For here in Palo Alto is a Community Theatre that comes as near being ideal as any we know. Community participation—municipal subsidy—isn't that a goal worth striving for?

Pasadena, California. Where? When? How?

Journalistically speaking these are questions. When applied to the Pasadena Community Playhouse, the first two may be answered easily. Where? Pasadena, California, a city which enjoys the largest leisure class of any community in the world, which in its experiments of socialized government has made a marked success, a city marked by beautiful civic buildings, thoroughfares, and boulevards, and blocks upon blocks of beautiful homes and modest cottages.

When? The Pasadena Community Playhouse was not founded, but stranded! Its original birth pang was when Gilmor Brown got off the train in Pasadena as the head of a little company of professional players. In those parlous days, just prior to and after the beginning of the war, it was difficult for a professional stock company to find a place for itself in any community. Mr. Brown, ever sensitive to the winds of public tendency, created and secured the interest and cooperation of a number of talented amateurs, and in November, 1918, organized the Pasadena Community Playhouse Association on an amateur basis with a Board of Directors of responsible citizens and a variable group of actors.

How? How was the Pasadena Community Playhouse organized? Through the personality and genius of one man—Gilmor Brown. Harriet L. Green, in her book *Portrait of a Man—and an Idea,* wrote:

"It is significant that Gilmor Brown did not arrive at the theatre through struggle or indirection. He was born to it, and he was born in North Dakota. This means that he was born to that outpost, pioneer, barnstorming theatre of the far west whose devotees had to rely so largely on unlimited energy, ingenuity and sheer theatrical bravado to maintain a professional existence. His father, Orville A. Brown, of English descent, was born in Illinois; his mother, a Gilmor of Scotch ancestry, was born in Georgia. In both could be perceived that mingling of shrewd, practical common sense with a robust spirit of adventure, so characteristic of American pioneer stock. With perhaps just a touch of the dreamer, the visionary, added.

"The boy, along with the usual public school education, early acquired familiarity with the practical mechanics and craftsmanship of the stage as practiced in small western stock companies. As soon as he was old enough, he made his way east where he could contact the traditions, methods and personalities of the larger theatre. He found a place with the Ben Greet Players, then fresh from England and attracting favorable attention in New York and elsewhere. After touring the country with them, he worked again in Western stock and road companies, then enjoying their golden era of prosperity in the rapidly developing country. Wherever he might be, he lost no opportunity to increase both his technical and theoretical knowledge of everything pertaining to the stage. In Chicago he had the good fortune to come under the notice of a highly gifted and experienced woman, Mrs. Milward Adams, who not only gave him valuable instruction but through her recognition of his capabilities inspired the self-confidence and courage necessary to their development. 'A woman with a rare power of evoking personality,' he says of her gratefully today.

"When the little group of Savoy Players came to Pasadena in 1916, Gilmor Brown was, as he has been ever since, a member of a closely united family. With him were his father and mother, his brother Frank, and his sister-in-law, Virginia Lykins Brown, who still at lengthening intervals brings her breezy comedy and sure sense of humor to the Playhouse stage. . . .

"So there is Gilmor Brown in his office at the Playhouse every morning, rapidly discharging routine duties and interviewing a panoramic succession of actors, playwrights, patrons, visitors, workers and associates who press for attention. In the afternoon he is not always in his office. He may be conducting rehearsals or classes, or giving a lecture, or in conference with committees on costume, production, casting, publicity, the School of the Theatre; or he may be at the warehouse or on the stage with the art director or the stage carpenter or electrician; or at a Board meeting discussing the graver problems of policy, finance, membership, play selection and other functions centering in that body. Or he may be over at 'Western' in Los Angeles, choosing costumes for an important production, or at the playbrokers' arguing the matter of royalties, or attending to any one of a hundred other responsibilities that ultimately devolve on him.

"Evening usually finds him again in his office. There may be distinguished visitors from home or abroad who come up between the acts of the performance; there are diplomatic problems of personality and temperament to be dealt with, the clash of conflicting egotisms to adjust; and always—and this I think is closest to his heart of all—the endless procession of theatre-loving youth; eager, hopeful and ambitious or frustrated and bewildered, all seeking the counsel and encouragement, the opportunity and inspiration which they fondly believe can open to them the magic doors of their heart's desire. Small wonder that he sometimes goes home to that favorite recreation of highly responsible and active minds—the detective story!"

In trying to sketch the history of the Pasadena Community Playhouse, the personality of this one man must constantly be kept fresh in mind to understand this institution's success. Next to Gilmor Brown there is in the Playhouse Association another figure who, to the insiders at least, must loom large in the history of the Association's development. That man is Charles F. Prickett. There has long been a legend about the Playhouse that the young people of the theatre often speak of these two men as "The Great God Brown and His Archangel Prickett." Charles Prickett is probably one of the most astute business managers of the theatre in this country today. He has veritably made theatre management a science. His innovation of the salary percentage based upon weekly income has enabled the Playhouse to maintain a staff of sixty-odd persons throughout the years of the depression, yet give the individuals the benefit of every dollar that came into the box office.

Prickett's innumerable graphs, pamphlets, and promotion material which the Playhouse has generously scattered throughout the country has created better business organization and management of Community Theatres.

The story of the life of the Playhouse has been told so many times and in such great detail that it need only be outlined. The Association first began working in a little broken down theatre on Fair Oaks Avenue. There an inadequate stage and an uncomfortable auditorium presented an opportunity for the enthusiasm of Brown's first players to win an audience which soon expanded the walls of this little temple into the now magnificent palace of the theatre on El Molingo Avenue.

Before the theatre are great palm trees, the insignia of the Pasadena Community Playhouse. Three flat steps lead into the large patio. On the right stands a fountain which splashes coolly throughout the evening. Beyond, in an arcade, heavy oak doors lead into the lobby where pleasant-faced and gaily-uniformed youngsters act as ushers. Once in the auditorium one realizes that in fifteen years taste in theatre architecture has changed. In 1925 this rococo and flamboyant Spanish auditorium was the latest word. Today it needs simplification, and undoubtedly when money and time are available, Brown will see to it. However, despite this fulsome architectural detail, there is an aesthetic quality in the surroundings. For the auditorium is not harsh, stern, austere, or imposing. The colors are warm, the tiling is gay, the curtain intriguing, the ceiling rich in wavering light, and the whole creates the realization that "This is a theatre."

Behind the curtain is a stage upon which more than seven hundred productions have been presented. Upon that stage every recognized playwright of the world has had at least one of his plays produced. There one may have seen the only production of "Lazarus Laughed"—possibly O'Neill's greatest effort—every play that Shakespeare ever wrote, the performances of thousands of young, middle-aged, and elderly people, and dozens of settings from the brushes of some of America's best designers. The Pasadenan, who has made the Playhouse a weekly ritual, is able to sit back and say: "I have experienced in these past years the pleasure of the greatest and most catholic theatre in the world today."

Off the patio, to the right, a staircase under a trellis leads into a small auditorium with a stage at each end. Here every two weeks throughout the year is presented either a new production by an unknown playwright or an experimental production given by the seniors of the School of the Theatre. The Laboratory Theatre of the Playhouse is perhaps one of the most valuable adjuncts to the American theatre, for this is the only group that constantly favors the new playwright, allowing him an opportunity to create with living material the images of his mind. *Stage* magazine in June, 1937, awarded the outstanding palm of that year in the Community Theatre field to the Laboratory Theatre, and it then said: "Most significant was Gilmor Brown's newly established laboratory theatre at the Pasadena Playhouse. The climax of its season of twelve full-length original plays was the presentation of Harold Igo's American trilogy 'Ohio Doom,' 'America Mass,' and 'Steel.' . . ."

Gilmor Brown has a private theatre known as the Playbox, which has no legal connection with the Playhouse, but is a favorite offspring. In this unique theatre, built in the rear of Mr. Brown's home, is one of the most radical experimentations in theatre in the world. Mr. Brown occasionally does an original script there, but more frequently gives exotically different productions of the world's great and little known classics of the theatre.

For ten years or more, the Playhouse has conducted a school which has served as added revenue to the ever-demanding coffers of the Playhouse and has enabled hundreds of youngsters to get an admirable training in their chosen profession. There is no theatre school in the United States, outside of the universities, that can compete with the Pasadena Playhouse in equipment, personnel, variety of subject matter, and scope of theatre instruction and technique.

Portland, Oregon. An All-embracing Membership.

While Portland has a population of only three hundred thousand— enough to support an active Little Theatre—it has a "metropolitan area" of well over a half million. There are many outlying towns in Oregon and southwestern Washington, within easy commuting distance, which are contributing active and audience support in increasing numbers. The Portland Civic Theatre is the only legitimate theatre producing regularly within a radius of two hundred miles; only economic limitations of the theatre prevent its spreading its influence over a very wide territory.

For almost a quarter of a century the city has been interested in community drama. For a good many years that interest was spasmodic; plays were produced at irregular intervals, in drawing rooms or public parks or in old buildings; there was no formal organization. In 1927, for the first time, a definite season was attempted; a director was engaged, a board organized to handle the administrative end of the business, a name was adopted. On March 22, 1929, the Portland Civic Theatre was incorporated as a nonprofit organization having for its object "The promotion and development of dramatic art, for the purpose of the education and culture of the members and the citizens of the City of Portland and the State of Oregon."

Since then the Portland Civic Theatre has dedicated itself to maintaining a high standard of play production, to developing discriminating taste on the part of its growing audiences; and especially to offering opportunity for expression and development to everyone who earnestly desired it. A fixed policy for public tryouts was adopted early by the Board of Trustees; there are no social barriers to limit participation. People from all walks of life meet on common ground. Some have come who are on relief; they rub elbows with lawyers and business men, teachers and Junior Leaguers, housewives and club women.

There is no age barrier to consider, for six-year-old Tiny Tim is as much a factor in the theatre success as the eighty-six-year-old man from Devon, who year after year has looked forward to participation in one of the theatre's plays as the highlight of an otherwise drab existence. He is on relief, and car fare to rehearsals and performances must be supplied by some sympathetic Board member, if he is not to walk weary miles.

Between these extremes of youth and old age are boys and girls, men and women, grandfathers and grandmothers, who are finding in this non-professional theatre a happy opportunity for study and development. To the student of a nearby college who went without food that he might save car fare and so be able to accept a part in "Yellow Jack"; to the middle-aged street conductor who developed undreamed-of ability as an actor; to the talented Junior Leaguer and to the shy waitress who wanted to know good literature and good drama—to these and countless others the Civic Theatre has opened the door to a new world.

During the 1935–36 season, over five hundred people responded to the tryout notices in the daily papers; two hundred twenty-five acting parts were filled by the people of Portland and adjacent communities; only twenty-four people played more than one part and about fifty per cent of the entire number were new to Civic Theatre activities. This does not take into account the scores who over the years have been interested in the arts and crafts of stage production—in stage design, in building, painting, and the like. The Civic Theatre employs only its director, an executive director, and an office secretary. All work is done by volunteer enthusiasts.

One of the difficult problems faced by the Civic Theatre early in its existence was the need of providing adequate and satisfying opportunity to *all* those who appealed for help. Try as it would, only a small percentage of those registering a desire for active work could be placed in the casts of major plays. A series of workshop productions was inaugurated, but these too failed to absorb the list of applicants. Finally, five years ago, after careful study and with some apprehension, it was decided to organize a Civic Theatre School. The Board of Trustees thought that a school would offer not only a greater outlet for activity, but also a training in voice, diction, posture and fundamentals of acting for those who wished to use it as an avocation.

The Board visioned its productions as laboratories for the students of stagecraft, where theories would find practical application. It also recognized a new and insistent demand for instruction in radio work, and decided to pioneer in that field; it responded to a growing interest in the art of playwriting, and besides creating a study class, inaugurated an annual state-wide playwriting contest. Thus, the Civic Theatre School got under way.

Fortunately, a number of competent teachers with exceptional technical training enthused over the new venture and cooperated to the fullest extent. Classes had to be held in office buildings, in churches and theatres—in rent-free space with meagre equipment; yet students registered in great numbers. Old and young, rich and poor, sought to improve and enrich their personalities that they might meet more successfully the problems of their everyday lives.

The Portland Civic Theatre has been justly proud of its school. In two successive years it produced "Alice in Wonderland" in a city park, for the Portland Rose Festival Association; it has been called on several times to write and produce radio skits for the Community Chest; it repeated "Ah, Wilderness" in the Public Auditorium at the request of the Will Rogers Memorial Committee, and has inaugurated a midsummer Shakespeare Festival of wide appeal.

So high have been its academic standards and so notable its faculty that last season Reed College, through Mr. Dexter Keezer, President, granted college credit to any of its students completing work in the school. This season it became affiliated with Oregon's State System of Higher Education, through the Portland Extension Center of the University, and now has fifty enrolled students working toward degrees.

One of the school's most interesting courses was organized at the instance of the director of auditoriums of the Portland Public Schools. Designed primarily for teachers, directors of recreational activities, supervisors of children's organizations, and the like, this class teaches the principles and practices of directing children's dramatics, including the use of drama in the presentation of history, geography, English, music and art: distinctly pioneer work in the Pacific Northwest.

It need not be pointed out that such a program of education, entertainment and service could not have been carried on without adequate local support. The activities of the Civic Theatre are financed primarily by widespread membership. Dues are $3.50 a year, and each membership includes a season ticket for the current plays. Membership dues, box-office receipts and school tuitions have been adequate to keep the theatre going, free from debt, all during the trying years of the depression.

This is not to suggest that there have been no hardships. Ever since the inception of the Portland Civic Theatre, its plays have been produced in an auditorium designed for a concert hall. The stage is only eighteen feet deep, thirty-four feet wide; there is no grid; dressing rooms are inadequate, and scenery, furniture and props have to be carted upstairs whenever a shift in scenes is necessary.

The Civic Theatre has accepted these limitations as a challenge to its ingenuity and has produced beautiful plays with rare technical skill. Now, however, this auditorium has been converted into a moving picture theatre and the new owner was reluctant to allow the theatre even to conclude its 1937–38 season there. A group of business men, sympathetic to the Civic Theatre, combed the city for a new location, but found nothing available.

There is no legitimate theatre in Portland and, therefore, practically no touring companies ever visit it. Last season "Tobacco Road" and "Three Men on a Horse" played here in large movie houses to indifferent audiences.

This year there is no prospect of a single professional company stopping in this city, and responsibility for presenting contemporary drama to the citizens of Portland and its environs rests wholly upon the Portland Civic Theatre. If the theatre is not able to solve its housing problem, then the Civic Theatre and the Civic Theatre School must cease to function as educational and cultural agencies in the community.

Early in 1938 the Civic Theatre had an exceptional opportunity to acquire a thirty-year lease on a small movie house in an acceptable location, and at the same time to buy at a reasonable figure adjoining property on which a modest building could be erected to care permanently for the school and the theatre's workshop. The Board of Trustees counts among its members some of the finest legal, financial and administrative leaders in the city, and it was the considered judgment of this group, after careful study, that only by courageously facing the responsibility involved in such an undertaking could the future of the theatre be assured.

The officers and members of the Portland Civic Theatre believe that the art of the theatre is one of the greatest of the arts; that it is the younger generation's birthright to benefit by its values; that it is an educational factor and an instrument of culture today, as it has been in centuries of history. They further believe that the Portland Civic Theatre has for ten years been a worthy exponent of this art, and that its contribution to the life and development of the northwest is too notable to be allowed to die.

Reno, Nevada. "We Take Pride in . . ."

"We take particular pride in the fact that since we first organized, we have always run on a carefully prepared budget and not only have kept to it, but also have ended each season with a clear profit." So, with pardonable pride, Edwin Semenza, the director of the Reno Little Theatre, points out that his organization, created as it was in the middle of the depression, has managed to make for itself a laudable box office record.

Back in 1935 Edwin Semenza and ten other serious theatre-minded people banded together to form a dramatic club. They faced several problems, one of which was the marked apathy on the part of the townspeople of Reno toward the term "little theatre," because several abortive attempts had been made to start such a movement there. One organizer even succeeded in raising several thousand dollars to build a theatre without first offering a single play. Nothing was ever heard further of a play or of the money. Another attempt was made a few years later. This group presented a first play, but the proceeds were swallowed up in some mysterious fashion and the leading organizer left town.

With this background to overcome, the new group was determined to present a complete season of plays and allow the townspeople to draw their own conclusions as to whether they were worthy of encouragement or not. They were fortunate in starting with a group large enough to cast their first play, and since all people in the group had had previous amateur experience, they had a remarkably successful presentation of "Three-Cornered Moon," which was followed by "Goodbye Again," "Post Road," "Cradle Song," "Oliver, Oliver," (which Semenza confidentially says—"even under the title of 'Mary at Leisure,' stunk") and "The Trial of Mary Dugan."

From the first play, this group, which was the nucleus of the Reno Little Theatre, played to packed houses, which testifies that their ability to sell tickets was second only to their histrionic talents.

Among the early problems of the Reno Little Theatre was their first brush with censorship when the second production, "Goodbye Again," as staged in the high school auditorium, resulted in an abrupt necessity to move somewhere beyond the reach of an officious member of the Board of Education. So they moved to the Civic Auditorium, as it is laughingly called; for the auditorium is the progeny of an architect's nightmare. It consists of a tiny lecture platform at one end of a large barren flat floor which seats fifteen hundred people. The stage is ten feet deep and twenty-four feet wide, and the off-stage space consists of two small rooms which serve as dressing room, store room, Green Room; and as the Little Theatre members cryptically remark—"The lack of toilets always speeds up the tempo of our last acts!"

From the description above, it is readily seen that it was an absolute necessity for the group to find a permanent headquarters somewhere else. At first a workshop was established in an idle dance hall, then in a garage, and finally in an abandoned house which served for the remainder of the first year.

The summer between the first and second years was spent in an entire reorganization of the club. They were fortunate to secure the help of Mrs. Sylvia Regan, formerly of the New York Theatre Union, who is now with the Mercury Theatre. They incorporated as a non-profit organization, governed by a Board of Directors of seven people. Membership in the acting company was open to anyone in the city, and after a concerted ticket drive, five hundred and fifty season tickets were sold for the second season. On the strength of this budget, four plays were produced.

A production of "Elizabeth the Queen" proved to be the high point of this season, and with its remarkable success, they were definitely accepted as a source of inspiration in the community life of Reno.

This season was concluded with a small cash balance, more equipment, and increased patronage. In fact, the income was exactly double that of the first year.

At the beginning of the third season there was a windfall: an abandoned potato chip factory; and in 1938, after ousting the rats with which the place was infested, they constructed there a small stage, a workshop, offices, paint rooms, and so forth.

In the third year, the director was hired on a full time basis; before that, he had been able to serve only part time. During that year their income trebled that of their first season.

It is interesting to note that they have on file more than one hundred people eligible for acting and that they have made efforts to draw together in a back-stage group of their own. The Board of Directors consists of seven people, each of whom acts as chairman of some production committee or necessary theatre service.

The entire responsibility for the production is placed directly on the Board of Directors whose spearhead, of course, is the professional coach. By placing complete control of the organization in the hands of the Board, they have in their own words "eliminated any possibility of our actors trying to dictate the policy of the whole group." This may seem highly autocratic in form, but actually it is very successful in practice and it is surprising to note how often this form of artistic dictatorship functions most efficiently in the essentially democratic form of Community Theatre.

The Reno Little Theatre is faced with the necessity of making its season a financial success. Therefore, the choice of plays to date has been largely determined by box-office appeal. The audience is certainly cosmopolitan in its interests. A large transient population clamors for Broadway hits which they may have missed at home or wish to see again. A portion of the audience likes artistic plays, another group wants to see only comedies, while still another element is satisfied to accept whatever seems to make a balanced program. The schedules of the Reno Little Theatre show that they have tried to maintain a balance of one farce, one comedy drama, a straight comedy, a serious drama, and one costume play.

During the year free classes in acting are given by the director for the benefit of the back-stage group, who feel that they need more experience in elementary training. These also allow the more experienced to work on different types of characterization. It is also noteworthy that the Reno Little Theatre has been conducting a one-act play contest with a small prize and a guarantee of production for the winner.

The primary aim of the Reno Little Theatre has been that of service to the community. That they have succeeded is shown clearly by the fact that at least one twentieth of the entire population of Reno attends each of their plays. Each season over two hundred persons find recreation and creative outlet by actual participation in the productions.

Through their radio programs and one-act plays, which are occasionally donated to worthy organizations in the community, many hundreds of other people are contacted by the Little Theatre.

They have recently launched a campaign for a theatre building of their own, and are making every effort to jolt their audiences into awareness of the difficulties under which they are forced to work. As a result, they have been given a former exposition building ideally situated in one of the city's parks. The architectural plans have been drawn for a model small theatre, seating approximately five hundred, with a large stage and workshop facilities.

Edwin Semenza has attempted to approach the problems of policy from a very practical viewpoint, for he says: "I believe the strength of a Community Theatre lies in the ability of the producing group to anticipate the needs and desires of its audience before that need is openly expressed by the paying public. Whenever a producing group fails to anticipate those needs and changes, it loses its position of leadership and falls a prey to the forces of dissension."

Mr. Semenza also goes on to say that if any friends of the Community Theatre Movement are contemplating taking the well-known "cure" in Reno sometime in the next few seasons, they are most welcome to drop into the Little Theatre and enjoy some real "wild western" hospitality.

San Carlos, California. Who's a Coward?

"Quick curtain . . ."

How can you have a quick curtain when it won't work that way? Looks like an impasse, eh? The answer is—darken the stage! One can always turn out a light in a hurry—and the San Carlos Players did.

That's the way they solved one problem—but there were others. For instance, how could a lady be discovered bound, gagged, and tied to a chair at the right of the stage at the end of the first act—when the only entrance is left, and there's no backdrop? Simple. Tie her up before the performance starts!

Thus with one make-shift and another, this group of players under the leadership of Harold Jones has enlivened the community of San Carlos, as well as Veterans' Hospitals in the Bay region, with a number of comedies.

It all started at a meeting of the San Carlos Community Club in September, 1926. "Let's do a play!" someone said, and they did.

To prove their nerve, the San Carlos Players chose a sketch for their opening effort whose title was appropriately enough, "Who's a Coward?" and when they had proved that they were not, another Community Theatre was added to the roster. Their past twelve years have seen production of a long list of plays, including "The Count of Monte Cristo," "Rip Van Winkle," "Oliver Twist," "Mrs. Wiggs of the Cabbage Patch," "Rebecca of Sunnybrook Farm," and some twenty others.

This is a good place to point out that San Carlos is a fine example of the great sensitivity that exists between almost all Community Theatres and their audiences. For this group plays to an audience that would be bored to death with any amateur production of "End of Summer," "The Second Man," or "Private Lives," but which has demanded two week runs of "The Girl from Out Yonder."

It is not the duty of a Community Theatre to foist upon patrons a pseudo-sophistication that is foreign to their instincts. Thus, while the above list of plays may not compare aesthetically with the repertory of Cleveland or Pasadena, it is nevertheless a list chosen with a great deal of discrimination.

The San Carlos Players allow themselves to act as a benefit organization for various Parent Teachers Associations, Volunteer Firemen, clubs, churches, etc. They give numerous benefits throughout the year resulting in a guarantee for their overhead and an immense amount of good will from all their sister groups. It is noteworthy of the Community Theatre Movement that you often find the theatre group is supporting every other type of cultural and club activity in its home town.

Harold Jones, who since the beginning of the San Carlos Players has been intensely interested in their work, writes his opinion of the relation of the Community Theatre to its locale: "It should be run for the good of other organizations . . . to give those who enjoy the stage a chance to see real dramas . . . and to keep this mode of entertainment alive in a younger generation who may some day, God willing, tire of talkies and canned dramas that are spewed on the radio."

Jones ended his comments with: "The Community Theatre is valuable because of the great pleasure it gives those who enjoy acting to mingle in a group of people who all enjoy the same hobby." In other words, he, like so many other people, believes that the value of a Community Theatre lies in its democratic promotion of cultural neighborliness.

The following description of the San Carlos Players is taken from Ethel Bogardus' story about them in the *San Francisco Examiner*.

They have a regular troupe. Jones, the moving spirit, is a graduate of the "ten-twent'-thirt's," with stock experience in everything. There are eight members to the troupe. Thelma Wright, leading lady, stars in the "westerns," comedy leads, and ingenues. Elizabeth Hopkins does the character roles, and heavy women's parts. Wilma Martin is soubrette, and handles the dramatic roles. Margaret Jones, with no stage experience to her credit, has made a hit in comedy roles. In ordinary life West Mallory handles the "heavy" work in a garage, but on play night he's a juvenile, character comedian, or "short heavy." Then there's Harry Gee who has displayed an unexpected flair for comedy. Clarence Wright is the "baby" of the cast— but he's also stage and business manager, juvenile and heavy.

San Diego, California. A Promising Future.

It is difficult to write coherently of the condition of the Community Theatre in San Diego for at the present time theatrical activities in that city are going through a very active stage of evolution.

It seems that originally there was a group of players banded together under the name of The Barn Players Club, founded by Mrs. J. William Fisher in the fall of 1933 with $85 that was left over in the treasury of the San Diego University Women's Club. Seventy-five dollars of this was spent for the first month's rent of an old mansion in San Diego and the remaining $10 was used for clearing up the barn in the rear. With the friendly cooperation of the society editors of the local papers, no great difficulty was experienced in calling together a group of drama lovers.

It was planned to convert the mansion into a club residence for young women, the income of which would go to pay for the entire establishment. This would then allow the barn to be developed and expanded without the necessity of high overhead.

Mr. David Young was the first director and under his guidance a number of interesting productions were given. However, the new home of the Barn Players Club seemed to be doomed from the beginning as the possibility of the sale of this valuable property was ever in the wind. The blow finally fell and the Barn Players were forced to look for another location.

In the meantime a group of distinguished San Diegans had organized themselves as the "Save the Globe" Committee. They tried to interest the Barn Players in the prospect of establishing a unified Community Theatre with headquarters in the Globe Theatre which was reconstructed and fireproofed by a WPA grant in cooperation with the city government. But for some reason the Barn Players chose to keep their identity and moved to the Bandim House in the Old Town, which is the Mecca for thousands of tourists throughout the year.

In the meantime, the Community Theatre at the Globe apparently faces a substantial future. Under the direction of Mr. Luther Kennett it has given a number of productions, each of which has been an improvement over the previous one. So the Community Theatre looks forward to making for itself definite and permanent place in the cultural life of San Diego.

San Francisco, California. Rats and Spectators.

San Francisco's foremost Community Theatre, The Wayfarers, celebrated their seventh anniversary in March, 1938, with that supreme test of ambition and talent, the Shakespearian Festival. "Othello," "The Merchant of Venice," and "Hamlet" were produced in repertory form—three nights each—with the turnaway houses for each performance a far cry from their inauspicious beginning seven years before.

In 1931 seven young people in San Francisco realized that they were stage-struck. Motivated by the common desire to act and be of the theatre, they banded together under the leadership of Jack Thomas and took the name of "The Wayfarers."

Commercial Street in San Francisco is a narrow, spectacularly unkempt alley, starting at the waterfront and rather carelessly losing itself in the bowels of Chinatown. The block adjoining the Embarcadero, or waterfront, is a polyglot of Scandinavian seamen's pubs, sailors' missions, and sundry union halls, graced with marvelous forethought at the first corner by the Harbor Police Station, while across the street as a more politic gesture stands Harbor Emergency Hospital. In this "genteel" setting, the hardy Wayfarers rented a second story loft directly across from the hospital. Hammer, brush, and needle were wielded long and often and March 21, 1931, saw the original subscribers arrive and, with hasty glances at the surroundings, enter 74 Commercial Street for Opening Night.

Ascending a long, narrow stairway, Mr. and Mrs. Guest noticed weirdly crayoned concrete walls reflecting the candlelight. Through a small foyer at the top they entered a long narrow room done in wine-red beaver board against vari-colored beams, one white, one yellow, etc., with candles set in art metal sconces along the wall. Comfortably seated, each guest found cigarettes and matches in a tray in front of every bench, to be divided among the four which it accommodated. By eight-thirty all fifty-two seats were taken, a gong sounded somewhere in the distance and a young woman in formal evening gown made a graceful rite of snuffing each candle; the hand-painted muslin curtain parted and the first of four one-act plays was on.

Critics from the daily papers were not long in "discovering" The Wayfarers' loft and no professional troupe ever read their reviews with more appreciation—whether favorable or otherwise. "Hard by the Ferry Tower" aptly described the work connected with its operation. Perforce everyone was employed during the day in other more mundane though lucrative capacities, and construction, set building, reading, selecting or even writing the next play, making of costumes, rehearsals, printing and mailing of subscription lists—in fact all work—was done at night or over week-ends. Incidentally, this situation has not changed and has several times given rise to the question: Have The Wayfarers found the long-sought substitute for sleep?

This era was definitely the experimental stage, as no one in the group could have been considered well versed in acting, directing, scene design, lighting effects, or any branch of stagecraft. References, trade journals and the contemporary stage were avidly followed and discussed, but for the most part effects were worked out by the trial and error method. This, coupled with intelligence and imagination, undoubtedly accounts for The Wayfarers' reputation for striking originality in all phases of their work.

After two years of presenting one-acts and short plays written by the members and San Francisco literary people, Ibsen's "A Doll's House," their first full-length play, was produced successfully. The reaction to this, by both cast and audience, was so favorable that a production was scheduled for every month and a half, each running nine nights. "Volpone," "Othello," "Don Juan," "Camille," and "Hamlet" followed in rapid succession.

However, off-stage noises such as rollicking Viking chanteys by the Norse rovers in the nearby groggery, the noisy arrival of the "Black Maria" next door, and the subsequent siren of the ambulance starting out to retrieve the wounded Irish, were not conducive to a spasmodic Oswald holding his audience spellbound in "Ghosts." In addition, word had apparently spread amongst the terrier-sized rats of the waterfront that The Wayfarers had furnished the place in cozy style for them; aside from sitting on the rafters in the flies and watching the performance, they were reported to have twice disputed the occupancy of a seat with guests. Space was at a premium on the stage, sixteen feet deep, with a proscenium nine feet wide and eight high. All these factors, together with an increasingly large subscription list incapable of being seated at 74 Commercial Street, were instrumental in the decision to find larger quarters.

A building housing in succession a church, a gymnasium, and a marionette theatre was available on Clay Street near Van Ness. Two Federal Housing Loans were obtained and the building was completely done over; a lobby as large as the original theatre was done in paneled Firtex and painted blue-gray. The floor was raised and inclined in the theatre proper and forest-green benches, alternately covered with green and yellow-red canvas cushions, were installed sufficient to seat a hundred and eight guests. The original color of the first theatre was repeated in painting the auditorium wine-red with six Shakespearian murals crayoned on the Firtex wall—each depicting one of the Bard's better-known plays.

The stage was patterned after a combination of three of Max Reinhardt's European stage designs, using a circular-step apron. This terminates in an arched opening on either side which is utilized for an entrance-exit in apron scenes played in front of the main curtain. One of the few plaster domes in America today forms the permanent backing to the stage and has proved invaluable in acoustical, lighting, and setting purposes. If necessary, the action of the play is taken across the apron into the audience and lighting equipment is such that any effect may be obtained from dawn at Elsinore to the murky sub-surface shadows of Maxim Gorky's "Lower Depths."

The nucleus of the group is composed of ten people, with an acting membership of thirty-five. The organization is entirely self-supporting, relying for revenue on guests' subscriptions and members' dues ($1.00 monthly). It is totally devoid of sponsors and with the possible exception of wigs and make-up The Wayfarers depend upon themselves for all theatre needs. Of the seven original Wayfarers, four are still active: Jack Thomas, Jerald Elwood, Margaret and Lawrence Kempton. Thomas has been author, director, producer, actor, financial savior and guiding spirit of The Wayfarers and has recently opened a School of the Theatre in conjunction with its regular operation. Jerald Elwood has gained a reputation for his artistic and imaginative sets and lighting.

This theatre is most impressive and has an atmosphere of excitement about it. Many San Franciscans whose instincts for theatre are being given excellent guidance and outlet make up the organization. It is to be hoped that success will not tend to "professionalize" this group, for to destroy the community link and spirit of cooperation, which is now the very life blood of The Wayfarers, would be a sad blow to the possibilities of establishing a really great theatre in San Francisco.

Scobey, Montana. A Gallant Start.

The Scobey Community Players were organized in 1937 by Reverend A. S. Bellinger, a progressive Methodist minister of that city. His intention at that time was to confine the activities of the Players to members of his congregation who were interested in such a movement. However, public interest was aroused to such an extent that applications were received from several outsiders and it became almost at once a community affair.

Winifred Haun has written a letter concerning the trials and hardships that many theatres in smaller communities undergo. We shall let her speak for herself:

"Not unnaturally the financial problems of the Scoville Community Players were acute from the beginning and there have been no groups to speak of for the last ten years—and also all too many of the community must receive aid from the federal government.

"They chose as their first play 'The Blue Bag,' an interesting, fast-moving comedy with, they considered, box-office appeal and no royalty. Also, it required but one interior set—there being only one set in town (which had to be borrowed) and that an interior. However, the cast entered into the spirit of the thing and carried it off with remarkable success and to the complete satisfaction of their 'public.' They then took the show to several outlying towns, where they played to capacity houses, and at the same time eased the money situation somewhat.

"The winters in Scobey are long and very severe, and the handicaps under which they labored were most trying. They made their own curtain of black sateen—for which they had to borrow the money until after the show opened. They rehearsed just any place where they could find an empty corner—were able to rehearse on the stage, with sets and props, just once before the performance. But of such trials are troupers made!

"So far the Players have no theatre of their own, as they are still greatly hampered by lack of money. However, aside from that, there have been no buildings available that would be suitable for their purpose until very recently, and for one of which they are now negotiating.

"During the summer of 1938 they practically disbanded as Reverend and Mrs. Bellinger had been transferred to another post and two others of the group had moved away. However, the remaining members, with the addition of some new ones, are already planning to reorganize, bigger and better than ever, in the near future. The program for this season will include "A Doll's House," "The Tavern," and others (with an eye to the box office), contemporary one-act plays, the study of Shakespeare, Ibsen, O'Neill, Maxwell Anderson, and others.

"The local broadcasting station has approached them to broadcast short plays and skits once a week, sponsored by local concerns, starting in the fall and continuing indefinitely. This, of course, is a big incentive and they are eagerly looking forward to this event.

"An extensive program of serious study and the presentation of worthwhile plays is being planned for the coming season. The Players will be directed by Winifred Haun who has in the past twelve years been connected with the Southern California Repertory Theatre, the Sunset Players and the Imperial Valley Community Players. Everyone of this small group of players in Scobey is talented, hard-working, serious and ambitious!"

The Wayfarers Civic Repertory Theatre of San Francisco presents "Othello."

Scene from pantomimic interpretation of "The Ballad of Reading Gaol."

Wayfarers Civic Repertory Theatre, San Francisco.

First gravedigger in "Hamlet."

"Oliver Oliver" set.

Reno Little Theatre.

"Personal Appearance."

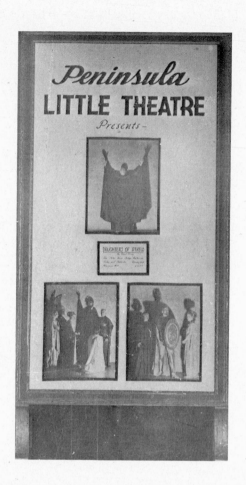

The Peninsula Little Theatre of Burlingame, California, presents "Daughters of Atreus."

Set for original three-act "Little Acorns Grow" by North Baker.

Peninsula Little Theatre.

Miniature set for "The Dark Tower" (20″ to 1″).

"The Silver Cord" at Burlingame.

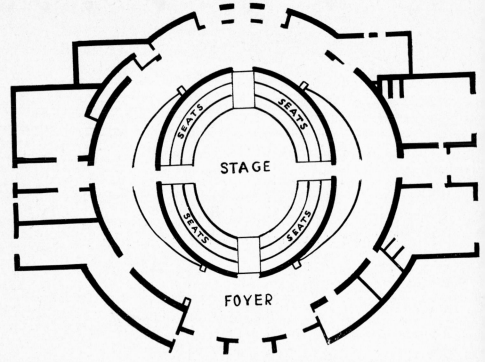

Plan of the Penthouse Theatre, Seattle, Washington.

The Cheyenne Little Theatre Players present "Holiday."

A University Civic Theatre production in Denver: "Abraham Lincoln."

Palo Alto
Community
Playhouse.

Foyer.

Auditorium
and stage.

Henry cools off after another secretary leaves him.

He asserts his masculinity by tweaking Miss Smith's nose.

The Community Theatre at Palo Alto presents "Springtime for Henry" with the audience on all sides.

"So you shot him in the Touraine. Why?" "Because he was a Frenchman—" "Any other reason?"

"Had enough of my wife!! Who the hell do you think you are?"

"Noah" at Palo Alto.

Kathleen Norris in the Palo Alto Community Players' production of "The Swan." (Photo by Archie London.)

"Pygmalion" at Palo Alto.

The Little Theatre of Eureka, Montana, presents, strangely enough, "An Old Kentucky Garden."

Utah State Little Theatre's attempt at "Julius Cæsar."

Dr. Pedersen, president of Utah State Little Theatre Board, appears in Drinkwater's "Abraham Lincoln."

Padua Hills Theatre, Claremont, California.

Scene from the Coloquio, medieval Mystery play which has been performed in Mexico for the past 300 years. It is given at Padua Hills Theatre each Christmas.

A street scene from one of the Mexican plays at Padua Hills.

The Mexican Players at Padua Hills present "Las Canacuas."

Mexican Players: The moon and a star being brought into the churchyard at dusk during the Fiesta of San Ysidro.

The Playbox presents "The Faun," by Knoblauch.

Five productions by the Pasadena
Community Playhouse Association.

Laboratory   Theatre's
production of "Steel."

"Autumn Crocus" at The Playbox.

The Pasadena Community Playhouse Association presents on its main stage
"Major Barbara" and "Back to Methuselah."
(Photographs by Eaton, South Pasadena.)

A scene from the Pasadena Community Playhouse production of "Back to Methuselah." (Photograph by Eaton, South Pasadena.)

Seattle, Washington. . . . The Way of the Pioneer, Like That of the Transgressor, is Hard.

Seattle, the Queen City of the Northwest, may justly be proud of the added culture that two of its newest pioneers have brought to its fame. Mr. and Mrs. Burton James, who came to Seattle some fifteen years ago, after five years on the staff of the Cornish School of the Theatre, resigned to undertake what had long been a cherished dream of theirs; namely, to create for Seattle a real civic theatre.

According to Mr. Joseph B. Harrison, president of the Board of Trustees of the Civic Theatre, the first step was unspectacular enough. As he says, it consisted, on a summer's day in 1928, of renting half a vacant store building on University Way between 42nd and 43rd streets (at this writing recently restored to its pristine vacancy). Mrs. James paid the first month's rent from her own purse; Mr. James negotiated a typewriter, and The Playhouse had not merely a name, but a home. The office was sketchily furnished, largely with an assortment of furniture that was the gift of Fred H. Parks. It was discovered, too, that in taking these quarters The Playhouse had accidentally acquired a rehearsal hall and a workshop for building scenery: a fairly large back room.

That bare, narrow little office soon became a busy workshop. A campaign for season subscriptions, largely by telephone, was launched. To Seattle's eternal credit it responded generously, at once. There were more than fifteen hundred subscribers that first year, most of whom paid their $5.00 for a season ticket before a performance had been given or there was any concrete assurance that they would receive anything at all for their money.

The nucleus of the acting company had been gathered during the early months of the summer; rehearsals began in September, and in October, 1928, the curtain rose at the Metropolitan Theatre on the first performance of the first production of Seattle's new Civic Theatre, the premiere of Sean O'Casey's "Juno and the Paycock."

Of the names the first program carries, only three remain on The Playhouse roster today—Florence and Burton James and Glenn Hughes—although one, Marion Litonius, returned to the acting company in 1938 after an absence of eight years. The rest are scattered, mostly to New York and Hollywood; one, Hazel Nagley, who played Juno, is dead.

In the season following this historic opening night, thirty-one performances of seven plays were given. The schedule was sporadic, a week-end of showings every month or so. "The Romantic Young Lady" and "The Wild

Duck" set the season's record for length of run; each achieved the happy distinction of a grand total of six performances. Only two of the plays were presented at the Metropolitan; theatre rental in the downtown area soon proved prohibitive. So, with its third production, "The Romantic Young Lady," The Playhouse moved its performances to the auditorium of the Woman's Century Club, at Harvard and Roy Streets.

Here the Civic Theatre made its home for the remainder of the first season and for the whole of the second. Here, too, productions were staged only at intervals, roughly a month apart. There were seven again that second year, and performances numbered only thirty-four, three of these in Everett—The Playhouse's first experiment in touring.

The fact that the Civic Theatre must have a home of its own to function properly, to grow in usefulness, artistic stature and community influence, was apparent from the beginning. Persistent efforts to this end over a period of two years, dating from the very inception of the institution, were ultimately crowned with success. This was no small achievement; the Civic Theatre had no building funds and no property and was determined to be self-sustaining. Yet, by a combination of perseverence, good luck and a happy conspiracy of time and circumstance, financing was arranged.

Building operations began in the summer of 1930. Few who sit in the simple, charming auditorium of The Playhouse now recall that its walls once housed offices and storage for a clay and tile firm. The art of Arthur Loveless, noted Seattle architect, by revision and additions on the adjoining corner lot, transformed the erstwhile storehouse into an admirable working theatre, one of the finest examples of its type in America.

The opening of the new building and The Playhouse's third season was originally set for October 23rd. But builders', like lovers', vows are notably unreliable, and it was not until a week later that the formal premiere could be held. Even then the curtain was a full hour late in rising; building inspectors, firemen, and workmen moiled backstage, and electricians worked in the back of the auditorium during the performance with laudable but unsuccessful efforts to be quiet. But the play (Bernard Shaw's biting "Major Barbara") did "go on." Thus inaugurated, The Playhouse has been the Civic Theatre's home ever since.

In the midst of that first season in the new building came that phenomenon of phenomena—"Peer Gynt," the greatest success in Playhouse history. There had been qualms about attempting it because of its magnitude and the expense for incidental music, but as the production took shape in rehearsal the feeling grew that it stood a good chance of equaling the Civic Theatre's long-run record, twelve performances, set earlier in the season. Some brave souls thought with great good luck it might run as many as fifteen.

Then things began to happen. As soon as the seat sale was opened, before a performance was given, the entire first week was sold out; before the end of that week the rest of the month was gone and before anyone knew it, seats were selling a month in advance and continued so until near the end of the run. In this, its first presentation, "Peer Gynt" played thirty-nine performances, at the first thirty-two of these people were turned away nightly for want of room, notwithstanding the fact that it was played at the highest seat-scale The Playhouse has ever had. It ran from the first week in February into the month of May and in that time some thirteen thousand playgoers thronged to see it. They came from everywhere—throughout the state of Washington, from Oregon, British Columbia, Idaho, and Montana, and one woman made the trip from San Francisco to Seattle to see it. (This was the beginning of the wide circle of patrons The Playhouse now enjoys throughout the Northwest.)

That original thirty-nine-performance run of "Peer Gynt" has yet to be surpassed. In the course of two revivals, the first in the summer of 1932, the second in the season of 1935–36, the total performances now stand at sixty, all of them at The Playhouse. This is exceeded by Talbot Jennings' "No More Frontier," which has been played a hundred and ten times, but only fifty-six of these in Seattle.

"Peer Gynt" marked, it would seem, the Civic Theatre's achievement of a full artistic stature. In the seasons that followed successive productions grew in scope, calibre and beauty (the 1932 Goethe Centennial production of "Faust" was one of the high-water marks) until The Playhouse shortly found itself in the forefront of institutions of its kind in America—one, it was put, of the "Big Four" among the regional theatres of the United States.

Along with this the Civic Theatre's sphere of activity grew apace. In the season of 1931–32 The Playhouse inaugurated its Annual Summer Drama Festival, the first on the Pacific Coast. Each summer its special program, composed of new productions and revivals from the repertory of past seasons, has drawn thousands of tourist playgoers to Seattle from every state in the Union and its audiences have numbered visitors from more than a dozen foreign countries.

Once a year original scripts have been given their premieres at the Civic Theatre in an effort to afford a hearing for the work of native writers. Six such have been staged: "In His Image," by Garland Ethel; "Leading Man," by William Alden Kimball; "The Chaste Mistress" and "Mad, Bad and Dangerous to Know," by Marianne King; "L'Envoi" and "Funny Man," by Albert M. Ottenheimer.

An effort was made, too, to provide a means of articulating the artistic

gifts of racial and language groups of Seattle, and to this end such productions as "Kolokola," the Russian musical revue, and "In Abraham's Bosom,"
with an all-Negro cast, were staged.   From the last, another of The Playhouse's outstanding successes, notwithstanding the fact that the national bank
holiday broke the back of its run in 1933, sprang more or less directly the
fine Negro Repertory Company of the Federal Theatre Project which came
into being and achieved nation-wide repute under Civic Theatre sponsorship
and direction in the season of 1935–36.

What gives both proof and promise of being The Playhouse's greatest
achievement, however, is its new child, the Washington State Theatre,
America's first and only state theatre.

The interrelation of the theatre and education was recognized from the
inception of the Civic Theatre.   Witness, for example, the annual production for young people during the Christmas holidays, begun with "Rip Van
Winkle" in The Playhouse's first season, a practice which has continued un-
broken throughout the theatre's history.   But during the fourth season, with
the first production at the Civic Theatre of Shakespeare—"Romeo and Juliet"
—a new phase was entered upon in the form of special week-day matinees
for the high school students of Seattle, in collaboration with the school authorities of the city.   Only three high schools were represented that first year,
but within the next two seasons special performances were being given for
every high school and junior high school in Seattle.   And at the same time
large numbers of students traveling long distances from outlying communities, unprompted, revealed the interest in and need for such opportunities
beyond Seattle.

So, in 1936 the Washington State Theatre, created by The Playhouse, the
State Department of Education, and the Rockefeller Foundation, came into
being—a professional touring company which makes a circuit twice each year
of Washington and near-lying communities in other states, playing Shakespeare, classic and romantic productions at matinees for high school students
and evening performances for the general public.   Audiences totaling nearly
seventy thousand saw the first two productions, "The Comedy of Errors" and
"No More Frontier," in its initial season of 1936–1937, and it has been
hailed in the realms of both the theatre and education as one of the most
significant developments in the field of either in a generation.

The long road the Civic Theatre has come in a decade of achievement is
best seen in the list of productions it has staged.   "Boy Meets Girl" was the
seventy-fifth.   Represented in this repertory of seventy-five plays are fifty-four
playwrights, from Shakespeare to Noel Coward, from Goethe to Clifford
Odets, representing twelve different nations.   The opening night of the tenth
season was The Playhouse's nine hundred thirty-seventh performance.   At-

tendance records for the first few seasons are unfortunately incomplete, but the audiences of nine seasons number between a hundred and fifty and two hundred thousand.

The Playhouse has run a good course. But, happily, the goal lies still beyond and there is a long way yet to go.

Taft, California. A Theatre Is Surrounded by Oil Wells.

Taft is the center of one of the world's largest oil producing districts. The actors and the audiences of this Community Theatre come from all parts of the surrounding country, which includes three cities, Taft, Fellows, and Maricopa, and numerous outlying districts and oil leases. The entire community is more or less isolated, cut off on all sides by miles of desert given over principally to the production of oil.

In the summer of 1935 original plans for the formation of a Community Theatre were drawn by Van James, Director of Dramatics for Taft School District. Community leaders were contacted, newspaper publicity printed, and invitations issued to all who might be interested in helping form a Community Theatre for the neighborhood.

A meeting was called in October, and the Taft Community Theatre was formed with Van James as director. In some respects the organization is distinctive. So far as we know it is the only one located in a strictly oil community. And it is unique in its set-up. The Taft Community Theatre activities are sponsored by the Taft Coordinating Council (an association composed of representatives of various civic bodies interested in community welfare) with the cooperation in various ways of the Kern County Department of Recreation, the Taft Union High School and Junior College District, the Taft School District, the Works Progress Administration, and the National Youth Administration. Although sponsored in this way the group is independent, dictates its own progress and policies, and is entirely self-supporting.

This Community Theatre is unique also in the degree of authority vested in the director, who is the only officer appointed by the sponsor, the Taft Coordinating Council. All other officers, committee members and workers are directly responsible to the director, and are appointed by him.

Membership in this unique organization is made up largely of oil workers, whose ranks are rounded out by professional and business people. No dues are charged, costs of production being met by ticket sales and program advertising. Profits from plays are put into a reserve fund which is used to finance future activities. Deficits are met through this fund, or by voluntary contributions from members if necessary.

Their greatest problem is a constantly shifting membership. Many of the assistants and actors who are oil workers are often transferred at short notice to other districts. A problem peculiar to an oil district is the transfer of a worker to another "shift" which may make him unavailable for rehearsal during certain periods. Still another problem exists in the selection of plays for the heterogeneous population of an oil community.

The plays, which run for three nights, are usually given in one or the other of the school auditoriums, both of which are well equipped. The workshop and storage building for scenery are located in an abandoned machine shop which has been adapted to their use. Volunteer help in play production is supplemented by stage carpenters, costumers, clerks, and so forth, provided by the Works Progress Administration, and the National Youth Administration, in cooperation with county recreational heads.

They endeavor to make their group function as they feel a Community Theatre should. They believe in Taft that the theatre has two principal objectives: (1) to furnish recreation for those in the community who are interested in dramatics and (2) to provide worth-while stage entertainment for the public.

Van James, the enterprising director of this group, says: "The theatre should grow as much as possible out of the life of the community. Each community has its particular possibilities which may be realized, and its definite limitations; some communities have very special social problems which set them apart. The program to be presented depends to a very large extent upon the intellectual and social characteristics of the locality in which a group functions.

"We believe strongly in discussion groups and lectures which will help in the dissemination of culture through the theatre.

"We believe that a Community Theatre should be democratic, and that positions in the organization as well as roles in plays should be apportioned on the basis of interest and ability, not on so-called 'social position.' In casting our plays we use people in all walks of life. The leads in the four plays of last season were, respectively, a teacher, the wife of an office clerk, an oil fields superintendent, and a meat cutter. One of the production managers was a prominent local newspaper writer, another a WPA worker. Petty snobbery has no place in a Community Theatre.

"A Community Theatre expects a great deal of support from the community. Individuals, organizations and clubs are required to spend time and money in furthering the theatre movement. Too often the members of a theatre group hold themselves consciously (sometimes ostentatiously) aloof from the life of the community in which they live, adopting a superior attitude. This aloofness contrasts strangely with their demands for community support.

If theatre workers expect aid they should justify their stand. In other words, they should do everything possible to make their organization a part of the life of the community. This group should constitute one of the forces which contribute to the culture and welfare of the community as a whole. There are many ways in which a city or locality can be made to feel proud of having a Community Theatre, many ways in which a Community Theatre can cooperate with local agencies in building the community and serving the citizens."

Tucson, Arizona.   A Theatre in the Temple of Music.

"For the past decade, The Tucson Little Theatre has been producing plays, but it has not succeeded in being recognized as a necessary part of Tucson's community life." This sentence is from the 1937 announcement of new policies adopted by the Tucson Little Theatre. It is a brave theatre that can admit its own failure and its own weakness, especially in such brave words as "we believe that our failure is not owing to such alleged errors as an unfortunate choice of play, director, actor or administrator, but to something more basic: that we have been attempting to operate without either a clearly defined goal or a trained leader who could devote all his time and energy toward getting us there."

Up to the beginning of 1937, direction of the plays given by the Little Theatre had been passed from hand to hand, and the entire theatre suffered because of dependence upon the spare time of individuals to function efficiently as theatre directors. At the beginning of this season, Edward Reveaux was appointed the director of the Tucson Little Theatre. Very quickly he was able to bring new benefits to the members of the Little Theatre. He was able to coordinate a tremendous surge of interest and energy into a high morale and excellent standards of production for the main stage shows. Workshop groups were arranged for those who wished more technical training in costuming, make-up and stage craft. Study groups were created for those interested in the history of the theatre and drama analysis. Mr. Reveaux hopes that soon extra consideration may be given to playwriting and play direction.

When we visited Tucson, Beryl Hamilton took us over to their workshop which is housed in a large auditorium of Cathedral Hall. There the old stage is used for rehearsals and the auditorium proper for the painting of scenery and the building of larger props; small side rooms are used for costumes, storage space, libraries, directors' rooms, etc.

The Directors of the Tucson Little Theatre believe that there is but one valid reason for the existence of their organization, and that is, as they express it themselves: "To keep Tucson's love of the theatre alive and justified by the production of good plays and the fostering of creative writing."

Tucson feels that the theatre is a place for entertainment rather than sermons; that their theatre should not be given to plays whose content creates extra burdens and harsh reminders to audiences that are seeking emotional release. Therefore the Tucson Little Theatre has very challengingly said that they will "ask far more of their playwrights than is offered by the hack pens of Broadway and the motion pictures. The play script should offer the basis for a rollicking evening in the theatre, but it should also do its part toward making that evening at once rich, satisfying, and significant."

Tucson's ambitions center on the hope of acquiring the place where they now give their main productions, the Temple of Music. This handsome building seems strangely familiar and Miss Hamilton confesses that it is the Pasadena Community Playhouse reversed. In other words, the main stairway in Pasadena is on the right-hand side as you enter—in Tucson, it is on the left; otherwise the main buildings seem identical.

If the Tucson Little Theatre does acquire this Temple, they will have a plant which is large enough to serve their functions for many years. They may achieve this ambition soon for they are doing an excellent job in bringing the living theatre to an important section of America.

Yuma, Arizona.   A Theatre Blooms in the Desert.

Yuma, too, is many miles from the glittering lights of Broadway. But they have their own theatre, produce plays, and are making a valiant effort to establish a Community Theatre.

Their director is Mrs. Kenneth A. Grow. When she arrived in Yuma, they had already produced Channing Pollock's "The Fool." Due to Mrs. Grow's experience in dramatic work in Indianapolis, she was appointed director for their next play, "Dude Ranch" by Richard Wilkinson.

Rehearsals were held in the members' homes, and the play was given in the high school auditorium. It was well attended and a profit was made. This the players blew for a $50 royalty play, "The Silver Cord." It flopped.

The audiences thought it too serious in tone, saying, "We have enough tragedy at home—give us something light, something entertaining."

So the players gave them an opus called "One Mad Night" by James Reach. There were two full houses and the townspeople thoroughly enjoyed the production.

But the members of the group still thought they should produce more serious plays, something in the nature of adult entertainment rather than farces better suited to high schools, so their next offering was "Accent on Youth."

These were the comments: "It was good, but not as good as 'Dude Ranch' or 'One Mad Night.' " "I didn't like the swearing!" "I didn't like the boldness and frankness of the play!"

But as Mrs. Grow says, "They get all this in the movies, but when their local friends are putting on the play they don't like it!"

By this time the treasury was empty. In order to pay two months' back rent on an old theatre that they had renovated they gave a very light play, "Aunt Abby Answers an Ad," and came out $20.00 ahead to start the fall season.

They have lots of fun putting on these plays, and the actors don't neglect the social side, either, for parties are held and good times in the group keep them together.

The members are mostly young people who, according to Mrs. Grow, "Like the spotlight, but don't like to work for it. Rehearsals are poorly attended because something more 'important' keeps them away, and jealousy has retarded the progress. The older people are not yet sufficiently interested to take a guiding hand. It's the heat and the desert—but despite these sappers of one's initiative, we are going ahead. We are planning several plays for this coming winter—and have some new members to help us."

A year ago Mrs. Grow also organized a Community Children's Theatre, which was sponsored by the County Recreation Department. They gave two plays and had large audiences. The children were very cooperative.

So in Yuma they are striving to create their own theatre—and are succeeding, despite the many handicaps to be overcome.

And Other Theatres of the West

Altadena, California.

The Theatre Americana came into being early in 1935, and is now a flourishing, progressive organization. Unique among theatres, its purpose—as the name implies—is the production of plays which portray the American scene and theme. With this in mind, they conduct a prize play contest for original scripts.

Burbank, California.

The Burbank Theatre Guild is now ten years old. From September to June, without interruption, they are either busy rehearsing a play or actively in production.

Carmel, California.

In a town of less than three thousand inhabitants, Carmel has had, at one time or another, as many as four and sometimes five little theatre groups operating simultaneously. From these groups directors have gone on to fame and fortune, and the works of well-known writers in some cases have been written directly for Carmel production. Today Carmel's Community Theatre is an active group using eighty or more people in the various branches of theatre work. George Marion, the actor, whose daughter, Marie Marion Barnett, directs the Civic Little Theatre of Corpus Christi, Texas, lives in Carmel and takes an interest in the work being done.

Cheyenne, Wyoming.

Founded in 1930, this group at the close of the 1937–38 season had produced some thirty-five plays. Their membership is around five hundred, with dues as low as $2.00 a year. There are twelve directors on the staff, who are representative of the service clubs, business and professional men, schools, and the Woman's Club of Cheyenne. Their scenic designers are two of the leading architects of the city, who devote a considerable part of their time not only to designing the sets but also helping build and paint them. They have two directors, Barrie O'Daniels and William Fernando DeVere, both of whom have had long experience on the professional stage. All of their plays are held at the Consistory Temple, one of the best equipped stages in Wyoming. The activities of this group are sponsored and encouraged by the Wyoming Consistory.

Egan, California.

This Little Theatre was one of the first of the small groups to flourish in and around Los Angeles. It was housed in a garret at the top of an old loft building, and had what is probably the smallest stage in the world; capacity audience in the auditorium is one hundred twenty-five. It did not depend for its support upon the good will of the bank and the banker, and consequently could present its plays to a selected audience. The group disbanded for a time, but when last heard from had reorganized with a much larger membership, and had secured another auditorium for productions.

Lamar, Colorado.

Organized in October, 1936, this is the only Community Theatre group in Southeastern Colorado. They do four plays a year. The theatre is sponsored by the Lamar Chamber of Commerce and with this backing it is felt that in the near future it will be able to have its own playhouse, in conjunction with a civic building.

Monrovia, California.

The Gold Hill Players in this Southern California city opened their seventh season in 1938. Four major productions are given each year and monthly workshop meetings are held during the season, at which time a one-act play is given and an open forum held with topics discussed of interest to theatre workers. The Players are a community group with membership open to all. They have their own theatre building.

Oakland, California.

The Oakland Theatre Guild, which operates under the sponsorship of the Oakland Woman's City Club, is a newcomer to the field. Organized in September, 1937, it began its first year with five productions. The season of 1938-39 saw Thomas Backos, formerly of the University of California, as the director of the Guild. An intensive subscription campaign made possible the production of four plays during the year, with a three-night run for each. The Guild does not claim to be original in its response to the question of what a Community Theatre should be, but is able to state its credo very wisely as: "Primarily an outlet for those who are interested in acting and theatrical work . . . A place for diversion . . . opportunities for congenial work . . . and for those in the community who want to get away from the humdrum activities of their daily life."

Phoenix, Arizona.

This group is over fifteen years old. Each season its presents some eight full-length plays. Walter Ben Hare has been the guiding light of the group, which, composed largely of students, often uses townspeople in productions—

and certainly in the audiences. Sometimes plays are taken to nearby towns, and visitors to Phoenix speak highly of the work being done in this theatre.

Santa Fe, New Mexico.

The Atalya Players of this city were the first to produce "God's In His Heaven" by Philip Stevenson, which was published by the Theatre Union of New York. Mr. Stevenson resides in Santa Fe.

Stockton, California.

It was in the fall of 1924 that the Little Theatre presented its first play to a Stockton audience; a religious drama entitled "The Rock." The players were greeted by a very small house, but since then no cast has played to such a small audience. Little Theatre membership has grown steadily until it has a prominent and vital place in the life of the community More than a thousand people now witness each production. The history of this Pacific Little Theatre is a record of the remarkable development of the dramatic artistry of its director, DeMarcus Brown.

Tacoma, Washington.

This was one of the first Little Theatres in the Northwest. For five years it maintained its own playhouse. Then the City of Tacoma decided to put a street leading to the markets right through the theatre, and the building was torn down. For two years they crawled into their shell and talked things over. Then, undaunted, they started again and secured a time-honored landmark, Scandinavian Hall, for their theatre, and play production went on.

VI. STAGE-STRUCK AMERICA—A SUMMING UP

When Did It Actually Begin?

Although the Community Theatres of America have apparently developed since 1900, "amateur dramatics" are not that young in this country. Even the early settlers loved to act—and did. As far as we know, the first "home talent" play ever done in this country was in the year 1598!

For this information we are indebted to Mary Austin, who said: "The first play produced in the United States was at San Juan, forty miles from Santa Fe, in 1598. Col. Ornate's soldiers gave the play and the Indians were the spectators. It was called 'Los Moros y los Christianos,' and the Spanish conquerors carried it all around the world. I saw it produced here forty years ago, but I cannot find a copy of it now. I am trying to get one from the Philippines. We think the Little Theatre Movement very new, but every settlement and outpost in New Mexico in those early days had its little band of players and many of them their own community plays. I have collected manuscripts and data about nearly one thousand of them."

The Spaniards started something nearly four hundred years ago. And America has been stage-struck ever since.

There is great academic debate among the communities of the South as to just when the first theatre was established. We'll let Charleston, South Carolina, and Williamsburg, Virginia, fight it out. But it is known that the students of William and Mary College gave amateur plays as far back as 1735.

At Harvard College the students anticipated George Pierce Baker and his famous 47 Workshop Theatre by two hundred and fifty years. Benjamin Colman wooed the muses in 1690 and wrote a tragedy entitled "Gustavus Vasa," and his fellow students acted it out before a quaking audience. Perhaps this was the first attempt in America to "produce an original play written by one of our own group."

Some sixty years later, in 1750, a group of amateurs in Boston on a make-shift stage in a coffee house performed "The Orphans" by Otway. But it didn't "go over" very well, and the City Fathers were shocked and outraged. They soon put a stop to this nonsense, and laws were passed forbidding indecent play-acting in that metropolis. Incidentally, Boston now has some sixty groups of amateur players, all doing very well indeed, and even in some instances encouraged and abetted by the authorities.

But maybe in those early days they were still remembering the disgraceful goings-on at Merry Mount along about 1625. Here was perhaps the first community participation in New England. The leader of this group was that wicked but gay-hearted rascal, Mr. Morton. William Bradford in his *History of Plymouth Plantation* says of him and his group, "And Morton became lord of misrule, and maintained (as it were) a schoole of Athisme. They allso set up a May-pole, drinking and dancing aboute it many days togeather inviting the Indean women, for their consorts, dancing and frisking togither, and worse practises. Morton likewise (to shew his poetrie) composed sundry rimes & verses, some tending to lasciviousness, and others to the detraction & scandall of some persons, which he affixed to this idle or idoll May-pole."

Of course, Thomas Morton was a very bad boy. But there was community participation of a sort in Merry Mount, even though it was the sort of thing that had best be forgotten quickly.

However, he did write the first poem in New England, a hymn to Bacchus, and it was sung as he has recorded, "with a chorus, which they performed in a dance, hand in hand about the May-pole, whiles one of the company sung, and filled out the good liquor like gammedes and Jupiter."

But there was much too much drinking in his group, and Mr. Morton was sent back to England in disgrace. Yet there had been community participation of a sort, and there the matter had better rest.

The next outbreak of amateur theatricals came during the Revolutionary War. It wasn't the townspeople who acted. Congress had forbidden that. It was the British soldiers, the visiting firemen of that period. For their own amusement, and for charity, they gave plays. And these "dramatic societies" flourished until the Revolutionary War came to an end.

Of course in the south, putting on plays became a recognized part of the social activity. Perhaps one of the first amateur groups was that of the Thalian Association in Wilmington, North Carolina, established about 1790. And those who have read *Gone With The Wind* will recall mention of the amateur plays given in Atlanta during those trying times.

Out in the west the first Community Theatre was probably at Salt Lake City, Utah. Here Brigham Young first built a church, then a school, and then a theatre. The first performance in this playhouse was on January 17, 1853.

In California the first community participation was at Santa Barbara, California. Here Jose Lobero, a romantic Italian adventurer, opened a tavern. His other contribution to the social life of Santa Barbara was, first of all, musical. He recruited an orchestra from the town and drilled it himself. But wanting something bigger than that, he plunged into opera. He drew casts from the community, coached and directed them, managed the productions, supplied the orchestra, and sang the leading roles himself!

And then he built a theatre of adobe. Six months were spent in rehearsals of the opening bill, and the first performance, as nearly as it can be placed, was in 1873. The theatre became the center of the social life of Santa Barbara. And in this city the Community Theatre of the present day bears the name of this early pioneer in the arts: the Lobero Theatre.

These early beginnings are mentioned merely to show that community drama is part of our national heritage. While it is true that the European Little Theatres of Antoine, Reinhardt, and Stanislavsky gave impetus to the movement in 1911 and thereabouts, amateur participation in the theatre had been in existence in America long before even Antoine's great-great grandfather wore swaddling clothes.

Even while Antoine was getting his start in France, about the year 1887, there were dramatic groups flourishing in this country. Some of these groups are in existence today.

Stage Societies As Such

One of the oldest and most exclusive stage societies in this country is the Comedy Club of New York City. They gave their first play on February 13, 1885—and obviously hadn't even heard of Antoine at that time. They have continued to produce plays ever since. This is a very modest group. The directors seldom make a report of their activities in the papers. Their plays are presented for their own amusement and the entertainment of their members and friends.

They have their own charming and adequate playhouse on East Thirty-sixth Street in New York, just off Park Avenue. Here a remodeled stable contains a small auditorium, workrooms, and reception rooms, literally lined with photographs, displaying debutantes of many a season and their gallant escorts in wig and buckskin as they once trod the boards. Here in this tiny playhouse they have club nights, rehearsals, and often try out new plays.

The membership, which is by invitation only, includes seventy-five who are actively engaged in play production, and many more associate members who subscribe and provide audiences.

From this group occasionally one of the members strays onto Broadway. Hope Williams, before she became a professional and played Linda in "Holiday," often acted with the Comedy Club. Also Harold Gould from time to time had played a role in a Broadway production. And when "The Warrior's Husband" was a one-act play it was first produced by the Comedy Club.

Another similar group of players which started before the turn of the century is the Montclair Dramatic Club of Montclair, New Jersey. Their first play was given on November 11, 1889. Since then they have averaged two productions each year. Their membership is limited, by invitation only, and the price of a season ticket is $15 a year. This entitles the holder to eight tickets, four for each production.

In Indianapolis, Indiana, the Indianapolis Dramatic Club was organized in 1890, and since that time has regularly given plays each year—three a season—including the years of the World War and through the depression. This club is purely social with a limited membership of five hundred. The members are elected by the Board of Directors. There has always been a waiting list for memberships. Usually the younger members are children and grandchildren of the founders and the members. There have been four generations of one family in the club, a great-granddaughter of one of the founders was admitted to membership in 1937.

The Board of Directors reads like a list of *Who's Who in Indiana*. Among those who have served as officers of this Dramatic Club and on the Board of Directors are Booth Tarkington, one of the early presidents and also director of the first plays; Morris Ross, third president of the club and dramatic critic of the old *Indianapolis Journal*, the man who first brought Julia Marlowe to the attention of the theatre-going public; Walter Connegut of the New York Theatre Guild; Hewitt Howland, formerly editor of *Century Magazine* and well known at the present time in literary circles in New York; the late Senator Albert Beveredge; the late William C. Bobbs of Bobbs, Merrill and Company, publishers; and others equally prominent.

The dues are $10.00 a year. The only other source of revenue is in the form of guest tickets, which can be purchased only for out of town guests by the members. At the present time Ricca Scott Titus of the professional theatre is the director. She has been associated with this club for the past seven years, and (with the exception of the scenic artist and the stage crew, union members since they use a downtown theatre in Indianapolis) is the only paid employee.

Among other groups of this nature must be included the Players of Providence, Rhode Island. They were organized in 1909, and have ever since then given about five productions each year. Their membership is limited and annual dues are $8.00. Seats are sold only to members. The only paid employee of this group is a general handy man.

They have their own playhouse, made possible through funds left by Henry A. Barker. This theatre, called the Barker Playhouse, was acquired in 1932 and is but a stone's throw from the spot where the players started their career.

In Philadelphia the Plays and Players have been in existence since 1911. A group interested in play production, with Mrs. Otis Skinner as their first president, rented a small clubroom and stage on the second floor of the old Philadelphia library building. Here they presented their plays, designed the sets, made the costumes and did the acting. Eleven years later they outgrew their headquarters, so a theatre at 1714 Delancey Street was purchased and thoroughly renovated with the cooperation of leading artists in Philadelphia. It soon became known as one of the finest amateur dramatic clubhouses in the country.

Ten plays are presented each season, and the membership, which exceeds six hundred, is composed of prominent Philadelphians. Although this club has never put tickets to its productions on public sale, it has given performances for other organizations.

These dramatic clubs are largely social in their organization. While it is community participation of a sort, it is participation by invitation only. They cannot be classed as Community Theatres to the same extent as groups where the banker acts on the same stage with the baker. They make no effort to serve the community as such, and yet they fulfill a very definite place in the artistic and cultural life of the cities where they flourish. Their productions are outstanding and their purpose is sincere.

Other groups in smaller cities, starting as more or less private dramatic clubs with limited memberships, have, as the years rolled by, let down the bars. They have admitted rather freely to their membership all applicants who display a desire to work, and the plays have been thrown open to the general public.

In some cities a selected few still directs the policies (as in Hutchinson, Kansas), but the active workers are from the community at large, and the man in the street can see the play if he buys a ticket.

It is an oft-repeated argument in many groups just what is the best policy to follow; whether to keep the group small and select, or admit anyone who desires to join. In Ashland, Kentucky, the roll of active members is kept small—only workers are allowed. This method works in Ashland. In Harrisburg, Pennsylvania, anybody can join. In Columbus, Ohio, the group is conducted on a club basis with the membership limited, but that limited membership is governed only by the seating capacity of the theatre. And Columbus has an outstanding group.

There is no definite answer to the question. And yet it has been discovered in many cities that the greater the community participation, the greater the success.

Certainly no group may fear failure when a few theatre-minded and hard workers keep their hands at the helm, and guide the destinies of the players through thick and thin. In some cities (as in Lake Charles, Louisiana, and Mason City, Iowa) one person kept the interest alive.

Given in any community a baker's dozen or less who are not afraid of passing defeat, and see clearly the vision ahead—the Community Theatre will stand stoutly against storms.

Groups That Have Had Their Swan Song

No record would be complete without the sad mention of some communities where theatres have flourished and then have closed their doors. The reasons for their demise may be illuminating.

From 1924 to 1934 the Drama Club of Lancaster, Pennsylvania, produced five plays each season. In 1932 they had over five hundred members and $1200 in the bank. The bank closed its doors and did not reopen.

"We finished the season on a shoestring and with gritted teeth because we were obligated to give our subscribers five productions," says Mrs. Kenneth O. Bates. "In addition we had a paid director whose contract called for $200 per month for three more months after the jolly bank closing. The next year we struggled through three productions with local, volunteer amateur directors and had only moderate success. At present the Drama Club of Lancaster is moribund. I write it regretfully."

At Greenwood, Indiana, the Community Players played with increasing success from 1920 to 1932. With an organization numbering a hundred and fifty in a town of two thousand they attracted state-wide attention.

But, says Clyde Lemasters, "The Community Players have been defunct since 1932 for lack of aggressive and interested leadership."

The Civic Theatre Guild of New Castle, Pennsylvania, jogged along for four years. "High overhead (although we did not have any paid officers or director), public apathy, and internal jealousies were the rocks upon which our group came to grief," writes Arthur M. Brown.

The closing of the Georgian Little Theatre of Evanston, Illinois, which existed for two seasons, was peculiar to a great, rich suburb. It folded ultimately as did other potentially good theatres—such as the North Shore Civic Theatre—because of the lack of general audience interest. This seems a paradox when one realizes that the Drama League of America, whose purpose was to increase and stimulate audience attendance at the theatre, was organized in Evanston.

The first Community Theatre in Iowa was at Waterloo in the pioneer days of 1917. For a time they had their own playhouse, a remodeled Methodist Church, seating a hundred and fifty-five. Plays every month, with work-shop programs included, were given.

Then the director went to war, and when he returned from service in the army the playhouse had been rented to a tailor. For a time the productions were given in the local opera house, but unlike the experience of the Bangor-Brewer Little Theatre of Bangor, Maine, it did not prove either exciting or stimulating. There had been so much more fun and so much more joy in the work when they had had their own playhouse and were their own boss. Interest could not be maintained, and when the director moved on to the greener pastures of New York, play production on an intensive scale ceased. A few theatre-lovers still continued to present plays at rare intervals, but listlessly.

Yet certainly the Community Theatre at Waterloo, a pioneer in its day, set the standards for Iowa. It paved the way for other cities in that state. And as one of the first Community Theatres, it deserves an honored place in the history of the movement in this country.

Another group that was an inspiration to dramatics in its state was the Ypsilanti Players of Ypsilanti, Michigan. Founded in 1915 by Daniel L. Quirk, Jr., this group served its community for fifteen years. Even today, according to Mr. Quirk, hardly a week passes but that someone refers to the work done by these Players. Certainly today no gathering of theatre-lovers and community drama enthusiasts in Michigan is complete without the presence of Mr. Quirk. And while the Ypsilanti Players are no more, the ideals fostered by these Players lingers, serving as a model for other theatres in Michigan.

Thus one can see the bitter problems that confront struggling groups. Aside from bank failures, which can happen to anyone, lack of inspired leadership, internal jealousies, lack of audience interest, and a lack of a home of their own, have all caused some theatres to close their doors.

But there is always the hope of revival. For love of the theatre never dies, and a new generation is coming along. Something must be done for them!

What's in a Name?

The majority of theatre groups organized from 1910 to 1930 rightly called themselves "Little Theatres." They were just that; tiny playhouses, usually with a small seating capacity and therefore "little."

But no longer can these theatres be called "little." When it is realized that the majority of groups now in existence have an active membership of over one thousand persons (Marshalltown, Iowa, has a membership of fifteen hundred, and Charleston, West Virginia, some twenty-five hundred members), and the estimated yearly attendance at these theatres approaches fifteen million persons; calling this movement the Little Theatre Movement is a contradiction.

So, many leaders have tried to change the name. Perhaps this is because "Little Theatre" has been associated in the past with groups such as George Kelly satirized in his play "The Torchbearers." Too, the professional theatre had a habit of looking down its nose at "little theatres"—which, though in some cases funny, have today outgrown the jokes and jibes at their expense, though the flavor lingers.

Kenneth Macgowan in *Footlights Across America* writes: "For myself, I am far from enamored of the words Little Theatre and Little Theatre Movement . . . Civic is an absurd title for any theatre that is not supported out of public funds. . . I prefer Local Theatre as a phrase for all the efforts which spring out of decentralized, noncommercial activity."

But the majority of groups born since Mr. Macgowan wanted to call them "Local Theatres" didn't take eagerly to the suggestion. Since they began actually serving the community, and their doors were thrown open to the community, the word "Community" or "Civic" crept into their names.

It was Percy MacKaye who first thought of the name, "Civic Theatre."

"I originated that name," he told us, "and according to my best recollection, the first time it was ever printed occurs in a sentence of the preface to my volume, *The Playhouse and the Play*. I well recall sitting up all one night, in my studio at Cornish, New Hampshire, thinking intensely for an apt and perfectly new name by which to call this new conception of the theatre which then filled all my thoughts—a theatre wholly divorced from commercialism. At about 5 A.M., as dawn was coming up over the hills, it came to me, 'The Civic Theatre—that's what I'll name it.'

"Before long the name was widely taken up, and often badly misapplied. In after years I came to wish that I had named it instead, 'The Communal Theatre,' and I still think that would have been a better term for its intrinsic ideal."

But since 1909, when *The Playhouse and the Play* was published, much has happened. Already there is one city—Palo Alto—which has a theatre supported by taxation. And certainly it has the right to call its theatre, "The Civic Theatre of Palo Alto." Other cities, working toward that goal, also have the right to use the word "Civic" somewhere. As long as a theatre is serving the entire community, and its doors are open to all citizens, and the ideal is service, why not?

Look, for a moment, at the names of the one hundred and five theatres, whose stories we have told:

	EAST	SOUTH	MIDDLE WEST	WEST	TOTAL
LITTLE THEATRE					
Little Theatre—and unashamed (With Variations)	4	18	4	5	
Le Petit Théâtre du Vieux Carré		1			
Little Country Theatre ...			1		
Very Little Theatre				1	34
CIVIC (Somewhere in the title)					
Civic Little Theatre	1				
Civic Players	1		2		
Civic Theatre	1	1	2	4	12
COMMUNITY (Somewhere about)					
Community Playhouse ...	1	1	1	2	
Community Theatre	2	1	4	3	
Community Players	2	1	1		
Community Little Theatre.				1	20
THE PLAYERS (Of one sort or another)					
Players (Merely Players) ..	5	2	6	2	
Players Guild	1				
Players Club		1	1		
Players Workshop			1		
Playmakers			1	1	
Playhouse	3	2			
Plays and Players	1				27
A NAME ALL THEIR OWN					
Candlelight Theatre	1				
Workshop	1				
Mark Twain Masquers ...	1				
Footlight Club	1				
Footlight Players		1			
Town Theatre		1			
Vagabonds		1			
Repertory Group			1		
Actors Guild			1		
Resident Theatre			1		
Harlequins			1		
Wayfarers				1	12

Of all the 105 groups only 34 call themselves "Little Theatres." The next popular name has something to do with "Players." Following not so far behind are "Community" and "Civic," and tagging along in the rear are those groups who have a distinctive name all their own.

But after all, what's in a name? And whether they call themselves, "The Town Theatre," "The Footlight Players," "The Harlequins," "The Mark Twain Masquers," "The Resident Theatre," or "The Plays and Players," all are Community Theatres, serving their communities and having community participation as their goal.

It is interesting to note that there are more so-called "Little Theatres" in the south than in any other part of the country; more "Civic" or "Community" theatres in the middle west and west. What does that prove? Probably nothing at all.

But a simple explanation may be that the majority of newly organized groups have taken some variation of community or civic in their names, and also in the middle west and west numerous established groups changed their names to denote more fully their real purpose as they outgrew their infant "Little Theatre" days.

Far from being so impertinent as to suggest that those groups now calling themselves "Little Theatres" change their titles, we can only urge that no matter what the name, the ideal of community participation is never lost. And we can also only hope that new groups will consider carefully an appropriate name.

When Organized and by Whom

In many cities, long before the present existing theatre group was organized, amateur plays were given. Hutchinson, Kansas, started in 1873. Various groups had presented plays in San Antonio, Texas, prior to the founding of the Little Theatre there in 1927. The same is true of Nashville, Tennessee, and other cities. It wasn't until the professional theatre failed these communities, that permanent and carefully organized groups were established.

When the "road" collapsed completely groups organized and planned definitely for yearly programs and continuous play production. The dates given in the stories of these theatres is the year in which this well defined program was established.

Tabulating these dates:

on record

	EAST	SOUTH	MIDDLE WEST	WEST	TOTAL
1877	1				1
1911		1	1		2
1912					
1913	1				1
1914			1		1
1915			1		1
1916	1	1		1	3
1917	1		1		2
1918			1		1
1919		2	3		5
1920		4			4
1921		1			1
1922		2	1		3
1923	3	2	2	1	8
1924	2				2
1925	1	1	1	1	4
1926	1	1	2	1	5
1927	2	4	1	1	8
1928	1	1	2	1	5
1929	2	1	1	2	6
1930	1	2	3		6
1931	1		1	3	5
1932		1	1		2
1933	4	1	1	3	9
1934		2	3	2	7
1935	3	3		1	7
1936		1	1	1	3
1937				2	2
1938	1				1

The growth of the Community Theatre Movement has been slow and rather evenly divided through the years.

The theatres established before 1920 were in the larger cities. Those formed after 1930 are found in smaller centers, indicating that successful dramatic expression in the larger communities inspired the neighboring towns and villages to do likewise.

It is also interesting to note that the greatest number of theatres established in any given years were in the years from 1933 to 1935. Seemingly hopeless depression years while we were living through them; they taught the average American use of leisure time.

Forced by necessity to slow down in the production of material things— denied them in many instances—men and women of America found time to discover themselves. And in discovering themselves they naturally turned to the creative arts of the theatre.

There was little sitting down and bewailing their losses. With true American spirit and "gumption" they were up and about; learning to endure hardships together, they also came to learn to play together.

Of the groups mentioned:

> By 1915—6 were established,
> By 1920—15 more—a total of 21,
> By 1925—18 more—a total of 39,
> By 1930—30 more—a total of 69,
> By 1935—30 more—a total of 99,
> By 1938—6 more (and a great many whose stories are not told here)— a total of 105.

The Community Theatre Movement is growing, spreading more and more into towns and cities throughout the nation. America is pioneering in the arts—discovering for itself the joy of creative endeavor—finding its soul in artistic expression.

This pioneering has not been done by one class of individuals, one self-appointed group of trained leaders in theatrical arts. Who did start these theatres? What sort of person or persons were they?

There's an interesting conclusion to be drawn from the table on page 337.

No one type of individual or organization is responsible for the beginnings of the Community Theatres of this country. The Drama League of America did much to foster and encourage groups in the beginning. But only six of the theatres discussed herein actually owe their present established groups to the inspiration of the Drama League.

The Women's Clubs of America have done much to aid and abet culture—but only four have started Community Theatres.

The National Recreation Association has started three groups going. The Speech Arts Clubs only one. The Association of University Women has founded two groups, and the War Community Service only one.

More individuals working alone have organized theatres than the concerted efforts of organized clubs. Considering the number of retired professional actors and actresses in this country you would think that more of them would have turned their talents to community drama. Among the individual drama enthusiasts, surely here can be found a representative group of people; from society matrons to stage-struck young men, from office workers to students of the drama.

Just as each group today, each Community Theatre has among its workers all classes of people, and is representative of a cross section of its city— so in the beginnings of these groups there is a cross section of the representative citizens and cultural leaders of the country at large.

CLUBS OR ORGANIZATIONS

	EAST	SOUTH	MIDDLE WEST	WEST	TOTAL
Drama Study Clubs	1	5			6
Women's Clubs	2	2			4
National Recreation Association	1		1	1	3
Speech Arts			1		1
Association of University Women	1			1	2
War Community Service ..		1			1
Total 17					

BY INDIVIDUALS

	EAST	SOUTH	MIDDLE WEST	WEST	TOTAL
Retired Professionals	1	1	2	1	5
Ministers of the Gospel ..	1	1		1	3
School Teachers	3	3	4	4	14
Newspaper Men	1		2		3
Y.W.C.A. Secretary	1				1
Jewish Community Leader			1		1
Merely a Drama Enthusiast and Theatre Lover * ..	7	2	8	2	19
Total 46					

JUST A GROUP OF PEOPLE

	EAST	SOUTH	MIDDLE WEST	WEST	TOTAL
GOT TOGETHER **	7	14	11	10	42
Total 42					

---

* Such inspired leaders pioneering alone at first as Mrs. Ina K. Trissel in Mason City, Iowa; Robert Olewiler in his Candlelight Theatre; Rosa Hart in Lake Charles, Louisiana, Mrs. Frederick Shedd in Columbus, Ohio—and others.

** We wish we knew who the leaders in these groups were, but perhaps there was no one person—and we like to think that the idea seized upon several at one and the same time—spontaneously. "Let's organize," says one. "Okay," cry others present—and the thing is done.

How Did They Build Their Theatres?

Once organized, the first headache is, "Where shall we give our plays?"

Usually, in the beginning, most groups used the nearest available auditorium. And like wandering gypsies some groups have played hither, thither, and yon. Any old stage in any old place; troubles and hardships dogging their footsteps.

No wonder then the cry, "Let's have our own theatre!"

Often it was the first available empty building—no matter what its past history. A stage was erected. Seats were put in, and a theatre was born.

Far better to have a place to call "home" than a rented auditorium with a grumbling janitor or a suspicious landlord.

Some groups became dissatisfied with makeshift theatres. As their audiences grew in numbers, as their position and place in the community became firmly established, they built their own theatres.

How many groups have their own playhouses? Of the Community Theatres whose stories have been told here: thirteen in the east; in the south seventeen; in the middle west, twelve; and in the west, eleven groups; a total of fifty-three Community Theatres in the United States owned and operated; dedicated to the ideals of community drama. And some other groups, whose stories are not told here, have their own playhouses.

The table summarizes the building aspects of these theatres:

HOW THESE THEATRES WERE BUILT

	EAST	SOUTH	MIDDLE WEST	WEST	TOTAL
Built by members themselves	8	9	7	7	31
The gift of an individual	4	2	2	2	10
By appeal to the general public	1	1			2
City built	1	1			2
An individual gave part, the members the rest		1	2		3
WPA—or Uncle Sam		1			1
A city gave part of the funds, the members subscribed the rest		1			1
A real estate company				1	1
From the treasury of a school		1	2	1	4

The fact to be observed is that in most cases the Community Theatres of America were built by the members themselves. Obviously these theatres are the Theatre of Democracy. No one person or group of persons built these theatres brick by brick and stone by stone—but the theatre lovers of each community who have erected their playhouses.

Of these theatres, those which are new buildings built especially for the purpose of housing community drama, there are:

> In the east 2
> In the south 7
> In the middle west 6
> In the west 4

The total score on remodeled buildings is:

REMODELED INTO A THEATRE

	EAST	SOUTH	MIDDLE WEST	WEST	TOTAL
Church	3	3	3	3	12
Barn	2	1	1	1	5
School		1		1	2
Old Opera House	2	2	1	1	6
Speakeasy	1				1
Fair Grounds Building ..				2	2
Library	1				1
Farmyard	1				1
Laundry		1			1
Morgue	1				1
Engine House		1	1		2
Dance Hall		1			1
Once a private home		1	1		2
Factory (potato chip) ...				1	1
Store				1	1
Paper Mill	1				1

And no less than eleven groups have announced their intentions to build their own playhouses and have already started plans and organized campaigns toward that end.

Many groups, though playing at the present time in rented auditoriums, maintain their own workshops in which they make their own scenery and conduct rehearsals.

To new and aspiring groups, these words of advice. Build your own theatre! Preferably let it be one built by your own members. A rich uncle who gives you a theatre is not to be scorned, but be careful lest there are strings attached. Be independent. Stand upon your own feet. Have a home of your own—no matter at what sacrifice.

But if you can't afford at first to build a new playhouse, find a vacant building and remodel it. Better a forlorn and jaded barn than the finest rented auditorium in the city.

The failure and the ultimate collapse of many groups is due simply to the fact that they didn't have a home of their own. Establish a definite center for your dramatic activities. This is the thing that will hold your group together in the long run.

And once you do decide to build your own theatre—and seek plans for a theatre building, consult with your local architect, of course. But first obtain from either the Pasadena Community Playhouse or *Theatre Arts*

Monthly their already designed plans for a Community Theatre. It may prove a short cut to perfection.

What About a Director?

It is only under proper leadership that the Community Theatres will grow and flourish. Next to having its own theatre, the most important acquisition of a successful group is the right director.

Getting the right director is like getting married. A group hiring one takes a chance on looks, previous experience, and then trusts to luck. Compatibility is something that only time can answer.

Directors obviously fall into two classes: professional and amateur. These directors are scattered about the country as follows:

	EAST	SOUTH	MIDDLE WEST	WEST	TOTAL
Professional Directors—Paid...	20	24	23	13	80
Volunteer Directors—Unpaid..	6	7	5	7	25

In his *Civic Theatre* Percy MacKaye says: "It is not enough that the policy of the theatre be safeguarded by the trusteeship of reliable citizens or institutions. The execution of its policies can only be carried out efficiently by artists of high professional standards."

Which means, of course, that the professional director must not only know and love the theatre, but must also be a creative artist in his own right.

Yearly the colleges and universities are graduating young directors fresh from classes in Play Production (M.W.F. at 10). They know how to produce plays in a million-dollar college theatre with tons of scenery, bushels of spot lights, and enough velvet drapes to clothe the nakedness of all the dowagers in the world. But what about getting the same effect on an improvised stage in a rented stable?

Out of nothing at all, he must be able to create the magic of theatre; out of a bit of unbleached muslin and paint produce a set; out of a bucket improvise a spot light; out of cheesecloth give the illusion of velvet. All the theories in the world won't help him then. But in time he will learn.

Besides this ability to create, there is something that is even more important for the ideal Community Theatre director.

He must know and love people! *feeling for thea.*

He must understand the peculiarities of the men and women under his direction, and forgive them for what they do. (Perhaps that is what is called a sense of humor.) He must love people for their own sakes—and must be able to be at ease and understand the idiosyncrasies of the banker as he must understand and be friendly with the baker. He must be a "good mixer." At the same time he must represent the dignity of the theatre he is directing. It's a tough spot to be in.

Artist, teacher, civic leader, humanitarian. In short, the ideal director should be a combination of God and David Belasco.

Find him!

Broadway—Moscow—or Folk Drama?

What kind of plays to give?

"What plays shall we give?" is the cry.

In Dobbs Ferry, New York, they believe that only plays of literary worth should be attempted. In Hartford, Connecticut, they found that the way to success was in doing the recent Broadway hits—be they ever so lowly.

Most Community Theatres, however, have found that a balanced diet gives the best results. Something for the highbrow—something for the lowbrow—and something just for fun. In that way, the exacting tastes of every community are satisfied—and the Literary Lady who Likes Pirandello and the Tired Business Man who Wants to Laugh both can find something likeable during the year.

But always in the background is the complaint about the payment of royalty. There is never a meeting of Community Theatre directors and workers but that someone raises this question. Meetings have been called to discuss the problem. But what can be done?

Nothing at all! If a group must do a play—they should also be willing to pay the royalty asked. If the local merchants contributed nails, paint, lumber, muslin; if the printers produced the programs free of charge; and if the Public Service companies gave electric current without cost—then perhaps those who object to paying royalty would have just reason to complain.

There is only one answer. Write to the play publisher—tell him honestly and truthfully the size of your auditorium, the seating capacity and the number of performances you intend to give. Tell him also what you charge for admission—in brief, what your total gross at the box office for capacity performances would be. Then politely inquire if, under these circumstances, a special reduction might be made. Most publishers are only too willing to make an adjustment on royalty. And, also, most experienced and established Community Theatre directors do not quibble when it comes to paying royalty. We hope for all time this may be the last and final word on the royalty question.

But, of course, if you still object—there's one thing you can easily do. You can write and produce your own plays. Perhaps that's not a bad idea at all.

There's hardly a theatre in the country but that at one time or another has produced original plays by its members. A complete count would probably reveal that many more new plays are being done each season in Community Theatres than on Broadway. Some of these plays may not be masterpieces of contemporary drama, but the efforts are honest and sincere.

Some of these plays have won fame and fortune. Notable, of course, is the one-act play "The Cajun" by Ada Jack Carver. Submitted in the Playwriting Contest conducted by the Little Theatre of Shreveport in 1926, "The Cajun" was awarded first place. It had its first production in Shreveport and was then taken to New York by this group and entered in the Little Theatre Tournament conducted by Walter Hartwig. Here it was given second place. Published later by Samuel French, it has been widely produced throughout the country.

Mention must be made also of the success of the original plays first presented in Wisconsin, many of which have been published and produced elsewhere. Of course, the Folk Plays of the Carolina Playmakers need no further comment.

One of the most popular full-length plays almost universally done by Community Theatres during the past few years is "Gold in the Hills, or the Dead Sister's Secret" by J. Frank Davis. Unknown to Broadway, it has been an outstanding success throughout the country. It had its premiere at the San Pedro Playhouse by the Little Theatre of San Antonio, Texas.

Both the Pasadena Community Playhouse and the Cleveland Play House give hearings to new scripts. The Little Theatre of St. Louis has had an annual play contest.

Here and there throughout the country is emerging a native drama; plays written by native playwrights, unknown to Broadway. It is a healthy sign. A dramatic literature of the highways and byways, of the hearthstones and street corners of America is being born.

The astute champion of these native playwrights is Barrett H. Clark. Urging that young playwrights turn their attention to the theatres away from Broadway, in his pamphlet, *West of Broadway,* originally published in the *New York Times* of October 27, 1935, he says: "A time will come when playwrights, unable or unwilling to write precisely the kind of show that professional managers want or think their audiences want, will turn elsewhere, seeking a public that is different, perhaps simpler, certainly less jaded and less conventional minded, less used to slickness and smartness, a public that will occasionally be willing to hear new themes, eloquence, even the delicate and splendid lines of poetry—in a word be moved by the sort of beauty that is hard to sell or keep going in our centralized market place."

As in the past Community Theatres have given every possible encouragement to actors and scenic designers, so the time must come when they will give this same encouragement to the playwright.

Let original plays be written and produced (the only way a playwright learns is through production) and in time who knows where the divine spark may strike and a great dramatist emerge?

Stay Home, Young Actor

We are also indebted to Barrett H. Clark for a comment he made in *West of Broadway* upon an observation of the Community Theatres: "Judging by the answers I got last spring during my 10,000 mile journey around the country, at least 95 per cent of the young people have no intention of going into the 'profession'; they are working for the joy of it; in order to become teachers in high schools and colleges, and to work in Little Theatres. The remaining 5 per cent are headed or think they are headed for New York."

We have seen how today the Community Theatres are a proper training ground for the ambitious youngster who wishes to make a career of the theatre. And from these theatres several have gone forth and made a name for themselves, not only on the stage in New York, but also on the screen in Hollywood. What word of encouragement or discouragement can be given to young hopefuls now casting a longing eye toward distant vistas?

The passing of stock and the road has made Community Theatres increasingly important as a stepping stone, not only to the commercial theatre but also to the motion pictures. Marian Robertson, a talent scout, considers Community Theatre training invaluable to the aspirant for a film career.

However, to one ambitious youngster Miss Robertson had this to say: "Stage experience is a prerequisite for picture work. The present system of film production makes it well nigh impossible for you (no matter how long your eyelashes or how striking your personality) to keep pace with the seasoned actors and actresses already in Hollywood, if you lack training.

"Count yourself lucky if there is a Community Theatre in your neighborhood, where you can learn cooperation along with stagecraft, and at the same time live like a human being.

"The picture industry spends thousands seeking talent and arresting personalities in every field allied to the drama. Do your job at home superlatively well, and Hollywood will come looking for you."

Truer words were never spoken. So stay home, young actor and young actress. If you are really as good as you think you are—Hollywood will find you. In the meantime, that job during the day may be dull, but there's a pay check every Saturday night. And there's also all the fun and glamor of backstage to be found in your Community Theatre—without any of the heartaches and disappointments of the professional theatre.

On to Success

Practically every problem that may arise in community dramatics has been solved by some group in one way or another. If you examine the stories of the struggles and the triumphs of the various Community Theatres, somewhere an answer to the difficulty that faces your group will be found: in radio, in the friendliness of greeting cards, in a school of the theatre, in the support of public officials, in social activities, in the awarding of prizes, the publication of a magazine, the promotion of a children's theatre, the establishment of an experimental workshop, and so on. There seems to be no one way toward success. But the application of new ideas and new schemes may prove not only stimulating, but also valuable in interesting new members and bringing new workers into the fold.

However, one goal should always be paramount with every group. The plays produced should be of such a high standard that they will please the general public. They should be so well done that the casual passer-by will purchase a ticket and then want to come back again.

And from all the Community Theatres one other thing is also apparent. There was a time in the 1900's when the theatre was handed to our fathers and grandfathers on a silver platter. They went to a play—sat through a play—and then toddled home.

Today we have learned that the greatest enjoyment in living is to create theatre for our own pleasure. America has discovered that the fun of doing it for one's self is greater than having it done for us.

And despite the seeming popularity of the radio and the movies—rather than destroying in us the desire to create, these things have not only stimulated that desire but also increased it—paradoxical as it may seem.

Certainly today more people are participating in the active production of plays and attending the production of these plays than ever before.

Five hundred thousand to a million workers in Community Theatres! And close to fifteen million persons attend their plays! The theatre is not dead!

And this is only the beginning: for the Community Theatres are becoming deeply rooted in the life of their communities—and the complete story can be told only fifty years from now.

An Experiment to be Tried  arena.

Certainly one of the chief functions of community drama is experimentation. Merely to repeat Broadway successes in the Broadway manner isn't enough. The Community Theatres must be alive to the new and the unusual —both in the presentation of new plays and also in the manner of production.

From Seattle, Washington, comes an interesting experiment. Here Glenn Hughes, Executive Director of the Division of Drama at the University of Washington, has originated a new approach to play production.

Mr. Hughes in the summer of 1932 experienced, as he says, "a strong revulsion against typical amateur theatricals." There was a waning audience interest in the productions at the University. The only theatre at their disposal was an auditorium seating two thousand persons, with a badly proportioned stage, uncomfortable seats, and poor acoustics. "The actors did not develop in their art, the audience was friendly but not enthusiastic—the whole program was commonplace."

So he spent many afternoons during the summer of 1932 thinking things over; of the early Greeks, and their circular dancing-place, wherein the first actors spoke; of the occasional suggestions made by modern theorists on application of circus technique to modern plays.

"But has anyone in the modern world actually established a theatre with the play in the center and the audience on all four sides?" he asked himself. He thought not. Then here was an opportunity to combine intimacy and novelty.

After looking about for a suitable place, he found, atop a sixteen-story hotel near the University, a modern penthouse. He marked off a stage twelve feet square in the center of the room, bought sixty folding chairs, some indirect lighting units, and put four one-act plays into rehearsal.

The experiment proved a success. The demand for seats was greater than the accommodations. So the next season they moved their theatre downstairs to the ballroom of the hotel, where, with the use of raised platforms for the audience, they were able to accommodate between a hundred and fifty and two hundred persons.

"The popularity of the 'circus' technique as applied to drawing room comedy was unmistakable," says Mr. Hughes. But the audiences were still growing, and in January, 1935, the theatre was moved to some lodge rooms near the campus. They called themselves "The Penthouse Theatre."

This theatre was opened in April, 1935, and offered performances to the public every week thoughout the year until April, 1938; five perform-ances a week, with each play running six weeks.

There is a theatre now being built on the campus of the University of Washington, especially designed and constructed for this type of production.

Mr. Hughes suggests that, for such a theatre, it is desirable, though not essential, to choose plays which require only one setting.

"It is artistically preferable," says Mr. Hughes, "to set the 'stage' and leave it. . . Unfortunately there are not enough first-rate comedies of one setting to keep a theatre going steadily. When we have to change settings, we do . . . unaffectedly in full light, with the audience enjoying the labors. When this occurs I am always reminded of the Chinese theatre, with its similarly frank handling of properties . . . our audiences do not seem to have their enjoyment of the play—and their belief in it—curtailed by the entr'acte activities. It has even occurred to me at times that such a practice is more sophisticated than the traditional one of lowering a curtain and pretending that the fairies have whisked the piano out of sight.

"At the beginning and end of an act lights substitute for a curtain. Actors enter in the dark to take their places and exit during the blackout at the end. They practice these blind entrances and exits during rehearsals, and become very skilful at judging distance and direction. The aisles and central acting area are heavily carpeted so that the actors' footsteps are not heard, and it is always a thrill to the audience to have the lights come up after a few seconds' interval and discover a complete cast onstage. The elec-trician has a time chart worked out during rehearsals, so that he knows just how much time to allow before turning up the lights.

"It must not be assumed, however, that this method of production is simple, and that it is bound to succeed. Actually it is difficult. . . Illu-sion . . . must be created by a sharp definition of the central acting area, by carefully concentrated lighting, and by the ability of the actors to create their imaginative world without the help of background. . .

"When a play is well directed and well acted in a properly arranged theatre of the Penthouse type, it takes on a reality which cannot be attained in a conventional theatre. . . Three rows of audience is ideal. More than that is a risk. And each row should be elevated sufficiently to allow for sight lines. Even the first row should be elevated above the level of the play-ing area. . . There must be considerable movement—at least a change of position. . . The furniture . . . must be chosen carefully in regard to height. . . .

"In a Penthouse theatre one looks across at a considerable portion of the audience, face to face. He can watch at least two thirds of those present without effort. . . In farce and light comedy this double interest operates most effectively. Therefore, the Penthouse method of production dramatizes the audience as well as the play, and presents one more theatrical effect which the motion picture theatres cannot offer."

Already this experiment of Glenn Hughes has been tried in other cities. St. Paul has found it effective. Virginia Vogt reports its success in Lewistown, Montana. And recently in the workshop of the Civic Theatre of Palo Alto, California, "Springtime for Henry" was given in this style.

It is recommended to other groups who are seeking a novel and unique method of play production.

VII. DECLARATION OF A NATIONAL POLICY

A Suggestion from Broadway
The Drama League Starts the Ball Rolling
The National Theatre Conference Steps In
The Existing State and Local Organizations
Is a National Organization Necessary?
Toward National Unity

A Suggestion from Broadway

When the Pepper-Coffee Bill was being discussed in Washington during the winter of 1938, and everybody including Burgess Meredith were airing their private opinions on the state of the theatre and what should be done about it, one man spoke up and made what we consider the most pertinent remark.

This was Brock Pemberton, New York producer. In quoting him the *New York Times* of February 8, 1938, concluded by saying: "He suggested that if a permanent theatre project were to be established, a start might be made through the Little Theatre Movement."

A sane suggestion, Mr. Pemberton—and an idea worth serious consideration. But the great question is, "How?"

Some eight or so years ago a group of New Yorkers, seated about a table, gathered together directors and Community Theatre workers from various parts of the country, and made an effort to start some sort of a national organization. They made cute little suggestions, being theorists and never having actually worked in a Community Theatre in their lives. They thought, for instance, it would be too, too wonderful if cities some hundreds of miles apart, say like San Antonio and Dallas, Texas, would both give the same plays. Then Dallas would box up their settings and ship them to San Antonio, while San Antonio would send by express their settings to Dallas. This would save the labor of making two sets of scenery, so thought the consulting graybeards.

But they didn't take into consideration the fact that perhaps Dallas might not want the San Antonio settings, and vice versa. Nor could they anticipate the howls of dismay from the scenic committees when they were to be told they didn't have to paint a set. Neither did they take into account the fact that shipping a lot of scenery to another town would actually cost more than painting that same set at home.

So suggestions from these theorists, who were only meaning to be helpful, didn't get very far. The directors sneaked out of the meeting, woefully shaking their heads—and nothing happened.

Nothing much has happened from organizers at a distance who have made attempts to bring the Community Theatres together. Their efforts have all been well meant. But an organization cannot be forced upon Community

Theatres from the top down. If a national organization of Community Theatres is to eventually come about, it must come from the various groups themselves.

The Drama League Starts the Ball Rolling

However, certain organizations have taken a step in this direction—and the right step. The first to point the way to leadership was the Drama League of America. Perhaps no other organization in this country during the years of its functioning did so much to aid and assist the various theatre groups being born throughout the country.

In 1910 the Drama League was founded in Evanston, Illinois. At first its purpose was the study of the drama and the encouragement of the professional theatre. Its aim, among other things, was to bring to the small towns better plays than otherwise they would get. They organized audiences; clubs in various cities took up the study of plays, and there was an intelligent citizenry awaiting the spoken drama in towns and cities throughout the United States.

But the road declined, and the professional theatre failed these drama-lovers.

The Drama League decided that something must be done. According to Mrs. A. Starr Best, one of the founders of the League, "In 1913 at its convention in Detroit, Michigan, the Drama League took the first step toward starting general interest in the direction of Little and Community Theatre activity, then entirely in embryo. The discussions of one entire day outlined the idea to the delegates, and the directors of the only three Little Theatres in America at that date were present to suggest activities. Thus, the Drama League took the initial step in this now great movement.

"The first Little Theatre Conference was called in Pasadena in 1924 by the Drama League. It was largely attended by directors and representatives. And the Drama League was enjoined to formulate some play for coordinating the Little Theatre activity and standardizing its effort.

"Sensing at once the tremendous opportunity furnished by Little and Community Theatres to rural and remote communities entirely cut off from professional attractions, the League outlined a plan for establishing such groups throughout each state. This department was called The Little Theatre State Circuit Committee and carried on extensive experimental work in Iowa until its activity was hampered by the lack of funds."

For years, with Sue Ann Wilson as executive secretary, the Drama League maintained a clearing house for information about Little Theatres. It also maintained a placement bureau for directors, and this service was rendered free of charge.

/ Through its Little Theatre Foundation an attempt was made to bring the theatres together in closer unity. The Drama League felt that the quickest and sanest solution to the problem lay in cooperation with the extension divisions of the state universities and colleges especially equipped for drama training, who would bring to the communities the resources of the intensified training of the educational institution, supplemented by the broader contacts of a national organization. Following this suggestion many universities inaugurated through their extension divisions a drama service. It was a start in the right direction. But unfortunately, the Drama League suspended activities in 1931, due to a lack of funds to carry on the work.

The Community Theatre Movement lost its best friend. And as a kindly and inspiring godmother the debt these Community Theatres owe to the Drama League must never be forgotten.

The National Theatre Conference Steps In

Then in June of 1931, Kenneth Macgowan, aided and abetted by the American Association for Adult Education, called together some twenty-six community and university directors for a conference in Evanston, Illinois. One of the purposes of this meeting was to discuss the formation of a national organization.

Many problems confronting Community Theatres were thrown into the arena: production, budgets, royalties, building and financing the theatre, and all the other headaches.

From this meeting the National Theatre Conference was formed. Mrs. Edith J. R. Isaacs, editor of *Theatre Arts Monthly*, stepped in and took control.

There were two types of membership; active, with voting powers, and associate. For the active membership any regularly organized theatre (as represented by the principal executive thereof) producing not less than three full-length plays each year or their equivalent (three one-act plays were considered the equivalent of one full-length play), and expending an annual budget for production of at least $1000, could belong. Also any regular college theatre or producing group. Associate memberships were open to any junior college, high school, organization or individual interested in the work of the National Theatre Conference.

To these members various types of service were offered, some gratis, and others for such fees as the council, controlling the organization, decided upon.)Play releases were prepared. Plans for theatre buildings and estimates of cost were drawn up. There was a placement bureau for directors, for which an added fee was charged. There was a monthly news letter to the membership. Also traveling exhibits were made ready and a library service was placed at the disposal of those who were inclined to read books.]

The membership fee, entitling the holder to the above privileges, was $25. The response from Community Theatre groups was not overwhelming. Twenty-five dollars was a lot of money to pay for play releases when the same information was offered free by all the play publishers. The number of groups needing advice on the problems of theatre architecture and building was negligible. The established theatre groups did not need advice nor help on production problems, being more or less familiar with the various books on the subject. And the problems of the smaller groups who didn't spend a thousand dollars a year and therefore couldn't belong went unanswered.

The result was that the majority of active members were representative of college and university theatres. And the regional conferences held by the National Theatre Conference became hot spots of academic discussion and debate, with the Community Theatre delegates sitting in the background and pondering over the occasional vulgar use of a split infinitive.

Then the National Theatre Conference began to have trouble with its budget. A meeting to dissolve was held, and after a stormy session at eleven o'clock one night it was finally agreed on by everyone to disband. But at seven o'clock the next morning the phone began to ring, and all the delegates were called for an eight o'clock conference to be confronted with the news that the Rockefeller Foundation had given them a grant.

And since the Rockefeller Foundation gives money in the interest of adult education, at present the majority of members of the National Theatre Conference are professors and directors of university theatres, with only a few Community Theatre directors thrown in for good measure.

Their policy has been definitely established. It is that the National Theatre Conference shall exist only for the purpose of conducting round-table discussions; and the three problems that they have under discussion are (1) the subsidy of playwrights; (2) library service; and (3) an investigation of the royalty situation, which Barclay Leathem of Western Reserve University at Cleveland, Ohio, is conducting.

Since the university leaders in the drama field are chiefly interested in their own problems, they are not representing the Community Theatre Movement. It is all well and good, of course, for the university and college theatres to have this grant from the Rockefeller Foundation, but it doesn't answer a need for the Community Theatres. These are, at the moment, in so far as the National Theatre Conference is concerned, sitting on the doorstep.

And while for the present, or even the immediate future, the possibilities of any national organization of Community Theatres seems rather doubtful, there is, however, a ray of hope.

There are in several states organizations already existing that include Community Theatres.   Some of these are under the patronage of the state universities, following the suggestion of the Drama League.   Others, more local in character, embrace groups within limited areas.

The Existing State and Local Organizations

It was in 1910 that Thomas H. Dickinson took the first step toward the organization of the now active and flourishing Wisconsin Dramatic Guild.

He founded the Wisconsin Dramatic Society which, although associated with the University of Wisconsin, was yet independent and had individual memberships in all parts of the state.   Among the outstanding charter members were Zona Gale of Portage and Mrs. Laura Sherry of Milwaukee.

Shortly after the organization of the Wisconsin Dramatic Society, Professor Dickinson began editing a small magazine called *The Play Book,* in which he outlined the ideals of this society.

"Around us," said Professor Dickinson, "people are talking a new language, not in terms of politics and science, but in terms of the simple things of living out of which a natural art comes.   This we would make our language . . . The goings-on in things dramatic today have a much broader reference than merely to the stage.   They refer to a society discovering itself. . . . We will be alert rather than authoritative; we would rather learn than be considered learned.   We will talk about the traditions of the middle west, believing that in the rich human background of our history there is soil for an art.   We will talk about our people; Norwegians, Swedes, Germans, French, Anglo-Saxons, with transplanted instincts toward art, welded into a mass different from that of the fatherland, rich with promise.   We will show that you cannot conceive of a completed society without conceiving of its theatre."

And that is exactly what they have done in Wisconsin.   Slowly but surely they continued to build toward a permanent organization.   In 1928 the then established Community Theatre groups of Wisconsin were brought together and the Wisconsin Dramatic Guild formed.   A Bureau of Dramatic Activities under the University of Wisconsin Extension Division with Ethel Theodora Rockwell in charge was established.

This Bureau acts as a general clearing house for the Guild.   And they are prepared to give advice and offer assistance on all matters pertaining to the theatre and theatre production.

The Wisconsin Dramatic Guild is a state organization composed not only of the Community Theatres in Wisconsin, but also dramatic clubs in schools, churches, social and fraternal associations, and industrial plants of the state. Over one hundred such groups now belong to the Guild.

One of its chief activities is the annual Dramatic Festival, at which play tournaments are held, and addresses and demonstrations of dramatic technique given by people of note. It has been the policy of the Guild to encourage the writing of original plays and to emphasize the regular production of plays in schools, churches and communities as the most valuable of their recreational and cultural opportunities.

Original playwriting has become the most interesting and significant development of the Guild. In 1935, for instance, over sixty plays were submitted in the annual Original Play Tournament, and fifteen of these were considered worthy of production in the Festival. Up to date about two score of Wisconsin plays have been published and are winning awards and appreciation in other states.

When Glenn Frank was president of the University of Wisconsin, he said: "The art of the theatre, like the art of literature, has been damned by professionalism. We have wandered far from the days of folk drama when even the souls of simple folk found expression in dramatic form. The next great dramatic renaissance in America will come when we become active enough in mind and rich enough in spirit to begin the creation of a folk drama and a folk theatre in America."

In thinking of folk drama in America one naturally turns to Frederick H. Koch, founder of the Carolina Playmakers at the University of North Carolina in Chapel Hill. Here truly is America's Folk Theatre. Established in 1918, these Playmakers, under the leadership of Dr. Koch, have in the past twenty years given over fifty series of experimental productions of new plays. And when one realizes that each series includes at least three and sometimes more original plays, the total number makes an amazing record.

In 1923 the Carolina Dramatic Association came into being. And ever since that time they have had an annual Festival and State Tournament at Chapel Hill. The purpose of the Carolina Dramatic Association is to encourage dramatic art in the schools and communities of North Carolina; to meet the need for constructive recreation; to promote the production of plays, pageants, and festivals; and to stimulate interest in the making of a native drama.

At the Fifteenth Annual Festival held in March, 1938, there was a total of one hundred and thirty-one member groups enrolled, including besides Little and Community Theatre groups (in the minority), groups from country high schools, junior high schools, junior community clubs and WPA

groups, city high schools, junior and senior colleges, and the dramatic divisions of Women's Clubs. Two hundred and thirty-five players and one hundred and fourteen stage technicians had a part in the plays produced at the
Festival. One entire week was given over to it, and the total attendance for
the week was nearly five thousand.

But like the Wisconsin Dramatic Guild this state organization of North
Carolina is not exclusively composed of Community Theatre groups. But it
is a step in the right direction, even though the problems of a production
group in school or college are not the same as those of a Community Theatre.

Among other state organizations are those of Florida and South Carolina.

The Theatre Institute of South Carolina was organized in the spring of
1936, and has done little more than have semi-annual meetings in Greenville,
Columbia, and Charleston. One of its purposes is an annual Little Theatre
Tournament with all the groups, community and academic, in South Carolina, participating. The prime mover in this association is Arthur Coe Gray
of Furman University of Greenville.

In the fall of 1937, the Gainesville Little Theatre, through its president,
Dr. Sigismond Diettrich, invited twenty-two similar organizations in the state
of Florida to a conference for the purpose of effecting a State Federation of
Little Theatres. On December 3 and 4, 1937, representatives from the other
groups in the state met at Gainesville and the Federation was formed. Dr.
Diettrich of the local organization was elected first president, and present
plans of the Federation are ambitious for fostering dramatic entertainment in
Florida.

And there have been murmurs from Georgia that Mrs. Piercy Chestney
of Macon is laying plans to bring the Community Theatres of that state together. Also in Iowa, Walter Stone of Burlington has some such scheme
up his sleeve. What may ultimately happen remains, of course, to be seen.

And out in Montana, Kay Fetterly of Eureka believes that "the Community Theatre should be a movement—state wide, even national in scope."
She is of the opinion that there should be a way so to organize state groups
that as a result of such organization a National Community Theatre would
evolve.

In the meantime two organizations of smaller scope are flourishing. One
is the Westchester County Association of Westchester County, New York,
and Greenwich, Connecticut. This was organized in 1928 and is affiliated
with the Westchester County Recreation Commission with headquarters at the
Civic Center in White Plains. It is a federation of Community Theatre
groups, drama sections of Women's Clubs, and high school dramatic organizations. It is governed by an executive board elected by representatives
of the member groups, with the exception of a paid secretary who is ap-

pointed by the Recreation Commission. Its purpose is to give service to all phases of dramatic activity to its member groups and, where possible, to anyone in the county interested in dramatic work.

They publish a bulletin five or six times a year with news of local productions. They have yearly drama conferences which are attended by well known people in the field of both Community Theatres and the professional theatre. Also a yearly tournament is held with all the groups competing, and occasionally they have given plays with the cast selected from outstanding members of groups throughout the county.

In making the announcement for one of the annual tournaments, the bulletin contained a suggestion to the competing groups that they must not take their participation too seriously.

"After all," the bulletin went on to say, "it is not a life and death matter. We entered for the fun of it, because of our desire for expression and our love for the Little Theatre and all that it suggests. The Community Theatre is primarily and essentially social. We are able to meet friends and make contacts that are interesting to us. The Tournament, therefore, when reduced to the lowest terms, is a market place where we may present our wares and where our talents may be judged. It is a place where we may try our abilities and have them measured according to competent judges. But above all, the Tournament offers a most pleasant week's entertainment in which competition will stimulate each group to do its best.

"We, in our individual groups, are perhaps inclined to oscillate ourselves and be smugly satisfied that we are doing good work and having a lot of fun in the meanwhile. We forget the advantages of pitting our abilities and potentialities against those of our neighbors. We are apt to overlook the fact that we can learn a good deal from other groups in nearby localities about various angles in play production. Only by clashing our talents against others do we get the best out of ourselves and really find out how good or how bad we are."

This seems a healthy and wholesome approach to the keen competition of a tournament. And certainly if community participation in the theatre begets neighborliness in the community, tournaments will broaden the scope and beget neighborliness among surrounding towns and cities.

Another important organization is the Los Angeles County Drama Association. There are probably more Little Theatres to the square inch in Southern California than any state in the Union. They flourish in halls and barns, attics and studios. Some have all the spontaneity of a mushroom, being nothing short of disguised dramatic schools with a promise to the paying pupils that the Hollywood magnates will attend, their pockets fairly bursting with concealed contracts. Many others, of course, are sincere.

The Los Angeles County Drama Association serves all the theatres in its area, holding tournaments, offering prizes for the best original play, publishing a magazine, and doing everything it can to encourage the amateur theatre.

In Longmeadow, Massachusetts, Ruth Miller in 1935 started the Down East Associates. The first conference was held on May 25th of that year.

Miss Miller says, "We had the idea, no money, but plenty of enthusiasm. We sent invitations to about thirty groups within a sixty-mile radius hoping a few would respond. We acquired the service of five important people to direct round-table discussions, and sat down and waited. Up to within ten days of the Conference we had heard from two groups in the immediate vicinity. Then the responses came pouring in. At the Conference there were about 120 people representing 22 Community Theatre groups."

Out of this conference representatives of about ten groups banded together, and the Down East Associates was born. They exchange news of activities, visit one another's productions, and hold a general meeting at least once a year.

Then there is the Ohio Theatre Conference, which operates through Western Reserve University and the Cleveland Play House. The Northern California Drama Association is sponsored by the San Francisco Recreation Commission. And in Arizona is the Arizona State Drama Association, including in its membership college faculty, students, high school teachers, members of women's clubs, and other individuals and institutions interested in the drama.

These and other similar state associations are pointing the way toward what may ultimately be a country-wide movement, out of which a unified method of cooperation and possibly a national organization may spring.

Is a National Organization Necessary?

It is only too obvious that a national organization of some sort is needed. Here and there little danger signs are appearing that may threaten the life and existence of the Community Theatres. They have grown too rapidly and spread too fast to be completely ignored as the ungainly stepchild of the theatre.

In the June 11, 1938, issue of *Billboard* there was a brief story to the effect that Actors' Equity was considering the possibilities of taking over the "little theatres" in order to stimulate increased employment among its members. And a committee was formed headed by Blanche Yurka to study several suggestions along these lines.

"Move to professionalize the little theatre was suggested to council," reads the item, "as a means of relieving the employment situation among actors who are ineligible for or who have shunned the Federal Theatre Project as a means of employment. If the move is found practicable by the committee, Equity will make an exhaustive study of the possibilities of Equity companies playing theatres which in the past have exhibited amateur talent, with a view toward having things ready by fall."

If anything comes of this suggestion, it is to be hoped that both Equity and the local stage-hands' unions will recognize that amateur or community dramatics hinge upon the enthusiasm of discriminating and intelligent individuals, and that anything that tends to spoil their pleasure or aesthetic appreciation of their efforts will destroy the entire Community Theatre Movement.

The Community Theatre Movement exists not from a desire to commercialize the theatre and make money for the sake of making money, but from the genuine desire for creative endeavor and artistic expression—be it ever so humble. It springs from the wish of the individual to add a cultural interest to his every-day life. He enters into the activities of his Community Theatre of his own free will and choosing, and not from any craving for monetary gain.

Should Equity move into the Community Theatres and take over their stages—what would happen? It would mean, of course, the establishment again of professional stock companies.

But what of the Community Theatre actor—the banker and the baker who have found enjoyment in this leisure-time activity? Would he quickly turn from active participation to becoming again a part of a submissive audience? Hardly that. He'd start all over again in some remodeled barn or old church—and would flourish side by side with the professional stock company, probably borrowing spotlights and exchanging views on the proper interpretation of a part. Certainly the Community Theatre actor would be only too ready and willing to cooperate with the professional.

During the past twenty or thirty years while the Community Theatres have been spreading their wings, perfecting their organizations, producing their own plays since Broadway left them stranded for lack of the spoken drama, and building their own playhouses, the professional theatre has turned a condescending glance in their direction. And now that the Community Theatres have become firmly rooted in their communities, the professional theatre is casting a look of dismay in their direction.

The professional theatre is one thing. Community Drama is quite another. The two, working together, could make the real American theatre. If one is stamped out, the other loses its best friend.

On the one hand the tributary theatres of America furnish the fresh blood and enthusiasm for the professional theatre, for from the Community Theatres are coming the young actors and playwrights of tomorrow. On the other hand the professional theatre furnishes the goal for those who aspire toward a career in the theatre. They are like a couple of quarreling relatives, bound together by a common purpose, and loving and hating each other in the same breath. The two working together could create our National Theatre.

We have seen how in Charleston, West Virginia, guest stars from the professional stage have furnished a new inspiration to the Kanawha Players. The experience was good for both the professional and the amateur. In Washington, Pennsylvania, stage hands were paid to sit in the audience. They survived the ordeal.

Certainly the Community Theatres have kept alive the interest of the audiences for the spoken drama throughout the country, and more than one group has sponsored the appearance in their city of a "road show."

And while the professional theatre has in its various branches organizations and official spokesmen for these organizations, there is at the present no spokesman for the Community Theatres. Were there such a recognized leader, no doubt, in any emergency which might arise the professional theatre workers and the Community Theatre leaders could come to a mutual understanding that would work toward the benefit of both parties.

It is for this reason that we feel a national organization of Community Theatres is necessary.

Even in 1912 Percy MacKaye in his chapter on "Scope and Organization" in *The Civic Theatre* foresaw this need. And he made the suggestion, "First: Appoint and empower a committee of national standing to act as sponsors for the civic theatre ideal, and for the wise application of that ideal in all American communities that desire it."

But how? That is the problem.

Toward National Unity

Toward a national association of Community Theatres efforts to organize from the top down have failed of their own weight. You can no more force the independent theatre groups to unite than you can force a community to organize a Community Theatre. If a national organization is to come about, it must come from the various groups themselves. There is already the example of organizations and associations in several states and counties.

Separate and individual Community Theatre groups, firmly established, have taken the time to look about them, and have extended the friendly hand of greeting to their neighboring Community Theatres. They have found an exchange of ideas helpful. They have enjoyed being hosts to other groups. And tournaments have brought together for a drama festival, at least once a year, the theatre-minded residents of some states.

To tell other states what to do would be wrong. If the need for a state association of some sort is felt, it will come about naturally. And that, of course, is what has happened under inspired leadership in some states. It is what will happen in others.

And just as each individual Community Theatre has met and solved its own problems in its own way, so should these states not yet organized meet and solve their problems.

In time perhaps each state association would pause to look at the work being done in the neighboring states. Then perhaps regional associations might spring into being, and the theatres of the east, the south, the middle west, and the west would unite in friendly cooperation.

And the next step after that, obviously, would be a national organization. Growing slowly, from the bottom up—not from the top down—it would be firmly rooted in the very heart and hearthstones of the Community Theatres.

Again we quote from Percy MacKaye's *Community Drama*, where in 1917 he said: "Neighborliness in a little town may beget the neighborliness of nations."

Such an ideal is not impracticable. Let each Community Theatre now in existence never forget this ideal of neighborliness. It should begin at home, and then overflowing into surrounding communities spread through the entire nation—and perhaps, in time, across the seas.

When this finally happens, the Theatre of Democracy, which has sprung into being in our generation, will come into its own.

"These things lie before us, awaiting our own will and organization." So prophesied Percy MacKaye in *The Civic Theatre* in 1912. "Forty or more state theatres—from the Theatre of California to the Theatre of Massachusetts. . . . A thousand municipal theatres—from the Theatre of San Francisco to the Theatre of Boston. . . . Leading and harmonizing these, one national theatre at Washington, endowed by the federal government. All these, organized by civic leaders, safeguarded to perform their highest functions, directed by experts in theatrical art, dedicated to cultivating—creatively in artists, critically in audiences—the liberal art of a drama of democracy."

Tonight in your town a play is being given. The stage is set. In the dressing-rooms the actors are slipping into their costumes and putting on their make-up. The property lady is busy making a last final check-up. The electrician is testing his lights.   The director is here, there, and everywhere see-ing that everything is in readiness.

The ushers are on hand in the auditorium.   An expectant audience is be-ginning to arrive.   They find their seats.   The lights are lowered.   There is a glow from the footlights upon the curtain.   A moment's pause.   And the play begins.

All over America there are CURTAINS GOING UP.

APPENDICES

APPENDIX A

THE COMMUNITY THEATRE GROUPS OF AMERICA

1. *Introduction*

From time to time come reports of the existence of various Community Theatre groups. A pleasantly phrased letter is sent asking for information. In some instances an opaque silence follows—and the letter with its stamp falls into oblivion. Perhaps the group is hiding its light under a bushel. Perhaps it has forgotten to pay its bills and quickly has changed its name and carries on under a pseudonym. (There are such cases—rare it is true—but they exist.)

Perhaps a few groups will now ask: "Why didn't you mention us?"

We can only reply, "Why didn't you write in?"

So here we offer a list of the towns and cities in America where at one time or another Community Theatre groups have flourished, are flourishing, and perhaps will flourish again. We don't claim this list to be in any measure complete at the present writing: neither the cities nor the names of the group. But we do know that at one time or another in the past thirty years, a Community Theatre group by that name has put on plays in the towns and cities listed.

2. *Where Community Theatres Have Flourished*

ALABAMA, 7. Anniston, Little Theatre; Bessemer, Little Theatre; Birmingham,* Little Theatre; Mobile,* Little Theatre; Montgomery, Theatre Guild; Selma, Drama League Players; Syacuga, Little Theatre Players.

ARIZONA, 3. Phoenix, Little Theatre; Tucson, Little Theatre; Yuma, Community Theatre.

ARKANSAS, 5. El Dorado, Little Theatre; Fort Smith, Community Players; Hot Springs, Little Theatre; Little Rock, Little Theatre; Pine Bluff, Little Theatre.

CALIFORNIA, 49. Alameda, Island City Players; Alhambra, Community Players; Altadena, Theatre Americana; Bakersfield, Little Theatre; Berkeley,* The Playmakers; Beverly Hills, Community Players; Burbank, Theatre Guild; Burlingame, Peninsula Players; Carmel, Arts and Crafts Little Theatre; Claremont,* Community Players; Compton, Community Players; Culver City, Community Players; Eagle Rock, Community Players; El Monte, Community Players; Escondido, Community Arts Club; Eureka, Little Theatre; Fresno, The Players; Glendale, Community Players; Hollywood, Community Players; Inglewood, Community Players; Laguna Beach, Community Players; Long Beach, Community Players; Los Angeles, Civic Players; Oakland, Community Playhouse; Oxnard, Community Players; Pacific Palisades, Westwood Hills Players; Palo Alto,* Civic Theatre; Pasadena,* Community Playhouse; Pomona, Theatre Guild; Redlands, Community Players; Redondo Beach, Community Players; Riverside, Community

* Has its own playhouse.

367

Players; Ross Valley, The Players; Sacramento, Community Players; San Bernardino, Community Players; San Carlos, The Players; San Diego,* Community Players; San Francisco,* The Wayfarers; San Gabriel, Community Players; San Marino, The Guild; San Rafael, Players Club; Santa Ana, Community Players; Santa Barbara,* Players Club; Santa Monica, Community Theatre Guild; Sierra Madre, Community Players; South Pasadena, Little Theatre; Vallejo, Community Players; Westwood Hills, Theatre Guild; Whittier, Community Players.

COLORADO, 6. Colorado Springs,* Community Players; Crested Butte, Community Players; Denver,* Civic Theatre; Greeley, Community Theatre; Lamar, Community Theatre; Pueblo,* Community Players.

CONNECTICUT, 17. Bridgeport, Little Theatre League; Bristol, Community Players; Danbury, Drama League; Greenwich, Community Players; Hartford, Mark Twain Masquers; Litchfield, The Players; Middletown, Little Theatre; Milford, Dramatic Club; New Haven, Elm City Players; New Britain, Little Theatre Guild; North Stamford, The Neighborhood Players; Norwalk, Silvermine Guild; Redding Ridge, Little Theatre Guild; Torrington, Civic Players; Stony Creek, Parish Players; Washington, The Dramalites; Waterbury, Civic Theatre.

DELAWARE, 3. Arden, Repertory Players; Norwalk, Air Castle Players; Wilmington, Little Theatre.

DISTRICT OF COLUMBIA, 1. Washington, Civic Theatre.

FLORIDA, 17. Clearwater, Little Theatre; Daytona, Community Players; Fort Myers, Little Theatre; Fort Pierce, The Masque; Gainesville, Little Theatre; Jacksonville,* Little Theatre; Lakeland, Community Players; Miami, Civic Theatre; Orlando, Little Theatre; Palm Beach, Community Players; Pensacola, Little Theatre; St. Augustine, Little Theatre; St. Petersburg, Little Theatre; Sarasota,* The Players; Tampa, Community Players; West Palm Beach, Community Players; Winter Haven, Little Theatre.

GEORGIA, 10. Albany, Little Theatre; Atlanta, Studio Club; Athens, Little Theatre; Augusta, Little Theatre; Barnesville, Little Theatre; Columbus, Little Theatre League; Macon,* Little Theatre; Savannah,* The Playhouse; Valdosta, Sock and Buskin Club; Waycross, Town Theatre.

IDAHO, 1. Boise, Drama Club.

ILLINOIS, 33. Aurora, Dramatic Club; Austin, Little Theatre; Bloomington, Community Players; Carbondale, Players Club; Centralia, Little Egyptian Theatre; Champaign, Theatre Guild; Chicago, The Mummers, Repertory Theatre; Decatur, Drama Guild; Elmhurst, Community Players; Englewood, Rotary Little Theatre; Evanston, Georgian Little Theatre and North Shore Circuit Theatre; Freeport, Winneshiek Players; Galesburg, Community Theatre; Glencoe, The Threshold Players; Hinsdale, The Players; Joliet, Little Theatre; Jacksonville, Municipal Theatre; La Grange, Community Players; Lanark, The Players; Lockport, Dramatic Club; Moline, League Players; Oak Cliff, Little Theatre; Oak Park, Little Theatre; Ottawa, Drama Club; Peoria,* The Players; Quincy,* Community Little Theatre; Rock Island, Attic Players; Springfield, Community Players; Waukegan, The Serio-Comic Players; Western Springs, Little Theatre; Winnetka, Community Theatre.

INDIANA, 12. Decatur, Dramatic Club; Elkhart, Little Theatre; Evansville, Community Players; Fort Wayne,* Civic Theatre; Gary, Civic Theatre; Goshen, Community Players; Greenwood, Community Players; Indianapolis,* Civic Theatre; La Porte, Little Theatre Club; Muncie, Civic Theatre; South Bend, Little Theatre; Spiceland, Little Theatre Club; Terre Haute, Community Theatre.

IOWA, 22. Bedford, Civic Theatre; Bloomfield, The Players; Burlington,* The Players Workshop; Cedar Rapids,* Community Players; Council Bluffs, Little Theatre; Davenport, The Players; Des Moines,* Community Theatre; Dubuque, Town Players; Emmetsburg, Community Players; Fort Dodge, Community Theatre; Knoxville, The Players; Malverin, Dramatic Club; Mason City, Little Theatre; Marshalltown, Community Theatre; Mystic, Dramatic Club; Newton, Little Theatre Ass'n; Ottumwa, Community Theatre; Prairie City, Community Players; Rock Island, The Playcrafters; Sioux City, Little Theatre; Waterloo, Community Theatre; Webster City, The Players.

* Has its own playhouse.

KANSAS, 4. Fort Scott, Thespian Players; Frankfort, Little Theatre; Hutchinson, Community Theatre; Ottawa, Players Club.

KENTUCKY, 3. Ashland, Little Theatre; Fort Thomas, Community Players; Louisville,* Little Theatre Company.

LOUISIANA, 8. Algiers, Little Theatre; Arcadia, Little Theatre; Baton Rouge, Little Theatre Guild; Lafayette, Community Players; Lake Charles, Community Theatre; Monroe, Players Club; New Orleans,* Le Petit Théâtre du Vieux Carré; Shreveport,* Little Theatre.

MAINE, 3. Bangor-Brewer, Little Theatre; Eliot, Little Theatre; Waterville, Little Theatre.

MARYLAND, 5. Baltimore,* Vagabond Players; Brunswick, Dramatic Club; Catonsville, Little Theatre; Centreville, Little Theatre; Hagerstown, Community Players.

MASSACHUSETTS, 26. Amesbury, Little Theatre; Arlington, Rotary Players; Belmont, Dramatic Club; Boston,* Footlight Club; Brookline, The Amateurs; Cohasset, Dramatic Club; Concord, The Players; Fitchburg,* The Workshop; Lawrence, Community Players; Lenox, Brotherhood Players; Leominster, Community Players; Methuen, Little Theatre; Milton, Community Players; New Bedford, The Players; Newburyport, The Players; Northampton, Amateur Players; Pittsfield, Town Players; Roxbury, Little Theatre Players; Quincy, Community Players; Springfield, Players Guild; Taunton, The Players; Walpole, The Footlighters; West Newton, The Players; Westfield, Little Theatre; Williamstown, Little Theatre; Worcester, Players Club.

MICHIGAN, 17. Allegan, Community Players; Battle Creek, Little Theatre; Benton Harbor, Community Theatre; Birmingham, Village Players; Dearborn, Players Guild; Flint, Community Drama League; Grand Rapids, Civic Players; Green Bay, Little Theatre; Jackson, Masque Players; Kalamazoo,* Civic Theatre; Lansing, Civic Players Guild; Monroe, Community Players; Petersburg, Little Theatre; Pontiac, Little Theatre; Port Huron, Little Theatre Guild; Saginaw, Little Theatre Players; Ypsilanti, Little Theatre.

MINNESOTA, 8. Clinton, Community Players; Duluth,* Little Theatre; Hibbing, Community Players; Minneapolis, Civic Theatre; St. Paul, The Players; Virginia, Little Theatre; Winona, Little Theatre; Winthrop, Little Theatre.

MISSISSIPPI, 4. Columbus, Theatre Guild; Hattiesburg, Little Theatre; Jackson, Little Theatre Players; Natchez, Little Theatre Players.

MISSOURI, 8. Canton, Dramatic Club; Cape Girardeau, Community Theatre; Columbia, Dramatic Arts Club; Kansas City,* Resident Theatre; St. Joseph, Little Theatre; St. Louis, Civic Theatre and Little Theatre; Springfield, Drury Players and Pill Box Little Theatre.

MONTANA, 10. Billings, Little Theatre; Bozeman, Little Theatre Ass'n; Eureka, Little Theatre Club; Fort Peck, Little Theatre; Kalispell, Community Theatre; Lewistown, Little Theatre; Red Lodge, Little Theatre Ass'n; Ronan, Little Theatre; Scobey, Little Theatre; Thompson Falls, Little Theatre League.

NEBRASKA, 5. Fremont, Little Theatre; Hastings, Little Theatre; Kearney, Drama League Players; Lincoln, Little Theatre; Omaha,* Community Playhouse.

NEVADA, 1. Reno,* Little Theatre.

NEW HAMPSHIRE, 1. Concord, Community Players.

NEW JERSEY, 54. Annandale, Middlebrook Players; Arlington, Little Theatre; Atlantic City, Allied Arts Theatre; Bayonne, Little Theatre Group; Bellville, Little Theatre Guild; Bloomfield, Community Players; Boonton, Little Theatre; Bordertown, Community Players; Camden, Playcrafters; Chatham, Community Players; Clinton, Contemporary Club; Cranford, Dramatic Club; Deal, Monmouth Players; Dover.* Little Theatre; Dunellen, Middlebrook Players; East Orange, Little Theatre; Elizabeth, Civic Theatre; Fairlawn, Redburn Players; Fanwood, Band Box Theatre; Florham Park, Afton Players; Gloucester, Playcrafters; Glouster, Laboratory Players; Hackensack, Bergen Players; Harrison, Collective Theatre; Hoboken, Little Theatre; Jersey City, The Players; Lakewood, The Playhouse; Lincoln Park, Lincoln Park Theatre; Linden, Westfield Community Players; Madison, Green Door Players; Maplewood, Placidian Players; Montclair, Dramatic Club; New Brunswick, Habima Guild; Newark, The Players; Nutley,

* Has its own playhouse.

Little Theatre; Passaic, Theatre Guild; Paterson, Neighborhood Players; Phillipsburg, Little Theatre; Plainfield, Kenyon Players; Rahway, Probasco.Players; Ridgewood, Joe Jefferson Players; Roselle, The Players; Rutherford, Little Theatre Guild; Short Hills, Paper Mill Playhouse; Sterling, Footlighters; Summit, The Playhouse; Tenafly, Ridgewood Dramatic Players; Trenton, Players Club; Watchburg, Valley Players; West Orange, Dorklip Players; Westfield, Community Players; Woodcliffe, Community Players; Union City, Laboratory Players; Vineland, Footlighters.

NEW MEXICO, 2. Albuquerque, Community Players; Santa Fe, Community Players.

NEW YORK, 39. Albany, The Players; Alfred, Footlight Club; Bath, Little Country Theatre; Bronxville, Woman's Club Players; Buffalo,* Studio Theatre Players; Chatham, Community Players; Dobbs Ferry,* Civic Theatre; Douglaston, The Players; Elsmere, Community Players; Forest Park, Community Players; Glens Falls, Little Theatre; Great Neck,* Community Players; Hamilton, Little Theatre; Jamestown, Players Club; Larchmont, The Players; Mamaroneck, Community Drama Society; Mount Vernon, Community Theatre; New Rochelle, Huguenot Players; New York City,* Amateur Comedy Club; Niagara Falls, The Players; Perry, Perry Grange Players; Plattsburg, Little Theatre; Port Chester, Sawpit Players; Port Washington, The Players; Poughkeepsie, Community Players; Rochester,* Community Players; Rye, Community Players; Scarborough-on-Hudson, Beechwood Players; Scarsdale, Spotlights Players; Schenectady, Civic Players; Southold, The Players; Syracuse, Little Theatre; Tarrytown, The Players; Troy, The Masque; Utica, The Players; Valhalla, Valhalla Players; West Point, The Players; White Plains, Contemporary Club; Yonkers, Little Theatre.

NORTH CAROLINA, 21. Asheville, Little Theatre; Cary, Dramatic Club; Charlotte,* Little Theatre; Derita, The Players; Durham, The People's Theatre; Fayetteville, Little Theatre; Goldsboro, Wayne Players; Greensboro, Little Theatre; Greenville, Little Theatre; Hickory, Players Guild; Hobgood, Community Players; Jamestown, Twin-Village Players; Lenoir, Little Theatre; Manteo, Elizabethan Players; Raleigh, Little Theatre; Reidsville, Little Theatre; Rocky Mount, Little Theatre Players; Valdese, Old Colony Players; Wilkesboro, Community Players; Wilmington, Thalian Ass'n; Winston-Salem, Little Theatre.

NORTH DAKOTA, 3. Fargo,* Little Country Theatre; Grand Forks, Dakota Playhouse, Hamilton, Community Theatre.

OHIO, 29. Akron, Weathervane Players; Antioch, The Players; Canton, Little Theatre; Chillicothe, Little Theatre; Cincinnati,* Civic Theatre; Cleveland,* The Playhouse; Cleveland Heights,* Civic Theatre; Columbus,* Players Club; Conneaut, Community Players; Cuyahoga, The Players; Elyria, The Playmakers; Glendale, Lyceum Players; Hamilton, Community Theatre; Lima, Community Players; Mansfield, Community Players; Massillon, Community Players; Miamisburg, Town Players; Mingo Junction, Community Players; Norwood, Little Theatre Community Players; Portsmouth, Little Theatre; Shaker Heights, Shaker Players; Springfield, Civic Theatre; Steubenville, Histrionic Club; Toledo,* Repertoire Little Theatre; Urbana, Community Players; Westerville, Cap and Dagger Club; Willoughby, The Players; Youngstown, Little Theatre; Zanesville, Little Theatre Guild.

OKLAHOMA, 6. Bartlesville, Little Theatre Guild; Chickasha, Dramatic Club; Oklahoma City, Civic Theatre; Ponca City, Legion Players; Tulsa, Little Theatre; Yukon, Little Theatre.

OREGON, 4. Eugene,* The Very Little Theatre; Portland,* Civic Theatre; Salem, Little Theatre Club; Silverton, The Playmakers.

PENNSYLVANIA, 30. Allentown, Civic Theatre; Altoona, Little Theatre; Beaver, Little Theatre; Bethlehem, Plays and Players; Butler, Little Theatre Group; Curtisville, Community Players; Dallastown, Community Players; Doylestown, Theatre Guild; Easton, Little Theatre; Erie,* Community Players; Greensburg, Little Theatre Players; Harrisburg, Community Theatre; Hazleton, Little Theatre; Lancaster, Little Theatre; Latrobe, Plays and Players Club; Lock Haven, Community Players; Oil City, Studio Players; Philadelphia,* Theatre League and Plays and Players; Pittsburgh, Civic Theatre; Reading, Little Art Theatre; Red Lion, Little Theatre; Scranton, Drama League Players; Sunbury, Little Theatre; Titusville, Little Thea-

* Has its own playhouse.

tre; Washington, Community Theatre; Wayne, Footlighters; Wilkes-Barre, Little Theatre; Wilkinsburg, Theatre Guild; Williamsport, Community Players; York, Little Theatre.

RHODE ISLAND, 6. Hope Valley, The Players; Kingston, Community Players; Pawtucket, Community Players; Providence, The Players; Wakefield, Community Players; Westerly, Community Players.

SOUTH CAROLINA, 5. Charleston,* Footlight Players; Columbia,* Town Theatre; Florence, Pinewood Players; Greenville, Little Theatre; Spartanburg, Palmetto Players.

SOUTH DAKOTA, 2. Gettysburg, Community Players; Sioux Falls, Little Theatre.

TENNESSEE, 8. Caplesville, The Little Players; Chattanooga,* Little Theatre; Cleveland, Little Theatre; Johnson City, Little Theatre Guild; Knoxville, Little Theatre; Lebanon, Cumberland Players; Memphis,* Little Theatre; Nashville,* Community Theatre.

TEXAS, 55. Abilene, Little Theatre; Amarillo, Black Mask Players; Austin, Community Players; Bastrop, Little Theatre; Beaumont, Little Theatre; Belton, Little Theatre; Brownwood, Little Theatre; Bryan, Little Theatre; Clarendon, Little Theatre; Cleburne, Community Theatre; Colorado, Little Theatre; Commerce, Little Theatre; Cooper, Little Theatre; Corpus Christi, Civic Players; Corsicana, Little Theatre; Dallas,* Little Theatre; Del Rio, Little Theatre; Denison, Little Theatre; Denton, Little Theatre; El Paso, Little Theatre; Fort Worth,* Little Theatre; Gainesville, Little Theatre; Galveston,* Little Theatre; Georgetown, Mask and Wig Club; Glidden, Little Theatre; Greenville, Little Theatre; Houston,* Little Theatre; Jacksonville, Little Theatre; Livingston, Little Theatre; Lubbock, Little Theatre; Mercedes, Little Theatre; Mexia, Little Theatre; Oak Cliff,* Little Theatre; Paducah, Little Theatre; Palastine, Civic Dramatic Club; Pampa, Little Theatre; Paris, Little Theatre Players; Pharr, Valley Little Theatre; Plainview, Little Theatre; Port Arthur, Little Theatre; Quanah, Little Theatre; Ranger, Little Theatre; San Antonio,* Little Theatre; San Juan, Little Theatre; San Marcos, Little Theatre; San Sabo, Little Theatre; Sherman, Little Theatre; Temple, Little Theatre; Texarkana, Little Theatre Club; Tyler, Little Theatre; Vernon, Little Theatre; Waco, Little Theatre; Weslaco, Little Theatre; Wichita Falls, Little Theatre Players; Winnsboro, Little Theatre.

UTAH, 4. Coalville, Little Theatre; Logan,* Little Theatre; Ogden, Weber Little Theatre; Salt Lake City, Little Theatre.

VERMONT, 6. Barre, Barre Players; Bennington, Theatre Guild; Brattleboro, Dramatic Club; Burlington, Theatre Club; Dorset, The Players; St. Johnsbury, Little Theatre.

VIRGINIA, 11. Alexandria, Columbian Players; Ashland, Little Theatre; Bowling Green, Little Theatre; Fort Humphries, Little Theatre; Lynchburg,* Little Theatre; Norfolk, Little Theatre; Richmond, Little Theatre League; Scottsville, The Players; Taylorstown, Little Theatre; Waynesboro, Fairfax Players; Winchester, Little Theatre.

WASHINGTON, 8. Aberdeen, Community Playhouse; Bellingham, Theatre Guild; Centralia, Civic Dramatic Club; Hoquiam, Community Players; Seattle,* Civic Theatre, Penthouse Theatre; Spokane, Drama League Players; Tacoma, Little Theatre.

WEST VIRGINIA, 6. Charleston, Kanawha Players; Elkins, Little Theatre Guild; Fairmont, Community Players; Huntington, Community Players; Wheeling, Little Theatre; Williamstown, Players Club.

WISCONSIN, 17. Ashland, The Strollers; Beaver Dam, Little Theatre; Bremerton, Drama Guild; Glidden, Little Theatre; Green Bay, Little Theatre; Janesville, Players Club; Lake Geneva, Belfry Players; Madison, Civic Theatre; Menomonie, Little Theatre; Milwaukee, Wisconsin Players; Neenah, Players Guild; Racine, Community Players; Ripon, Ripon Players; Sheyboygan, Community Players; Superior, Little Theatre; Waukesha, The Players; Wisconsin Rapids, Little Theatre.

WYOMING, 4. Caspar, Community Players; Cheyenne, Little Theatre; Evanston, Little Theatre; Laramie, Little Theatre.

* Has its own playhouse.

The Constitution and By-laws of Community Theatres

1. *A Model Isn't Necessary.*

Unfortunately there is no such thing as a model constitution and by-laws for Community Theatre groups. Each community has its own problems. And constitutions vary. They can also be amended.

But as a sample of a constitution under which certain groups work, the following is offered.

2. *From the Little Theatre of Glidden, Wisconsin.*

CONSTITUTION

ARTICLE I

NAME

This Club shall be called the Glidden Little Theatre Group.

ARTICLE II

OBJECT

The object of this club shall be to stimulate the production of good plays at a minimum charge to the public and to foster greater interest in reading and acquiring good plays.

ARTICLE III

OFFICERS

The officers of this club shall be a President, Vice-President, Secretary, Treasurer and a Dramatic Director.

ARTICLE IV

ANNUAL MEETING AND ELECTION

Section 1. The annual meeting shall be held the second regular meeting in May.

Section 2. All officers except the Dramatic Director shall be nominated and elected by ballot at the annual meeting, to serve for one year. They may be re-elected for one term only.

Section 3. The officers, together with the Chairmen of Standing Committees, shall constitute the Executive Committee.

Section 4.   In case of a vacancy occurring during the club year, the Executive Committee shall appoint a member to fill the post, except the presidency, in which case, the Vice-President automatically becomes the President.

ARTICLE V

MEMBERSHIP

The membership shall be unlimited.

ARTICLE VI

AMENDMENTS

This Constitution may be amended at any regular business meeting of the club provided that the proposed amendment has been presented in writing at the previous business meeting.

BY-LAWS

ARTICLE I

DUTIES OF OFFICERS

Section 1.   The President shall preside at all meetings at which she is present; shall exercise general supervision over the affairs and activities of the club and shall serve as member ex-officio on all standing committees.

Section 2.   The Vice-President shall assume all duties of the President in the latter's absence.

Section 3.   The Secretary shall handle correspondence for the club and keep the minutes of each and every meeting, said minutes to be an accurate record of all business transacted.

Section 4.   The Treasurer shall receive all club funds and pay out funds only by order of the Club.   She shall keep an itemized account of all receipts and expenditures.

Section 5.   The Dramatic Director shall cast all plays, appoint a production staff and direct all plays.

ARTICLE II

MEETINGS

Section 1.   The regular meetings of the Club shall be held on the second and fourth Tuesdays of each month from October to June at 7:45 P.M. at places designated by the Program Committee.

Section 2.   Any regular meeting may be postponed by the President with the concurrence of the Vice-President and Secretary.

Section 3.   Special meetings may be called at any time by the President with the concurrence of the Vice-President and Secretary.

ARTICLE III

QUORUM

Two-thirds of the membership shall constitute a quorum.

ARTICLE IV

COMMITTEES

Section 1. Committees shall be appointed by the President.

Section 2. The Standing Committees shall be as follows: Program, Social, Library, Auditing.

ARTICLE V

PLAYS

Section 1. The number of plays produced each year shall be left to the discretion of the Dramatic Director, but dates chosen shall not conflict with other important civic functions.

Section 2. No benefit performance shall be given for any organization, nor shall the Little Theatre Group sponsor any performance for any other organization.

ARTICLE VI

EQUIPMENT

No equipment shall be loaned to any other organization or individual.

ARTICLE VII

FUNDS

All funds shall be used for the producing of better plays and for the purchasing of better equipment.

ARTICLE VIII

PARLIAMENTARY AUTHORITY

Gleason's Parliamentary Digest shall be authority upon all questions not covered by the Constitution and By-Laws.

ARTICLE IX

AMENDMENTS

The By-Laws may be amended at any regular business meeting of the Club by a two-thirds vote; notice of said amendment having been given at the previous regular business meeting.

A QUESTIONNAIRE FOR PROSPECTIVE MEMBERS

1. *Where Do You Belong?*

In order to find out new members' aptitudes, interests, and in what particular activities they wish to engage, most Community Theatres submit a questionnaire listing the various activities of the theatre. You pay your dues, you state your preference, and you go to work!

2. *From the Shaker Players, Shaker Heights, Ohio.*

CHECK SHEET FOR SHAKER PLAYER ACTIVITIES
1935–1936 Season

To the Board of Trustees,
Shaker Players, Inc.,
Shaker Heights, Ohio.

I am willing to contribute to the success of our 1935–1936 season by assisting in the activities checked below. Please notify me to which activities I am assigned.

PUBLIC PLAYS

...... Acting * ...... Properties ...... Scene Design ...... Costuming
...... Play Reading ...... Scenery Painting ...... Make-up ...... Stage Lighting ...... Back Stage Crew.

WORKSHOP AND RADIO PLAYS

...... Acting * ...... Costuming and Properties ...... Directing
...... Play Writing ...... Radio Players ...... Prompting

ADMINISTRATIVE

...... Publicity ...... Ushering ...... Programs ...... Box Office
...... Typing or Addressing ...... Subscription Desk

SOCIAL

...... Hostess ...... Women's Committee ...... Refreshments
...... Registrar

NAME ....

ADDRESS ....

PHONE ....

* Members trying-out for parts are also expected to assist in other activities.

3. *From the Macon Little Theatre, Macon, Georgia.*

THE MACON LITTLE THEATRE
MACON, GEORGIA

Dear Member:

In order to organize the program and work of The Macon Little Theatre, it is necessary that certain information be furnished the officers by each member. With this in view, I am asking that you fill out and return the enclosed questionnaire to the undersigned as soon as practicable.

  I. I will try to interest ...... persons as members of the Theatre. Mail me ...... membership blanks. (Strike if not needed)
 II. I desire for this season the following types of plays numbered in order of preference. (Please number your preferences)
     Recent New York successes not yet staged in Macon:
     (a) Acknowledged modern "masterpieces." (b) An experiment with an original play. (c) A group of one-act plays. (d) A revival of classics. (e) Children's plays for special performances.
III. I suggest the following plays for production this season: (List name and author)
 IV. I should enjoy and am willing to work for the Little Theatre in the capacity of: (Please check)

(a) Actor.
(b) Player of small parts.
(c) Art director, scenery designer.
(d) Stage manager.
(e) Carpenter.
(f) Painter of scenery.
(g) Electrician.
(h) Costumer.
(i) Assistant to the director-prompter.
(j) Making-up.
(k) Ticket seller (In box or outside—check)

(l) House manager.
(m) Publicity writer.
(n) Usher.
(o) Executive or committee worker.
(p) Stenographic worker.
(q) Music. (Name instrument)
(r) Assistant to any of the above work. (Mention which)
(s) I would be willing to devote ...... hours each play to the above work.
(t) I would rather work: (a) Mornings, (b) Afternoons, (c) Nights. (Please check)

  V. The dressing rooms, library, lounges and offices of the Little Theatre building need furniture and furnishings of every possible sort. If you have any furniture or furnishings you would care to contribute, please list them below and state where and when they may be secured. In listing furniture or furnishings, please state size.

Davenports	Mirrors	Piano
Tables	Chairs	Divans
Pictures	Stools	Desks
Bookcases	Towels	Carpets
Draperies	Clocks	Curtains
Radio	Rugs	Shades
Floor lamps	Table lamps	Tapestries

Books (List on back)	Phonograph	Tools (list)
Flowers	Potted plants	Records (list)
Chests	Medicine cabinet	Bureaus
Dressers	Dressing tables	Typewriter
Filing cases	Pens, pencils, office supplies	

VI. For presentations, various properties will be needed. If you can lend properties for presentations, please indicate below the description of them so the property man's catalogue can carry the list to be called for when needed. Specify the length of time properties can be kept. They will be well cared for and insured, and returned when specified. (Every possible thing will be needed, from an antique highboy to a pair of riding boots, size eleven)

(Signed) ....

Member

Address ....

Telephone Number ....

A Contract for the Director

1. *A Letter Has Been Sufficient.*

Three steps are usually taken when a director for a Community Theatre is engaged. First the Board of Directors examines carefully his references, the record of his past accomplishments, and also gazes thoughtfully at his photograph. It's very important to know what a director looks like.

If he passes this hurdle a letter is written him, extolling the advantages of living in the community, its charms, its desirability as a health resort, and the blessings that will be his if he comes to direct this group of players.

In the meanwhile the prospective director has not been idle. He has been inquiring of the former directors of this particular group just what the town is like, why he didn't stay, and what the problems of the group happen to be. If it doesn't sound good, and he doesn't need the money, a polite letter declining the offer is sent. But if he has a favorable report, he accepts the call.

Then it's time for a contract to be drawn up between the two parties.

Signed by both the president and the secretary, a letter may serve as a contract.

2. *A Good Contract to Sign.*

Here is what seems to be a simple, direct, comprehensive contract; fair to both parties, and a model of its kind.

STATE OF ....

COUNTY OF ....

THIS AGREEMENT made and entered into this ...... day of ...., by and between the ...., Party of the First Part, and ...., Party of the Second Part,

WITNESSETH:

1. Party of the First Part hereby appoints the Party of the Second Part Director of the .... for the season ...., and that is to say, September 15, ..., to June 15, ..., and the Party of the Second Part hereby accepts the aforesaid appointment on the terms and conditions hereinafter set forth, which are hereby agreed to.

2. That in consideration of the services to be rendered by the Party of the Second Part as Director, the Party of the First Part agrees to pay the Party of the Second Part the sum of .... dollars in nine equal installments on or before the 15th day of each month of said term, commencing October 15, ..., and ending June 15 .....

3. Party of the Second Part agrees to present seven productions to be of four performances each during said season, offering as many "repeats" and out-of-town performances of said productions as to the President and/or the Executive Committee of the .... in agreement with the said Director, may seem advisable.

4. Party of the Second Part agrees to present each of the aforesaid seven productions according to the following schedule and within the times therein provided:

First—Between October 6 and October 23.
Second—Between November 10 and December 27.
Third—Between December 8 and December 25.
Fourth—Between January 20 and January 29.
Fifth—Between February 17 and March 2.
Sixth—Between April 21 and April 30.
Seventh—Between May 5 and May 15.

5. Party of the second part agrees to keep all activities and expenditures, under his direction, within the limits of the budget as adopted by the Executive Committee and/or the Board of Governors, and Party of the Second Part agrees to make no expenditures in excess of that provided by the aforesaid budget without the written approval of the Executive Committee or its duly constituted representative.

6. Party of the First Part, subject to the aforesaid provisions and restrictions, hereby grants to the Party of the Second Part exclusive authority with reference to (a) choice of cast, (b) creation of productions within budgetary limits, and (c) selection of plays except that as to this item the said Director is to submit for the approval of the Board a list of not less than ten plays from which the productions for the year are to be chosen by agreement between said Director and the Board of Directors, such lists to be submitted not later than September 15 .....

7. It is agreed that the Costume, Property and Stage Staff Committee and their respective chairmen be selected by the Director, with the approval of the President.

8. Party of the Second Part agrees to co-operate with and foster the activities of the .... and do the utmost to advance the interest of the Party of the First Part.

9. In addition to the compensation hereinabove provided for, it is understood and agreed that the Party of the Second Part shall share in any income received by the Party of the First Part over and above the amount of the annual budget fixed by the Board of Directors for the .... season in the following proportions: ......% of such overplus to the amount of ...... dollars; ......% of any excess over that; any amount due hereunder to be ascertained at the close of the season on June 15, ..., and any amount then found to be due to be then payable.

IN WITNESS whereof the ...., by its President and its Secretary, has caused its name to be hereunto subscribed and its seal to be hereunto affixed, and the said .... has hereunto set his hand and seal, both in triplicate, the date and year first above written.

This is a good contract. If you are a director, just graduated from the Drama School, and get a contract like this—sign it!

RULES FOR A TOURNAMENT

A Survey Is Made.

After a careful survey of the various rules for conducting and judging the one-act play tournaments held throughout the country, Mrs. Mabel Foote Hobbs drew up a comprehensive set of rules. In her lively and pertinent article, "Lo—the Poor Judge," published in *Recreation* (the magazine of the National Recreation Association, 315 Fourth Avenue, New York, N. Y.), she sums up these rules, and gives advice on conducting a tournament.

For the gracious permission to reprint this we are indebted not only to Mrs. Hobbs, but also to the Editors of *Recreation.*

TOURNAMENT SUGGESTIONS

The following suggestions were selected from ten different set ups, ranging from the most experienced to the simplest tournaments.

Suggested Tournament Rules

I. The contest is open to all non-professional dramatic groups in . . . No professional actors shall be employed in the presentation. A professional director does not come within the restrictions mentioned, as long as he does not act a part in the tournament.

II. Not more than . . . groups may compete. Registration of intention to enter the contest must be made by . . . and registrations are accepted in order of their receipt. Name of play and cast need not be announced at that time.

Note: Mr. Carl Glick, who was one of the first to introduce the state tournament, offers the following suggestions. An invitation to participate, with the rules attached, is sent by the tournament committee to each eligible group by registered mail, receipt card requested. The reply of acceptance, which the committee asks the groups to send by registered mail, indicates that the entrants are willing to abide by the rules. This method eliminates any possible misunderstanding through lost mail.

III. Name and synopsis of play must be in the hands of the committee by. . . . No two groups shall give the same play. The first group to submit the play shall be given the preference. No player may act in more than one play.

IV. An entrance fee of . . . will be charged each contesting group, payment to be made not later than . . . Each competing group will receive gratis . . . tickets. These may be disposed of for . . . apiece, thus covering the cost of entrance fee and perhaps the royalty for the play. There will be no expense to the contestants for rental of the theatre.

Note: The rental and general expenses govern the amount of the entrance fee.

V. Entries are limited to strictly one-act plays with casts of at least four people. Musical and dancing specialties are barred. Only one set is allowed. The curtain may be dropped to denote passing of time. Maximum playing time shall be forty minutes.

Note: The time limit varies from thirty to forty-five minutes, but the majority of rules place a forty-minute limit. The New Haven Drama Tournament bars original plays, one act from a long play, and plays that have been presented in the tournament during the past four years.

VI. Each contesting group must be responsible for the royalty on its own play, and the receipt for payment to the play agents must be presented to the committee twenty-four hours before the performance. Failure to comply with this rule will be considered an automatic withdrawal from the contest, with forfeiture of the entrance fee.

Note: This rule, which is in general use, is taken from the Pittsburgh Drama League set up.

VII. Each group will be allowed one hour during the afternoon of the day of their performance for rehearsal, making it possible for the actors to gauge their voices and become familiar with the stage. Full dress rehearsal is not possible at this time.

VIII. All scenery, properties and effects of each group must be at the theatre on the morning of the day it is to play. These must remain in charge of the tournament committee until a decision has been reached by the judges as to the prize plays that are to be presented at the final performance. Groups must remove properties as soon as they are eliminated from the contest. Transportation to and from the theatre is at the expense of each group which is also responsible for the care of costumes and properties.

IX. All plays will use the same drapes as a background.

Note: Most tournament committees are desirous of getting away from all kinds and types of stage scenery and the expense of elaborate settings. This rule is especially valuable when groups of different financial standing are competing.

X. No persons are permitted backstage except those connected with the play being presented at the time.

Note: Backstage space is always limited. Each group should have full use of the stage without any handicap during the presentation of their play. Groups will wait in their dressing rooms until the time of their appearance when they must be ready to take charge of the stage as soon as the previous play is over.

XI. The preliminary contests will be on the first . . . nights, four plays given each night. The preliminary judges will select the four best performances and these four will be presented in the final contest, usually held the first night following the preliminaries. The committee will group all plays entered as seems best from the standpoint of artistically arranged programs.

XII. There will be two sets of judges—one for the preliminary contest and one for the final. These will be selected by the Drama Tournament Committee.

XIII. The cup will be awarded to the play judged best by the final judges. The cup is to be held by the winning group for one year. It will again be competed for in the next tournament. The group winning it three times, not necessarily in successive tournaments, will become the permanent owners.

Rules for Judging Play

I. *Diction:*
   (a) Could the actors be heard (1) with difficulty (5), (2) clearly (10).
   (b) Was the diction of the actors fair (5), good (10) excellent (15).

   NOTE: Diction to cover pronounciation, accurate dialect fitting quality of voice.

II. *Acting:*
   Was the acting of the group as a whole fair (10), good (20), excellent (30).

   NOTE: Acting to include smoothness of performance and general cooperation of players. Do the actors play to each other, no one trying to out-do another, each actor giving his best for the good of the play and the rest of the group?

III. *General effect:*
   Fair (5), good (10), excellent (15) (Make-up, costuming, and properties must be appropriate for play.)

IV. *Interpretation:*
   Was the interpretation of the play as a whole fair (10), good (20), excellent (30).

   NOTE: Interpretation, the meaning of the play as brought out by the actors, and the degree to which the audience realized it. Direction including tempo.

Name of Group	Diction, 25% (a) 10% (b) 15%	Acting, 30%	General Effect, 15%	Interpretation, 30%	Total Percentage
1.					
2.					
3.					
4.					
5.					

A Guide for the Selection of the Best Actor and Actress

In the Little Theatre of Macon, Georgia, each year an award is made to the best actor and the best actress of the year.

Here are the instructions to the judges. And also, it seems to us, a comprehensive standard by which to judge good acting.

RULES

(The Little Theatre of Macon, Georgia)

I. Diction:
    (a) Could the player be heard, with difficulty (5); clearly (10).
    (b) Was the diction of the player fair (5); good (10); excellent (15).

    NOTE: Diction to include pronunciation, accurate dialect, fitting quality of voice, enunciation, word value in interpretating lines.

II. Acting:
    Was the acting of the player fair (10); good (20); excellent (30).

    NOTE: Acting to include smoothness of performance, characterization (that is, emotional and intellectual understanding and rendition of lines and character), pantomime, poise (or stage presence), co-operation (or teamwork), that is no effort on the part of the player to feature *himself* at the sacrifice of the other players; fitting into his rightful relation to the work of the other players.

III. Interpretation:
    Was the interpretation of the role by the player fair (10); good (20); excellent (30).

    NOTE: Interpretation to include the success with which the player got into the skin of the character; the degree to which the audience seemed to realize it; the effect of the performance upon the audience (as determined by laughter, applause, comments, etc.).

IV. General Effect:
    Was the general effect of the player fair (5); good (10); excellent (15).

NOTE: General Effect to include the appropriateness of costuming (and the success with which the player wears his clothes), make-up, posture (whether walking, standing, or sitting), charm, appeal, etc.

NOTE: The ratings given above are not arbitrary. If, for instance, you feel that a player is better than "good," yet not so good as "excellent," given an in-between rating. Take No. II—"good" is 20%; "excellent," 30%. If you consider the player better than "good" yet not "excellent," why not give the player 25%? Or take No. IV. Should you consider the player's general effect better than "good," yet not "excellent," why not rate the player 10-plus.

. . . . . .

SCORE SHEET ON PETTICOAT FEVER

Name of Player	Diction, 25% (a) 10% (b) 15%	Acting, 30%	Interpretation, 30%	General Effect, 15%	Total Percentage
Man					
Woman					

(a) I consider .... the best man player, and ....
the best woman player, *so far this season.*
  NOTE: Give your reasons on reverse of this paper.
(b) I consider .... and .... tie for first place as the best man player, so far this season.
  I consider .... and .... tie for first place as the best woman player, so far this season.
   NOTE: If the men tie and the women do not, or vice versa, use both (a) and (b).
   NOTE: Use other side of paper for general comment, if any.

Signed ....

IMPORTANT

Please send this Score Sheet to Mrs. Chestney IMMEDIATELY after the play.
Do NOT send the other two sheets—keep them for reference throughout the season.
From now on ONLY Score Sheets will be sent the judges, so be certain to preserve the other two attached sheets carefully for the rest of the season.

How Do They Spend Their Money?

1. *Home Town—Home Spent.*

When they hear that Hollywood spends one million or more dollars on the production of a super-colossal-terrific film, and how Broadway producers with the right angel think nothing of sinking fifty thousand dollars in the production of a play, it is little wonder that the treasurers of Community Theatres gasp and speculate on how it is done.

Sets have been made for as little as $10, including drayage, as in Macon, Georgia. And there are other groups that have spent about that much or even less.

One thing is most apparent: the monies paid at the box offices of the Community Theatres—with the exception of royalties and that part of the director's salary which goes for a well-earned vacation in the summer—is all spent in the community itself. It isn't like the old days of the road shows coming in and taking money out of the town. Earned in the community— spent in the community. That's the principle of the Community Theatre. Secretaries of the Chambers of Commerce please note!

2. *What One Production Costs in Nashville, Tennessee.*

Break-down for the production of "High Tor":

Royalty	$125.00
Scripts	12.50
Costumes	25.00
Lumber	33.68
Paint	5.28
Lights	27.88
Make-up	5.00
Rope, hardware	26.39
Publicity	47.00
	$307.73

Permanent yearly expenditures divided by six productions:

House	
Coal	$42.10
Electric current	43.25
Rent	100.00
Maintenance	33.32
Telephone	12.50
Salaries	
Director	200.00
Scene carpenter	66.67
Janitor	33.32
	531.16

Total:

Production expense	$307.73
General overhead	531.16
	$838.89

3. *Peoria Players—Peoria, Illinois.*

TREASURER'S REPORT 1937–1938

RECEIPTS		DISBURSEMENTS	
Balance forward	$700.68	Heat & Light	$968.24
Memberships	5787.50	Water	18.50
Benefit Ball	915.50	Janitor	970.90
Jefferson T. & S. Bank Loan...	500.00	Advertising	2.70
Publicity	45.00	Membership Campaign	73.50
Rent	285.00	Benefit Ball	238.00
Productions	1484.40	Building Improvements	333.54
Incidentals	14.50	Equipment	1021.95
Advertising	3.70	Office Help	220.00
Check not cashed 348	5.96	Indebtedness (standing)	454.00
		Jefferson T. & S. Bank	500.00
	$9742.24	Interest	78.50
		Office Supplies, etc.	181.51
		Tickets	81.50
		Publicity	253.30
		Telephone	102.70
		Taxes—real estate	161.00
		Taxes—social security	27.34
		Productions	2647.00
		Insurance	767.23
		Building Maintenance	141.80
		Incidentals	172.60
		Junior Department	39.03
		Memberships returned	24.00
			$9478.84
		Balance	263.40

4. *Consolidated Box Office Report, 1937–38.*

OLD FORT PLAYERS' SEVENTH SEASON

Fort Wayne, Indiana

	Goodbye Again	Alison's House	Murder Arranged	Accent On Youth	Butter & Egg Man	Stage Door	White Wings	Petrified Forest	Totals	Average
Main Floor:										
Season Tickets.........	1100	965	890	1064	815	1150	715	1030	7,729	966
Cash Sales............	118	151	190	153	115	244	204	131	1,306	163
Complimentary........	65	75	81	65	63	84	87	61	601	75
Totals............	1303	1191	1161	1282	993	1478	1006	1222	9,636	1204
Balcony:										
Season Tickets.........	15	2	4	6	4	6	—	62	99	12
Cash Sales............	232	203	132	273	190	430	198	186	1,894	237
Complimentary........	8	—	—	12	—	—	—	—	20	2
Totals............	255	205	186	291	194	436	198	248	2,013	251
Grand Totals.........	1558	1396	1347	1573	1187	1914	1204	1470	11,649	1455
Box Office Sales.......	$127.25	$137.60	$156.12	$153.35	$121.45	$253.90	$173.80	$123.90	$1,347.37	$168.42
Attendance:										
Thursday............	362	327	331	323	311	558	304	333	2,849	356
Friday..............	511	461	429	519	402	648	339	457	3,766	471
Saturday............	685	608	587	731	474	708	561	680	5,034	629
	1558	1396	1347	1573	1187	1914	1204	1470	11,649	1456

Note. These figures do *not* include the attendance at "Aaron Slick," "At Curtain Time," Children's Theatre productions or the sales of the entire house to Clubs for special performances.

5. *First Time on Any Stage in San Antonio, Texas.*

The cost of production of an original play in a Community Theatre, "Gold in the Hills," by G. Frank Davis, is here noted. Royalty was not paid on this production, as the author, being a resident of San Antonio, granted special permission for this premiere.

RECEIPTS:

Subscription and members ...	$901.75
Sales at box office	740.25
Exchange tickets	82.50
Student tickets	32.25
	$1759.75

EXPENSES:

Typing parts for play	$26.00
Music	4.25
Photographs for publicity ...	33.25
Tickets	2.75
Announcement cards to members	16.50
Clerical work	5.00
Newspaper publicity	12.28
Street card cards	6.50
Window display cards	3.70
Scenery material	14.18
Properties	13.99
Drayage	20.25
Costumes	27.70
Wigs	18.85
Rental auditorium	150.00
Stage hands	65.00
Programs	30.60
Make-up	2.48
Box office	20.00
Telephone	4.00
Incidentals—supper to cast...	10.00
Director's guarantee	600.00
	$1087.28
Profits	$672.47

The Plays Produced by Community Theatres

1. *What Play Shall We Give?*

Often people write for advice on the selection of a play. The writer of one of these letters states: "We want to do a sure-fire comedy with a small cast and settings that aren't too difficult. We have four very good women, and five men who have talent. Do you know of a play that would fit our group? And, oh yes, I forgot to say that our best woman is perfectly excellent in serious parts, and two of our men have a decided flair for comedy."

It's next to impossible to answer such letters. Conducting a matrimonial agency would be easy in comparison. And even in a matrimonial agency, who would want to select a blonde for a perfect gentleman a thousand miles away?

In selecting a play there are three things to do. First write to play publishers for catalogs. Among the leading play publishers are:

Walter H. Baker, 178 Tremont Street, Boston, Massachusetts.
Dramatists Play Service, Inc., 6 East 39 Street, New York, N. Y.
Samuel French, 25 West 45 Street, New York, N. Y.
Frederick B. Ingram, Gansert Building, Rock Island, Illinois.
Row, Peterson, and Co., 1911 Ridge Avenue, Evanston, Illinois.
Dramatic Publishing Co., 59 East Van Buren Street, Chicago, Illinois.
Longmans, Green and Co., 114 Fifth Avenue, New York, N. Y.
Fitzgerald Publishing Corp., 14 East 38 Street, New York, N. Y.
Penn Publishing Co., 925 Filbert Street, Philadelphia, Pennsylvania.

Play lists of tried plays and recommended plays together with other pertinent information may be secured from:

Drama Department, National Recreation Association, 315 Fourth Avenue, New York, N. Y. (Plays for all ages, and seasonal plays.)
National Service Bureau, Federal Theatre Project, 1697 Broadway, New York, N. Y. (Christmas plays, classic English plays, children's plays, little known one-acters, new and unproduced plays, early American, and so forth.)
Drama Book Shop, 48 West 52 Street, New York, N. Y. (Specializes in finding plays for you and has many suggestions to offer.)
Mrs. Ina K. Trissel, Drama Book Shop, Mason City, Iowa. (Handles plays of all publishers.)

Then what may make matters much easier is to write also to the extension division of almost any state university; they have prepared lists of plays and copies of plays, which they will gladly loan for reading; this makes selection easier.

The following lists of the plays produced by a few of the Community Theatres throughout the country may well solve many problems of play selection inasmuch as they embrace a very wide range of possibilities.

2. *Nineteen Years of Play Production at Columbia, South Carolina.*

PLAYS PRESENTED AT THE TOWN THEATRE 1919–1938.
(Not including one-act plays.)

The Misleading Lady	Charles Goddard & Paul Dickey
The Unchastened Woman	Louis K. Auspacker
Beau Brummel	Clyde Fitch
Prunella	Housman & Barker
The Gipsy Trail	Robert Housman
The Dummy	O'Higgins and Ford
Nearly Married	Edgar Selwyn
The Stronger	Giacosa
Believe Me Zantippe	Frederick Ballard
Alice in Wonderland	Adapted by Dan Reed
Clarence	Booth Tarkington
Why Marry?	J. L. Williams
Questioning Fate	From Affairs of Anatole—Schintzler
The Great Divide	Wm. Vaugh Moody
The Man Who Married a Dumb Wife	Anatole France
Ladies Laugh Last	Knowles Entriken
No Dogs Allowed	Rebecca Dial (Prize Play)
Enter Madame	Gilda Varesi & Don Byrne
Seventeen	Booth Tarkington
Ali Baba and the Forty Thieves	Dramatized by Lady Bell
The Piper	Josephine Peabody
Jack and the Beanstalk	Adapted by Dan Reed
This Age	Jane Trenholm Bradley (Prize Play)
Home Brew	Dan Reed
Dulcy	Kaufman & Connelly
A Christmas Carol	Dramatized by Dan Reed
Lady Windermere's Fan	Oscar Wilde
Mr. Pim Passes By	A. A. Milne
Hilda	Frances Gibbes Keith (Prize Play)
Undertow	Rebecca Dial (Prize Play)
Torchbearers	George Kelly
The Lighted House	Dorothy Heyward
The Mollusc	Hubert Henry Davies
A Successful Calamity	Clare Kummer

PLAYS PRESENTED AT THE TOWN THEATRE 1919–1938.—*Continued.*

Importance of Being Earnest	Oscar Wilde
Patience	Gilbert and Sullivan
Romance	Edward Sheldon
You and I	Philip Barry
The Cricket on the Hearth	Charles Dickens
The Concert	Herman Bahr
Sun Up	Lulu Vollmer
Romeo and Juliet	Shakespeare
Aladdin and the Lamp	Dramatized by Daniel Reed
Ruddigore	Gilbert and Sullivan
Arms and the Man	Bernard Shaw
The Truth	Clyde Fitch
Snow White and the Seven Dwarfs	Dramatized by Daniel Reed
Her Husband's Wife	A. E. Thomas
The Face	Frances Gibbes Keith
Princess Ida	Gilbert and Sullivan
The Charm School	Alice Duer Miller & Robert Milton
A Doll's House	Ibsen
The Show-off	George Kelly
Justice	John Galsworthy
Aren't We All	Frederick Lonsdale
He and She	Rachel Crothers
March Hares	Harry Wagstaff Gribble
The Patsy	Barry Connors
The Circle	Somerset Maugham
The Pigeon	John Galsworthy
The Swan	Franz Molnar
Paris Bound	Philip Barry
Cinderella	Dramatized by Harry Davis
Meet the Wife	Lynn Starling
Wappin' Wharf	Charles S. Brooks
School for Scandal	Sheridan
Robin Hood	Dramatized by Harry Davis
Outward Bound	Sutton Vale
Tons of Money	Evans & Valentine
Holiday	Philip Barry
Seven Keys to Baldpate	George M. Cohan
Sleeping Beauty	Dramatized by Harry Davis
The Young Idea	Noel Coward
Fashion	Mrs. Anna Cora Mowatt
Up There	Frances Gibbes Keith
On Approval	Frederick Lonsdale
Hay Fever	Noel Coward
Candida	Bernard Shaw
The Knave of Hearts	Belford Forrest
Hedda Gabler	Ibsen
Three Live Ghosts	Frederick Isham

David Garrick	Tom Robertson
First Mrs. Fraser	St. John Ervin
Hamlet	Shakespeare
Little Women	Louisa Alcott
If I Were Queen	Josephine Caldwell Withers
She Stoops to Conquer	Oliver Goldsmith
Camille	Alexander Dumas, Fils
Expressing Willie	Rachel Crothers
The Gondoliers	Gilbert and Sullivan
Fanny Dorini	Belford Forrest
Julius Caesar	Shakespeare
When Ladies Meet	Rachel Crothers
The Crime at Blossoms	Mordaunt Shairp
Anna Christie	Eugene O'Neill
The Mikado	Gilbert and Sullivan
Broken Dishes	Martin Flavin
The Trial of Mary Dugan	Bayard Veiller
Macbeth	Shakespeare
The Late Christopher Bean	Sidney Howard
H. M. S. Pinafore	Gilbert and Sullivan
Another Language	Rose Franken
The Marquise	Noel Coward
Charley's Aunt	Brandon Thomas
Her Master's Voice	Clare Kummer
Othello	Shakespeare
Racketty-Packetty House	Frances Hodgson Burnett
The Ghost Train	Arnold Ridley
Caroline	Somerset Maugham
The Pirates of Penzance	Gilbert and Sullivan
East Lynne	Mrs. Henry Wood
Hi-ways and By-ways	Belford Forrest
Grand Hotel	Vicki Baum
Mr. Dooley, Jr.	Rose Franken & Jane Lewin
Let Us Be Gay	Rachel Crothers
Double Door	Elizabeth McFadden
Heidi	Johanna Spyri
Faust	Goethe
Personal Appearance	Lawrence Riley
The Dragon	Lady Gregory
The Drunkard	William Smith
The Royal Family	Geo. S. Kauffman & Edna Ferber
The Happy Husband	Harrison Owens
The Silver Cord	Sidney Howard
Rip Van Winkle	Joseph Jefferson
Coquette	Geo. Abbott & Ann Preston Bridges
Master Skylark	John Bennett
Yeomen of the Guard	Gilbert and Sullivan

3. *The First Fifty Plays from Denver, Colorado.*

THE PLAYS PRODUCED DURING THE NINE SEASONS 1929–38

Season 1929–30

Candida	George Bernard Shaw
Why Not?	Jesse Lynch Williams
Redemption	Leo Tolstoi
Dear Brutus	Sir James M. Barrie
The Adding Machine	Elmer Rice

Season 1930–31

The Ship	St. John Ervine
The Rose and the Ring	Harris Deans
Outward Bound	Sutton Vane
The Whiteheaded Boy	Lennox Robinson
Craig's Wife	George Kelly
Hay Fever	Noel Coward

Season 1931–32

The Road to Rome	Robert Emmett Sherwood
When the Red Army Marches	Harry L. Baum
The Silver Cord	Sidney Howard
The Emperor Jones	Eugene O'Neill
Once in a Lifetime	George Kaufman and Moss Hart
Rancour	Lynn Riggs

Season 1932–33

Distant Drums	Dan Totheroh
These Few Ashes	Leonard Ide
The Crime at Blossoms	Mordaunt Shairp
Passing Through Lorraine	Lionel Hale
Good Friday	John Masefield
Murder on the Second Floor	Frank Vosper

Season 1933–34

He	Alfred Savoir
Twelfth Night (25th Production)	William Shakespeare
The Sacred Flame	Somerset Maugham
The Watched Pot	H. H. (Saki) Munro
Solid South	Lawton Campbell
East Lynne	Mrs. Henry Wood

Season 1934–35

A Pre-season Presentation of "The Mollusc" by H. H. Davies

You Never Can Tell	George Bernard Shaw
The Barker	Kenyon Nicholson
The Roof	John Galsworthy
The Mad Hopes	Romney Brent
Criminal At Large	Edgar Wallace
Nothing But the Truth	James Montgomery

Season 1935–36

Yellow Jack .... Sidney Howard
The Romantic Young Lady .... G. Martinez Sierra
Ladies of the Jury .... Fred Ballard
Noah .... Andre Obey
Ladies in Waiting .... Cyril Campion
Goodbye Again .... George Haight and Allan Scott

Season 1936–37

A Pre-Season Presentation of "Murder in the Cathedral" by T. S. Eliot

Judgment Day .... Elmer Rice
The Old Ladies .... Rodney Ackland
Is Life Worth Living? .... Lennox Robinson
The Second Man .... S. N. Behrman
Hail Nero! .... Mary Stocks
Post Road .... Wilbur Daniel Steele and Norma
Mitchell

Season 1937–38

The Distaff Side .... John Van Druten
Minick .... George Kaufman and Edna Ferber
Abraham Lincoln (50th Production). John Drinkwater

Season 1929–30, Maurice Gnesin, Director
Seasons 1930 to 1938, Walter Sinclair, Director

4. *The First Hundred Plays from Kalamazoo, Michigan.*

1929–30
  New Toys
  Meet the Wife
  Wedding Bells
  The Patsy
  Mr. Pim Passes By
  In the Dark
  Icebound
  Mrs. Bumpstead-Leigh
  Kempy
  The Dover Road
  Kindling
  The Show-off
  Enter Madame
  Pomeroy's Past
  Children of the Moon
  Machinal
  Minick
  Rip Van Winkle
  The Swan
  Young Woodley
  The Courageous Mrs. Hardy

1930–31
  Paris Bound
  A Doll's House
  Expressing Willie
  The Silver Cord
  Lady Windermere's Fan
  Beyond the Horizon
  The Queen's Husband
  Arms and the Man
  Grumpy
  Holiday

1931–32
  The Constant Wife
  Cock Robin
  Dulcy
  Little Women
  The Criminal Code
  A Successful Calamity
  The Adding Machine
  Tea for Three
  Loyalties
  Ned McCobb's Daughter
  Once in a Lifetime

1932–33
  Philip Goes Forth
  The Bad Man
  Candida
  The Young Idea
  Little Women
  Berkeley Square
  The Circle
  Michael and Mary
  The Skin Game
  Anna Christie
  Uncle Tom's Cabin
  Petticoat Influence
1933–34
  Hay Fever
  Journey's End
  Brief Moment
  Nine Pine Street
  A Kiss for Cinderella
  Elizabeth the Queen
  One Sunday Afternoon
  Liliom
  Criminal-At-Large
  Goose Feather Bed
  Twelfth Night
1934–35
  As Husbands Go
  Ten Minute Alibi
  Biography
  Pirates of Penzance
  The Master Builder
  They Knew What They Wanted

The Truth About Blayds
Both Your Houses
Taming of the Shrew
Her Master's Voice
1935–36
  Fly Away Home
  Noah
  Kind Lady
  Mrs. Wiggs of the Cabbage Patch
  Sweeney Todd
  Oliver Oliver
  Yellow Jack
  The Distaff Side
  Another Language
  The Present Greatness
1936–37
  The Late Christopher Bean
  Bury the Dead
  Accent on Youth
  The Sea Gull
  Fresh Fields
  Inheritors
  Dangerous Corner
  Call It a Day
  Yellow Jack
1937–38
  The Marquise
  The Sheppy
  First Lady
  Libel
  Penny Wise
  The Road to Rome

5. *Sixty-one Years of Play Production.*

The plays given by the Footlight Club of Jamaica Plain, a suburb of Boston, Massachusetts, in the past sixty years of its existence constitute practically a history of playwriting.

PLAYS OF THE FOOTLIGHT PLAYERS

A Scrap of Paper
The Babes in the Wood
The Rose of Amiens
Betsy Baker
Two Can Play at that Game
Doing for the Best
Victims
A Widow Hunt

David Garrick
Dot; or, The Cricket on the Hearth
Our Boys
She Stoops to Conquer
New Men and Old Acres
Married in Haste
Caste
A Lesson in Love

Randall's Thumb
Our Girls
Partners for Life
The Heir-at-Law
The Spark
Tom Cobb
The Chimney Corner
Women's Privilege
Still Waters Run Deep
Money
Sweethearts
Domino
Old Heads and Young Hearts
The Parvenu
The Two Roses
The Rivals
Cyril's Success
Picking up the Pieces
The Snow-ball
Apples
The Higher Education
An Unequal Match
Blow for Blow
On Guard
Taming the Truant
Engaged
Ours
Midsummer Madness
Old Love Letters
A Household Fairy
To Oblige Benson
The Lancers
False Shame
A Game of Cards
The Pilgrim Sons
The Romances of a Poor Young Man
Rain and Shine
Bad Advice
The Palace of Truth
Our Boys
Masks and Faces
Diplomacy
School
London Assurance
Esmeralda
The Pink Letter
Cesar Girodot's Will

A Morning Call
A Russian Honeymoon
Young Mrs. Winthrop
Plot and Passion
Red or White?
False Pretensions
A Fool for Luck
Second Thoughts
What Fools These Mortals Be
The Magistrate
Sweet Lavender
The Gray Mare
The Ladies' Battle
In Honor Bound
The Porter's Knot
For One Night Only
Everybody's Friend
Woodbarrow Farm
The New Boy
Liberty Hall
Duke of Killicrankie
Second in Command
Rosemary
The Manoeuvres of Jane
Because She Loved Him So
When We Were Twenty-one
The Tyranny of Tears
Mrs. Temple's Telegram
Seven-Twenty-Eight
Mrs. Gorringe's Necklace
Love in Harness
The Mollusc
Her Husband's Wife
The House Next Door
Cousin Kate
Jack Straw
Green Stockings
The Dictator
The Two Mr. Wetherbys
Ann
The Marriage of Kitty
Trelawney of the Wells
Mollentrave on Women
Kindlings
Eliza Comes to Stay
The Romancers
The Twelve-Pound Look

PLAYS OF THE FOOTLIGHT PLAYERS—*Continued.*

A Collection Will be Made
The Bracelet
Just to Get Married
The Younger Generation
The Bonds of Interest
Overtures
Trifles
Playgoers
Art and Opportunity
The Superior Miss Pellender
The Noble Lord
At Night All Cats Are Grey
The Dear Departed
The Clever ones
Heartbreak Hours
Belinda
The Monkey's Paw
Wurzel-Flummery
The Crimson Cocoanut
Alice Sit by the Fire
Magic
The Bishop's Candlesticks
The Ship
The School for Scandal
The Inconstant Lover
The New Word
The Boy Comes Home
The Temperamentalists
The Choice
The Fountain of Youth
The Enchanted Cottage
X = O
Androcles and the Lion
Tea for Three
Success
Luca Sarto
I'll Leave It to You
The Tempest
What Might Happen
Wedding Bells
Not Herbert
The Whiteheaded Boy
The Intimate Strangers
The Witness for the Defense
The Electra

Dr. Knock
Cock Robin
The Celebrity
The Queen's Husband
To Have the Honour
Hay Fever
Berkeley Square
Dandy Dick
Jim the Penman
Tom Pinch
The Schoolmistress
An Unequal Match
The Weaker Sex
A Gold Mine
The Tyranny of Tears
His Excellency the Governor
The Rogue's Comedy
The Rajah
Love on Crutches
The Jilt
The Rivals
Lady Huntworth's Experiment
Christopher, Jr.
The Importance of Being Earnest
Miss Hobbs
The Mask and the Face
Brief Candle
Mr. Prohack
One Hundred Years Old
The Young Idea
Martine
The Unattainable
Murder on the Second Floor
The Joyous Season
The Tavern
The Breadwinner
Hail Nero
Laburnum Grove
The Man Who Pays the Piper
On Stage
Charity Begins
Bees on the Boat Deck
Penny Wise
Viceroy Sarah

A Representative Community Theatre Library

General

1. *Scheme and Estimates for a National Theatre*—William Archer. Duffield, 1908.
2. *Little Country Theatre*—A. G. Arvold. Macmillan, 1922.
3. *The Theatre Through Its Stage Door*—David Belasco. Harpers, 1919.
4. *Community Drama in Theory and Practice*—Louise Burleigh. Little, Brown, 1917.
5. *The New Spirit in Drama and Art*—Huntley Carter. Kennerly, 1913.
6. *The Art Theatre*—Sheldon Cheney. Knopf, 1925.
7. *The New Movement in the Theatre*—Sheldon Cheney. Kennerly, 1914.
8. *On the Art of the Theatre*—Gordon Craig. Small, Maynard, 1924.
9. *Towards a New Theatre*—Gordon Craig. Dutton, 1913.
10. *Little Theatre Organization and Management*—Alexander Dean. Appleton, 1926.
11. *The Community Playhouse*—Clarence J. De Goveia. Huebsch, 1923.
12. *Insurgent Theatre*—Thomas H. Dickenson. Huensch, 1917.
13. *Making the Little Theatre Pay*—Oliver Hinsdell. Samuel French, 1925.
14. *The Story of the Theatre*—Glenn Hughes. Samuel French, 1928.
15. *Theatre*—Edith Isaacs. Little, Brown, 1927.
16. *Toward a Municipal Theatre*—Frederick Koch. University of North Dakota, 1916.
17. *Footlights Across America*—Kenneth Macgowan. Harcourt, Brace, 1929.
18. *The Little Theatre in the United States*—Constance D'Arcy Mackay. Holt, 1917.
19. *The Playhouse and the Play*—Percy MacKaye. Macmillan, 1909.
20. *Civic Theatre*—Percy MacKaye. Kennerly, 1912.
21. *Community Drama*—Percy MacKaye. Houghton Mifflin, 1917.
22. *The Theatre of Today*—Hiram K. Moderwell. Dodd, Mead, 1914.
23. *Work of the Little Theatre*—Clarence Arthur Perry. Russell Sage Foundation, 1933.
24. *The People's Theatre*—Romain Rolland. Holt, 1918.
25. *Theatron—An Illustrated Record*—Clarence Stratton. Holt, 1928.

Acting

26. *Acting*—Crafton and Royer. Crofts, 1928.
27. *Acting and Play Production*—Andrews and Weirick. Longmans, Green, 1925.
28. *Amateur Acting and Play Production*—Wayne Campbell. Macmillan, 1931.

399

29. *Modern Acting*—Helena Chalmers. Appleton, 1930.
30. *Problems of the Actor*—Louis Calvert. Holt, 1918.
31. *Elementary Principles of Acting*—Edward and Alice MacKaye. Samuel French, 1937.
32. *Problem-Projects in Acting*—Katharine Kester. Samuel French, 1937.
33. *Modern Acting: A Manual*—Rosenstein, Haydon, and Sparrow. Samuel French, 1936.
34. *Masks or Faces?*—William Archer. Longmans, 1888.
35. *Training for the Stage*—Arthur Hornblow. Lippincott, 1916.
36. *On Actors and the Art of Acting*—George Henry Lewes. Brentanos.
37. *The Art of Rehearsal*—George Bernard Shaw. Samuel French, 1929.
38. *Magic of Speech*—Vida Ravenscroft Sutton. Pitman, 1936.
39. *The Voice: Its Production and Reproduction*—Stanley and Maxfield. Pitman, 1933.
40. *The Technique of the Speaking Voice*—James Murdoch. Stephens, 1915.
41. *Speech Craft*—Elsie Fogarty. Dutton, 1931.
42. *Self-expression through the Spoken Word*—Crafton and Royer. Crowell, 1928.
43. *Technique in Dramatic Art*—Halliam Bosworth. Macmillan, 1926.

Play Production

44. *Problems of Acting and Play Production*—Edwin C. White. Pitman, 1938.
45. *The Improvised Stage*—Marjorie Somercales. Pitman, 1932.
46. *Practical Stage Directing for Amateurs*—Emerson Taylor. Dutton, 1923.
47. *The Book of Play Production*—Milton Smith. Appleton, 1926.
48. *The Art of Play Production*—John Dolman, Jr. Harpers, 1928.
49. *Play Production in America*—Arthur Edwin Krows. Holt, 1916.
50. *The Process of Play Production*—Crafton and Royer. Crofts, 1926.
51. *Producing in Little Theatres*—Clarence Stratton. Holt, 1921.
52. *The Practical Theatre*—Frank Shay. Appleton, 1926.
53. *Amateur Stage Management and Production*—Charles S. Parsons. Pitman, 1931.
54. *Dramatics for School and Community*—C. M. Wise. Stewart Kidd, 1923.
55. *Technique in Dramatic Art*—Halliam Bosworth. Macmillan, 1926.
56. *Shakespeare for Community Players*—Roy Mitchell. Dutton, 1919.

Stagecraft and Scenery

57. *Equipment for Stage Production*—Arthur Edwin Krows. Appleton, 1928.
58. *Practical Stagecraft*—Mary Helen Hynes. Baker, 1930.
59. *Scenery*—Harold Helvenston. Stanford University Press, 1931.
60. *The Scenewright*—Andre Smith. Macmillan, 1926.
61. *Stage Decoration*—Sheldon Cheney. Day, 1927.

62. *Runnin' the Show*—Whorf and Wheeler. Baker, 1930.
63. *Stage Scenery and Lighting*—Selden and Sellman. Crofts, 1930.
64. *Theatre Art*—Victor D'Amico. Manual Arts Press, 1931.
65. *Modern Theatre*—Irving Pichel. Harcourt, Brace, 1925.
66. *The School Theatre*—Roy Mitchell. Brentano, 1925.
67. *Scenery for the Theatre*—Burris-Meyer and Cole. Little, Brown, 1938.
68. *Drawings for the Theatre*—Robert Edmond Jones. Theatre Arts, 1931.
69. *Scenery and Lighting for School and Little Theatre Stages*—Samuel Selden. University of North Carolina Press, 1928.

Lighting

70. *Stage Lighting*—Aldred and Ridge. Pitman, 1936.
71. *Lighting for the Non-Professional Stage Production*—Powell and Rodgers. Drama Book Shop, 1931.
72. *Lighting the Amateur Stage*—Henning Nelms. Theatre Arts, 1931.
73. *Stage Lighting*—Theodore Fuchs. Little, Brown, 1929.
74. *Theatre Lighting*—Louis Hartman. Appleton, 1930.
75. *Glossary of Stage Lighting*—Stanley McCandless. Theatre Arts, 1927.
76. *The Lighting Art*—M. Luchiesh. McGraw, Hill, 1917.

Make-up

77. *The Art of Make-up*—Helena Chalmers. Appleton, 1930.
78. *Guide to Theatrical Make-up*—Charles S. Parsons. Pitman, 1934.
79. *Modern Make-up*—Gall and Carter. Banner, 1928.
80. *Time to Make Up*—Richard Whorf. Baker, 1930.
81. *Make-up*—John Baird. Samuel French, 1930.

Costumes

82. *Costuming a Play*—Grimball and Wells. Century, 1925.
83. *A Study of Costume*—Elizabeth Sage. Scribner, 1926.
84. *Clothes: On and Off the Stage*—Helena Chalmers. Appleton, 1928.
85. *Historic Costuming*—Nevil Truman. Pitman, 1936.
86. *Costumes and Scenery for Amateurs*—Constance D'Arcy Mackay. Holt, 1930.
87. *Stage Costuming*—Agnes B. Young. Macmillan, 1933.
88. *Costume through the Ages*—Mary Evans. Lippincott, 1930.
89. *A Book of Dramatic Costume*—Dabney and Wise. Crofts, 1930.
90. *Costuming the Amateur Show*—Dorothy Lynne Saunders. French, 1937.

And Just for Fun

91. *The Theatre of Tomorrow*—Kenneth Macgowan. Boni, 1921.
92. *Scenes for Student Actors*—Frances Cosgrove. French, 1937.
93. *My Life in Art*—Stanislavsky. Little, Brown, 1924.
94. *Lost April*—Sydney Thompson. Crowell, 1938.

95. *Who's Who in the Theatre*—John Parker.   Pitman, 1939.
96. *Theatre and Stage*—Harold Downs,   Pitman, 1934.
97. *A Study of the Modern Drama*—Barrett H. Clark.   Appleton, 1928.
98. *At 33*—Eva Le Gallienne.   Longmans, Green, 1934.
99. *Are We All Met?*—Whitford Kane.   Mathews and Marrot, 1931.
100. *Our Theatre Today*—Herschel Brickel.   Samuel French, 1936.

Tomorrow—and Tomorrow—and Tomorrow

New Community Theatres are being born continually. Established groups are making changes and growing.

For subsequent editions of this book and revisions, we should like to have the proper names and addresses, not only of the many groups we have been unable to mention, but also corrections in the addresses of known theatres.

So please fill in this page—tear it off on the dotted line—and mail it to us:

Carl Glick and Albert McCleery
CURTAINS GOING UP

c/o Pitman Publishing Corporation
2 West 45 Street
New York, N. Y.

NAME OF GROUP ....

PERMANENT ADDRESS ....

CITY AND STATE ....

YEAR ORGANIZED ....

BY WHOM ORGANIZED ....

HAVE YOU YOUR OWN THEATRE? ....

HOW WAS IT BUILT? ....

WHAT WAS THE BUILDING ORIGINALLY? ....

SEATING CAPACITY ....

VALUE OF THEATRE PROPERTY ....

HAVE YOU A PROFESSIONAL DIRECTOR? ....

IF SO, WHO? ....

IF NOT, HOW? ....

NUMBER OF MEMBERS......... ACTIVE PARTICIPANTS YEARLY? ....

NUMBER OF PLAYS PRESENTED YEARLY ....

TOTAL PRODUCTIONS TO DATE ....

WHAT ARE YOUR SPECIAL PROBLEMS? ....

OTHER COMMENT—USE ADDITIONAL SHEETS IF NECESSARY

       SIGNED ....

       POSITION ....

       ADDRESS ....

       ....

INDEX

Theatre
and Stage

FIFTY-SIX CONTRIBUTORS.   HAROLD DOWNES, Editor

2 *vols.   Cloth.   7¼″ x 9½″.   1308 pages.   Profusely illustrated. $10.00.*

The whole field of the amateur stage, to the last detail, covered in the most expert, instructive, stimulating and practical fashion. From the organization of an amateur group, through production of every type of entertainment, down to the minutest bit of business, here is a vast store of fact and authoritative opinion. Whatever your particular concern, whether with production or direction, with staging, lighting, costuming, make-up or acting, with music or ballet, with Sophocles, Shakespeare, Gilbert and Sullivan, Eugene O'Neill or Noel Coward, you will find your own particular problems discussed by noted authorities who understand them from your own angle.

SUBJECTS DISCUSSED

The Past and Future of the Amateur Movement

The Critical Faculty

Reading a Play for Production

The Play's The Thing

Acted Drama as an Educational Instrument

The Work of the Producer

Producing
Naturalistic Drama — Farce — Comedy—Tragedy—Romantic Drama — Shakespeare — Revue — Opera

Aspects of Production

Musical Production

Acting
In Naturalistic Drama— Farce — Comedy — Tragedy — Romantic Drama — Shakespeare

The Authentic Drama of the Theatre

Theory and Practice of Stagecraft

Modern Make-Up

Stage Costuming

Stage Effects and Noises Off

Modern Stage Lighting

Stage Movement

Aspects of Dramatic Technique

Theatrical Dancing

Stage Dancing

The Little Theatre and Its Stage

Business Organization and Management

Home-Made Lighting Apparatus and Scenic Equipment

Dictionary of Stage Terms

Topicalities in Shakespeare

The Theatre in the Study

Music in the Theatre

Festivals and Competitions

Aspects of Criticism

Amateurs and Revue

Religious Drama

Voice, Speech and Gesture

Going on the Stage

Law in the Theatre

Stage Faults and Short Comings

Women in Drama

The Children's Theatre

Practical Points in Ballet Production

Music and the Amateur Stage

Playmaking and Imaginative Education

Famous Players of the Past

Health and the Stage

Amateurs, Playwrights, and Productions

Play Readings

Convention and Conventionality

The Organization of a Playwrights' Club

Acting of Plays in Foreign Languages

Gilbert and Sullivan Opera

Pageants

——————*Write for descriptive list of Theatre books*——————

PITMAN PUBLISHING CORPORATION, 2 West 45th Street, New York

THEATRE AND STAGE SERIES

Other volumes in preparation

Acting for the Stage

By SYDNEY W. CARROLL
Foreword by St. John Ervine
Cloth. 5½" x 8¼". 149 pages. **$2.00.**

As actor, manager, producer, author, and dramatic critic, Mr. Sydney W. Carroll is known and appreciated by all who are interested in the theatre and the stage. Believing that without moral or spiritual encouragement the most strenuous struggle to achieve a position in the theatre can accomplish little, he wrote this book not so much to instruct as to inspire. Nevertheless, in it he has, with the facility and the authority of the expert, combined pertinent comments on different aspects of acting with practical advice to make the volume appeal to professional and amateur alike.

Problems of Acting and Play Production

By EDWIN C. WHITE
Foreword by Flora Robson
Cloth. 5½" x 8¼". 176 pages. **$2.50.**

Not only has the actor to discover the author's intentions and make the most of the material that is put before him, but he has also to communicate his interpretation to the audience. This twofold duty involves numerous problems of acting technique, and it is these that form the subject of Mr. White's book. The author discusses in detail the use of speech, movement and gesture on the stage, and also makes constructive suggestions with regard to play production. It is above all a practical book, and the assistance that it gives will be welcomed by all who are actively concerned with the theatre.

———————*Write for descriptive list of Theatre books*———————

PITMAN PUBLISHING CORPORATION, 2 West 45th Street, New York

Historic Costuming

By NEVIL TRUMAN

Cloth. 7" x 9½". 152 pages. Illustrated. **$3.00.**

Convenient and practical reference manual of costume from classical times to days just past. An interestingly written story and also a reliable guide, as garments are illustrated and described so that they may be reproduced accurately. The dress of all social classes is studied, and concise "at a glance" tables make the information instantly available. Special topics, such as armor, and the garb of the clergy, receive attention. The application is to Britain primarily, but also to Europe generally. All concerned with historic drama or spectacle will welcome the careful arrangement, clear classification, and concise summaries of practical data, while others as well will not fail to appreciate the decided social and historical interest of the material and of the abundant illustrations.

Stage Lighting

By C. HAROLD RIDGE and F. S. ALDRED

Cloth. 7¼" x 9½". 130 pages. Fully illustrated. **$2.25.**

Effective lighting is of such profound importance in any stage production that everyone connected with such work will welcome this comprehensive and practical book. Both the artistic and the technical sides receive full consideration. Not only are theory and principles discussed, but practical details are studied and explained. The book is a complete guide to what can be done and to the exact methods of doing it. Possible effects are surveyed, and actual apparatus and its use is fully explained. The most elaborate modern installations are described, and so also are the devices by which amateurs with limited facilities contrive satisfactory effects. Such instructive and well organized chapters as those on color plots and color mixing contribute significantly to available knowledge, and offer invaluable guidance for practical use.

———————*Write for descriptive list of Theatre books*———————

PITMAN PUBLISHING CORPORATION, 2 West 45th Street, New York